The African Liberation Struggle: Reflections

Godfrey Mwakikagile

Copyright © 2018 Godfrey Mwakikagile
All rights reserved

The African Liberation Struggle: Reflections
Godfrey Mwakikagile

First Edition

ISBN 978-9987-16-010-5

New Africa Press
Dar es Salaam, Tanzania

Contents

**Biographical Profile
and Personal Recollections**

Africa in The Sixties

The Struggle for Mozambique

**The Rhodesian Crisis:
The Struggle for Zimbabwe**

**American Involvement in Angola
and Southern Africa**

The Struggle Against Apartheid

**Appendix:
The Land Question**

Africa's Racial Land Divide

**Namibia:
Landless In The Land Of The Brave**

In South Africa, Land Apartheid Lives On

Land inequality in SA a 'ticking time bomb'

Introduction

THE liberation struggle in the countries of southern Africa still under white minority rule – and in the Portuguese colony of Guinea-Bissau/Cape Verde in West Africa – was one of the most important chapters in the history of Africa since the advent of colonial rule.

It was also one of the most dramatic events, a momentous upheaval driven by outright war and a combination of political, diplomatic and economic pressure exerted by the international community on the white minority governments to relinquish power to the black majority and other non-whites in those countries.

This work focuses on that critical phase in the history of Africa. It includes a biographical profile and personal recollections of the author and others concerning important events which shaped the anti-colonial struggle and the fight against apartheid on a continent whose countries were the last to win independence.

The work focuses on the liberation struggle from the 1960s to the 1990s in the countries of southern Africa.

The author witnessed some of those events. He was also a victim of some of the racial injustices perpetrated against blacks in his home country, Tanganyika, during colonial rule.

He writes from personal experience. When the Organisation of African Unity (OAU) was formed in

Addis Ababa, Ethiopia, in May 1963, Tanganyika (now Tanzania) was chosen to be the headquarters of the OAU Liberation Committee. All the African liberation movements went on to open their offices in Tanzania's capital Dar es Salaam. Many refugees fleeing oppression in the countries of southern Africa also went to live in Tanzania.

The author was a young news reporter in Dar es Salaam in the early seventies and got the chance to know some of the freedom fighters and their leaders who were based there during those days. He also interviewed a number of them and has provided an additional perspective to his work as a primary source of some of the material included in his book.

It was one of the most important periods in the history of post-colonial Africa.

Most countries on the continent had won independence by 1968. The toughest struggle was in the few strongholds of white supremacy in the southern part – Mozambique, Rhodesia, Angola, Namibia, apartheid South Africa – and in the Portuguese colony of Guinea-Bissau/Cape Verde in West Africa. The struggle finally ended in victory. As President Nyerere once said:

"Throughout history, nationalist struggles have had one end: victory."

Biographical Profile and Personal Reflections

Godfrey Mwakikagile was born in the town of Kigoma in western Tanganyika – what is now mainland Tanzania – on Tuesday (6AM), 4 October 1949.

He was baptised Godfrey on Christmas day, 25 December 1949, as a member of the Church Missionary Society (CMS) among whose supporters was Scottish explorer and missionary-doctor, David Livingstone, of the London Missionary Society.[1]

Dr. Livingstone campaigned against slavery and the slave trade but also helped pave the way for the colonisation of Africa.[2]

In his book, *The Mind of Africa*, renowned Ghanaian philosopher Dr. Willie Abraham described colonialism, as an imperial phenomenon, in terms of its hostile nature. As he put it:

"Colonialism is aggression." – (Willie E. Abraham, *The Mind of Africa*, London: Weidenfeld, 1962, p. 152).

Colonialism robbed the people of their natural right to live in a state of independence which is itself a state of nature even in political and social organisations formed by the people themselves, not just in a state of nature before the formation of social and political states which only validated and legitimised the natural state of independence of individuals and communities. Man is born free. Freedom is a natural right which is restored after independence is regained; it is never gained for the first time. It existed before colonisation. And it is never given. Never. Colonial rulers were forced to relinquish power.

Missionaries from Europe were some of the earliest trail blazers of the colonial enterprise in Africa and played a role in robbing Africans of their natural right to live free and even to own land in some cases. As Jomo Kenyatta said:

"The white man came and asked us to shut our eyes and pray. When we opened our eyes it was too late – our land was gone." – (Jomo Kenyatta, quoted by Godfrey Mwakikagile, *Africa in The Sixties*, New Africa Press, 2014, p. 130; G. Mwakikagile, *Africa After Independence: Realities of Nationhood*, 2009, p. 51; G. Mwakikagile, *Africa 1960 - 1970: Chronicle and Analysis*, p. 134; G. Mwakikagile, *Africa and the West*, 2000, p. 5. This witticism is attributed to Jomo Kenyatta by various sources including Kenyan Professor Ali Mazrui in his book, *Political Values and the Educated Class in Africa*, University of California Press, Berkeley and Los Angeles, 1978, p. 108, among other works).

Christianity was incompatible with colonialism. Yet it was used to facilitate imperial conquest of Africa, consolidate colonial rule, and even pacify African nationalists when they were fighting for independence. Some of the most prominent African nationalists were Christian. As Professor Ali Mazrui stated in his book, *Political Values and the Educated Class in Africa*:

"The process of pacific socialization was in part based on western Christianity as transmitted in the black world. Kenneth Kaunda, Albert Luthuli, Martin Luther King were all products of a devout upbringing in Christian terms. Even Nkrumah had many of his earlier sensibilities fundamentally affected by the impact of Catholicism....

Just as Saint Augustine had once allied Christianity with the concept of *Pax Romana*, so Christianity later came to be linked to the whole vision of *Pax Britannica*. In Africa Christianity came to be associated particularly with colonization.

In one of his early speeches of the 1940s, Jomo Kenyatta is said to have compressed into a witticism a feeling of disaffection shared by many other nationalists: 'The white man came and asked us to shut our eyes and pray. When we opened our eyes it was too late – our land was gone.'

Much later Albert Luthuli, himself a devout Christian, came to feel keenly the handicap which his religion was experiencing in the age of nationalism in Africa. Luthuli lamented: 'The average African says the white man is the cause of all his troubles. He does not discriminate between white men and see that some come here for material gain and others come with the message of God'....

The message of Jesus had been used to encourage submission from the natives. The message had not been presented as a call for 'non-violent *resistance*' but at best for 'non-violence.' Christianity could even be interpreted to mean 'non-resistance' – a coming to terms with those in authority, whoever they might be. 'My kingdom is not of this earth' – this declaration came to imply what E.H. Carr called 'a boycott of politics.'" – (Ali A. Mazrui, *Political Values and the Educated Class in Africa*, Berkeley and Los Angeles: University of California Press, 1978, pp. 108, 109).

Kenyatta's witty remark – on how European conquerors used the Bible to blindfold Africans and swindle them out of their land – articulated in nationalistic terms, captured the essence of the collective sentiment of many Africans across the continent, as Godfrey Mwakikagile has demonstrated in his book, *Africa and the West*, among other works.

Kenyatta even questioned the fairness of Christian symbolism, black versus white, as taught by European conquerors, in which all the forces of evil were black and whiteness represented righteousness. He gave it a literal interpretation in racial terms and demanded a reversal of the two symbols:

"Kenyatta has felt that the entire interpretation of the Bible as propagated by Europeans was calculated to vindicate the superiority of whiteness over blackness. The forces of evil were 'black,' the angels 'white.' In January 1962 Kenyatta called for a reinterpretation of Christianity and for a reversal of symbolism as between those two colours. See *The Guardian* (Manchester), 30 January 1962." - (Ali A. Mazrui, *Towards a Pax Africana: A Study of Ideology and Ambition*, London: Weidenfeld and Nicolson, 1967, p. 276).

It is a subject Godfrey Mwakikagile has also addressed in his book, *Africa and the West*, among other works. He contends that colonisation of Africa "was an invasion"; so was penetration of the continent by foreigners spreading bad influence and polluting African minds as a form of cultural imperialism which sometimes led to the destruction of Africa's cultural and spiritual wellbeing.

He further asserts that even after the end of colonial rule, Africans have not recovered from the devastating impact of colonialism including physical and psychological wounds inflicted on them by their European conquerors who turned them into beasts of burden and objects of ridicule and contempt.

Conquest of the mind was the worst form of colonisation, stripping Africans of their dignity and humanity and turning their conquerors into role models, looking up to them as the best specimen of mankind and fountain of wisdom, instead of seeing them as predators of body and soul; in spite of some of the mutual benefits derived from the interaction between Africa and Europe in an asymmetrical relationship – coloniser versus colonised – tipping scales in favour of the conqueror. – (Godfrey Mwakikagile, *Africa and the West*, Huntington, New York: Nova Science Publishers, Inc., 2000, pp. 4 – 6).

According to his autobiography, Godfrey Mwakikagile was born at Kilimani Hospital and lived with his parents in one of the government houses for government employees in Mwanga, on a street with the same name, in the town of Kigoma when his father worked as a medical assistant at the same hospital.

He later moved to Ujiji with his parents where his sister Maria was born at a Roman Catholic hospital. The rest of his siblings were also born in different parts of the country: Morogoro, Mbeya, and Tukuyu.

He was named Godfrey by his aunt, Isabella, one of his father's younger sisters, and lived in different parts of Tanganyika – Western Province, Coast Province, Southern Highlands Province, and Southern Province – in his early years.

He was, according to his birth certificate, baptised by Reverend Frank McGorlick (from Victoria, Australia), a Scottish minister of the Church Missionary Society in Kigoma his parents belonged to. But he was brought up as a member of the Moravian Church at Kyimbila, three miles south of the town of Tukuyu, in Rungwe District in what was then the Southern Highlands Province in colonial Tanganyika, as he has stated in his books, *Life in Tanganyika in The Fifties* and *My Life as an African: Autobiographical Writings*.

The church was built by the Germans in 1912, as mentioned below, and ministered by them, although according to some reports, it was built in 1907.

But there are historical records showing that 1907 was

an important year in the history of Moravians at Kyimbila. That was the year when a missionary was sent to work there. It does not necessarily mean the church also was built in the same year simply because a missionary was assigned to the area. According to a historical work, *The Moravian Church in Tanzania Southern Province: A Short History*:

"Kyimbila Station: This station is just seven kilometres from Lutengano. The distance from Kyimbila to Rungwe is about 20 kilometres....The decision was reached to send a missionary in 1907, who was to perform all pastoral duties (at Kyimbila)." – (Angetile Yesaya Musomba, *The Moravian Church in Tanzania Southern Province: A Short History*, Nairobi, Kenya: Institut Francais de recherche en Afrique (IFRA), 2005, p. 36).

Historical works also show the role the Germans played in establishing Kyimbila not only as a mission but as a plantation:

"There were some attempts to establish rubber plantations in the southern highlands region. The missionaries of the Hermhuter Mission at Kyimbila in Langenburg District successfully established a plantation of *Landolphia stolzii busse*. In 1907 they had planted four hectares with 4,000 vine plants and 2,000 support trees." – (*African Economic History*, African Studies Center, Boston University, 1993, p. 126).

The church at Kyimbila was built in an area where they also established a tea estate in 1904 which did not become fully operational on commercial basis until 1926.

The first Moravian Church in Rungwe District was established near Mount Rungwe in 1891. According to the history of Moravian missions:

"The Berlin Missionary Society was already at work in German East Africa; with that Society the Moravian Church did not want to compete and, therefore, to prevent friction or overlapping,...the two Societies, working side by side, will found stations north of Lake Nyassa....

In 1891 the campaign began. For twenty-three years the chief leader and superintendent of the work in German Nyassaland was Theodore Meyer, son of Henry Meyer, the pioneer in Hlubiland. One of his colleagues was a Swiss, Theophilus Richard, and these two, pushing north from Lake Nyassa, discovered, at the foot of Mt. Rungwe, a spur of the Livingstone Hills, a splendid sight for the first station. The date was August 21st.

The two men had never beheld a more gorgeous scene. On the north-west rose Mt. Rungwe; on the west lay a dense forest; on the south-east lay the teeming dales of Kondeland; and gazing southwards towards Lake Nyassa....

Rungwe seemed an ideal site for a mission-station. The land was high, the water pure, and the air clear and bracing." – (Joseph E. Hutton, "A History of Moravian Missions," Internet Archive).

The founding of the Moravian Church near Mount Rungwe was followed by the establishment of two missions at Lutengano and Ipyana in 1894.

Lutengano Moravian Church is three miles southwest of Kyimbila. Godfrey Mwakikagile had a second baptism at age 14 at Lutengano Moravian Church under Reverend Mwatonoka in June 1964 when he was on holidays for one month from boarding school at Mpuguso Middle School. He was in Standard Eight and in his last year at Mpuguso.

Other mission stations were established by the Moravians in Rungwe District and beyond in about fifteen years, some of them in neighbouring Mbeya District:

"In 1903 they opened a Training College for

Evangelists, and in 1910 they opened a Normal School, and thus Rungwe (mission near at the foot of Rungwe Mountain) became the centre of widespread evangelistic and educational activity.

For twenty years the Brethren were engaged, not merely in building a model Christian village at Rungwe, but in attempting to christianize the whole surrounding neighbourhood. In this work they employed twenty missionaries, fifty-three native helpers, thirty-seven native evangelists, and twenty-seven volunteer assistants. And in each of the five districts mentioned, strong stations, surrounded by many preaching places, were founded.

In Kondeland, besides Rungwe, they founded Rutenganiot (1894), Ipiana (1894), Mueia (1907), and Kyimbila (1912); in Bundah, Isoko (1900); in Nyika, Mbozi (1900); in Usafwa, Utengulet (1895); and in Mawanda, Ileya (1906).

In addition, however, to these head stations, the Brethren had also thirty-five out-stations and one thousand and eighty-one preaching places. The number of converts rose to 1,955; the number of schools was 144; and the number of scholars attending them, 4,949....

The missionaries..., in some cases,...introduced entirely new forms of industry. At Rungwe there was a carpenters' shop and wood-working establishment; there sixteen large saws could be seen working at once; and the natives learned to manufacture beams, joists, boards, doors, cupboards and chairs, and other articles of domestic furniture. At Utengule there was a large boot factory. At Kyimbila there was a rubber plantation.

Some of the missionaries introduced Muscat donkeys, said to be able, unlike horses, to resist the attacks of the tsetse fly; others planted rice in the lowlands and potatoes in the hilly districts; others introduced sheep and a new and hardier breed of cattle; others cultivated coffee and tea; and others, with varying success, introduced strawberries, gooseberries, plums, peaches, apricots, oranges, lemons, grapes, and other fruits previously unknown to the natives....

Formerly the natives had few implements; now they became experts in the use of hoes, knives and axes. At the head stations the Church as such generally owned a large tract of land...and the natives preferred to live near a station...partly because they felt sure that their children would be well educated." – (Ibid.).

About a quarter of mile north of Kyimbila Moravian Church, which was in the midst of a large tea plantation, was Kyimbila Primary School.

The pastor of Kyimbila Moravian Church was Godfrey Mwakikagile's great uncle (grand uncle), Asegelile Mwankemwa, who was the younger brother of his maternal grandmother Tungapesyaga (Tunga) Mapunga Mwankemwa. Mapunga (Mwamapunga) was their mother and Godfrey Mwakikagile's great-grandmother. They were the only siblings who grew into adulthood; the third-born, a boy, died in childhood.[3]

Asegelile Mwankemwa was the first African pastor of Kyimbila Moravian Church.

Godfrey Mwakikagile's mother, Syabumi Mwambapa (her maiden name), was brought up by her uncle Asegelile Mwankemwa and by her mother Tungapesyaga. She lived with her uncle after her parents died. She was almost 14 years old when her mother died.

Her mother went to live with her brother Asegelile Mwankemwa after her husband Mwambapa, Godfrey Mwakikagile's maternal grandfather, died – and was buried – in Mpumbuli village, Kyimbila, in 1929, about two miles west of Mwankemwa's residence. But he had roots in Mwakaleli, immediate biological ties with the Mwambapas and the Mwasomolas there, lineal descendants of the same family. For example, his elder brother (Godfrey Mwakikagile's grand uncle) used the name Mwasomola. Yet he was also Mwambapa as

Mwambapa's biological son. The Mwasomolas were Mwambapas and Mwambapas, Mwasomolas. Godfrey Mwakikagile's great-grandfather was also Mwambapa.

There was a Mwambapa who was born in 1773. He was featured in *Science News*, *The Geological Survey Department of Tanganyika* and *Tanganyika Notes and Records* as a witness to a volcano which erupted from Mount Kyejo northwest of Selya in the eastern part of Rungwe District when he was about 25 years old:

"An approximate dating of the flow was made possible by the fact that Andulile Kajigili had sufficient record of his ancestry, and of the tradition embodied in his account, for it to be asserted that the original narrator was one Mwambapa, that the flow took place when he was a young man of about 25, and that this must have been about a.d. 1800. As Mr Harkin points out, Mwambapa's account 'might well apply to a present-day eruption.'" – (*Science News*, Issues 4- - 34, Penguin Books, 1956, p. 121).

A report in *Memoir – Geological Survey Department of Tanganyika* stated:

"Andulile Kajigili kept some record of his ancestry, and by tracing back with him it was possible to construct a family tree with approximate dates as follows: - Mwambapa Born 1773 Died 1853. Kajigili Born 1841 Died 1919....The eruption took place when Mwambapa was a young man of about 25 years and can therefore be dated as approximately 1800 A.D. (vii) Volcanological History. – The volcanological history of Kiejo...." – (*Memoir – Geological Survey Department of Tanganyika*, Issue 3, 1960, p. 19; Albert Mathieson Quennell, *Tanganyika Notes and Records* - Issues 35 – 50, 1955, p. 20).

Tungapesyaga and Asegelile Mwankemwa also had

roots in Mwakaleli. They moved to Kyimbila from their home in Mwakaleli.

Syabumi's mother Tungapesyaga died in 1943 and was buried on her brother's family compound in Katusyo about five miles southeast of Tukuyu.

That is also where Syabumi was born, on 8 November 1929, in the same year her father died. She was brought up on the same compound together with her first cousins, the children of Asegelile Mwankemwa, and with her brothers and sisters. One of Syabumi's cousins, Lugano Mwankemwa who was born on 25 November 1933, married a childhood friend of her husband. Their husbands came from the same area the two cousins came from.

In the 1940s, Syabumi and her cousins attended Kyimbila Girls' School headed by the British feminist educator Mary Hancock. Hancock was also a friend of Julius Nyerere and his family since the 1950s before Nyerere became prime minister and then president of Tanganyika:

"Maureen Cowan and March Hancock have told me about Tabora Girls' School, of which both have been headmistresses. Miss Hancock is a devoted friend of the Nyerere family; while Julius and Maria Nyerere were struggling with financial difficulties, two of their children lived with her." – (Judith Listowel, *The Making of Tanganyika*, London: Chatto & Windus, 1965, p. 428).

And as William Edgett Smith stated in his book, *We Must Run While Others Walk: A Portrait of Africa's Julius Nyerere*:

"Miss Mary Hancock, a peppery little Englishwoman who had come to Tanganyika in 1940 'to help the black people, as we called them then, has recalled, 'Oh, that man, how he thinks! The civil servants in Musoma couldn't see why I remained his friend after he declared for Uhuru. We civil servants had to be careful, you know --- we couldn't attend political meetings. I would say, 'He's my friend. If you can'r differentiate, I can. Well! You should have seen the civil servants change when it became clear that he was winning.'" – (William Edgett Smith, *We Must Run While Others Walk: A Portrait of Africa's Julius Nyerere*, New York: Random House, 1972, p. 84; W. E. Smith, *Nyerere of Tanzania*, Faraday Close, Worthing, UK: Littlehampton Book Services, 1973, p. 65; The New Yorker, Volume 47, Issues 27 - 35, 1971, p. 84).

Mary Hancock was the district education officer (DEO) of Musoma in the 1950s when she first met Nyerere and his family. Musoma was Nyerere's home district. – (Pat Holden, *Women Administrative Officers in Colonial Africa 1944 – 1960*, Oxford Development Records Project, 1985, p. 194).

She later, in the late fifties, became a provincial education officer (PEO) for the Lake Province and was based in Mwanza, the provincial capital.

Mary Hancock played a major role in the education of girls in colonial Tanganyika and after independence.

She was born in 1910 in England and went to Tanganyika in 1940 to work as a volunteer teacher. She became headmistress of Tabora Girls' School in the Western Province.

She also taught at Kyimbila Girls' School three miles south of the town of Tukuyu in Rungwe District in the Southern Highlands Province in the 1940s and founded Loleza Girls' School in the town of Mbeya in the same province during the same period.

She became a citizen of Tanzania and a senior education inspector. She was elected member of parliament in 1970. Fondly known as Mama Hancock, she died in October 1977:

"In 1970, she was nominated to Parliament by the

women's organisation, Umoja wa Wanawake wa Tanzania (UWT) and elected by the National Assembly (Parliament). Mama Hancock was a much loved and respected figure. A requiem mass was celebrated by the Cardinal Archbishop in Dar es Salaam Cathedral on 28th October." – ("Obituary: Mary Hancock," *Tanzanian Affairs*, August 1977 – January 1978).

Godfrey Mwakikagile remembered his mother Syabumi talking about Mary Hancock – as a devoted teacher and very strict disciplinarian – during her days as a student at Kyimbila Girls' School in the same area where her uncle Asegelile Mwankemwa served as pastor of the Moravian Church.

It was one of the few, very few, girls' schools in the whole country. Machame in the region of Mount Kilimanjaro was also one of them:

"Both Kyimbila and Machame Government girls' schools have had girls in Standard IX this year and about twelve girls are, in spite of difficulties, continuing to Standard X in 1950. Kyimbila School has become in many ways a centre of social life for the District....

At Kyimbila, the Government girls' school in the Southern Highlands Province, a successful performance was given of the *Merchant of Venice* adapted to the circumstances of a production in Swahili." - (Tanganyika Department of Education, *Tanganyika Territory, Annual Report of the Education Department 1944*, Dar es Salaam, Tanganyika, pp. 22, 18).

In the 1950s, Godfrey Mwakikagile also went to school at Kyimbila, a primary school for boys and girls. One of his teachers there, Eslie Mwakyambiki, was later elected member of parliament representing Rungwe District. He was also appointed by President Nyerere to serve in the cabinet as deputy minister of defence and national service.

There was also a land dispute between Kyimbila Tea Estate and the congregation of Kyimbila Moravian Church which had a sad ending:

"In 1951, the African congregation of Kyimbila Mission turned to the UN, desperate for help. They felt betrayed by their own missionaries who had apparently sold the church lands to a tea estate without informing the congregation. They were told that all the buildings would have to be torn down within a year. The mission owned the land freehold, and it had the legal title to sell it." – (Ullrich Lohrmann, *Voices from Tanganyika: Great Britain, the United Nations and the Decolonization of a Trust Territory, 1946 – 1961*, Munster, Germany: LIT Verlag, 2008, p. 311).

The tea estate won the case and the church was demolished in the sixties. The congregation found another site farther north, away from the estate, and rebuilt the church but with a different architectural design.

When the original church building went down, so did its history. People of the younger generation, and those who were born after it was torn down, have no memory of it. It was a historical building and would have served as a reminder of the area's history and the coming of German missionaries to the region had it been left intact. It is as if it had never even existed. After the spot where it stood was taken over by the tea estate, the memory was also erased, except in the minds of those who knew where the church was during the old days when Asegelile Mwankemwa became the first African pastor and continued to serve the congregation in the following years.

The sons of the Kyimbila Moravian Church pastor Asegelile Mwankemwa also used another family name, Mwaiseje, as their surname; for example, Itika Mwaiseje, the last-born child, about whom Godfrey Mwakikagile has written in some of his writings stating that he was one of the last two relatives to bid him farewell when he left Tanzania for the United States. He took a taxi to the airport to see Mwakikagile less than an hour before the plane left Dar es Salaam and had a farewell drink (Tanzanian beer) with him.

The other one was Godfrey Mwakikagile's first cousin Tunga Mwambapa, daughter of Johan Chonde Mwambapa, who worked at Dar es Salaam's international airport as a ground hostess and later married a general in the Tanzanian army whose career had striking parallels with that of her eldest brother who was also in the army. Each ended up being head of Tanzania's leading army officers' training school. Tunga was named after Tungapesyaga, her paternal grandmother, who was Godfrey's maternal grandmother.

Itika Mwaiseje's first cousin Syabumi, Godfrey Mwakikagile's mother, was also brought up by her elder brother Johan Chonde Mwambapa, a teacher, who was almost thirteen years older than she was. He was born in 1917. She was the youngest in their family and lived with him until she got married. She was married on Saturday (10 AM), 7 August 1948. She later followed in her uncle's footsteps and became involved in church activities teaching Sunday school.

One of her brothers, Amos Mwambapa, a teacher and World War II veteran born in 1914 (he fought in Burma), also became involved in church activities serving as a deacon of the Moravian church in their area. He was head teacher of Masebe Primary School, near Mpuguso Middle School, for many years.

Another brother, Benjamin Mwambapa born in 1922, pursued a career in law enforcement. He became head of the criminal investigation department (CID) in the ministry of home affairs in the government of newly independent Tanganyika in the early sixties in the town of Tukuyu serving Rungwe District.

When he joined the police force during British colonial

rule, Benjamin Mwambapa became a corporal and served as a driver for the head of the intelligence unit, then known as the special branch, in Mwanza, capital of the Lake Province (surrounding Lake Victoria) in northern Tanganyika; a position which facilitated his entry into the investigative field and his career advancement when he later became head of the criminal investigation department for Rungwe District after Tanganyika won independence.

Peter D.M. Bwimbo, who years later became head of security for President Nyerere and who knew Benjamin Mwambapa as a colleague during their early days in the police force, stated the following in a book he wrote about his career and as head of the president's security unit:

"After being promoted and becoming corporal on 1 January 1953, officers of the Special Branch in Dar es Salaam (the nation's capital) started, without my knowledge, watching me, observing and following me closely when I lived at the police barracks on Kilwa Road, in order to see whether or not my conduct and behaviour as well as my lifestyle would be compatible with someone who would be chosen to work in the Special Branch.

There was a sergeant at the police barracks on Kilwa Road known as Sergeant Pancras, a member of the Luo tribe (ethnic group). He is the one who came to me one day and told me the kind of job he was doing and that he had a message for me from high levels to go and see his boss in order to be interviewed and see if I could be transferred there if I passed the interview. I agreed, arrangements were made, and Sergeant Pancras took me to his boss, a white man, who interviewed me and I passed. Together with other qualifications, he also wanted to know which languages of the tribes in the Lake zone I knew, besides Swahili and English, and I named them.

I agreed to be transferred to Mwanza starting 1 April 1953. The head of the barracks, Officer Commanding Barracks, on Kilwa Road, Dar es Salaam, was Mr.

Pamment who was eventually transferred to Sarawak (in Malaysia).

I left Dar es Salaam on a train, third class, and arrived in Mwanza where I found the head of our department, John Press. I joined my colleagues, Sergeant Said Nassoro, Henry, Corporal Lucas Ogutu, Corporal Livingstone Wainaina and Inspector of Police Thomas Ogoya, Livingstone Lubega and others. All those officers were glad to welcome me when I arrived wth my wife Christina Magali binti (daughter of) Makongoro.

When Mr. Press was transferred, Mr. E.N.G.N. Brend came (Mr. Mtemba - Mr. Pipe), a name we gave him, without him knowing that, because he smoked a pipe. His driver for a long time during those days was Corporal Benjamini Mwambapa. Their personal secretaries were Miss Pat Quinlan, Miss S.E. Bailey, Miss Foggo and Miss B. Ross. They worked in Mwanza at different times.

My kind of transfer from the uniformed branch (of police officers wearing uniform) to the Special Branch was the procedure that was followed during colonial rule because the uniformed branch had many people and that was where every policeman was given basic training after being investigated and recruited. Those who were transferred from there were provided with other kinds of training depending on the kind of work that was done where they were being transferred. But all of us were in the same police force under the Commissioner of Police before this title was changed and came to be known as Inspector General of Police (IGP) a few years after independence.

After the Special Branch was abolished in 1963, it was replaced by the Department of National Security. The change was made to enable the Department to be free to employ its officers from other places (instead of being exclusively dependent on the police department). But in spite of that, the employment procedure, investigating prospective employees, remained the same at a high level of scrutiny to avoid employing people who were not suitable to work in this highly sensitive department.

I remember the first director of National Service (Jeshi la Kujenga Taifa – JKT – established in July 1963), David S. Nkulila, came from the police force before JKT merged with the people's army of Tanzania (Tanzania People's Defence Forces -TPDF – Jeshi la Wananchi wa Tanzania – JWT).

Even the first director of TAKUKURU – (Taasisi ya Kuzuia na Kupambana na Rushwa – TAKUKURU – Prevention and Combating of Corruption Bureau – PCCB, formerly Anti-Corruption unit), Geoffrey Sawaya, came from the police force." – (Peter D. M. Bwimbo, *Mlinzi Mkuu wa Mwalimu Nyerere: Wasifu wa Mlinzi wa Kwanza wa Mwalimu Nyerere (1960 - 1973)*, Swahili Edition, Dar es Salaam, Tanzania: Mkuki na Nyota Publishers Ltd., 2015, pp. 16 – 17. Translated from Swahili to English by Godfrey Mwakikagile in G. Mwakikagile, *The African Liberation Struggle: Reflections*, New Africa Press, 2018, pp. 21 - 22).

Benjamin Mwambapa's career spanned two critical periods in the history of Tanganyika, later Tanzania, from the colonial era to independence and symbolised the transition and the changes the majority of the employees in the first government of independent Tanganyika went through during those years.

Syabumi had another elder brother, Andengenye Mwambapa, an active member of the Moravian Church who also became an elder of the church and whose son, Brown Mwambapa, became a Seventh-Day Adventist (SDA) pastor in Tanzania. And her daughter Maria Kasuka, Godfrey Mwakikagile's sister, married a Seventh-Day Adventist pastor Anyitike Mwaipopo.

Syabumi also had two elder sisters, Mbage and Nyambilila. Born in 1925 and the immediate elder sibling of Syabumi, Nyambilila also became an active member of the Moravian Church in her area and got involved in church activities in varying degrees.

And one of their cousins, Mbutolwe, a daughter of their uncle Asegelile Mwankemwa, became deeply involved in church activities as a missionary worker and an itinerant preacher spreading the Gospel.

Their brother Johan Chonde Mwambapa, simply known as Chonde or Chonde Mwambapa, was also the father of Brigadier-General Owen Rhodfrey Mwambapa who was the head of the Tanzania Military Academy, an army officers' training school at Monduli in Arusha Region in the northeastern part of the country, whose alumni include army officers from South Africa, Uganda, Kenya, Zambia, Seychelles, Rwanda, Lesotho and other countries. It is one of the leading military academies on the continent.

Born in 1945, Owen Mwambapa graduated as an army officer (lieutenant) from Sandhurst, a royal military academy in the United Kingdom, in the sixties.

Godfrey's younger brother, Lawrence Anyambilile Mwakikagile, was also a lieutenant in the national army, the Tanzania People's Defence Forces (TPDF), and participated in the Uganda-Tanzania War, also known as the Kagera War, which started on 30 October 1978 and ended on 11 April 1979. He retired with the rank of captain in 1996. And their younger sister, Gwangu Kasuka, was married to a sea captain, John Mwakibete. She was named Gwangu by her grand uncle Asegelile Mwankemwa.

The patriarch of the family, Asegelile Mwankemwa, died in September 1983.

Godfrey's father, Elijah Mwakikagile, attended Malangali Secondary School, one of the top schools in colonial Tanganyika. His classmates at Malangali, where he was head prefect, included Jeremiah Kasambala who became a cabinet member under President Julius Nyerere after Tanganyika won independence from Britain, and

John Mwakangale who, during the struggle for independence in the 1950s, became one of the leaders of the independence movement in Tanganyika. Elijah's maternal uncle, Eliakim Simeon Mwaibanje who was the younger brother of his mother Rahel (Laheli) Kasuka Mwaibanje, paid for his education.

The parents of Rahel (Laheli) Kasuka and Eliakim Simeon Mwaibanje were Kasofu Mwamwaja and Mary Iseke. They had other children all of whom, together with Rahel (Laheli) and Eliakim, were born in Mpata village in the ward of Kabula in Selya in the eastern part of Rungwe District.

Another maternal uncle of Elijah Mwakikagile, Jotham Mwaibanje, was the father of Oscar Mwamwaja, one of Tanzania's first commercial airline pilots. Oscar was named after his grandfather Kasofu Mwamwaja whose other children with Mary Iseke were Kilabo Ndaga, Amos, Jane, and Anyegile. Kasofu Mwamwaja and Mary Iseke were Godfrey Mwakikagile's great-grandparents.

Oscar Mwamwaja was the co-pilot of an Air Tanzania plane, a Boeing, 737, that was hijacked on 26 February 1982 and forced to fly from Mwanza, Tanzania, to London Stansted Airport in the United Kingdom. The aircraft was on a domestic flight.

The pilot was Deo Mazula, elder brother of George Mazula who, together with his brother, was also among the first commercial airline pilots in Tanzania. George was also a classmate of Godfrey Mwakikagile at Tambaza High School in Dar es Salaam. Another classmate was Mohamed Chande Othman, also known as Othman Chande, who became chief justice of Tanzania appointed by President Jakaya Kikwete.

The hijacked plane had 99 passengers. The pilot and co-pilot were assisted by a crew of three. After stopping in Dar es Salaam, Deo Mazula was forced to fly the plane to Nairobi in Kenya, Jedda in Saudi Arabia, Athens in Greece, and finally the United Kingdom where he landed at Stansted about 30 miles northeast of London.

A British defence ministry spokesman said "there are contingency plans involving military units" at Stansted. The hijackers threatened to blow up the plane if security forces attempted to storm in.

The police refrained from storming the plane fearing they would endanger the passengers. But anti-terrorist units were already in position ready for an assault on February 27th, one day after the plane was hijacked in Tanzania and flown to the UK.

The hijackers said they wanted to see Britain's foreign secretary, Lord Carrington, and Tanzania'a high commissioner (ambassador) to Britain, Amon Nsekela. Carrington was then on an official visit to Kenya.

They also demanded to speak to Oscar Kambona, Tanzania's former minister of foreign affairs who had fallen out with President Nyerere and who was then living in exile in London.

A crackled radio message from the pilot, Deo Mazula, to the controllers at Stansted international airport that was later broadcast on BBC, said:

"We have a request. Would like the following persons to meet the aircraft on arrival: The Tanzanian high commissioner in London and the British foreign minister and Mr. Oscar Kambona." – ("Hijacked Jetliner Arrives in Britain," *The New York Times*, 28 February 1982).

But negotiators ended the ordeal before Kambona arrived on the scene. His younger brother Mattiya, also living in exile in London and who was a fierce opponent of Nyerere like his brother, said in a radio interview that he did not believe his elder brother would meet the hijackers.

The hijackers, all in their early twenties, wanted President Nyerere to resign. They claimed to be members of a movement which their leader alternatively described as the "Tanzania Youth Democratic Movement" and the "Tanzania Youth Revolutionary Movement." There was no such movement or political organisation in or outside Tanzania demanding change in the country.

Their level of education was low, between primary school and secondary school, from standard 7 to standard 12.

The hijacking ended when the hijackers surrendered on February 28th. There were five hijackers, all related through birth and marriage. There were two pairs of brothers and one a brother-in-law. His sisters were married to the eldest brother in each pair:

"A 48-hour hijacking drama that began in East Africa ended tonight...with the surrender of...(the) young terrorists and the release of more than 90 hostages....

Security sources here said that explosives were found wired to the aircraft doors and placed in a toilet. The hijackers had threatened to blow up the plane, a Boeing 737, at 10:30 Saturday night. 'Please Bring 100 Coffins.'

'We are going to blow the plane,' one terrorist said in talks with airport officials. "We are going to die now. Please bring 100 coffins at once.'

The only known casualty was the co-pilot, who was injured when he was...shot...in the waist just before the plane arrived in Athens. The hijackers, who were taken into custody this evening, were armed with knives, pistols, submachine guns and grenades. However, some of the arms were said to have been made of wood or plastic.

According to the police, the terrorists were seeking the overthrow of the President of Tanzania, Julius K. Nyerere. They were identified as members of a left-wing group that describes Mr. Nyerere as a traitor who has suborned Marxist ideology.

The drama was brought to an end by the intervention of Oscar Kambona....Once Mr. Kambona arrived at Stansted, which is in the county of Essex, about midway between London and Cambridge, the terrorists began to release the hostages. Later on Saturday night they freed a pregnant mother and her 5-year-old son. At noon today (Sunday, 28 February) four women, a man and a baby girl were freed.

Then at 2:30 P.M., seven men and three women were set free. The injured co-pilot was released at 3:15 P.M. and 41 passengers were allowed to leave at 4. P.M. About an hour later the rest of the hostages walked down the ramp and the hijackers surrendered.

Robert Bunyard, the Chief Constable of Essex, said all of the hijackers were in their early 20's. 'The people are all safe,' he said." – (R.W. Apple, Jr., reporting from Bishop's Stortford, England, 28 February 1982, Special to *The New York Times*, "4 Tanzanian Hijackers Surrender; 90 Hostages Are Freed in Britain," published in *The New York Times*, 1 March 1982. See also "A Hijacking of a Tanzanian Aircraft," *Tanzanian Affairs*, 1 July 1982; "Former Hijacker Arrested," *Tanzanian Affairs*, 1 January 1991).

The co-pilot, Oscar Mwamwaja, was shot by the leader of the hijackers. He underwent an operation at a hospital in the UK to remove a bullet from his body and returned to Tanzania.

Years later, one of the hijackers was arrested when he returned to Tanzania after serving eight years in prison in the United Kingdom:

"Musa Membar, who took a free ride to Britain aboard an Air Tanzania Boeing 737 which he hijacked with four other youths in 1982, was arrested on September 14th 1990 when he crossed the Kenya-Tanzania border. He had been jailed in Britain for eight years. After his release he became a founder member of the Tanzania Youth Democratic Movement under the umbrella of a Tanzanian opposition front headed by Oscar Kambona, former

Foreign Minister who has been in exile in Britain since 1967.

Speaking in a BBC interview the other day, Mr Kambona denied any prior knowledge of Member's departure from London. 'He did not bid any of us farewell' he said.

In a letter from the Ukonga maximum security prison, where he is being held, Member said 'I returned to Tanzania ... to lead a peaceful campaign for multi-party democracy....' (*Business Times*, 19 October 1990)." – "Former Hijacker Arrested," *Tanzanian Affairs*, 1 January 1991).

Oscar Mwamwaja, who was Elijah Mwakikagile's first cousin, later became a commercial pilot training instructor at the Nigerian College of Aviation Technology in Zaria, northern Nigeria.

A former American Peace Corps teacher, Leonard Levitt – author of *An African Season*, the first book ever written by a Peace Corps – who taught Oscar Mwamwaja and Godfrey Mwakikagile at Mpuguso Middle School (1963 – 1964) wrote about his former students and his experiences in Tanzania in his article, "Tanzania: A Dream Deferred," published in *The New York Times Magazine* on 14 November 1982.

Other alumni of Mpuguso Middle School who went there in the late 1950s a few years before Godfrey Mwakikagile (1961 – 1964) and Oscar Mwamwaja (1962 – 1965) did include Brigadier-General Owen Rhodfrey Mwambapa, Godfrey's first cousin; and David Mwakyusa, President Nyerere's last personal physician who was with the Tanzanian leader until his last days when he died at a hospital in London, United Kingdom, in October 1999. Mwakyusa was also elected member of parliament representing Rungwe West and served as minister of health and welfare development under President Jakaya Kikwete during the same period.

The headmaster of Mpuguso Middle School in 1961, the year Godfrey Mwakikagile first went there and enrolled in Standard Five, Moses Mwakibete who was also his math teacher, years later became the registrar of the High Court of Tanzania. He was appointed judge of the high court by President Nyerere in 1973.

Geoffrey Sawaya, director of Tanzania's Criminal Investigation Department (CID) who presented evidence against the coup plotters in the 1970 treason trial at the High Court of Tanzania in nation's capital Dar es Salaam also was once headmaster of Mpuguso Middle School before he was later appointed CID director by President Nyerere. As Leonard Levitt stated in his article about Mpuguso, one of the leading schools in what was then the Southern Highlands Province (later divided into Mbeya and Iringa Regions), and about Tanzania in general:

"I first arrived in Tanzania in 1963, as a teacher in the Peace Corps, in the heady days just after independence from Britain. The school I was assigned to was in the southern highlands, in blue mountains shadowed by clouds and mist. It was a setting as pristine as the ideals that had brought me there.

The school was named Mpuguso, after the surrounding village of mud huts and shambas, small plots where farmers kept cattle and chickens and where they planted banana trees and tea and coffee shrubs. Mpuguso was an upper primary school - that is, it included grades 5 to 8, and the students' ages ranged from 10 to 20; proper birth records had not been kept. The school consisted of a complex of brick buildings: classrooms, dormitories, a dining hall and teachers' houses. Below the dining hall lay a large soccer field, the grass cut short by cattle the villagers led there to graze.

My students, nearly all of them boys, were as bright and hard working as any I'd ever known. Many walked 10 or 15 miles each day from their villages to Mpuguso.

During the masika, or long rains, when we wouldn't see the sun for days or weeks, they'd arrive each morning, barefoot and sopping wet in their white school uniforms, with long, green banana leaves over their heads. The boarders - those whose fathers owned enough cows to sell in order to pay the 150 shillings, or $20-a-year fees -studied in their classrooms until midnight by a kerosene lamp hung from a rafter. Hunched over their desks, they squinted and scribbled as the light became fainter and fainter.

The goal of each student was to pass his exam for secondary school, where there were places for only a quarter of them. Passing the exam was the first step necessary to leaving their villages and entering the modern world of the 20th century, which to them meant a world where everyone wore new clothes and shoes, listened to transistor radios and rode in cars and airplanes. To my students, this was the promise of uhuru, or independence from British rule.

Uhuru had been won by the young and charismatic President Julius K. Nyerere, who so eloquently urged a new and better life for Tanzania and for Africa. The son of an illiterate tribal chief from a village not unlike Mpuguso, Nyerere had been a teacher himself -hence his Swahili title of Mwalimu. Educated in Britain, he had translated Shakespeare's *Julius Caesar* into Swahili. More important, Nyerere had persuaded the British to quit Tanzania without firing a shot. Among Western liberals and intellectuals, he came to be regarded as a kind of African philosopher-king. He was perceived as a selfless leader, a man who disdained violence; a nonracist who offered Tanzanian citizenship to any European or Asian who wished to remain; a benevolent socialist who wished to rid Tanzania, indeed all Africa, of its triple plagues - ignorance, poverty and disease.

In retrospect, there was an almost touching naivete about all he sought to accomplish and about American eagerness to believe and support him. We Americans were certain that we could help transform Tanzania, quickly and painlessly, into a modern nation - one that would incorporate the best aspects of Western culture without sacrificing its own African identity.

And we were not alone. Tanzania came to be viewed as a model developing country. Billions of dollars and thousands of volunteers poured into Tanzania, not only from America, but also from Europe, Canada, Israel, the Soviet Union, China, Japan and even other undeveloped nations such as Brazil. Tanzania became the second largest recipient nation, on a per capita basis, of foreign aid in the world.

Despite the money and the hopes – and, to an extent, because of them – Tanzania today is a tragedy. Nyerere's political party - the only party in the country - now controls the Government, the military, the press. His ideals have atrophied into an ideology, called 'African Socialism,' that seems to combine the worst features of East and West. Business and industry have been nationalized and have become dependent on foreign subsidies. Corruption is epidemic. There are no goods in the stores, and no foreign currency to purchase spare parts when machines break down. If, outside Tanzania, the Mwalimu is still regarded as the eloquent champion of African and third-world aspirations, his own people are now poorer in almost every way than they were before independence.

In September 1981, 18 years after I first arrived in Tanzania, I returned to find my students, and from them, perhaps, to learn something of what had happened to the country. They were all as delighted to see me as I was to see them, and to my surprise they remembered even the most obscure details about our time together - words I'd spoken, lessons I'd taught, books I'd given them.

On the surface many members of this first generation of uhuru's beneficiaries appeared to have prospered. Of the 10 I saw, half had studied abroad; nearly all held

Government jobs. Yet there was a quality of despair and desperation about all of them. They were, without exception, disillusioned in some way: frustrated in their careers, disappointed in their lives, unfulfilled in their expectations. They seemed not to understand why the dreams they had been told were rightfully theirs had not been realized. For them, as for Tanzania, the road from the village to the 20th century had proved more tortuous than they or I had imagined.

Tanzania is not unique in any of this. Many, if not most, of the African nations that a generation ago gained their independence in a rush of self-confidence and optimism today resemble defeated nations, countries where prosperity now appears to be farther out of reach than ever, where basic freedoms have never been granted, where the participation of the people in the governments that rule them seem as remote as it was during the days of colonialism. Tanzania's decay is evident as soon as one arrives. I drive from the airport to Dar es Salaam in a sagging, unpainted airport bus whose rear door bangs open in the wind. It is a Sunday evening, and a gasoline shortage and a ban on Sunday driving have emptied the streets of cars. Green-leafed banana trees and mud-brown huts with corrugated roofs line the road, while barefoot children in unwashed shorts wander down dirt-filled side streets. In the dusk, once-white buildings appear yellow and brown, stained with dirt and neglect. Windows are broken, panes of glass missing. Downtown, along Independence Avenue, near the harbor, storefronts are bare of goods. There are, I learn, shortages of all staples - sugar, salt, butter, rice, soap, light bulbs. Each day a line of people winds around the block from a bakery, waiting for bread.

I am staying at the Kilimanjaro Hotel, which is said to be the best hotel in Dar es Salaam. It is nine stories high, with a balcony outside each room, and with a swimming pool. In this tropical city of two-and three-story buildings, it seems out of place. The hotel was built by the Israelis in the mid-1960's, and managed by them until Nyerere broke relations after the 1973 October War. Now it is managed by a Dutchman. Over the last six years, the Dutch have provided Tanzania with more than $300 million in aid.

My window overlooks the harbor to the Indian Ocean, where huge Soviet and Yugoslav ships lie at anchor while tiny wooden dhows of another age sail past them. Though the temperature and humidity in Dar both approach 100 degrees, the hotel's air-conditioning barely functions. At night, with my balcony doors open, the stench of the harbor at low tide floods my room. Some mornings there is no hot water. A valve has broken, the hotel operator explains, and there are no spare parts. A few months earlier, I learn, the water came out the taps mud-brown because the city's water system had run out of aluminum-sulphate purifier.

In the lobby of the Kilimanjaro I meet one of my former students, whom I will refer to here as Rashid. I remember him as a small, light-complexioned boy, younger than the others. Now, though he is still short, his color has darkened and he has gained weight, giving him the portly appearance of prosperity.

'So, Mr. Levitt. How are you?' he says to me, standing in the lobby. He is wearing slacks and an open-neck sport shirt, the dress of the urban Tanzanian. He smiles. 'How are things?'

This colloquialism reminds me of the fine linguist Rashid was. Remarkably, at Mpuguso, he learned to speak English with barely an accent.

'Do you remember the book you gave me, Mr. Levitt, when you left Mpuguso?' he says. 'Inside you wrote, 'To Rashid, you have been a pleasure to teach. I am sure one day you will study in the United States.' Well, Mr. Levitt, I have not yet been to the United States, but I have studied in Europe.'

We walk upstairs to the hotel lounge and order two

Kilimanjaro beers (which, when available, cost 20 shillings, or $2.50, a bottle) while Rashid begins telling me about himself. 'As I am sure you know, Mr. Levitt, I passed my exam for secondary school. After secondary school, I passed Form V and Form VI on my own and was accepted at the University of Dar es Salaam, where I received a degree with honors in international marketing. I am now,' he says proudly, 'the manager of a small, private tourist company. So you see, Mr. Levitt, I am doing very well.'

A few days later, I visit Rashid at his office. It is in an Indian, or 'Asian' - as Indians are called - section of the city, and consists of a small room off the sidewalk. The room is filled with old men in Muslim skull caps and long white gowns.

Perhaps to explain why his small tourist company is smaller than he indicated, perhaps because he decided he would rather confide in me than attempt to impress me, Rashid begins speaking in a rapid voice. 'You see, Mr. Levitt, with my degree in international marketing, I became an assistant manager with the T.T.C.,' he said, referring to the Government-run Tanzania Tourist Corporation, which has taken over most segments of Tanzania's once-lucrative tourist industry. 'I did very well there. I was sent to Sweden for a year's course of study. And I received a scholarship to study in France and was studying French in preparation.'

He pauses. 'Mr. Levitt, my superior was jealous of me. I was better educated than he, and he resented my success. A year ago, a woman tourist made a complaint against me, and my superior dismissed me. I was in Sweden at the time and was recalled. My scholarship to France was canceled. I was out of work for nine months. I was married to a young girl, and we had two small children. I had no money and the poor girl was so upset she ran away. I had to send the children back to my mother near Mpuguso.'

He waits for my reaction, but I can say nothing. I am

thinking of what those nine months must have been like for him - no job, no money, abandoned by his wife, left with the two small children. It would have been difficult for any man. For an African accustomed to traditional family roles, one can only imagine the pain.

'Mr. Levitt, life is not good here in Tanzania,' he says, now in a whisper. 'There is no longer opportunity here. The Government controls everything, and now that I no longer work for them they do not care about me anymore. I want to leave Tanzania. I want to move to Nairobi, to Zambia, even to Botswana, but without sponsorship they will not let me. When I lost my scholarship, I wrote to the French Government, but they said without Government sponsorship they could not give me one. Perhaps you know of some way I could go to the United States. Perhaps I could get a scholarship. There is nothing here for me anymore.'

There are two ways to travel overland to Mpuguso. A new tarmac road built by the Americans runs from Dar southwest to Mbeya, the regional capital of the southern highlands; from Mbeya, another new tarmac road, built by the Germans, runs south past Mpuguso, 50 miles away, and continues down to the Malawi border. The problem with these roads - all of which are foreign built - is that they are not maintained. Sections are filled with potholes; bridges are collapsing. Some are already impassable, so that now it takes more time to travel from, say, Dar to Arusha in the north than it did 20 years ago.

There is also the Tazara Railway, built by the Chinese, which runs from Dar to Mbeya, and then southwest into Zambia. Completed in 1976, it, too, has deteriorated - as I discover when I take it. The cars are dirty; toilets do not flush. The Tanzanians have not maintained the tracks and trains are out of service for days and weeks at a time.

I share my compartment with two Asians, a father and son. The father says he is a retired schoolteacher who owns a duka, or small shop, outside Mbeya. He has just returned from Canada, where two other sons have emigrated, and he says he and this son will soon be going there, too. Echoing Rashid he tells me, 'There is nothing here for us in Tanzania anymore.'

Unlike Uganda, where Idi Amin confiscated their businesses and then expelled them, Tanzania originally permitted Asians to live in relative calm and prosperity as its merchant class. Then, in 1977, Nyerere began abolishing the village dukas, virtually all of which were owned by Asians. Nonracist that he professes to be, Nyerere claimed the measure was not directed against the Asians but was, rather, in keeping with the philosophy of "African Socialism," a first step in nationalizing all business in Tanzania. For the Asians, the effect was little different from Uganda.

We arrive in Mbeya, about 50 miles from Mpuguso, early the next morning. I remember it as having been a lovely place set in the mountains, with purple jacaranda trees and Asian dukas lining its two main streets. In its center was the British settlers' Mbeya Club, with a bar, squash court and nine-hole golf course with 'greens' of black tar, and which only the year before uhuru began accepting African and Asian members. But now, as the train pulls into Mbeya, nothing seems familiar. The land is bare and dusty. A haze covers the mountains. We arrive at a white-brick station on the town's outskirts that had not existed when I was there. Later, when I walk through the town, I see many of the dukas have been shuttered. The windows of others are bare of goods. What does remain is the Mbeya Club. Its door is unlocked. Its brick walls have holes in them. Through its cracked rear window, I can look down the hill that had been the first hole of the golf course and that is now filled with half-completed mud-brick houses.

The Mbeya Hotel also remains, a relic of the colonial past where visiting Tanzanian dignitaries from Dar es Salaam are now put up and where, at night, at the bar, the elite of Mbeya's officials congregate. The hotel is seedy with age. The windows are broken or missing panes of glass, and its flowers have been destroyed by a herd of goats that grazes on the front lawn.

I introduce myself to the young African at the front desk, but I am unprepared for his reply. 'Are you the Mr. Levitt from Mpuguso school?' he asks. He introduces himself as Azim A. Mwinyimvua, though he prefers to be called Bwana Simba, or, in English, Mr. Lion. Bwana Simba remembers me, he says, because as a schoolboy he visited Mpuguso for a track meet and attended the Friday night debates when I was debate master. We had debated topics of the students' choosing, such as 'Resolved: It Is Better to Marry an Educated Girl Than an Uneducated Girl,' or 'Resolved: It Is Better to Have One Wife Than Many Wives.'

Bwana Simba, it turns out, is the manager of the Mbeya Hotel. He apologizes for the state into which it has fallen, explaining that although he studied hotel management in Nairobi and in Italy, there is no money and no trained staff to maintain its former standards. He does his best for me, however. He places me in the hotel's deluxe suite, which consists of a bedroom, sitting room and bathroom with a light bulb, and a chandalua, or mosquito net, with a hole the size of my fist. In the corners of the room, a stream of red ants eats away at the unbaked brick walls, which, in a few more years, I fear, will no longer exist. At meals, I am offered the finest carvings of goat meat, which come from the herd on the front lawn. Bwana Simba assigns special staff members to clean my room and serve my meals.

Yet sometimes at meals there is no meat, no bread, no milk, no sugar. Sometimes in the bar there is no beer, and Bwana Simba is forever using his ingenuity to procure these items. Each Saturday night he acts as a host at a disco and charges 30 shillings a head, then uses the money to purchase such items as curtains. Other money goes for soap or light bulbs, or for such minor luxuries as Coca-Cola or Fanta orange soda, which are smuggled in over the Zambian border or purchased, with a bribe, from the Government-run corporations that supply them. What he cannot purchase are new panes of glass; the materials no longer exist in Tanzania.

While I am at the hotel, Bwana Simba tells me he has received Government permission to attend a two-week course in hotel management in England. He awaits only the final call to proceed to Dar es Salaam. But the call never comes. When I leave the hotel and return to Dar es Salaam, he is still waiting. There is a group of Swedes living at the hotel. They are part of a Scandinavian aid program that from 1976 to 1980 provided Tanzania with more than $600 million. In Mbeya, the Swedes have built three factories to produce sweaters, wooden clogs and plastic toys. It is as ridiculous a project as can be imagined, for the raw materials are purchased abroad and the finished products are too costly to sell effectively on the export market. As for the Tanzanians themselves, they have little need for sweaters, clogs or plastic toys.

The factories have been operating since mid-1981, but because of the lack of water, electricity, diesel fuel and generator maintenance and breaking of the cooling pipes, they are operating at one-third capacity.

'Recently a Swedish aid official visited Mbeya,' says Thomas Gotting, the Swedish manager of the sweater factory. 'But he visited our factory for only five minutes, then gave a lunch at the Mbeya Hotel for the Africans where they all made speeches praising each other. You see, the Swedish Government gives 1 percent of its gross national product away in foreign aid. And the bureaucrats care only about giving it away, not if it does any good. The man who came here made no attempt to find anything of the kind.'

'In Sweden, people don't understand how much time it takes to learn,' adds Anders Otterstram, the Swedish technical adviser to the plastic toy factory. 'In Sweden it took us generations, with many mistakes. When I was home last year, I tried to explain this to people, but they do not listen. When I tell them things are not working in Tanzania, they call me -what is the English word? -they call me a racist.'

There is also a Peace Corps worker in Mbeya. The Peace Corps was dismissed in the late 1960's by Nyerere, ostensibly in protest against the United States' involvement in Vietnam. Meanwhile, in the villages, the Government spread rumors that Peace Corps workers were spies. Ten years later, in the late 1970's, Nyerere was feted at the White House by President Carter. Subsequently, he proposed that the Peace Corps return.

In keeping with its new image of pragmatism and practicality, as opposed to my generation's unskilled idealism, the Peace Corps worker in Mbeya is a forestry specialist. Her job is to plant trees, as the Tanzanians have denuded their hillsides by cutting down too many for firewood. The problem, she explains, is that the Tanzanians insist on planting European pine and cypress, which mature faster than the indigenous eucalyptus. But the pine and cypress do not retain the soil's moisture as well as eucalyptus does. Thus the topography is changing and the land is becoming dusty and bare.

In Mbeya I find one of my students, whom I will refer to as Henry, and who is now a teacher. Like Rashid, he was one of my brightest and most hard-working pupils. He was gifted in all subjects, but was especially interested in English and history.

He has grown a beard but I recognize him immediately. And he recognizes me. 'Levitt! Is it really you?' he shouts as I arrive at his school. He tells me he is not teaching English or history, as I'd imagined, but science. 'At secondary school my headmaster encouraged me to pursue a degree in agriculture,' he explains. 'I received a scholarship to study abroad - a six-year course in the

Soviet Union.'

He was there three years, he tells me, but returned home. 'I became sick there, Mr. Levitt. I could not work. I could not concentrate on my studies. I was laughing, and crying. I do not know why. I was sent back to my village and remained there an entire year. When I became better, I took this job.'

He tells me he does not enjoy teaching science and has applied to the university in Tanzania to complete his degree in agriculture, so that he can go abroad again. 'I want to travel. I want to go to the West, to Europe, to America. Then, after some years, I will return to Tanzania.' But without his degree, he says, he will be unable to leave Tanzania. 'Mr. Levitt, if I am not accepted at the university, I do not know what I will do.'

He also tells me he married last year. His wife is a teacher and she is three months pregnant. But he is not pleased about becoming a father as most Africans would be. He is afraid. 'When my wife has the baby and stops working, it will be very hard for us. It is very expensive here in Mbeya. I do not know how we will live.'

Listening to him, my former student who is now a man, who has traveled abroad and suffered a breakdown, who is married and is soon to become a father, I find myself thinking back 18 years to when he was a young boy in a white Mpuguso school uniform. Hard as he had worked, hard as he had studied, in retrospect his life seemed simple then. He had had a goal. He had succeeded. He had passed his exam, graduated from secondary school and gone on to study abroad. Yet something had gone wrong. He had achieved his goal, but his success had created other, unforeseen problems.

No longer was he content to be a teacher, to have a wife and children, as he might have a generation before. Now he wanted something else - to travel to the West -something, I feared, that now lay beyond his grasp. I imagine him waiting, like Bwana Simba, for a call from

Dar es Salaam, a call that, like Bwana Simba's, may never come.

Afterward, I invite Henry and his wife to the Mbeya Hotel for tea or Cokes. It is a treat for them, he tells me, as they can afford such luxuries only once a month. His wife, a lovely young woman of 23, wears her best clothes - perhaps her only dress clothes -a dungaree skirt and white blouse. Though she understands English, she is too shy to speak it. As they prepare to leave, he says to me, 'Mr. Levitt, I beg you not to write about me. I am ashamed of my life. I do not want people knowing about me.' I tell him I will change his name. I am to travel to Mpuguso the next day, so we agree to have lunch together when I return to discuss it further. But he never appears. I never see him again.

Mpuguso has also changed. It is no longer an upper primary school; instead, refresher courses for school teachers are now given there. One of Tanzania's proudest boasts is that it has provided free primary education for all school-age children. In each village I pass on the way to Mpuguso, a primary school stands by the side of the road. But while school children roam outside, most of the classrooms are empty.

At Mpuguso, I walk along dirt paths I remember, past rows of brick houses where we teachers lived, past my own brick house, where two African women sit in the doorway. A new row of classrooms has been built alongside our old ones, but when I look into the windows, they, too, are empty. Where are the students who worked until midnight by the light of a kerosene lamp? Where are the students who walked 10 to 15 miles to school each day? I remain in Mpuguso less than an hour, struggling to recapture something that, for me, is lost forever.

Before I return to Dar es Salaam, Bwana Simba takes me to a political rally. The rally is to be held in the stadium across from the hotel. It is organized by Nyerere's Revolutionary Party and is to celebrate the women of the region. And all that morning, the road into Mbeya is filled with dilapidated buses and open-backed trucks carrying loads of women from the outlying villages.

The rally's organizers have arranged a series of races for the women - 100-yard dashes, quarter- and half-mile runs and relays - and, as the women run, their kangas (colorful cotton material wrapped as a skirt or a dress) flap wildly around their legs. The crowd laughs and shouts in delight. Each winner is then brought to the podium and awarded a prize - a bar of soap, which, like so many items, is unobtainable in the stores.

When the races end, the speeches begin. The crowd has heard them all before and quickly grows restless. The women begin moving toward the stadium's two large gates, which have been locked to prevent their premature departure. Watching it all, my eyes travel upward to the green billboards emblazoned with Swahili slogans, political jargon of a long-forgotten age. 'Kazi Ndiyo Msingi Wa Maendeleo' - 'Work Is the Foundation of Progress.' 'Nchi Maskini Haiwezi Kuendelea Kwa Msingi Wa Fedha' - 'A Poor Country Will Not Progress If It Depends On Aid (Will not Develop Depending on Money).' 'Nchi Maskini Haiwezi Kujitawala Kama Inategemea Misaada Toka Nje" - 'A Poor Country Cannot Rule Itself If It Relies on Foreign Help.'

Reading these slogans, rendered absurd by the direction Tanzania has taken, I imagine a more apt one: 'Njia Ya Jehanum Inatengenezwa Kwa Nia Njema' - 'The Road to Hell Is Paved With Good Intentions.'

The reasons why Tanzania has become a mockery of its own slogans are, of course, complex. Some - such as the rising price of oil and turbulence in the world economy -were clearly beyond the small nation's control. Tanzania had always been a poor country, with few natural resources. Nyerere's well-meaning but authoritarian attempts to redistribute among the country's 18 million people what little wealth there was only led to a decline in production, to endemic corruption and, finally, to the withdrawal of thousands of citizens from the official economy and their return to the subsistence farming of their ancestors. Finally, Nyerere's Government has become as oppressive and out of touch with its own people as the colonial system he sought to replace.

Back in Dar es Salaam I meet with my student George. He is a communications officer for the meteorological department at the airport, an imposing-sounding title. He'd been an excellent student, with a gift for mathematics. He was older than most of the boys and he had a steadiness and maturity beyond that. He'd wanted to become an engineer. I expected much from him.

'Mr. Levitt,' he begins, 'you will be very disappointed in me when I tell you about my life.' He tells me that he passed his exam at Mpuguso and was accepted at Tusamaganga secondary school, one of the best-known in the country. But in 1967, his second year, he contracted a severe case of malaria. 'I was in Iringa Hospital five months,' he says. 'When I came out, I found I could not concentrate on my studies. And I especially could not concentrate on mathematics. I failed my exams. Mr. Levitt, you will not believe this, but I failed mathematics.'

So George dropped engineering and instead joined the meteorological department. 'But I am only a communications officer. Not a meteorological officer. I simply push papers. When I try to concentrate, to use my brain, I cannot.'

I meet a Canadian psychologist, Dr. Morris Block, at Dar es Salaam's Muhimbili Hospital. When I mention George to him, he offers to see him. Afterward, Dr. Bloch tells me George's symptoms suggest a mental disorder peculiar to educated Africans that has been reported in psychiatric journals He and Dr. William Lucieer, a Dutch psychiatrist at Muhimbili, explain there is no organic reason why one should be unable to concentrate as a result of malaria. Rather, Block and Lucieer say, for reasons doctors cannot explain, a surprisingly large number of educated Africans suddenly become depressed, unable to sleep or concentrate. The disorder, they say, usually occurs after emotional shocks or disappointments - in George's case, probably set off by the malaria.

Of all my former students, the most successful turns out to be Oscar Mwamwaja, who has become a pilot for Air Tanzania. It is a prestigious job, for there are few qualified African pilots. Of the 40-odd pilots at Air Tanzania, half are foreigners.

We meet on a Saturday evening in the lounge of Dar es Salaam's Kilimanjaro Hotel. Little Oscar - who was smaller than the other boys - is now tall and thin, a few inches taller than I. He is wearing his navy-blue Air Tanzania uniform and he walks with jaunty confidence, in the manner of pilots everywhere.

'I was in the States, you know,' he says. 'I trained for two years in Texas. I've also been to Europe and to India, where I trained to fly the 737's.' Watching him so poised, listening to him speak so casually of being a pilot, it is difficult to remember Oscar had once been a 'day boy' at Mpuguso school, living in a mud hut outside Tukuyu, walking six miles each day to and from school.

'Life is not good here in Tanzania now, Mr. Levitt,' he says, leaning toward me and lowering his voice. 'Our salaries have been cut. The best pilots are leaving the country.'

As he speaks, a young African plunks himself down at our table and sits staring off into space. Gradually, he joins our conversation. When he leaves, Oscar looks at me. 'Do you know him?' he asks. I shake my head. 'A stranger sits down at our table,' he says. 'Who is he? Maybe he is a spy. You know, Mr. Levitt, there are spies at all the hotels. They are there to spy on foreigners, like yourself.'

Although I was not to see Oscar again, I was to hear of him. Last February, after I'd left Tanzania, an Air Tanzania 737 on a domestic flight was hijacked by three men and forced to fly to London. There, the hijackers surrendered, released their passengers and read a proclamation demanding the resignation of President Nyerere.

A few weeks later, I received a letter from Rashid in Dar es Salaam. 'You will get a shock to learn that the Air Tanzania plane which was hijacked to London was being manned by Oscar Mwamaja as copilot,' he wrote.

Then last month, I received a letter from Oscar himself. He was in Nigeria. 'This surely will be a surprise for you,' he began, 'especially to hear from me being in Nigeria. ... Maybe you know I was involved in the hijacking which happened in Tanzania in February. That was a terrible experience.' He went on to say he had been shot in the back, but no major organs had been touched and in London the bullet had been removed. He said he had resigned from Air Tanzania and left the country 'for my peace of mind.'

He told me he was now working as a flying instructor in Nigeria, and that he hoped to go to the United States. He asked me to write him a recommendation to a university in California. He gave no indication that he had any intention of ever returning to Tanzania.

Even Oscar, the most successful of the young Africans I had known, no longer saw a future for himself in Tanzania. 'At the moment, I don't miss home much,' he wrote. 'I have a lot to do here and life isn't that difficult.'"
– (Leonard Levitt, "Tanzania: A Dream Deferred," *The New York Times Magazine*, 14 November 1982).

Besides Oscar Mwamwaja, another first cousin of Elijah Mwakikagile was Absalom Mwaibanje. He was the son of Eliakim Simeon Mwaibanje and attended Malangali Secondary School after Elijah did.

He was among the first civil servants in the government of newly independent Tanganyika from a school which – together with Tabora Boys, Tanga School and Old Moshi – produced a large number of people who went on to fill government positions, especially in the civil service, in the early years of independence when the country did not have many educated people.

Secondary school graduates formed the backbone of the civil service in Tanganyika, later Tanzania, during the post-colonial era. Among the alumni of Malangali – of other schools as well – were some of the people who played a major role in the struggle for independence in Tanganyika and in the new nation after it emerged from colonial rule.

Another alumnus of Malangali Secondary School was Amon Nsekela from Lupepo in Rungwe District. His contemporaries at Malangali included Elijah Mwakikagile, Brown Ngwilulupi, Jeremiah Kasambala and John Mwakangale. He also went to Tabora Boys.

Amon Nsekela later became a prominent figure in the government under President Nyerere. He served as permanent secretary in the ministry of foreign affairs soon after independence and held the same position in three other ministries at different times including the ministry of finance.

He was also the first chairman and director of the country's largest bank, the National Bank of Commerce, appointed by President Nyerere. He assumed the post in 1967only a few years after independence and served in that capacity for many years. He was also the first chairman of the Council of the University of Dar es Salaam and later served as high commissioner (ambassador) to Britain. He held many other high-level positions in Tanzania through the years from the 1960s to the 1990s.

A college, Dr. Amon J. Nsekela Bankers' Academy in the town of Iringa in the Southern Highlands, was named after him.

Another classmate of Elijah Mwakikagile at Malangali Secondary School was W.B.K. Mwanjisi who later became a doctor trained at Makerere University College in

Uganda. He was one of the early nationalists who gained national prominence in the political arena during the struggle for independence and held leadership positions at the national level in some organisations which fought for the rights of Africans and served as president of the national organisation of African government employees.

He was one of the most prominent members of TANU, the party that led the nationalist campaign, from the Southern Highlands Province. In 1954, he left government service and returned to Rungwe District in the Southern Highlands to work at a hospital in the town of Tukuyu, his home area.

During the struggle for independence, there were some Africans, including prominent ones, who compromised their "nationalist credentials" when they joined the United Tanganyika Party (UTP) of the British settlers who claimed Tanganyika was not ready for independence. But history was not on their side.

Before being actively involved in politics, another classmate of Elijah Mwakikagile at Malangali Secondary School, Jeremiah Kasambala, was the head of the Rungwe Cooperative Union in Rungwe District in the Southern Highlands Province, a position which thrust him into national prominence because of the major role cooperative unions - of farmers - across the country played in the struggle for independence. He was elected member of parliament representing Rungwe District and was appointed by President Nyerere as minister of trade and cooperatives, a portfolio that reflected his background as a leader of the cooperative union in Rungwe, one of the largest farmers' unions in Tanganyika. He also served as minister of industries, minerals and energy among other posts.

Besides being one of the leading figures in the independence struggle in Tanganyika, another Malangali alumnus, John Mwakangale, was also one of the leaders of the Pan-African Freedom Movement for East and Central

Africa (PAFMECA) founded in the port town of Mwanza on the shores of Lake Victoria,Tanganyika, in September 1958 under the leadership of Julius Nyerere.

PAFMECA mobilised forces and coordinated the struggle for independence in Tanganyika, Kenya, Zanzibar, Uganda, Nyasaland (renamed Malawi), Northern Rhodesia (now Zambia), and Southern Rhodesia (renamed Zimbabwe).

It was renamed the Pan-African Freedom Movement for East, Central and Southern Africa (PAFMECSA) after it was expanded to include the countries of southern Africa: apartheid South Africa, Bechuanaland (now Botswana), South West Africa (renamed Namibia), Basutoland (renamed Lesotho), and Swaziland.

John Mwakangale remained a prominent leader in the larger freedom movement which also played a major role in the formation of the Organisation of African Unity (OAU) in Addis Ababa, Ethiopia, in May 1963. The OAU was renamed the African Union (AU) in July 2002.

In 1958, John Mwakangale was one of the few African leaders who were elected to the Legislative Council (LEGCO), a colonial parliament of Tanganyika dominated by the British colonial rulers led by the British governor.

Members of LEGCO were elected on a tripartite system representing three racial categories: European, mostly British settlers; Asian, mostly Tanganyikans of Indian and Pakistani origin, a category which also included Arabs in terms of racial separation; and African – blacks who constituted the overwhelming majority of the population of Tanganyika but whose numerical preponderance did not overshadow racial minorities. Collectively, non-blacks were a significant minority.

Africans in Tanganyika – as in other British colonies including neighbouring Kenya, Uganda, Zanzibar, Northern Rhodesia and Nyasaland – were also subjected to indignities of colour bar similar to those under apartheid in South Africa, although not as rigid, yet equally humiliating.

There were signs designating racial categories. Toilets were labelled "Europeans," "Asians" and "Africans." Some hotels and bars were labelled "Europeans." Facilities for Africans were the worst. There were separate schools for Europeans, Asians and Africans.

The school Godfrey Mwakikagile attended in Dar es Salaam, Tambaza High School, was predominantly Asian. It was in an upper middle-class area of Upanga, designated – like the city centre – as a residential area for Asians. The head of the school during that period, Bori Lira, was the school's first African headmaster.

The students at the school were mostly Tanzanians of Indian and Pakistani origin even ten years after independence. It was once known as H.H. The Aga Khan High School, almost exclusively for Asian students, and changed its name to Tambaza after independence when the government decided to integrate all schools including Christian schools to enable Muslims and other non-Christians to enroll as students. Integration was mandatory.

Godfrey Mwakikagile was among the first African students to integrate the former H.H. The Aga Khan High School. And the hostel where some students stayed, known as H.H. The Aga Khan Hostel only a few yards from the school, was also overwhelmingly Asian. Mwakikagile was one of the few African students who stayed there.

It was a socially and racially stratified society. As Trevor Grundy, a British journalist who worked in Tanzania on the same newspaper where Godfrey Mwakikagile also worked as a news reporter during the same period, stated:

"I worked in Dar es Salaam (1968 - 1972) for one of the English papers....

Between 1933 and World War II there was next to no

development in Tanganyika. Hitler wanted his colonies back and the various British politicians thought it a good idea to return them - an act of appeasement to the German leader. So why spend money on something you're sooner or later give away?

After 1918, Tanganyika became a mandated territory under the League of Nations.

In African eyes, the British were no more popular than the Germans. The British turned Tanganyika into an undeclared apartheid state that was socially divided between divided Africans, Europeans and Asians....

(It was) British-style apartheid – their secret was never to give racial segregation a name." – (Trevor Grundy, "Julius Nyerere Reconsidered," 4 May 2015, africaunauthorised.com).

It is an observation made by a number of researchers including Professor Sarah L. Smiley. As she states in her paper, "The City of Three Colors: Segregation in Colonial Dar es Salaam, 1891 - 1961":

"My Dar es Salaam was one with little interaction between races and one where residents have strong ideas about where people belong. As a white American living in the traditionally Asian City Center, I was told by many people that I was out of place. The Dar es Salaam I experienced was *Mji wa Rangi Tatu* – the city of three colors.

To me these three colors are distinct, both in color and in geography, and represent three races in the city: whites, Asians, and Africans. That these colors are separate is a direct legacy of seventy years of segregation, first implemented by the German colonial government and later continued by the British colonial government.

Yet these three colors were never equal in terms of population; Dar es Salaam is, and always was, a majority African city. The city's African population was 90 percent in 1894 and 63 percent in 1957. During that same period, the city's European population was never more than four percent.

To call colonial Dar es Salaam a racially segregated city is not groundbreaking, since many scholars of the city have already done so. De Blij commented on the *de jure* racial segregation of Dar es Salaam among European, Asian and Arab, and African areas, and Leslie surveyed the city's many suburbs designed exclusively for the African population. Anthony and Mascarenhas both suggested that race served as the primary factor in Dar es Salaam's segregation, above class, ethnicity, religion, or occupation....

Building ordinances were subtle backdoor policies to segregate the city without an explicit focus on race. They divided Dar es Salaam into zones based solely on the types of buildings allowed in each zone. Zone 1 was for buildings of a European type, Zone 2 was for residential or commercial buildings, and Zone 3 was for native style buildings. These zones were distinct entities but had an important spatial component. Zone 1 occupied the city's premium land along the coast and was situated as far as possible from Zone 3 while Zone 2 served as a buffer between these areas.

Although these ordinances applied only to physical structures, they ultimately dictated the racial composition of these areas. in fact these areas acquired colloquial Swahili names; Zone 1 became known as *Uzunguni* (the place of Europeans), Zone 2 as *Uhindini* (the place of Indians), and Zone 3 as *Uswahilini* (the place of Africans)....

The British government maintained and strengthened racial segregation in Dar es Salaam in the absence of any official policy of segregation. This segregation did more than dictate the residential patterns of urban residents; the city was the site of social segregation as the government privileged the minority European population at the expense of the majority African population....

The end result of over one hundred years of racial segregation is *Mji wa Rangi Tatu*, a city with little interaction between races but clear notions about spatial belonging." – (Sarah L. Smiley, "The City of Three Colors: Segregation in Colonial Dar es Salaam, 1891 – 1961," *Historical Geography* Volume 37, 2009, pp. 178 – 179, 180).

The hierarchy of residential areas coincided with racial identity and served political purposes as well. The colonial rulers used Tanganyikans of Asian origin as a shock absorber - a buffer between Africans and Europeans to shield themselves from Africans. Some of the anger, caused by racial injustice, which should have been directed against the British colonial rulers was instead directed at Tanganyikan Asians. It was, nonetheless, a well-structured racial hierarchy to the detriment of Africans more than anybody else.

Smiley goes on to state:

"German rule in German East Africa officially began in 1887, and the government enacted some early forms of segregation before implementing its first building ordinance in 1891. During those four years the government seized eastern portions of the city from Africans and expelled them farther west....After 1912 the German government began to purchase land for a dedicaated African settlement, suggesting that it envisioned more strict segregation for the future....

The era of German colonial rule was interrupted by, and ultimately ended by, World War I. At the conclusion of the war, the Treaty of Versailles stripped Germany of its colonial possessions. The League of Nations Covenant mandated Tanganyika, formerly German East Africa, to Great Britain....The Mandate explicitly prohibited segregation and the unequal treatment of races....

Not only did the British government maintain and eventually expand the segregation implemented by the German administration, it repeatedly prioritized the needs of the European minority at the expense of the African majority....in fact a 1932 economic report suggested that too much money was spent on the European administration in a place where the needs of Africans were to come first....

Inequalities were especially evident in education. Before the end of World War II, Great Britain increased spending on education in Tanganyika Territory without providing education for Africans, an omission considered 'one of the least fortunate chapters in the history of the country under mandate.' After the war Britain began to spend more on African education, but spending levels remained disparate.

A 1955 grant supposedly allotted funding equally between European, Asian, and African education. The vast population differences – 21,000 Europeans, 80,000 Asians, and 8 million Africans – meant that African education received much less per person. These examples on education spending clearly show that the League of Nations did not prevent racial segregation or discrimination in Tanganyika in spite of the larger goal of the Mandate." – (Ibid., pp. 180, 181, 183).

This deliberate policy of systematic exclusion, segregation and discrimination which had its origin in the colonial administrations of both the German and British rulers of Tanganyika had a lasting impact that endures today decades after the country won independence. As Smiley points out concerning segregation in Dar es Salaam along racial lines, a policy that was implemented in other urban areas of colonial Tanganyika only in varying degrees but with the same objective in mind, to keep races apart, with whites having the most privileged status, it was impossible to separate residential designation from racial identity. Residential areas in Zone 1, of prime land, were designated "European," even if not explicitly so in semantic terms; Zone 3, "African."

The policy also led to racial friction and antagonism between Asians and Africans in Zone 3 which was referred to – and designated – as the "African area" but was also open to non-Africans since the British colonial rulers claimed the designation had nothing to do with race – the area had simply evolved into becoming "African" in terms of residence but never officially intended to be so. Smiley states:

"It is impossible for these (residential) zones to be simultaneously racially homogeneous and not about race at all....

One effect...was the intrusion of Asians into Zone 3; since the change permitted any type of construction in this area, some Asians took advantage of cheaper housing costs and increased business opportunities in this area. After World War II, the Tanganyika African Government Servants Association complained that Asians occupied all of the well-ventilated and hygienic homes in Kariakoo and were therefore contributing to the housing shortage and poor housing conditions of most of the city's African residents....The government was unwilling to stop this movement of Asians...since there was 'no policy of segregation of race'....

(Yet) conditions in Zone 3 remained poor (for racial reasons since the area still was mostly African in spite of the presence of some Asians - this comment added, not by Smiley). Zone 3 remained the only portion of the city that permitted construction of African style homes, and the government seriously underfunded this zone throughout colonial rule....

The government recognized that an official policy of racial segregation would violate the League of Nations Mandate but it clearly expressed interest in implementing such a policy and discovered ways to circumvent the Mandate. The desire to segregate Dar es Salaam was not expressed only by low-level officials. Even the governor of Tanganyika Territory, Horace Byatt, found segregation appealing:

'So far as segregation is concerned it is pretty clear to me that in this Territory we cannot adopt the principle of racial segregation as such, for that would lead us into a position...where we should be in conflict with the terms of the Treaty and the Mandate. There is a universal agreement as to the wisdom and necessity of segregation....We can, I believe, ensure proper segregation in actual practice by means of Building and Township Regulations. For example, though an Asiatic may buy a plot in the European residential quarter, we can require him to build on it a house of a type which would not suit his methods of life in that we should prohibit the existence of the Asiatic conception of a latrine....'

Certainly, as this quotation suggests, racial difference was a primary factor in why the British government segregated Dar es Salaam. Effectively the government achieved its goal by basing its building ordinance on racist assumptions. It assumed that only a European would want a flush toilet and that Africans were incapable of maintaining any structure other than a hut. Although these sanitation preferences could be linked to class, the government used racial categories when discussion these issues, suggesting its interests were in racial segregation rather than economic segregation." – (Ibid., pp. 183, 184).

Also, it was Africans who constituted the backbone of the economy. Yet they got virtually nothing in return. They paid the largest amount in taxes but saw nothing in terms of provision of services in their areas. In the 1940s, there wasn't even a water-borne sewage system in the African residential area of Dar es Salaam. Yet in 1942, more than 72 per cent of the city's residents were African. Residential segregation also reinforced social segregation. The British implemented this informal policy far more than the Germans did for historical reasons; they ruled Tanganyika longer than the Germans did and therefore had far more time and resources at their disposal to enforce it. As Smiley states:

"The British administration had nearly forty years to strengthen and expand the segregation begun by the Germans. It did so through deliberate actions that kept Europeans, Asians and and Africans physically and socially separate; by differentiating among the three zones in terms of housing and amenities, the government ensured that Dar es Salaam remained a city of three colors....In the absence of an official racial segregation policy, the British government was extremely successful in dividing Dar es Salaam (along racial lines)....

This trend of providing few benefits to Africans continued throughout British rule. In 1953 (eight years before independence) the majority of Africans in the Magomeni area did not have a bathroom or latrine. More so, this area had over 10,000 residents and only one public water point....(And) it was normal...for the city's Asians and Africans to live without electricity....The Colonial Development and Welfare Act did bring improved infrastructure to the city but unfortunately not all residents benefited equally from this policy. Europeans still received the best treatment while Africans often lived without basic amenities. Even when African areas did receive services, their scope and quality were often inferior to services in Zone 1 (for Europeans)....

On my trip to *Rangi Tatu* (also an African market area) I saw firsthand the racial divisions in Dar es salaam. I met one man who complained that many white researchers have passed through Mbagala asking residents about the quality of their lives, but many years later they are still without water and electricity. Why then should he talk to me? What would I do to benefit him? His response was not totally unexpected. He lives in one of Dar es Salaam's poorest neighborhoods, in an area that has been discriminated against since colonial rule.

Even with policies to increase development for Africans, Zone 3 areas still bear the ill-effects of too many years of neglect. After more than forty years of independence in Dar es Salaam, the legacies of colonial racial segregation and inequality are still very much evident....

The three zone urban plan implemented first by the German government and later expanded by the British government created stark divisions within the city.

What is especially interesting about these divisions is that they occurred without any direct policy of racial segregation. The colonial governments succeeded in segregating Dar es Salaam in the absence of an official state-sanctioned policy and without ever directly addressing the issue of race....The British adopted a seemingly innocuous building ordinance in the hope of securing the 'same advantages' as racial segregation....

The German and British uses of building ordinances certainly created a city of three colors. These three colors were not equal, with Africans comprising the overwhelming majority of Dar es Salaam's population. In spite of this dominance, the British government still privileged the European minority giving them premium residential plots, better amenities, and more funding....The British government was alarmed when native style huts encroached on Oyster Bay's European suburb but acted quickly to maintain the area's unofficial racial segregation....

In 1952 officials refused to let Europeans live in homes without electricity (which was normal for Africans)....

In light of these inequalities, it is no wonder that Dar es

Salaam became such a divided city....To call Dar es Salaam *Mji wa Rangi Tatu* (the city of three colours) is not a compliment on the city's diversity or cosmopolitanism; it is a recognition of its history of racial segregation and discrimination." – (Ibid., pp. 186, 190, 191, 192, 193).

Almost 60 years after independence, Dar es Salaam essentially remains a racially segregated city. This segregation spans the cultural and socio-economic spectrum with little prospect for fundamental change.

Godfrey Mwakikagile experienced that when he worked as a news reporter and lived in Dar es Salaam in the black areas of Tandika, Temeke and Ilala, products of decades of racial segregation and reflective of the systematic racialism instituted by the colonial rulers and fortified by other non-blacks – Tanzanians of Asian origin and Arabs – who don't want to integrate with blacks. That is one of the most prominent features of the city's identity even if some of the city's residents don't acknowledge colour consciousness as a fact of life. It is ruthlessly public in residential patterns in spite of the racial integration that has taken place in some areas through the years in the post-colonial era.

Godfrey Mwakikagile lived under this system of racial segregation and discrimination when he was growing up in Tanganyika in the fifties and sixties and wrote about it in his books, *Life in Tanganyika in The Fifties*, *My Life as an African*, *Africa and The West* and other works including *Nyerere and Africa: End of an Era* and *Tanzania under Mwalimu Nyerere: Reflections on an African Statesman*. For example, he vividly remembers the public toilet he and other Africans had to use at the bus station in the town of Mbeya in the Southern Highlands Province where he came from. It was labelled "Africans" and was filthy. The label on the toilet was still there even after independence, a chilling reminder of an inglorious past.

He remembers using the toilet during holidays when he

was a student, going to and from Songea Secondary School, a boarding school in southern Tanzania he attended from 1965 to 1968. He slept at the bus station – on the floor – with the other students as well as other passengers, all black. There were no chairs or benches.

The bus station in Mbeya, the capital of the Southern Highlands Province, was also the only one in town in those days. The buses were owned by the East African Railways and Harbours Corporation (EAR&H) serving the three East African countries of Kenya, Uganda and Tanganyika (later Tanzania) founded by the British colonial rulers.

There was also, in the town of Mbeya, the Mbeya Club exclusively for whites before independence; Mbeya School for white children, mostly of British settlers; and a residential area and houses for whites, again mostly British.

Godfrey Mwakikagile also spent a part of his childhood in Mbeya from 1954 to 1955. He and his family moved from Kigoma to Morogoro in 1952, and from Morogoro to Mbeya in 1954.

The years Godfrey Mwakikagile spent under segregation when he was growing up in different parts of Tanganyika shaped his thinking and perspective on race relations and on the impact of colonial rule on the colonised when he became a writer of non-fiction books about colonial and post-colonial Africa.

There was also racial discrimination in employment during colonial rule when Godfrey Mwakikagile was growing up in the fifties. His father was a victim of such discrimination when he worked for the colonial government and other British employers, as he has stated in his autobiographical writings.

The struggle for independence in Tanganyika in the 1950s, Mwakikagile's formative years, was partly fuelled by such racial injustices which, years later, became the focus of some of his writings.

He has written about that in his book *Life in Tanganyika in The Fifties* and other works including *Life under British Colonial Rule: Recollections of an African* in which he describes some incidents of racial injustice. One such incident involved his father when a white supervisor where he worked told him he could not have lunch in the office they shared or even put it on the table. But the supervisor could eat there.

Another one had to do with Godfrey Mwakikagile himself when, as a six-year-old walking to school with other boys, he was severely injured after being chased and bitten by a dog owned by a white couple who lived in a house the children went by everyday, on a public road, on their way to and from school.

Decades later, after 2017, he stated in his autobiographical writings that he still had a highly visible scar on his right knee where he was bitten by the dog. It was a large dog and it could have killed him.

The couple had two dogs, including a German shepherd, which used to chase the boys. They knew the children went by their house and saw them on their way to and from school everyday but did not tie the dogs or keep them on leashes.

The house was on a tea plantation at Kyimbila, the children passed through, and the husband was the manager of Kyimbila Tea Estate.

That was in 1956 when Godfrey Mwakikagile was in Standard One in primary school in Rungwe District in the Southern Highlands Province, as he stated in his books *Life in Tanganyika in The Fifties*, *My Life as an African*, *Life under British Colonial Rule* and *Tanzania under Mwalimu Nyerere: Reflections on an African Statesman*.

After being bitten by the dog, he stated in his autobiographical writings that he went on to school where he attended class without getting any help – there was no medical assistance at the primary school, not even a First Aid kit – until he returned home in the evening. He continued to go to school in the following days. And nothing could be done to the dog owners during those days. It was colonial rule, blacks did not have the same rights whites had, and knew their place as colonial subjects not as equal citizens in a racially divided society which was vertically structured not only to keep whites on top of other races, especially blacks, but also virtually above the law.

Godfrey Mwakikagile also stated in his autobiographical works that when he was bitten by the dog, the attack was seared in his memory but as a six-year-old he did not see it in terms of racism until he became a teenager. Years later, he stated in some of his writings that had the children been white, the white couple would probably not have allowed the dogs to roam freely knowing they could attack them.

The colonial rulers and many white settlers had total disregard for the wellbeing of Africans as Godfrey Mwakikagile himself experienced when he was growing up in colonial Tanganyika and almost lost his life when he was attacked by a dog owned by a white couple who did not care about the safety of African children, or any other blacks, passing by their house even though they walked on a public road. Such disregard for the wellbeing and safety of Africans was a continental phenomenon even if the parallels were not exact; it was the same experience and humiliation, nonetheless, be it in Tanganyika, Kenya, Guinea or Mali. As Godfrey Mwakikagile stated in his book *Africa and The West*:

"In all the African colonies, exploitation went hand in hand with degradation and brutality. In the Congo under the Belgian King Leopold II, Belgians chopped off the hands and arms of Africans who did not collect enough rubber from the forest. In Tanganyika, when it was German East Africa, Germans introduced forced labor and corporal punishment, virtually enslaving Africans, a practice which triggered the Maji Maji war of resistance from 1905 – 07 and covered almost half of the country. The uprising almost ended German rule which was saved only after reinforcements were rushed from Germany.

The French in West Africa also introduced forced labor. Some of the leaders of independent Africa toiled in those labor camps. Madeira Keita, a native of Mali who was active in the politics of Guinea before it won independence in 1958 and collaborated closely with Sekou Toure in founding the Democratic Party of Guinea, was one of them. In April 1959, he became Interior Minister of Mali, and in August 1960, he also became Minister of National Defense, holding two ministerial posts under President Modibo Keita. He related his experience as a conscripted laborer:

'Before 1945, there was a colonial regime with government by decree, the regime of the *indignat*. The *indignat* form of government permitted the colonial administration to put Africans in prison without any trial. Sometimes you were put in prison for two weeks because you did not greet the administrator or the commander. You were happy enough if they did not throw stones at you or send you to a work camp, because there was also forced labor at that time. In 1947, I met French journalists who were very surprised to learn that forced labor was nonvoluntary and not paid for. Transportation was not even covered; nor were food and lodging. The only thing that was covered was work.'

The conquest of Africa inexorably led to such brutality because its purpose was exploitation which has no room for compassion. It was an invasion we could very well have done without. The baneful foreign influence Africa is still subjected to is a result of that invasion. And we are now inextricably linked with our former conquerors, for better or for worse, in an international system which accentuates inequalities and from which no part of humanity can extricate itself.

But the materialism of the West, which has found its way into Africa with devastating impact, must be counterbalanced with the spirituality and sense of sharing of the African which animates his culture, indeed his very being." – Godfrey Mwakikagile, *Africa and The West*, Huntington, New York: Nova Science Publishers, Inc., 2000, pp. 14 – 15; Madeira Keita, "Le Parti Unique en Afrique," in *Presence Africaine*, No. 30, February – March 1960; and Madeira Keita, "The Single Party in Africa," in Paul E. Sigmund, ed., *The Ideologies of the Developing Nations*, New York: Praeger, 1963, p. 170. On the African uprising and war of resistance against German colonial rule in Tanganyika, see, among other works, G. C. K. Gwassa and John Iliffe, eds., *Records of the Maji-Maji Rising*, Dar es Salaam: Tanzania Publishing House, 1968).

Mwakikagile further stated in *Africa and The West*:

"The argument that we blacks are genetically inferior to members of other races is nothing new. It is a stereotype rooted in Western intellectual tradition and has even been given "credibility" by some of the most eminent thinkers of the Western world including Immanuel Kant, Georg Hegel, David Hume, and Baron de Montesquieu. Some of them did not even consider blacks to be full human beings.

As Montesquieu stated in *The Spirit of the Laws*:

'These creatures are all over black, and with such a flat nose, that they can scarcely be pitied. It is hardly to be believed that God, who is a wise Being, should place a soul, especially a good soul, in such a black, ugly body. The Negroes prefer a glass necklace to that gold which polite nations so highly value: can there be a greater proof of their wanting common sense? It is impossible for us to suppose these creatures to be men.'

The other philosophers were no less racist. According to Kant:

'The Negroes of Africa have received from nature no intelligence that rises above the foolish. The difference between the two races (black and white) is thus a substantial one: it appears to be just as great in respect of the faculties of the mind as in color.'

Hume:

'I am apt to suspect the Negroes...to be naturally inferior to the whites. There never was any civilized nation of any other complexion than white, nor even any individual eminent in action or speculation. No ingenious manufactures among them, no arts, no sciences...Such a uniform and constant difference could not happen, in so many countries and ages, if nature had not made an original distinction betwixt these breeds of men.'

And according to Hegel:

'Africa...is no historical part of the world; it has no movement or development to exhibit.'

It is a sentiment echoed more than 100 years later in contemporary times by many people including British historian Arnold Toynbee who died in 1975. As he put it:

'The black races alone have not contributed positively to any civilization.'

And in the words of that great humanitarian Dr. Albert Schweitzer:

'The Negro is a child, and with children nothing can be done without the use of authority. We must, therefore, so arrange the circumstances of daily life that my natural authority can find expression. With regard to the Negroes, then, I have coined the formula: 'I am your brother, it is true, but your elder brother"....

The conquest of Africa led not only to oppression and exploitation, but also to denigration of her culture and indigenous institutions. Africans, at least a vary large number of them, were brainwashed into believing that they had no history they could be proud of; that all their customs and traditions were bad, and that even their languages were bad.... When Africa was conquered by the imperial powers, she was also conquered by ideas...as a very effective weapon for conquering other people by conquering their minds....

There is no other continent which is endowed with so much in terms of natural resources. But there is also no other continent where it has been so easy for foreigners to take what does not belong to them....

Because of the pervasive nature of Western influence, its negative impact has reached all parts of the world, including Africa where the devastation wrought is difficult to contain because of the underdeveloped nature of our economies, and also because of our inability to resist such penetration. The sheer scope of such influence, as well as its negative attraction especially among the youth who are mesmerized by the glitter of the West, is mind-boggling and far beyond our capacity to resist it. That is especially the case in the cities which continue to attract millions of people in search of better – read, Western – life. It is a burden Africa cannot bear.

The West may have harnessed the forces of nature and pushed the frontiers of knowledge in many areas, from which Africa has indeed benefited as has the rest of the world. But Africa's contribution – material and spiritual as well as intellectual – to the growth of Western civilization has never been fully acknowledged. Nor has the destruction of African civilization by the West through imperial conquest. That is undoubtedly one of the saddest chapters in the history of relations between Africa and the West. As Immanuel Kant, although a racist, conceded in one of his works *Eternal Peace and Other Essays*:

'If we compare the barbarian instances of inhospitality...with the inhuman behavior of the civilized, and especially the commercial, states of our continent, the injustice practiced by them even in their first contact with foreign lands and peoples fills us with horror; the mere visiting of such peoples being regarded by them as equivalent to a conquest...The Negro lands,...The Cape of Good Hope, etc., on being discovered, were treated as countries that belonged to nobody; for the aboriginal inhabitants were reckoned as nothing...And all this has been done by nations who make a great ado about their piety, and who, while drinking up iniquity like water, would have themselves regarded as the very elect of orthodox faith.'

Africa has yet to recover from the multiple wounds inflicted on her by this Western invasion. But there is a glimmer of hope. And that is traditional Africa. In spite of all the devastating blows our continent has sustained from the West, traditional Africa continues to be the continent's spiritual anchor and bedrock of our values without which we are no more than a dilapidated house shifting on quick sand. It is to traditional society that we must turn to save Africa from the West, and also save ourselves – from ourselves." – (G. Mwakikagile, *Africa and The West*, ibid., pp. viii – ix, 208, 218).

Godfrey Mwakikagile also explained that East Africans who were born and brought up during colonial rule had more direct experience with racism than West Africans did because of the larger white population in East Africa with significant settler communities, especially in Kenya, although smaller and fewer in Tanganyika. Many of them had bitter experience with the colonial rulers and the white settlers because of the racial injustices perpetrated against them, including doubts about their intelligence and even common sense expressed by some whites. As he stated in his book *Africa and The West*:

"Colonialism, as a system of oppression and exploitation, not only continued to plunder Africa but sought to instill in the minds of Africans feelings of inferiority to justify such domination...This is just one example – what Colonel Ewart Grogan, the doyen of the white settlers in colonial Kenya and leader of the Kenya British Empire Party, said about Africans attending the renowned Makerere University College in Uganda:

'Just teaching a lot of stupid monkeys to dress up like Europeans. Won't do any good. Just cause a lot of discontent. They can never be like us, so better for them not to try.'

Another (Kenyan) settler in the 'Dark Continent' had this:

'I've actually got a farm hand who wears a tie – but the stupid bastard doesn't realize you don't wear a tie without a shirt!'

The implication is obvious. It is a sweeping indictment against all "native Africans" as a bunch of idiots.

Yet another one, Sir Godfrey Huggins, Prime Minister of Southern Rhodesia, acclaimed as a British liberal, shot point-blank at a press conference in London:

'It is time for the people in England to realize that the white man in Africa is not prepared and never will be prepared to accept the African as an equal, either socially or politically. Is there something in their chromosomes which makes them more backward and different from peoples living in the East and West?'" – (Godfrey Mwakikagile, *Africa and The West*, Huntington, New York: Nova Science Publishers, Inc., 2000, pp. 9 – 10, 69; Colin M. Turnbull, *The Lonely African*, New York: Simon and Schuster, 1962, pp. 89, 21, 90, 97; G. Mwakikagile, *Africa and The West*, p. 97: "A man with a flair for controversy and an outspoken racist, Grogan described himself as 'the baddest and boldest of a bold bad gang.' He also gained notoriety for publicly flogging Africans in Nairobi. The settlers from South Africa also came 'with the racial prejudices of that country. Frederick Jackson, Sir Charles Eliot's Deputy Commissioner, told the Foreign Office that the Protectorate was becoming a country of 'nigger-' and game-shooters.'" G. Mwakikagile, ibid, p. 113: "Colonel Ewart Grogan, a leader of the white settlers, bluntly stated: 'We Europeans have to go on ruling this country and rule it with iron discipline...If the whole of the Kikuyu land unit is reverted to the Crown, then every Kikuyu would know that our little queen was a great Bwana'"; E. S. Grogan, in the *East African Standard*, Nairobi, Kenya, 12 November 1910; Elspeth Huxley, *White Man's Country, Vol. I*, London and New York: Macmillan, 1935, pp. 222 - 223, 261 - 262; George Padmore, *Pan-Africanism or Communism?: The Coming Struggle for Africa*, London: Denis Dobson, 1956, pp. 255, 256).

The humanity of Africans, and their lives, meant absolutely nothing to many whites, demonstrated by the injustices and indignities black people suffered under colonial rule.

School children who grew up in the fifties were among

the victims. The problem was compounded by inequalities in the provision of funds and facilities for education. Meagre resources were allocated to education for African children in sharp contrast with the amount spent on schools for European and Asian children. The school Godfrey Mwakikagile attended was no exception. It was also the dawn of a new era in the history of Tanganyika.

He stated in his autobiographical works that the fifties which was a decade that preceded independence was a transitional period which symbolised the identity and partly shaped the thinking of those who grew up in those years as a product of both eras, colonial and post-colonial. They also served as a bridge between the two.

Godfrey Mwakikagile also stated in his works, *Life in Tanganyika in The Fifties* and *Life under British Colonial Rule* among others, that it was in the same year he was bitten by the dog that Princess Margaret visited Mbeya and Sao Hill in the Southern Highlands Province, as well as other parts of the country, in October 1956; a visit that symbolised British imperial rule over Tanganyika but also at a time when the nationalist movement was gaining momentum in the struggle for independence. The party that led the country to independence, Tanganyika African National Union (TANU), had been formed just two years before, in July 1954, and within months succeeded in mobilising massive support across the country in its quest to end colonial rule. Independence was inevitable.

Mwakikagile has written about other incidents of racial injustice and other subjects to show how life was in colonial Tanganyika in the fifties from the perspective of colonial subjects who hardly had any rights in their own country ruled and dominated by whites. Africans were lowest in the racial hierarchy, with Asians and Arabs ranked next to whites.

According to his autobiographical works, he grew up in a politically conscious family. His father knew some of the leading figures in the independence struggle who came from the Southern Highlands Province and other parts of Tanganyika.

They included Austin Shaba who did not come from the Southern Highlands Province but was his classmate at a medical training centre at the national hospital in Dar es Salaam and later became a cabinet member in the first independence cabinet serving as minister of local government. Shaba was also a member of parliament for Mtwara and later served as deputy speaker of parliament and as minister of health and housing.

Although Austin Shaba was brought up in Tanganyika, he lost his "citizenship" and cabinet post as well as other government positions in October 1968 because the government found out that both of his parents, who moved to Tanganyika from Nyasaland, were born in Nyasaland and were not Tanganyikan citizens. Therefore he himself was not a citizen and lost something he never had, although it had been assumed through the years that he was a citizen; he was not, according to the law. He and his parents came form Mzimba, Nyasaland.

There was also a time when Elijah Mwakikagile and Austin Shaba worked together when they were medical assistants. Years later, when Godfrey Mwakikagile was a news reporter, he stated that he once interviewed Austin Shaba on the telephone when Shaba was chairman of the Tanganyika Sisal Marketing Board based in Tanga. Shaba asked him: "Are you Elijah Mwakikagile's son? I know your parents and knew you when you were a child."

When he was growing up, Godfrey's parents told him about some of the people they knew, especially his father's classmates, schoolmates and co-workers who were involved in the nationalist movement during the struggle for independence. Godfrey knew some of them. They came from the same area where he grew up in Rungwe District.

Godfrey Mwakikagile has written about the "complex" race relations between Africans and the British settlers in those days and about many other subjects in his book, *Life in Tanganyika in The Fifties*:

"What makes this account particularly compelling is that he is an African whose own family experienced life under colonial rule. Interviewing many surviving actors, this book offers compelling primary evidence on the state of race relations at this delicate time before independence." – (British Empire Books, Authors, Bibliography, Historiography and Library: http://www.britishempire.co.uk/library/library.htm).

The book has had favourable reviews. A reviewer on amazon.com who lived in Tanganyika in those days stated the following:

"I grew up in Tanzania, and this book really takes me back home. The man tells how things were without hiding the bad times of the colonial era. But, I must say, he is NOT bitter and angry at the British like many other African writers. This story has its boring moments of course because life is like that. I found it very realistic and refreshing." – (Steve VN, "An African Growing up in Tanzania in the 1950s and 1960s," amazon.com, August 18, 2016, https://www.amazon.com/Life-Tanganyika-Fifties-Godfrey-Mwakikagile/dp/9987160123#customerReviews).

Another reviewer, also on amazon.com, wrote the following about the same book:

"I was there. What a beautiful country! Wonderful days, wonderful memories. The best of times. Brought tears to my eyes. I have yet to read a better book on Tanganyika in those days." – (Keith, "Tanganyika in the fifties – a decade to remember," amazon.com, July 7, 2006, https://www.amazon.com/Life-Tanganyika-Fifties-

Godfrey-Mwakikagile/dp/9987160123#customerReviews).

It was an era of delicate and sometimes tense race relations, with Africans confined to a subordinate status, being on the lowest rung of the racial hierarchy. Education meant nothing in terms of social status and earnings. Africans were never treated equal to Europeans, Asians and other non-blacks. Some of the earliest African nationalists were those who fought in World War II, an experience which fuelled nationalist sentiments among them when they returned home. One of them was Ali Sykes who played a major in forming the party that led Tanganyika to independence:

"One thing that Ally Sykes learned from these experiences was that he must come back and liberate Tanganyika from the yoke of imperialism. There were three different diets in the army designed on racial basis for Europeans, Asians and Africans. Back home salary grades were similarly designed along racial lines with Africans at the bottom rung. A fully qualified African doctor from Makerere was being paid half of what a semi-qualified Indian doctor was earning....

Returning to Tanganyika – today Tanzania – in the early 1950s, Sykes became a key activist in the liberation movement being one of the founder members of the Tanganyika African National Union (Tanu) the forerunner of Chama Cha Mapinduzi (CCM). He carried membership card number two while Julius Nyerere carried card number one." – (Douglas Kiereini, "Ally Sykes' Courage That Saw Tanzania Gain Independence," *Business Daily*, Nairobi, Kenya, 10 May 2018)."

African leaders, including Julius Nyerere, campaigning for independence were subjected to the same indignities which continued even after the end of colonial rule, especially during the early years, but drew a swift response from the new government which was predominantly black and multi-racial. As Mwakikagile stated in *Nyerere and Africa: End of an Era*:

"Mwalimu himself had experienced racial discrimination, what we in East Africa – and elsewhere including southern Africa – also call colour bar. As Colin Legum states in a book he edited with Tanzanian Professor Geoffrey Mmari, *Mwalimu: The Influence of Nyerere:*

'I was privileged to meet Nyerere while he was still a young teacher in short trousers at the very beginning of his political career, and to engage in private conversations with him since the early 1950s.

My very first encounter in 1953 taught me something about his calm authority in the face of racism in colonial Tanganyika. I had arranged a meeting with four leaders of the nascent nationalist movement at the Old Africa Hotel in Dar es Salaam. We sat at a table on the pavement and ordered five beers, but before we could lift our glasses an African waiter rushed up and whipped away all the glasses except mine.

I rose to protest to the white manager, but Nyerere restrained me. 'I am glad it happened,' he said, 'now you can go and tell your friend Sir Edward Twining [the governor at the time] how things are in this country.'

His manner was light and amusing, with no hint of anger.'

Simple, yet profound. For, beneath the surface lay a steely character with a deep passion for justice across the colour line and an uncompromising commitment to the egalitarian ideals he espoused and implemented throughout his political career, favouring none.

Years later his son, Andrew Nyerere, told me about an incident that also took place in the capital Dar es Salaam shortly after Tanganyika won independence in 1961 near the school he and I attended and where we also stayed from 1969 – 1970. Like the incident earlier when Julius Nyerere was humiliated at the Old Africa Hotel back in 1953, this one also involved race. As Andrew stated in a letter to me in 2002 when I was writing this book:

'As you remember, Sheikh Amri Abeid was the first mayor of Dar es Salaam. Soon after independence, the mayor went to Palm Beach Hotel (near our high school, Tambaza, on United Nations Road in Upanga). There was a sign at the hotel which clearly stated: 'No Africans and dogs allowed inside.' He was blocked from entering the hotel, and said in protest, 'But I am the Mayor.' Still he was told, 'You will not get in.' Shortly thereafter, the owner of the hotel was given 48 hours to leave the country. When the nationalization exercise began, that hotel was the first to be nationalized.'

Such insults were the last thing that could be tolerated in newly independent Tanganyika. And President Nyerere, probably more than any other African leader, would not have tolerated, and did not tolerate, seeing even the humblest of peasants being insulted and humiliated by anyone including fellow countrymen." – (Godfrey Mwakikagile, *Nyerere and Africa: End of an Era*, New Africa Press, 2010, pp. 501 – 502).

It was also at the Palm Beach Hotel where Stokely Carmichael (Kwame Ture) stayed when he went to Tanzania in November 1967; he was interviewed by the *Sunday News* and *The Nationalist*, Dar es Salaam, 5 – 6 November.

He gave a fiery speech at the University of Dar es Salaam in early 1968 denouncing racism which he himself would have experienced at the Palm Beach Hotel had he gone there before or soon after independence, as did the first African mayor of Dar es Salaam, Sheikh Amri Abeid, who assumed the post not long after Tanganyika attained sovereign status.

Professor Terence Ranger (1929 – 2015), a renowned British historian who specialised in African history and who taught at the University College of Rhodesia and Nyasaland (now the University of Zimbabwe) in Salisbury (renamed Harare in 1982) from 1957 until 1963 when he was deported in March by the white minority regime for supporting Africans in their quest for racial equality – he went to teach at the University of Dar es Salaam after he was deported – recalled the day Stokely Carmichael spoke at Tanzania's leading academic institution. As he stated in his book, *Writing Revolt: An Engagement with African Nationalism, 1957 – 67*:

"Early in 1968 Stokely Carmichael [Trinidadian-American civil rights activist] visited the College to give a lecture under the auspices of the Student Revolutionary Front. As the frogs croaked loudly in the pool outside, Stokely held his audience spellbound inside. A master orator, he could do more with a whisper than anyone else with a shout.

He had three messages. The first was that African students were the true proletariat and that they, guns in hand, must spearhead the revolution.

The second was that the major liberation movements could not be trusted. He attacked particularly the so-called 'authentic' movements, recognized as such by Soviet Russia - ZAPU, FRELIMO, and the MPLA. He offered to chair a debate between their representatives and spokesmen of the rival parties, ZANU included. (Wisely none of them took up the challenge). Giovanni Arrighi, now teaching in Dar and a strong supporter of ZAPU, was incandescent with rage, hissing to me that Stokely must be an agent of the CIA.

The third message was that it was necessary, but hard,

to hate the whites. It was easy to hate Asians, he said, but whites were so much admired and so dominant that one had to work really hard to hate them.

At one stage he was interrupted while students came up and mopped his brow with a large handkerchief.

A history student sitting next to me was shouting 'I do hate the whites, I do hate the whites,' pausing to whisper to me, 'I don't mean you, Professor Ranger.'

Stokely's then wife, Miriam Makeba, sang 'Nkosi Sikelel' iAfrika,' a moment of true emotion.

It was the only meeting I have ever been to at which it was impossible for me to raise a question or to make an objection.

The next day I visited the Refugee School, where the teachers thought their students would be interested to hear about 1896 (when blacks fought white settlers in Zimbabwe and lost). I took *Revolt* with me.

It turned out that Stokely had been there the day before. He had told the students that he was pleased they were passing exams but they must not take this white knowledge seriously. They must always be suspicious of whatever whites told them, and be most suspicious when a white told them something they liked to hear. They must always ask themselves what the motive was. So I encountered a very critical audience.

The first questioner told me that he had understood what I had said but that what he wanted to know was the function of it. Fortunately for me, he gave an example by adding:

'I think you have told us about 1896 because the Africans were defeated in the end and you want to discourage us.'

I determined not to knuckle under and fought back, grasping a convenient hammer which was lying on the desk. I asked whether Nyerere talked of Maji Maji because it had been defeated in the end and he wanted to discourage Tanzanians.

When they refused to believe that some Africans served on the white side in 1896, I showed them photos in the book (*Revolt*). 'But who took the photos?' they asked. Would that all audiences were so critical!

A very different repudiation of the book came when I arrived at UCLA in 1969. As I entered the elevator in the Bunche building, Donald Abraham wheeled himself out. 'I hold you personally responsible for the death of spirit mediums in Mozambique,' he said in passing.

Nor were the academic reviews all positive. Robert Rotberg wrote a particularly disobliging one for *African Historical Studies*." – (Terence Ranger, *Writing Revolt: An Engagement with African Nationalism, 1957 – 67*, Woodbridge, Suffolk, UK: James Currey; Harare, Zimbabwe: Weaver Press, 2013, pp. 178 - 170).

Stokely Carmichael's message had universal appeal in terms of struggle against racism, especially in the context of southern Africa where white minority regimes were in control during that period, with Tanzania being the headquarters of all the African liberation movements.

It was also a message that resonated with his audience at the University of Dar es Salaam and at the school for young refugees (Kurasini International Education Centre on the outskirts of Dar es Salaam) from southern Africa in a country where incidents of racism were nothing new, blacks being the main victims during colonial times and even after independence at the hands of other non-blacks as well, not just whites.

Godfrey Mwakikagile's home region, the Southern Highlands Province, was one of the areas of Tanganyika which had a significant number of white settlers, mostly British, during the colonial period and in the early years of independence.

Incidents of racial discrimination in the province were

not uncommon, including some involving his father in the town of Tukuyu, as he explained in his book *Life in Tanganyika in The Fifties*. He has, in the same book, written about other incidents when he himself was a victim of racism; incidents which he has also narrated in his other work, *Tanzania under Mwalimu Nyerere: Reflections on an African Statesman*.

It was also in the town of Tukuyu where the first meeting of the leaders of the white settlers met in October 1925 to discuss formation of a giant federation covering East and Central Africa – Kenya, Uganda, Tanganyika, Nyasaland, Northern Rhodesia and Southern Rhodesia – to consolidate imperial rule.

The conference was called by Lord Delamere, the leader of the British settlers in Kenya. Godfrey Mwakikagile wrote about that in his books, *Africa and the West* and *Africa After Independence: Realities of Nationhood*. As he stated in *Africa and the West*:

"In 1920, the protectorate of British East Africa became Kenya Colony...a fundamental transition...intended to consolidate the power of the white settlers.

In London the Secretary of State for the Colonies, Winston Churchill, speaking at an East African dinner...in January 1922...said the democratic principles of Europe were 'by no means suited to the development of Asiatic and African people.'

According to *The Times*, London, 28 January 1922, he stated that the intention was to enable British settlers in Kenya to have their own government, a situation similar to what led to the consolidation of white power in Southern Rhodesia and...to the eruption of guerrilla warfare years later by black nationalists in both countries....

Had such self-government been granted,...it would eventually have led to a declaration of independence by whites, making Kenya an independent 'white' nation like apartheid South Africa, Australia and New Zealand, and as Rhodesia attempted to do when it declared independence in November 1965, had black people in Kenya not unleashed Mau Mau.

There was such a determined attempt to consolidate white power that even a giant federation of all the British territories in East and Central Africa was considered. Settler leaders from the British colonies in the region met for the first time in October 1925 at Tukuyu, in the southwestern highlands of Tanganyika, to consider the proposal with the blessings of the British government. As George Bennett states:

'In Kenya Delamere was ready for (Governor Edward) Grigg's federation plans...(and) called a conference, at Tukuyu in southern Tanganyika, of settler leaders from the whole area from Kenya to Nyasaland and Northern Rhodesia. This was succeeded by others, at Livingstone (Northern Rhodesia) in 1926 and Nairobi in 1927.'

However, after the British Conservative Government fell in June 1929, hopes for any federation of East and Central African territories were also dashed....

Yet the Hilton Young Commission of the British government which issued a report on the failure of the proposed federation was condescending towards Africans, and its recommendations were endorsed by successive governments. As Bennett states:

'The Report itself describes (Africans as) 'the backward races' twenty centuries (2,000 years) behind the Europeans.'

That was tantamount to saying the interests of the indigenous people could never be considered equal to those of the members of the 'advanced' race. According to the Hilton Young Report:

'(Waiting) till the backward races have reached their (white settlers') standard is an impossible proposition which no virile and governing race could be expected to acquiesce in'....

Continued mistreatment of Africans led to increased political agitation...during the late 1920s and thereafter." – (Godfrey Mwakikagile, *Africa and the West*, Huntington, New York: Nova Science Publishers, Inc., 2000, pp. 88 – 89).

In his work, *Sidney Webb and East Africa: Labour's Experiment with the Doctrine of Native Paramountcy*, Professor Robert G. Gregory provided another perspective on Lord Delamere and the meeting of the white settler leaders he convened at Tukuyu:

"The idea of a federation in East and Central Africa was not new; it was almost as old as white settlement in Kenya....By 1925, when Griggs became Governor, Delamere had decided that federation was inevitable.

In October 1925, with characteristic zeal, he organized an unofficial conference. At Tukuyu, a remote outpost in southern Tanganyika, he met with twelve influential settlers from Kenya, Tanganyika, Nyasaland, and Northern Rhodesia to discuss closer union. He fed them canned food and champagne and by the end of the week had convinced them of the advantages of a federation. ...Sir Herbert Stanley, Governor of Northern Rhodesia, delivered the opening address, and Delamere as chairman presided over the other sessions.

But although Delamere at this time gained much prestige and was hailed as 'the Rhodes of East Africa,' he did not succeed in bringing the delegates to any agreement. Representatives from the Rhodesias (Northern and Southern Rhodesia) feared amalgamation with the

'Black North.'" – (Robert G. Gregory, *Sidney Webb and East Africa: Labour's Experiment with the Doctrine of Native Paramountcy*, Berkeley: University of California Press, 1962, pp. 64 – 65).

In the late 1920s and 1930s and even thereafter, British settlers, especially in Kenya, continued to campaign for a federation of the three East African countries – Kenya, Uganda and Tanganyika – they knew they would dominate. Nairobi, Kenya's capital, had, in the 1920s, virtually become the capital of the British East African colonies. The proposed federation was strongly opposed by African leaders who saw it as an instrument of domination to perpetuate imperial rule.

The Central African Federation, also known as the Federation of Rhodesia and Nyasaland (Northern Rhodesia, Southern Rhodesia and Nyasaland), collapsed for the same reason. Formed in August 1953 and dominated by Southern Rhodesia which had the largest number of white settlers among the three countries, it was dissolved in December 1963 because of strong opposition by African nationalists.

Founded in 1900 by the German colonial rulers and named Neu Langenburg, the town of Tukuyu where the leaders of the white settlers met to formulate plans on how to turn the entire region into a white dominion was and still is the headquarters of Rungwe District in the Southern Highlands. It was partly destroyed by an earthquake in 1919:

"During May and June, 1919, very severe seismic disturbances were experienced in the south-western portion of the Territory, which wrecked the Government station and several mission buildings in the Rungwe (former Langenburg) district and caused much damage at Songea....

At Tukuyu, (formerly Neu Langenburg) the shocks

occurred almost hourly till the end of the month, and at Songea 72 separate shocks were recorded. They appeared to emanate from the Livingstone Mountains and to travel in a north-easterly or north-westerly direction. All earth tremors were accompanied by heavy rumblings, whilst rumblings were frequently heard though no shock was felt." – (*Report on Tanganyika Territory, Covering the Period from the Conclusion of the Armistice to the End of 1920*, H.M. Stationery Office, Dar es Salaam, Tanganyika, 1921, p. 10; and Gerald Fleming Sayers, *The Handbook of Tanganyika*, London: MacMillan and Co., 1930, p. 28).

A hilly plateau with abundant rain (more than 100 inches every year) at an elevation of 3,000 - 5,000 feet above sea level with mountain ranges which form the walls of the Great Rift Valley reaching up to 8,000 – 10,000 feet or more in the peaks of the eastern range (Livingstone Mountains also known as the Kipengere Range), Rungwe District has very fertile soil and temperatures ranging from 40°F – 80°F; before climate change, temperatures were sometimes in the 30s and frost was common. The district is prone to earthquakes like other parts of the Southern Highlands.

John Mwakangale represented the Southern Highlands Province in the colonial legislature (LEGCO) where, together with his colleagues, he continued to campaign for independence.

The Southern Highlands Province in the southwest bordering Northern Rhodesia (now Zambia) and Nyasaland (now Malawi) was one of seven provinces of colonial Tanganyika.

The provinces were Western Province which was the largest; Lake Province, Northern Province, Central Province, Coast Province, Southern Province, and the Southern Highlands Province which was simply known as the Southern Highlands. The provinces were divided into smaller administrative units called regions in 1963.

After Tanganyika won independence in December 1961, John Mwakangale continued to be a member of parliament. He was appointed Regional Commissioner of the Southern Highlands in 1962 after serving as TANU provincial secretary for the same province.

Others who were appointed regional commissioners in the same year – and who had also served as TANU provincial secretaries of other provinces – were Richard Wambura, Samuel Luangisa, John Nzunda, S.J. Kitundu and J. Abdallah. S.A. Mtaki and S. P. Muro, who once served as TANU provincial chairmen, were also appointed regional commissioners.

During colonial rule, heads of provinces – all British – were known as provincial commissioners (PCs). Led by Nyerere, TANU – Tanganyika African National Union – was the nationalist movement that won independence for Tanganyika.

Humphrey Taylor, a British who served as a District Officer (D.O.) in Tanganyika from 1959 to 1962, wrote the following about John Mwakangale when he was a cabinet member serving as minister of labour under Prime Minister Nyerere:

"Soon after Tanganyika became independent, and near the end of my time as a District Officer in Njombe, I received a call from the British manager of the Commonwealth Development Corporation's wattle plantation and factory a few miles from the District Office. The factory took the bark that was stripped from the wattle trees and used it to make tannin. The workers there were on strike for higher pay, in part because they expected to earn more now that the country was no longer a British colony.

The manager called me because he was afraid that a large crowd of strikers near the factory might attack and damage it. He asked for police protection. I arrived a little while later with ten or fifteen African policemen. I cannot remember if they were armed with anything other than truncheons. It is possible that they also brought rifles. Anyway, everything passed off peacefully without a serious incident. The police and I stood for a couple of hours between the strikers and the factory. The strikers then dispersed and went away. There was no violence of any kind.

However the local union leader sent a fiery telegram to the Minister of Labour, John Mwakangale in Dar es Salaam, in which he wrote that there was a dangerous crisis with provocative action by the British colonial District Officer and the police and that there was a 'danger of the spilling of blood.' Mwakangale was believed to be the most aggressively anti-white or anti- British member of the government. He telegrammed back to say he was coming to Njombe the next day and he sent us a very sharp message criticizing my action and asking to meet with us as soon as he arrived.

At the start of the meeting he was very aggressive and hostile, but as he listened to the manager, the police and to me, he understood what had, and had not, happened. At the end of the meeting we went off and had some beers together.

A little while later, I was in Dar es Salaam to catch the plane on my way home at the end of my brief colonial career. As I was walking on a street there I saw a small group of African cabinet ministers, including Mwakangale, walking towards me on the other side of the street.

When he saw me, he dashed across the road, welcomed me enthusiastically, took me by the hand, and brought me across to meet his cabinet colleagues. He told me how sorry he was to hear that I was leaving Tanganyika." - (Humphrey Taylor, "Danger of Spilling Blood," The BritishEmpire, https://www.britishempire.co.uk/article/dangerofspillingblood.htm).

Professor John Iliffe in his book *A Modern History of Tanganyika* described John Mwakangale as a "vehement nationalist,"" an assessment underscored by some of the remarks Mwakangale made in parliament. According to Professor Paul Bjerk in his book *Building a Peaceful Nation: Julius Nyerere and the Establishment of Sovereignty in Tanzania* (pp.72 - 73):

"In October 1961, racialist sentiments sprang up even among his (Nyerere's) own party members when a proposal was brought forward to delay citizenship for non-Africans for five years after independence. Christopher (Kasanga) Tumbo urged for a distinction between 'native' and 'immigrant races.' A TANU member from Mbeya, J. B. Mwakangale, went so far as to call for the resignation of non-African ministers after independence. 'We have no proof of their loyalty. They are bluffing and cheating us,' Mwakangale alleged.

In response, Nyerere threatened that he and his ministers would resign if the assembly did not support TANU's policy. Nyerere denounced the hypocrisy of a policy favoring Africans in a country that was just about to emerge from a racially prejudiced colonial state. Visibly angry, he argued that once racial bias was introduced to Tanganyikan politics its logic would take a life of its own, leading to widespread ethnic animosity:

'A day will come when we will say all people were created equal except the Masai, except the Wagogo, except the Waha, except the polygamists, except the Muslims, etc...You know what happens when people begin to get drunk with power and glorify their race, the Hitlers, that is what they do. you know where they lead the human race, the Verwoerds of South Africa, that is what they do...

I am going to repeat, and repeat very firmly, that this Government has rejected, and rejected completely any ideas that citizenship with the duties and rights of citizenship of this country, are going to based on anything except loyalty to this country.'"

John Mwakangale also strongly opposed the recruitment of American Peace Corps to work in Tanganyika contending that they were there to destabilise and topple the government. "Wherever they are we always hear of trouble, you hear of people trying to overthrow the government. These people are not here for peace, they are here for trouble. We do not want any more Peace Corps." He was quoted in a news report, "M.P. Attacks American Peace Corps," which was the main story on page one published in the Tanganyika *Standard* (renamed *Daily News* in 1972), 12 June 1964.

John Mwakangale was also the first leader of Tanganyika whom Nelson Mandela met in January 1962 when Mandela secretly left South Africa to seek assistance from other African countries in the struggle against white minority rule in his home country.

Tanganyika was the first country in the region to win independence; it was also the first independent African country Mandela visited after he left South Africa for the first time on 11 January 1962.

He met John Mwakangale in Mbeya, the capital of the Southern Highlands Province. Mwakangale had been assigned to receive Mandela in Mbeya on behalf of the government of Tanganyika. After meeting Mwakangale, Mandela flew to Dar es Salaam the next day where he met Julius Nyerere.

Nyerere was the first leader of an independent African country Mandela met. In his autobiography, *Long Walk to Freedom*, Mandela recalled his meeting with John Mwakangale in the town of Mbeya and how, for the first time in his life, he felt free and proud to be in an independent African country:

"Early the next morning we left (Bechuanaland, now Botswana) for Mbeya, a town near the Northern Rhodesian border....

(In Mbeya) we booked in a local hotel and found a crowd of blacks and whites sitting on the veranda making polite conversation. Never before had I been in a public place or hotel where there was no color bar.

We were waiting for Mr. John Mwakangale of the Tanganyika African National Union, a member of Parliament and unbeknown to us he had already called looking for us.

An African guest approached the white receptionist. 'Madam, did a Mr. Mwakangale inquire after these two gentlemen?' he asked, pointing to us. 'I am sorry, sir,' she replied. 'He did but I forgot to tell them.' 'Please be careful, madam,' he said in a polite but firm tone. 'These men are our guests and we would like them to receive proper attention.'

I then truly realized that I was in a country ruled by Africans. For the first time in my life, I was a free man. Though I was a fugitive and wanted in my own land, I felt the burden of oppression lifting from my shoulders. Everywhere I went in Tanganyika my skin color was automatically accepted rather than instantly reviled. I was being judged for the first time not by the color of my skin by the measure of my mind and character. Although I was often homesick during my travels, I nevertheless felt as though I were truly home for the first time....

We arrived in Dar es Salaam the next day and I met with Julius Nyerere, the newly independent country's first president. We talked at his house, which was not at all grand, and I recall that he drove himself in a simple car, a little Austin. This impressed me, for it suggested that he was a man of the people. Class, Nyerere always insisted, was alien to Africa; socialism indigenous. – (Nelson Mandela, *Long Walk to Freedom: The Autobiography of Nelson Mandela*, Little, Brown and Co., New York, 1994,

p. 538).

Besides John Mwakangale and Jeremiah Kasambala, Brown Ngwilulupi, who was one of the founders and leaders of the main opposition party in Tanzania, Chadema, was also a classmate of Elijah Mwakikagile. He served as vice chairman of Chadema when the party was founded in 1992. Edwin Mtei was the party's chairman.

Mtei also wrote a book, *From Goatherd to Governor*, an autobiographical account of his rise from humble roots and poverty to the corridors of power in Tanzania, also in the regional context of East Africa and in the international arena.

Edwin Mtei worked with President Nyerere for many years. He was the first governor of the Bank of Tanzania, appointed by Nyerere in 1966, and later served as minister of finance. After he differed with Nyerere on economic policies, he left the cabinet and went to work at the World Bank in Washington, D.C., on Nyerere's recommendation. He supported structural adjustment programmes (SAPs) and other austerity measures including currency devaluation recommended by the International Monetary Fund (IMF) and which were to be imposed on Tanzania as a mandatory condition for financial aid to rejuvenate the country's economy.

Nyerere was strenuously opposed to that. He saw the measures as a deliberate attempt by the United States and other Western powers who dominate the IMF and the World Bank to reverse his socialist policies and force the country to mortgage its independence in order to get assistance from the world's financial institutions. He also said the draconian IMF measures would hurt the poor. He went on to say that IMF imposition of ready-made prescriptions on poor countries for their ailing economies as a condition for aid was unacceptable:

"Any serious Third World government will ask serious

questions. I cannot sign an agreement (with the IMF) and then have riots on the streets. You may be the economic experts but I am the political expert - allow me at least to say how much the people can take." – (Julius Nyerere at a press conference in Dar es Salaam, Tanzania, 22 November 1984, quoted by Godfrey Mwakikagile, *Economic Development in Africa*, Commack, New York: Nova Science Publishers, Inc., 1999, pp. 63 and 66; and in *Mwenge*, Tanzania Embassy Newsletter, Washington, D.C., November 1984. On the hardship on the poor caused by IMF conditions imposed on African countries, see also Joe Mensah, quoted by Colleen Lowe Morna, "Surviving Structural Adjustment," *Africa Report*, September-October 1989, p. 48, and by G. Mwakikagile, *Economic Development in Africa*, op. cit., p. 68; and Chinua Achebe, "Africa is People," in his Presidential Fellow Lecture to the World Bank Group, Washington, D.C., 1998).

The heavy-handed approach taken by the IMF ostensibly to fuel economic growth and alleviate the plight of the poor in developing countries prompted Nyerere to ask what came to be a famous question:

"When did the IMF become an International Ministry of Finance? When did nations agree to surrender to it their power of decision-making?" – (Julius Nyerere, quoted in "NO to IMF Meddling," *Daily News*, Dar es Salaam, Tanzania, 2 January 1980, quoted by Lawrence E.K. Lupalo, *Nyerere and Nkrumah: Shared Vision*, CreateSpace, Scotts Valley, California, USA, 2016, p. 41).

Nyerere also contended that IMF conditions for aid had not only made life worse for the poor but had not been helpful in improving the overall condition of developing countries. As he stated:

"I was in Washington last year (1997). At the World

Bank the first question they asked me was 'how did you fail?' I responded that we took over a country with 85 per cent of its adult population illiterate. The British ruled us for 43 years. When they left, there were 2 trained engineers and 12 doctors. This is the country we inherited.

When I stepped down there was 91-per-cent literacy and nearly every child was in school. We trained thousands of engineers and doctors and teachers.

In 1988 Tanzania's per-capita income was $280. Now, in 1998, it is $140. So I asked the World Bank people what went wrong. Because for the last ten years Tanzania has been signing on the dotted line and doing everything the IMF and the World Bank wanted. Enrolment in school has plummeted to 63 per cent and conditions in health and other social services have deteriorated.

I asked them again: 'What went wrong'? These people just sat there looking at me. Then they asked what could they do? I told them have some humility. Humility - they are so arrogant!....

It seems that independence of the former colonies has suited the interests of the industrial world for bigger profits at less cost. Independence made it cheaper for them to exploit us. We became neo-colonies. Some African leaders argued against Kwame (Nkrumah)'s idea of neocolonialism.

The majority of countries in Africa and the rest of the South are hamstrung by debt, by the IMF. We have too much debt now. It is a heavy burden, a trap. It is debilitating. We must have a new chance. If we doubled our production and debt-servicing capabilities we would still have no money for anything extra like education or development. It is immoral. It is an affront. The conditions and policies of the World Bank and the IMF are to enable countries to pay debt not to develop." – (Julius Nyerere, in an interview with Ikaweba Bunting, "The Heart of Africa: Interview with Julius Nyerere on Anti-Colonialism," *New Internationalist*, Oxford, UK, January-

February 1999; and in G. Mwakikagile, *Nyerere and Africa: End of an Era*, op. cit., p. 582).

Paying debts is an enormous burden African countries and others in the developing world continue to bear, prompting Nyerere in 1986 to ask:

"Must we starve our children to pay our debt?"

Although Mtei had fundamental differences with Nyerere on economic policy, he did not alienate Tanzania's founding father and remained on very good terms with him. That is why Nyerere recommended him for the IMF position as Africa's representative – director of IMF's African Department – after he left the cabinet; it was Tanzania's turn to choose one and Nyerere chose Mtei.

And when Mtei founded the opposition party Chadema, Nyerere predicted then (proved correct years later) that it was the only party - among all the new parties formed in the early 1990s - which had a clear programme and which would become the main opposition party in the country. Many of its founding members had been senior government officials and politicians who decided to leave the ruling party and provide a credible challenge to it in the political arena and chart a new course for the country.

Nyerere also advised the leaders of the opposition parties to unite and form one major party with a nationwide base of support to challenge the ruling party if they were to have a chance at winning elections instead of pursuing the goal as a divided opposition. It is an advice that has gone unheeded through the years, thus helping the ruling party – in stewardship of the nation for decades – to perpetuate itself in power.

Even Mtei, as the leader of the main opposition party in the country, did not seek unity with the other leaders – nor did they – to form one broadly-based national party, not an alliance of parties – to challenge the ruling party whose dominance on the political landscape and hegemonic control of the country tilted the balance in its favour in every election even without rigging electoral contests.

Mtei also once served as secretary-general of the East African Community (EAC) and was one of the most prominent Tanzanians in the nation's post-colonial history when he founded Chadema with Brown Ngwilulupi and other leading figures including Bob Nyanga Makani, the first secretary-general of Chadema and former deputy governor of the Bank of Tanzania. Makani also once served as Tanzania's deputy attorney general. He was later elected chairman of Chadema after Mtei stepped down.

The leadership of Chadema, when the party was formed, was nationally representative. Chairman Mtei came from the northeastern part of the country. Vice chairman Ngwilulupi came from the southwest, and secretary-general Makani from the lake zone comprising regions around Lake Victoria. There were also high-ranking officials representing western, central and coastal regions including the former island nation of Zanzibar, now semi-autonomous.

Brown Ngwilulupi (his father was Ngwilulupi Mwasakafyuka) who came from Rungwe District in the southern highlands was also a childhood friend of Elijah Mwakikagile. They came from the same village of Mpumbuli in the area of Kyimbila four miles south of the town of Tukuyu. John Mwakangale's home village was about five miles north of theirs near Tukuyu.

They were, together with John Mwakangale, classmates all the way from Tukuyu Primary School (in the town of Tukuyu) to Malangali Secondary School in Iringa District (then a part of the Southern Highlands Province) and later became relatives-in-law. Brown Ngwilulupi's wife, Lugano Mwankemwa, and Elijah Mwakikagile's wife, Syabumi Mwambapa, were first cousins.

Brown Ngwilulupi also went to Tabora Government School (in Western Province), also known as Tabora Boys, another highly-rated academic institution in colonial Tanganyika which Professor Julian Huxley described as "the Eton of Africa," patterned after the British school.

He attended Tabora School together with Amon Nsekela; Oscar Kambona who became Tanganyika's minister of defence and foreign affairs after the country won independence; and Kanyama Chiume who also became minister of foreign affairs in his home country of Malawi after independence. Both Kambona and Chiume held other ministerial posts at different times in their respective countries in the sixties.

Kanyama Chiume left Nyasaland in 1937 and went to Tanganyika to live with his uncle in what is now Morogoro Region in the eastern part of the country. He was about eight years old.

He grew up in Tanganyika where he attended primary school and secondary school before going to Makerere University College in Uganda. After he graduated from Makerere, he returned to Tanganyika where he became a secondary school teacher.

He spoke perfect Swahili and became one of the most eloquent "native" speakers of the language. He lived in Tanzania (and Tanganyika) longer – for decades since his childhood – than he did in Malawi (and Nyasaland) and was in that sense more Tanzanian than Malawian.

His classmates at Dar es Salaam Central School included Rashidi Kawawa who later became prime minister and vice president of Tanzania; Abdul Sykes and Ali Sykes who became some of the leading members of the nationalist movement in the struggle for independence; and Hamza Aziz who became the second indigenous Inspector General of Police since 1961 and later ambassador to the United States among other posts; he was buried with full military honours when he died in 2004. As Chiume stated in an interview with Benjamin

Lawrence of the Hoover Institution, Stanford University, on 13 November 1998:

"I was born on the 22nd of November in 1929...at Usisya, which is my home village,...in Nkhata Bay District, Nyasaland. I had my primary education in Tanzania, Tanganyika as it was then, because up to the death of my mother in 1937 when I was about eight years old, my uncle, who himself had been very much helpful to me and my mother...took me to Tanganyika where he was working as a head clerk under the district commissioner in Kiberege in the then Eastern Province.

And from there I went to Dar es salaam Central School where I had the rare privilege of going to the same class, same dormitory, for five years, with Rashidi Mfaume Kawawa, among many others, who later on became...the vice president and prime minister of Tanzania.

From Dar es Salaam, in 1946, after I had skipped one class, Standard Eight, I was selected as the only student from that school to go to Tabora Secondary School which was then the senior territorial secondary school in Tanzania (Tanganyika) for those who came from eight government junior secondary schools. This is the school to which Nyerere himself went. He was not a student at the time when I was there but he was teaching in a Catholic School (St. Mary's) just about a mile or so from Tabora (School).

And from there in 1949 after I had passed...Makerere College Entrance Examination – we also did Cambridge School Certificate Examination, we were the first people in that government school to sit for the Cambridge School Certificate Examination – I went to Makerere as a science student."

Kanyama Chiume also played a major role as one of the main leaders of the independence movement in Nyasaland (Malawi). After he and other cabinet members fell out with Malawi's President Hastings Kamuzu Banda in 1964, he returned to Tanzania where he lived for 30 years in Dar es Salaam before going back to Malawi in 1994.

During his years of exile in Tanzania, Kanyama Chiume worked as a features writer and editor at *The Nationalist*, the ruling party's daily newspaper, together with Benjamin Mkapa who was the managing editor before President Nyerere appointed Mkapa editor of the *Daily News*. Chiume also worked with the *Daily News* during that period.

Before joining the opposition, Brown Ngwilulupi was a member of the ruling party, TANU, renamed CCM, and served for many years as secretary-general of the country's largest farmers' union, the Cooperative Union of Tanganyika (CUT), appointed by President Nyerere. His younger brother, Weidi Ngwilulupi Mwasakafyuka, a former ambassador, also left the ruling party and joined one of Tanzania's opposition parties in the early 1990s and served as head of its foreign affairs division.

Godfrey Mwakikagile stated in his autobiographical works that he moved to Rungwe District in 1955 with his parents when he was 5 years old after living in different parts of Tanganyika – Kigoma, Ujiji, Kilosa, Morogoro, and Mbeya – where his father worked as a medical assistant for the British colonial government.

They also stayed in the area of Kandete, near Elijah Mwakikagile's elder sister Ngabagila Mwangolela (married name), in what is now Kyela District for many months in 1955 before moving to Kyimbila in Rungwe District in the same year.

His father was one of the few medical assistants in colonial Tanganyika. In a country with an acute shortage of doctors, medical assistants played a critical role in the provision of vital medical services.

Well-trained, they were, in many cases, a substitute for doctors during colonial rule and even after Tanganyika won independence. In fact, when Tanganyika won independence from Britain on 9 December 1961, it had only 12 doctors. As Professor John Iliffe of the University of Cambridge stated in his book, *East African Doctors: A History of the Modern Profession*:

"Medical assistants, normally with three years of medical training, and often much practical experience, had become the core of colonial medical systems....(In Tanganyika)...the Medical School opened (in 1963) but...by the mid-1960s it was realised that medical assistants were still needed and their training resumed in 1968." – (John Illife, *East African Doctors: A History of the Modern Profession*, Cambridge University Press, 1998, p. 128).

They were few in colonial Tanganyika, a vast expanse of territory of about 365,000 square miles with millions of people to serve. According to John Illife, there were only about 300 medical assistants in January 1961, in the whole country, the same year Tanganyika won independence. Tanganyika had a population of 12 million during that time.

Godfrey Mwakikagile stated in his autobiography that his father also worked at Amani Research Institute in Muheza District.

During German colonial rule, Amani Research Institute was world-renowned for its research in a number of areas including tropical medicine (for malaria and other vector-borne diseases among others), as well as biological and agricultural sciences and had highly trained scientists. It excelled in high-quality research and retained its international reputation under British rule after Germany lost its colony (Deutsch-Ostafrika – German East Africa – renamed Tanganyika) in World War I.

His father also worked in Handeni and then in Tanga before moving to Kigoma four months before Godfrey

Mwakikagile was born. Coincidentally, it was also in what is now Tanga Region where Godfrey's paternal grandfather, Kasisika Molesi Mwakikagile, died.

Born and brought up in Mwaja, Kyela, in what is now Mbeya Region, his grandfather went to work in Tanga and Muheza and worked there for a number of years. He died in 1937 and was buried at Power Station, Muheza, in the northern part of what was then known as the Coast Province.

His younger brother, Lamusi Mwakalinga (Mwakikagile), the only sibling he had, who was also born in Mwaja, lived almost his entire life in Kasumulu, Kyela. Their father was Kyoso Mwakalinga, Godfrey Mwakikagile's great-grandfather.

Godfrey Mwakikagile stated in some of writings that when he and his siblings were growing up, and before he went to boarding school in 1963, their paternal grand uncle Lamusi Mwakalinga used to visit them and their parents in Kyimbila, travelling on the bus from Kyela, a distance of about 30 miles.

Godfrey's father Elijah Mwakikagile was also born in what is now Kyela District in an area called Lwangwa in the ward of Busale but grew up in Kyimbila near the town of Tukuyu in Rungwe District. He was born on 25 October 1924.

Rungwe was the home district of Godfrey Mwakikagile's parents. Both were born and brought up in Rungwe District and were members of an ethnic group indigenous to that part of Tanzania.[4]

Rungwe District, ringed by misty blue mountains, is close to the border with Malawi and is located in the Great Rift Valley north of Lake Nyasa. And what is now Kyela District bordering Malawi was once a part of Rungwe District.

Godfrey Mwakikagile went to school in Tanzania and in the United States.

Tanganyika united with Zanzibar in 1964 to form

Tanzania.

Early years

Godfrey Mwakikagile attended Kyimbila Primary School (up to Standard 4) two miles south of the town of Tukuyu and Mpuguso Middle School (up to Standard 8) seven miles southwest of Tukuyu in Rungwe District in Mbeya Region in the Southern Highlands; Songea Secondary School (up to Standard 12 or Form Four) near the town of Songea in Ruvuma Region, and Tambaza High School (up to Standard 14 or Form Six) in the nation's capital Dar es Salaam.[5]

The headmaster of Songea Secondary School, Paul Mhaiki, when Godfrey Mwakikagile was a student there from 1965 to 1968, later in the early 1970s became director of adult education at the ministry of national education, appointed by President Nyerere. He was later appointed director of UNESCO's Division of Literacy, Adult Education, and Rural Development.

After finishing high school at Tambaza in November 1970, Godfrey Mwakikagile joined the National Service in January 1971, which was mandatory for all those who had completed secondary school, high school, college and university.

He underwent training, which included basic military training, at Ruvu National Service camp in the Coast Region. After that, he went to another national service camp in Bukoba on the shores of Lake Victoria in the North-West Region bordering Uganda.

The region was later renamed Kagera Region. Ugandan military ruler, Idi Amin, attempted to annex the region when he invaded Tanzania in October 1978.

Godfrey Mwakikagile once worked as a news reporter at the *Standard*, which was later renamed *Daily News*, and as an information officer at the Ministry of Information and Broadcasting in Tanzania's capital Dar es Salaam before going to school in the United States in November 1972.[6]

He left Tanzania on November 3rd and arrived in the United States on November 4th, three days before the US presidential election on November 7th the incumbent, Richard Nixon, a Republican, won against his Democratic opponent George McGovern in one of the biggest landslide victories in the nation's modern history.

He first joined the editorial staff of the *Standard* as a junior reporter when he was still in high school, in Form Five (Standard 13), in 1969.[7]

Coincidentally, his editor at the *Daily News*, Benjamin Mkapa, who also helped him to go to school in the United States, years later became president of Tanzania and served two five-year terms (1995–2005).[8]

He was the third president in the nation's history since the country won independence from Britain in 1961. Before then, Benjamin Mkapa served as Tanzania's minister of foreign affairs, among other ministerial posts, and as high commissioner (ambassador) to Nigeria and Canada, and as ambassador to the United States.

He also served as press secretary to President Julius Nyerere and was later appointed minister of information and broadcasting before assuming other cabinet posts – including serving as minister for science, technology and higher education – in the following years.

The president of Tanzania during that period, Julius Nyerere who led the country from 1961 to 1985, was the editor-in-chief of the *Daily News*. But his role was only ceremonial rather than functional.

Mkapa was preceded by Sammy Mdee as managing editor of the *Daily News*. Godfrey Mwakikagile joined the editorial staff when Mdee was the editor. After he was replaced by Mkapa, Mdee became Director of Information Service at the Ministry of Information and Broadcasting, appointed by President Nyerere, and later served as

Nyerere's press secretary and, after that, as a diplomat.

Godfrey Mwakikagile graduated from Wayne State University in Detroit in the state of Michigan, USA, in 1975 and was president of the African Students Union at that school.[9]

He also attended Aquinas College in Grand Rapids, Michigan, in 1976.

One of his professors of economics at Aquinas College was Kenneth Marin who once worked in Tanzania.[10]

It was just a coincidence that he went to Aquinas College where he ended up being taught by someone who had worked in Tanzania years before. He did not know anything about Professor Marin before then and met him at Aquinas College for the first time.

Here is another coincidence: Kenneth Marin worked in the multi-storey Co-operative Building on Lumumba Street, in Dar es Salaam, where Brown Ngwilulupi also worked as secretary-general of the country's farmers' union. The two knew each other well and used to have lively exchanges on a number of issues, as Professor Marin said in an economics class he taught at Aquinas College when he recalled his days working in Tanzania.

Godfrey Mwakikagile was in that class, one of four African students and the only one from Tanzania; three were Nigerian.

Professor Marin was a great admirer of President Nyerere as a leader and as an intellectual and said he used to go to the same church he did in Oyster Bay, Dar es salaam. They were Roman Catholic. He called him a world leader, not just an African leader, as Mwakikagile stated in his book, *Nyerere and Africa: End of an Era*.

He even read Nyerere's writings in class when he lectured on development economics and other Third World subjects. He also said Nyerere was an excellent writer and had thorough command of the English language. He also said the following about Nyerere in one of his lectures at Aquinas College: "He is one of the best world leaders we have today."

Professor Marin worked as an economist for the government of Tanzania in the late sixties and early seventies. He went to Tanzania in 1968 and served as an adviser to the government on capital mobilisation and utilisation. Before then, he worked as an economist for the United States federal government. He was appointed by President Lyndon B. Johnson to serve on Wage and Price Control during the mid-sixties. President Johnson appointed Professor Kenneth Marin as a member of the White House Consumer Advisory Council.[11]

In 1966, Professor Marin was a member of a U.S. State Department evaluation team that was assigned to review various performances in the economic and political arena in six South American countries.[12]

Years later, one of his students, Godfrey Mwakikagile, also ended up writing about economics, among other subjects, mostly about Africa. And coincidentally, Mwakikagile's first book, *Economic Development in Africa*, was also about economics.[13]

Writings

Godfrey Mwakikagile came into prominence in Tanzania and elsewhere after he wrote a major book about Julius Nyerere not long after the former Tanzanian president died.[14]

He is considered by many people, including those who have reviewed his books about President Nyerere in different newspapers, magazines and academic journals in a number of countries, to be an authority on Nyerere and one of his most prominent biographers.[15]

One scholar who cited Godfrey Mwakikagile as an authoritative source on President Nyerere was Professor David Simon, a specialist in development studies at the University of London and Director of the Centre for

Development Areas Research at Royal Holloway College at the university. Professor Simon published excerpts from Godfrey Mwakikagile's book on Nyerere in his compiled study, *Fifty Key Thinkers on Development*, published in 2005.[16]

During that time and thereafter, Professor David Simon was also the editor of the scholarly *Journal of Southern African Studies* and was on the editorial staff of another academic publication, the *Review of African Political Economy*.

Godfrey Mwakikagile's works have been getting serious attention among many people including academics in many countries who have also reviewed some of his books in scholarly journals.

His first book, *Economic Development in Africa*, was published in June 1999 and he has maintained a steady pace since then, writing books, as demonstrated by the number of titles he has on the market. He is one of Tanzania's most well-known authors and one of Africa's most prolific.

He has written more than 60 books since 1999 as his bibliography shows, mostly about Africa during the post-colonial era, and has been described as a political scientist although his works defy classification.

He has written about history, politics, economics, as well as contemporary and international affairs from an African and Third World perspective and is known for such works as *Nyerere and Africa: End of an Era*, and *Africa and the West*.[17]

Both have been favourably reviewed in a number of publications including the highly influential *West Africa* magazine (founded in 1917 and based in London) which reviewed two of his books in the same year; a rare accomplishment in such a major publication.

The books were reviewed by *West Africa* magazine editor Kofi Akosah-Sarpong, a Ghanaian who also once was a visiting lecturer and scholar-in-residence at the

University of Botswana. They were excellent reviews.

Godfrey Mwakikagile's book, *Nyerere and Africa: End of an Era*, his magnum opus and probably his most well-known title, was reviewed by *West Africa* magazine in 2002 three years after Nyerere died of leukemia in October 1999 at the age of 77.[18]

It was also reviewed by a prominent Tanzanian journalist and political analyst, Fumbuka Ng'wanakilala of the *Daily News*, Dar es Salaam, Tanzania, in October 2002 and is seen as a comprehensive work, in scope and depth, on Nyerere.[19]

Others who have reviewed the book include Professor A.B. Assensoh, a Ghanaian teaching at Indiana University in Bloomington, Indiana, in the United States. He reviewed the first edition of *Nyerere and Africa: End of an Era* in the *African Studies Review*, an academic journal of the African Studies Association, in 2003.

The same book was also reviewed by Professor Roger Southall of the University of the Witwatersrand (Wits), formerly of Rhodes University, South Africa, in the bi-annual interdisciplinary publication, the *Journal of Contemporary African Studies* (Taylor & Francis Group), 22, No. 3, in 2004. Professor Southall was also the editor of the journal during that period.

The first edition of *Nyerere and Africa: End of an Era* was published in November 2002, and the second, an expanded edition, in January 2005. The third edition, also an expanded version, was published in November 2006. The fourth edition, also expanded, was published in December 2008. And the fifth edition was published in 2010.

The book has also been cited by a number of African leaders including South African Vice President Phumzile Mlambo-Ngcuka in one of her speeches about African leadership and development in which she quoted the author.[20]

She was the main speaker at a conference of African

leaders, diplomats and scholars at the University of the Western Cape in South Africa in September 2006 when she gave her speech.

Although his books have been able to get the attention of some African leaders, it is impossible to know if they have had any influence on any of them. But the mere fact that they are cited by them shows that he is taken seriously as an author, not only in Tanzania but in other African countries and elsewhere.

One of Godfrey Mwakikagile's books, *Africa and the West*, which is a sweeping survey of the continent before the advent of colonial rule and during the colonial era as well as after independence, was also reviewed by *West Africa* magazine in its edition of 21–27 January 2002.[21]

The book, which was published in 2000, has been described as an appeal to Africans to respect their cultures, values and traditions and take a firm stand against alien ideas which pollute African minds and undermine Africa. It is also a philosophical text used in a number of colleges and universities in the study of African identity, philosophy and history. It is also a strong condemnation of the conquest of Africa by the imperial powers.

West Africa magazine, in its January 2002 edition, also described Godfrey Mwakikagile as an author who articulates the position of African Renaissance thinkers.

But in spite of his passionate defence of Africa, past and present, Godfrey Mwakikagile is also highly critical of some Afrocentric scholars who propagate myths about Africa's past and even reinvent the past just to glorify the continent, claiming spectacular achievements in the precolonial era in some areas where there were hardly any or none; for example, in advanced science, technology and medicine. They also inflate achievements in some areas.

He contends that "true scholarship requires rigorous intellectual discipline and entails objective enquiry and analysis of facts and evidence including admitting failures and shortcomings"; a position he forcefully articulates in his books *Africa and the West* and *Africa is in A Mess: What Went Wrong and What Should be Done*, among other works.

It is a position that led one renowned Afrocentric Ghanaian political analyst and columnist, Francis Kwarteng, to describe Godfrey Mwakikagile as a "Eurocentric Africanist" in his article, "End of the Dilemma: The Tower of Babel," on GhanaWeb, 28 September 2013, in which he discussed the role and the question of race, religion, and ethnicity in Ghana's politics and, by extension, in a Pan-African context including the African diaspora; which is a wrong characterisation of Mwakikagile since all his works are written from a purely African, not a Eurocentric, perspective.

In his article, Francis Kwarteng also cited one of Godfrey Mwakikagile's books, *Ethnic Politics in Kenya and Nigeria*, in his analysis of the role of ethnicity in national politics in Africa:

"Wole Soyinka rightly admits in *Of Africa* that if America, a racist country at that, can elect a person of African ancestry, a black man of Luo ethnicity, president, then, he sees no reason Kenya shouldn't learn from that—that precedent....

Soyinka believes Kenya's democratic process must allow enough political space for the accommodation of ethnic diversification, so that qualified minorities can also partake in leadership positions, principally the presidency....But Soyinka's Nigeria has its own fair share of problems, a cornucopia of them. A truism flies across Nigeria's social and political landscape that Hausas are born natural rulers....

Yet Nigeria has about 250 ethnic groups. So, what defines the criteria for Nigeria's multiethnic exclusivism from the presidential pie?....

This is not unique to Nigeria, however. The same thing happened in Ghana and Uganda, producing the likes of Idi

Amin. This phenomenon is captured in the Eurocentric Africanist Godfrey Mwakikagile's *Ethnic Politics in Kenya and Nigeria*."

In another article on GhanaWeb, 15 October 2013, Francis Kwarteng also stated:

"We all know how Western material culture and unholy spiritualism are destroying Africa. Corruption in Africa is proliferating like cancerous cells in the body politic. Corrupt African politicians collaborate with Western banking officials to secrete the people's money in Western banks, monies, which, however you look at it, either fortunately for the West or unfortunately for Africa, are reinvested in Western national economies. So, in the long run Africa becomes positively poorer and the West negatively wealthier. Analytically, this runs counter to the central thesis of Rodney's *How Europe Underdeveloped Africa*. In fact, it's what the Eurocentric Africanist Godfrey Mwakikagile calls 'Africa in a Mess.' This inverse relationship of economic bilateralism is unhealthy and must be critically addressed by Africa."

It is a case of Africans themselves, especially the leaders, contributing to the underdevelopment of Africa. Bad leadership including corruption in African countries is one of the subjects Godfrey Mwakikagile has addressed extensively in his books, especially in *Africa is in A Mess: What Went Wrong and What Should be Done*, *The Modern African State: Quest for Transformation*, *Africa After Independence: Realities of Nationhood*, *Africa at the End of the Twentieth Century: What Lies Ahead*, and *Statecraft and Nation Building in Africa: A Post-colonial Study*, and *Africa in Transition: Witness to Change*.

He contends that bad leadership is the biggest problem most African countries have faced since independence, and everything else revolves around it.

Africans of all ideological stripes agree corruption is one of the biggest problems African countries face. It is even acknowledged by some leaders. And a number of African scholars including Godfrey Mwakikagile have addressed the problem, proposing solutions to a seemingly intractable problem. As Francis Kwarteng stated in "A Political Coin of Three Sides: What Do We Actually Want?," GhanaWeb, 8 November 2013:

"Today's leadership has failed to show moral and social leadership in the face of mounting national crisis. Indeed corruption threatens the very future of the youth....President Mahama's book (*My First Coup D'état*) must be read in tandem with Wole Soyinka's *The Open Sore of a Continent*, Ali Mazrui's *The African Condition: A Political Diagnosis*, Molefi Kete Asante's *Rooming in the Master's House*, and Godfrey Mwakikagile's *Africa is in A Mess: What Went Wrong and What Should Be Done* and *Africa After Independence: Realities of Nationhood*. In fact, these bibliographies must be included in every secondary school curriculum as well as the curricula of teacher training institutions across the country. We may then use them as bibliographical platforms to ask students to come up with comprehensive solutions to our myriad national problems."

He stated in another article, "Africa Must Practice Its Own Democracy: A Moral Necessity," GhanaWeb, 17 October 2013:

"We were not the first to raise this question; others had before us!
Celebrated prescient leaders like Kwame Nkrumah made this philosophical mantra part of their political platform, so were others — Patrice Lumumba, Amilcar Cabral, etc. Literacy scholars like Chinua Achebe, and Ngugi wa Thiong'o; international economists like Dambisa

Moyo and Yaw Nyarko; political scientists like Ali Mazrui, Godfrey Mwakikagile, and Mahmood Mamdani; legal experts like Shadrack Gutto and Randall Robinson; world-renowned anthropologists and linguists like Cheikh Anta Diop and Théophile Obenga; and Afrocentrists like Molefi Kete Asante, Chinweizu, Maulana Karenga, and Ama Mazama had made similar arguments in the past few decades—via their prolific scholarship, organizations, and political activism."

One of the problems Africa faces in nation building is how to achieve unity in diversity in countries composed of different ethnic groups and threatened by ethno-regional loyalties and rivalries. It is one of the subjects Godfrey Mwakikagile has addressed in his books.

He has written extensively about ethnicity and politics in Africa in the post-colonial era and how the two phenomena are inextricably linked in the African political context. He has used case studies in different analyses of the subject in different parts of the continent.

One of his books, *Ethnicity and National Identity in Uganda*, has been described by Tierney Tully as "a great book, but very dense." A reviewer on amazon, UK, has described Godfrey Mwakikagile's work, *Uganda: The Land and Its People*, as a "very studious book about Uganda's history, politics, ethnic groups and social structure."

His other books on the subject include *Identity Politics and Ethnic Conflicts in Rwanda and Burundi: A Comparative Study*; *Burundi: The Hutu and The Tutsi: Cauldron of Conflict and Quest for Dynamic Compromise*; *Civil Wars in Rwanda and Burundi: Conflict Resolution in Africa*; *Ethnic Diversity and Integration in The Gambia*; *The People of Ghana: Ethnic Diversity and National Unity*, and *Belize and Its Identity: A Multicultural Perspective*, a scholarly work on the Central American nation founded by the British colonial rulers and African slaves as British Honduras and which, culturally and historically, is considered to be an integral part of the Afro-Caribbean region, hence of the African diaspora. Although written by an African, the book is an important part of Afro-Caribbean literature.

One American journalist who interviewed Godfrey Mwakikagile described him as an independent scholar who was also a widely read and highly regarded author.

Godfrey Mwakikagile responded by saying that he was just an ordinary African, like tens of millions of others, deeply concerned about the plight of his continent.

But there is no question that he is a serious writer whose writings are widely read even if he considers himself to be just an ordinary African like millions of his brethren across the continent and elsewhere.

In his book, *African Political Thought* (Palgrave Macmillan, 2012), Professor Guy Martin has described Godfrey Mwakikagile as one of Africa's leading populist scholars who refuse to operate and function within the limits and confines of Western ideologies – or any other external parameters – and who exhort fellow Africans to find solutions to African problems within Africa itself and fight the syndrome of dependency in all areas and create a "new African."

He goes on to state that all these African-populist thinkers are academics and deal strictly with ideas, without being directly involved in politics, although most of them are political scientists.

Professor Martin states in his book that some of the most prominent African-populist scholars include Senegalese scientist, historian and Egyptologist Cheikh Anta Diop (1923 – 1986), Nigerian political scientist Calude Ake (1939 – 1996), Burkinabé historian Joseph Ki-Zerbo (1922 – 2006), Tanzanian scholar Godfrey Mwakikagile, Kenyan political science professor, Mueni wa Muiu, and Daniel T. Osabu-Kle, a professor of politicial science from Ghana.

He goes on to state that all these scholars are also ardent Pan-Africanists and, for reasons explained in the book, he has devoted chapter eight exclusively to the thoughts, concepts and ideas of only four scholars: Mwakikagile, Ake, Osabu-Kle and Muiu. As he states in Chapter Eight, "The Africanist-Populist Ideology: Popular Democracy and Development in Africa," which he starts with a quotation from President Julius Nyerere:

"Africa...is isolated. Therefore to develop, it will have to depend upon its own resources basically, internal resources, nationally, and Africa will have to depend upon Africa. The leadership of the future will have to devise, try to carry out policies of maximum national self-reliance and maximum collective self-reliance. They have no other choice. Hamna! [There is none!] – Julius K. Nyerere, "Reflections," quoted in John S. Saul, The Next Liberation Struggle, 159.

As we saw in Chapter 7, Frantz Fanon's warning to African people, leaders, and scholars was that for popular democracy and development to succeed in Africa, they must stop blindly following the West: they must stop aping Western culture, traditions, ideas, and institutions; they must think 'outside of the box'; and, above all, they must be bold and innovative and develop their own ideas, concepts, and institutions based on African values, culture, and traditions. This alternative path to Western liberal democracy and capitalist development is precisely the line of thinking of an emerging African scholarship, exemplified by the four African scholars whose political ideas are examined in this chapter.

More specifically, this chapter reviews the ideas and values for a new, free, and self-reliant Africa put forth by African scholars who have the best interest of the African people at heart and thus advocate a popular type of democracy and development. However, unlike the populist-socialist scholars, the Africanist-populist scholars refuse to operate within the parameters of Western ideologies - whether of the socialist, Marxist-Leninist, or liberal-democratic persuasion - and call on all Africans to become the initiators and agents of their own development, with the ultimate goal of creating a 'new African.'" – (Guy Martin, *African Political Thought*, New York: Palgrave Macmillan, 2012, pp. 129 - 130).

Professor Guy Martin is also the author of *Africa in World Politics: A Pan-African Perspective* (2002); co-editor, with Chris Alden, of *South Africa and France: Towards a New Engagement in Africa* (2003); and, with Mueni wa Muiu, co-author of *A New Paradigm of the African State: Fundi wa Afrika* (2009). As Edmond J. Keller, professor of political science and former Director of the UCLA Globalization Research Center- Africa and of the James S. Coleman African Studies Center at the University of California-Los Angeles, stated in his review of Professor Guy Martin's book, *African Political Thought*, in one of the leading academic journals on African research and studies, *Africa Today*, Volume 60, Number 2, Winter 2013, published by Indiana University Press:

"The work is an ambitious survey. Martin is encyclopedic in his treatment of the subject of African political thinking. He demonstrates a comprehensive knowledge of African political thought throughout history. He has succeeded in his efforts to produce what is arguably the first real attempt to synthesize African political thought into a single thematic volume....

Martin begins his analysis by focusing on indigenous political thought dating back to ancient times (Kush/Nubia, sixth century BCE). He then brings his study up to the present...He systematically introduces the reader to the ideas of specific theorists and their biographies. He situates these thinkers in the context of their times.

Some were political activists, such as Amílcar Cabral, Samora Machel, Kwame Nkrumah, Julius Nyerere, and Steve Biko. Others were public intellectuals and academic theorists, such as Claude Ake, Godfrey Mwakikagile, Daniel Tetteh Osabu-Kle, and Mueni wa Muiu.

For the amount of ground covered in *African Political Thought*, this is quite a slim volume. The comprehensiveness of the book is its greatest strength. It touches upon most of the major African political thinkers....

It is interesting that the political thought of Meles Zenawi, the now-deceased political leader of Ethiopia, is not considered. Debate is currently raging as to whether or not, despite his views on Marxism, he was an original thinker."

Godfrey Mwakikagile is also featured as a major African author and scholar in the *Dictionary of African Biography, Volume 6* (Oxford University Press, 2011), edited by Harvard University professors, Emmanuel K. Akyeampong and Henry Louis Gates, Jr. As Professor Ryan Ronnenberg who wrote a profile of Mwakikagile in the *Dictionary of African Biography* (pp. 365–366) states:

"Godfrey Mwakikagile's childhood in the closing stages of Tanzania's colonial period made a significant impression on him. He witnessed colonial oppression firsthand, and the racist ideology that upheld it....

Indeed, the ideas of Pan-Africanism embraced by the early Nyerere government would resonate with Mwakikagile deeply, as he early on came to possess a deep and abiding respect for Africans and African Americans who preserved their culture in the face of racist ideology and institutions.

In his introduction to *Africa and the West* (2000), he wrote, 'Much as the conquest of Africa led to the denigration of the African personality, leading many

Africans to hate themselves by despising their heritage; an equally intense but opposite reaction was caused by this very invasion and conquest of our continent.'

Mwakikagile embraced Tanzania's independence, and the independence of the African continent as a whole, with fierce pride. 'I was too young to play a role in the independence movement, but old enough to know what Mau Mau in neighboring Kenya was all about, and who our leaders were: from Kwame Nkrumah in Ghana to Julius Nyerere in Tanganyika; from Nnamdi Azikiwe in Nigeria to Jomo Kenyatta in Kenya and Patrice Lumumba in Belgian Congo' (*Africa and the West*, 2000)

His experience also inspired his thinking regarding Africa and its relationship to the Western world, which led to several academic works dedicated to the subject.

Mwakikagile's early works focused on pressing issues in African studies, particularly the theory and realization of development in Africa. *Economic Development in Africa*, published in 1999, uses the rich case study of Tanzania's transition from socialism to free-market capitalism as a foundation for broader conclusions concerning the continent's development failures.

Mwakikagile writes about Africa as a whole in such a way as to suggest that he possesses not only a keen understanding of the way things are, but also a deep understanding of the way they should be.

The arcebically titled *Africa Is in a Mess: What Went Wrong and What Should Be Done* reflects on the decades since independence with pragmatism and regret, observing the loss of both leadership and ingenuity as the continent's intellectual elite settle abroad, while suggesting how this process might be reversed.

In fact, as the years have passed, and as those early optimistic moments after independence have slipped away, Mwakikagile has taken it upon himself to write about why Africa has fallen short of its vision.

Mwakikagile has translated his experience as a youth

in colonial East Africa and his adulthood in postcolonial Tanzania into provocative scholarship concerning topics vitally important to African studies.

Deeply invested in the ideas of Pan-Africanism that guided the Nyerere government, Mwakikagile has brought this perspective to bear upon a variety of crucial areas of scholarship, including postcolonial development, the African diaspora, and the late Julius Nyerere's career." – (Ryan Ronnenberg, "Godfrey Mwakikagile," in Emmanuel K. Akyeampong and Henry Louis Gates, Jr., eds., *Dictonary of African Biography, Volume 6*, New York: Oxford University Press, 2011, pp. 365 – 366).

Kofi Mensah, one of the people who reviewed Godfrey Mwakikagile's book *Africa is in A Mess: What Went Wrong and What Should Be Done* on amazon.com wrote the following about Godfrey Mwakikagile:

"He was one of the most promising intellectuals of our generation, and one of the most inspiring, to emerge out of the seventies, when he graduated from university."

In one of his lectures, Professor Abdul Karim Bangura of Howard University, a Sierra Leonean, cited Godfrey Mwakikagile as one of the major African thinkers. He used Godfrey Mwakikagile's book, *The Modern African State: Quest for Transformation*, among other works by different scholars, in his lecture, "The Democratic Project and the Human Condition across the African Continent" in January 2013 at Howard University and stated that his lecture was "based on the analyses of major African thinkers" including Godfrey Mwakikagile.

Godfrey Mwakikagile has also been invited to give lectures at different universities because of the books he has written. And his role as a public intellectual has been demonstrated in other ways. For example, he has been sought for interviews by BBC, PBS (America's public television network), and byVoice of America (VOA), among other media outlets. This is documented in the interview he had with the American journalist.

The interview, which focused on Julius Nyerere as a leader and on other subjects about Africa, is reprinted in its entirety in one of Godfrey Mwakikagile's books, *Nyerere and Africa: End of an Era*.

Although he has been exposed to Western cultures, was educated in the Western intellectual tradition and even lived in the United States for many years, his perspectives and philosophical conceptions have undoubtedly been shaped by his African upbringing and are deeply rooted in African cultures and traditions. And he rejects the notion that Africa was a blank slate until Europeans came to write on it.

He passionately argues that the history written about Africa by Europeans when they first went to Africa and even during colonial rule as well as after independence is not African history but the history of Europeans in Africa and how they see Africa and Africans from their European perspective or perspectives.

He also contends that traditional Africa has produced philosophers and other original thinkers whose knowledge and ideas – including ideas at a high level of abstraction – can match and even surpass the best in the West and elsewhere in the world. He forcefully articulates that position in his book, *Africa and the West*.[22]

And although he sees Africa as an indivisible whole, he also argues that all nations, include those in Africa, have different national characters. He looks at the concept of national character in the African context in one of his books, *Kenya: Identity of A Nation*, and makes a compelling case for this idea which is sometimes highly controversial.

The work is, among other subjects, a study of comparative analysis in which the author looks at the national characters of Kenya and Tanzania, thus demonstrating that nations do indeed have different national characters and have been that way throughout history.

Kenyans themselves have had to grapple with questions of identity, ethnic versus national, and how to reconcile the two for the sake of national unity, peace and prosperity. As Dr. George Nyabuga, a lecturer at Nairobi University, stated about Godfrey Mwakikagile's book, *Kenya: Identity of a Nation*, in his article, "Politics of East Africa," in *Oxford Bibliographies*, 29 November 2011:

"Ethnicity, identity, conflict, power, democracy, corruption, and governance are often mentioned as issues of interest when examining not only African but also East African politics. Sometimes these issues make it difficult for people within the countries of East Africa to develop appropriate characteristics with which to identify themselves. This is perhaps the issue that Mwakikagile tries to examine as many nation-states grapple with their multiple identities. However, in most instances many people identify with their ethnic groups whose consequences for politics in Africa are sometimes deleterious. In Kenya, ethnicity has been the cause of numerous conflicts, most recently the post-election violence of late 2007 and early 2008."

Tanzania is one of the few countries on the continent which have been spared the agony and scourge of ethnic conflicts, unlike Kenya which Godfrey Mwakikagile has used for comparative analysis in looking at the identities of the two neighbouring countries.

In his books, including *Nyerere and Africa: End of an Era*, he has also explained how Tanzania has been able to contain and even neutralise tribalism unlike other countries on the continent. As Keith Richburg, who travelled and reported on many African countries when he was *The Washington Post* bureau chief based in Nairobi in the 1990s, stated in his book, *Out of America: A Black Man Confronts Africa*:

"One of my earliest trips was to Tanzania, and there I found a country that had actually managed to purge itself of the evil of tribalism. Under Julius Nyerere..., the government was able to imbue a true sense of nationalism that transcended the country's natural ethnic divisions.... Tanzania is one place that has succeeded in removing the linguistic barrier that separates so many of Africa's warring factions. But after three years traveling the continent, I've found that Tanzania is the exception, not the rule. In Africa..., it *is* all about tribes."

One of Africa's most prominent political analysts, Kenyan columnist Philip Ochieng, articulated the same position. As he stated in his article, "Mwalimu Nyerere's Bequest to Mkapa a Tall Order," in one of Kenya's main newspapers, the *Daily Nation*, Nairobi, 16 October 1999:

"Tanzania (is) the most united country in Africa. This unity and sharp national consciousness was contributed to by (the) life-works of the Teacher (Mwalimu Nyerere).... He insisted on uniform Kiswahili throughout the Republic. During the three years that I worked in Dar es salaam I rarely heard any tribal language spoken."

He also stated in another article, "Africa's Greatest Leader," in *The East African*, Nairobi, 19 October 1999:

"(Under President Nyerere) Tanzania became the African country with the highest degree of national self-consciousness and has almost annihilated the bane of Kenya that we call tribalism.... At a time when Nairobi was drowning in crude elite grabbing, Dar es Salaam was a Mecca of the world's national liberation movements, and a hotbed of global intellectual thought.... Mwalimu Julius

Kambarage Nyerere is the most successful leader that Africa has ever produced since the European colonial regime collapsed 50 years ago."

One Kenyan reviewer of *There Was a Country*, a book about Biafra by Chinua Achebe who considered Nyerere to be the role model for African leaders, stated on amazon.com:

"Nyerere succeeded in creating the only non-tribal country in Africa where there is no tribalism..... I have seen... tribalism in Kenya and know how it works. And surely enough, we also have violence in almost every election we have because of tribalism."

President Ellen Johnson-Sirleaf of Liberia also said in a television interview that Nyerere was her role model. Wole Soyinka also considered Nyerere to be a role model other African leaders should emulate.

Godfrey Mwakikagile has written extensively about tribalism and contends that it is one of the biggest problems Africa faces and is the source of instability in many countries on the continent, including civil wars.

He undoubtedly has strong convictions but does not neatly fit into any ideological category. He expresses strong Pan-Africanist views in his writings and sees Africa as a collective entity and one organic body and has strongly been influenced by staunch Pan-Africanist leaders such as Kwame Nkrumah, Julius Nyerere, Ahmed Sekou Toure and Patrice Lumumba whom he also strongly admires.[23]

He says Africa does not have leaders of that kind anymore.

He also strongly admires Thomas Sankara as a man of the people like Nyerere and contends that among the new breed of African leaders, Sankara – who has been described as the African Che Guevara – showed great promise but was eliminated by some of his so-called compatriots working for France and other Western powers before he could realise his full potential the same way Lumumba was, eliminated by the United States and Belgium.

Godfrey Mwakikagile has written about Thomas Sankara in his book *Military Coups in West Africa Since The Sixties* and in *African Countries* among other works.

But some of his critics contend that he overlooks or glosses over the shortcomings of these leaders precisely because they are liberation icons and played a leading role in the struggle for independence and against white minority rule in Southern Africa.[24]

He also seems to be "trapped" in the past, in liberation days, especially in the seventies when the struggle against white minority rule was most intense. But that may be for understandable reasons.[25]

He was a part of that generation when the liberation struggle was going on and some of his views have unquestionably been shaped by what happened during those days as his admiration for Robert Mugabe, for example, as a liberation icon clearly shows; although he also admits in his book, *Nyerere and Africa: End of an Era*, that the land reform programme in Zimbabwe could have been implemented in an orderly fashion and in a peaceful way and without disrupting the economy.

But his admiration for Mugabe as a true African nationalist and Pan-Africanist remains intact; a position that does not sit well with some of his critics although he does not condone despotic rule as he clearly states in his writings.

He admires Mugabe mostly as a freedom fighter and liberation hero who freed his people from colonial rule and racial oppression and exploitation, and as a strong leader who has taken a firm and an uncompromising stand against Western domination of Africa.

And by remarkable contrast, his contempt for African

leaders whom he sees as whites with a black skin also remains intact. He mentions Dr. Hastings Kamuzu Banda as a typical example of those leaders.

He has written about Dr. Banda and other African leaders, among other subjects, in his book, *Africa After Independence: Realities of Nationhood.*[26]

Godfrey Mwakikagile also contends that only a few African leaders – Kwame Nkrumah, Julius Nyerere, Ahmed Sekou Toure, Gamal Abdel Nasser, Ahmed Ben Bella and Modibo Keita – strove to achieve genuine independence for their countries and for Africa as a whole and exercised a remarkable degree of independence in their dealings with world powers. And Mugabe was the only other leader who fit in this category, in spite of his shortcomings.

According to Ben Bella, the six leaders – Nkrumah, Nyerere, Sekou Toure, Nasser, Modibo Keita and Ben Bella himself – constituted what came to be known as "The Group of Six" within the Organisation of African Unity (OAU). In an interview in Switzerland in 1995 with Jorge G. Castañeda, the author of *Companero: The Life and Death of Che Guevara*, Ben Bella said the six leaders worked together secretly within the OAU on a number of issues including the Congo and African liberation, excluding other African leaders. It is a subject Godfrey Mwakikagile has also addressed in his book *Nyerere and Africa: End of an Era.*[27]

Godfrey Mwakikagile's background as a Tanzanian has played a major role in his assessment of many African leaders because of the central role his country played in the liberation struggle in the countries of Southern Africa, and not just in South Africa – the bastion of white minority rule on the continent.[28]

Zimbabwean President Robert Mugabe was one of the African leaders who had strong ties to Tanzania, Godfrey Mwakikagile's home country, since liberation days. Others with strong ties to Tanzania include Thabo Mbeki, former president of South Africa; Joaquim Chissano, former president of Mozambique; and Sam Nujoma, former president of Namibia.[29]

Tanzania, then known as Tanganyika, was also the first independent African country Nelson Mandela first visited when he secretly left South Africa for the first time in 1962 to seek support from other African countries for the liberation struggle in his home country. And Julius Nyerere was the first leader of an independent African country he met when he went to see him in Dar es Salaam during that time. It was also Nyerere who authorised the government of Tanganyika to give Mandela a travel document that enabled him to go to Addis Ababa, Ethiopia, to attend a conference of African leaders and to go to other African countries. Mandela wrote about that in his book *Long Walk to Freedom*:

"Because I did not have a passport, I carried with me a rudimentary document from Tanganyika that merely said, 'This is Nelson Mandela, a citizen of the Republic of South Africa. He has permission to leave Tanganyika and return here.' I handed this paper to the old Sudanese man behind the immigration counter and he looked up with a smile and said, 'My son, welcome to the Sudan.' He then shook my hand and stamped my document." (Nelson Mandela, *Long Walk to Freedom*, ibid., p. 176).

Newspaper background

In those days, Dar es Salaam, Tanzania, was the headquarters of all the African liberation movements, under the leadership of President Julius Nyerere, and Godfrey Mwakikagile got the chance to know many of the freedom fighters who were based there when he worked as a young news reporter in the nation's capital.[30]

They included Joaquim Chissano Joaquim Chissano who was the head of the FRELIMO office in Dar es Salaam and who later became the minister of foreign affairs and then president of Mozambique when his country won independence after 500 years of Portuguese colonial rule.[31]

Many other freedom fighters who were based in Dar es Salaam, Tanzania, also went on to become national leaders in their respective countries after the end of white minority rule in Southern Africa. And they all still have strong ties to Tanzania even today.

Tanzania played a big role in supporting the African liberation movements not only by giving sanctuary to the freedom fighters but by providing them with military training and guerrilla bases and by supporting them financially because of Nyerere's leadership. As the legendary British journalist David Martin stated after interviewing Nyerere one day:

"I remember one day sitting in his office questioning that a number of African countries had not paid their subscriptions to the OAU Liberation Committee Special Fund for the Liberation of Africa. He looked at me for some moments, thoughtfully chewing the inside corner of his mouth in his distinctive way. Then, his decision made, he passed across a file swearing me secrecy as to its contents. It contained the amount that Tanzanians, then according to the United Nations the poorest people on earth, would directly and indirectly contribute that year to the liberation movements. I was astounded; the amount ran into millions of US dollars.

It was the practice among national leaders in those days to say that their countries did not have guerrilla bases. Now we know that Tanzania had many such bases providing training for most of the southern African guerrillas, who were then called 'terrorists' and who today are members of governments throughout the region....

Tanzania was also directly attacked from Mozambique by the Portuguese. But, in turn, each of the white minorities in southern Africa fell to black majority political rule and Nyerere saw his vision for the continent finally realized on 27 April 1994 when apartheid formally ended in South Africa with the swearing in of a new black leadership." – (David Martin, "A Candle on Kilimanjaro," in *Southern African Features*, 21 December 2001).

Tanzania was also threatened by the apartheid regime many times. South Africa's defence minister, P.W. Botha – who later became president - publicly stated in 1968 that countries which support "terrorists" – freedom fighters – should receive a "sudden hard knock," in pointed reference to Tanzania, which had the largest number of guerrilla camps, and Zambia which also had a number of such bases. According to *Africa Contemporary Record*:

"By 1968 the potential threat of escalating guerilla attacks became elevated to a top priority of the South African regime....This threat was taken a stage further on April 24 (1968) by the Commandant-General S.A. Melville, former head of the S.A. Defence Force, who said that South Africa already had sufficient justification and provocation for retaliation against countries which 'harboured' and encouraged terrorists whose only intention was to penetrate South Africa or South West Africa. He supported the Minister of Defence's view that such countries should receive a 'sudden hard knock.'

On April 25, the Deputy Minister of Police, Mr. S.L. Muller, informed parliament on information about fresh groups of 'terrorists' gathering in Zambia....Accodring to Muller, there were in Zambia '19 training and transit camps for terrorists as well as officers of all the African subversive organisations'....the South African Minister of Defence, Mr. P.W. Botha, warned on April 5 (1968) that countries aiding and inciting terrorism and guerilla warfare against South Africa could eventually provoke South Africa into 'hitting back hard'....

The Rhodesia rebel Minister of Law and Order, Mr. Lardner Burke, extending the state of emergency at the beginning of 1968, said that the number of 'terrorists' waiting in Zambia and Tanzania to cross the Rhodesian border continued to mount. The South African Deputy-Minister of Police, Mr. S.L. Muller, said Tanzania posed 'the greatest potential threat to the Republic.' He claimed there were '40 camps in Tanzania for the training of terrorists and all the offices of subversive organisations'.

A new external service of Radio Tanzania was inaugurated in 1968 to assist in 'propagating the ideological principles of the liberation movements in Tanzania.'

Tanzania's relations with its southern neighbour, Malawi, continued to decline in 1968 for three reasons. First, because of Dr. Banda's growing relations with South Africa. Second, because Malawi accuses Tanzania of supporting its exile Ministers, like Mr. Chipembere, in subversive activities. And third, because of frontiers disputes.

Malawi's territorial claims to districts in Tanzania provoked President Nyerere to retort that Dr. Banda was 'insane'; but, he warned, 'Dr. Banda must not be ignored; the powers behind him are not insane'....

A Tanzanian note in January, 1967, objected to maps which showed the Malawi-Tanzanian boundary as running along the eastern and northern shores of Lake Nyasa. Tanzania contended the boundary passes through the middle of the lake and that the change was made illegally by the British government on the declaration of the Rhodesian Federation.

Dr. Banda counter claimed that the lake had always belonged to Malawi, and that he had every right to change its name to Lake Malawi. The Portuguese Foreign

Minister, Mr. Nogueira, supporting Malawi in March, recalled that under a Portuguese-British treaty still in effect, Malawi owned one part of the lake and Portugal the other.

By September, 1968, Dr. Banda had not only laid further claim to four districts in Tanzania, but to four Zambian districts as well. Speaking at the Malawi Congress Party's annual convention on September 17, Banda said that 'the real boundary' between his country and Zambia should be the Luangwa River, thus incorporating the whole of the Zambian eastern province. At the same time he announced he was putting the first of many gunboats on Lake Nyasa to start patrols as an answer to Tanzania's 'claim.'

Dr. Nyerere described these claims as 'expansionist outbursts which do not scare us, and do not deserve my reply.'

On September 27, President Kaunda said his country could not establish diplomatic relations with Malawi until claims to Zambian territory had been renounced....(and) challenged Dr. Banda 'to go ahead and declare war on Zambia'....

Suspicious that Swaziland's independence on September 6 (1968) was more apparent than real, President Nyerere declined to permit Tanzania to be represented at their celebrations....

On May 17, Mr. Vorster (the prime minister), speaking at the National Party's 'twenty years of Nationalist rule festival,' said that slowly but surely an army would be built up in certain Central African States for an eventual 'now or never' attack on South Africa....'These people have put it very clearly that they will abandon their plans only if South Africa is prepared to hand over to the Blacks'....Two days before, on May 15, at a summit meeting of 14 Central and East African leaders in Dar es Salaam, full support was promised to the guerilla movements fighting in Southern Africa." – (Colin Legum and John Drysdale, eds., *Africa Contemporary Record: Annual Survey and Documents 1968 – 1969*, London: Africa Research Limited, 1969, pp. 291, 292, 249, 373 - 374, 220, 180, and 250).

Dr. Banda's territorial claims extended to Mozambique; he even tried to convince Nyerere in the early sixties to share the territory with him. As Nyerere said years later:

"In 1961 we became independent. In 1962, early 1962, I resigned as prime minister and then a few weeks later I received Dr. Banda. We had just, FRELIMO had just been established here and we were now in the process of starting the armed struggle.

So Banda comes to me with a big old book, with lots and lots of maps in it, and tells me, 'Mwalimu, what is this, what is Mozambique? There is no such thing as Mozambique.' I said, 'What do you mean there is no such thing as Mozambique?' So he showed me this map and he said: 'That part is Nyasaland. That part is part of Southern Rhodesia. That part is Swaziland, and this part, which is the northern part, Makonde part, that is *your* part.'

So Banda disposed of Mozambique just like that. I ridiculed the idea, and Banda never liked anybody to ridicule his ideas. So he left and went to Lisbon to talk to Salazar about this wonderful idea. I don't know what Salazar told him. That was '62." – (Julius K. Nyerere, at an international conference, University of Dar es Salaam, Tanzania, 15 December 1997, in Godfrey Mwakikagile, *Nyerere and Africa: End of an Era*, Pretoria, South Africa: New Africa Press, 2010, pp. 556 - 557).

Mozambique won independence in 1975 after almost 500 years of Portuguese colonial rule with its territory intact; so did Angola, in the same year, from the same colonial power. Three countries in southern Africa remained under white minority rule: Rhodesia, Namibia, and South Africa.

In 1976, the American secretary of state, Henry Kissinger, went to Tanzania and met with President Nyerere three times – once in April, twice in September – in an attempt to help find solutions to conflicts in the countries of southern Africa still under white minority rule, especially Rhodesia where the white minority had unilaterally declared independence, excluding the black majority from the government.

Nyerere was chairman of the Frontline States – Tanzania, Zambia, Mozambique, Angola and Botswana – in the struggle against the white minority regimes and was critical to finding solutions to conflicts in the region. As David Martin stated about Nyerere's prominent status and the meetings he had with Kissinger:

"Tanganyika became independent on 9 December 1961 and a year later...the country became a republic. For the next 24 years Nyerere was to fill the African and international stage like a colossus.

When he met the astute American Secretary of State Henry Kissinger for the first time in Dar es Salaam in 1976, the two men began a mental verbal fencing match of David and Goliath proportions. One began a quote from Shakespeare - some of whose works Nyerere translated into Swahili setting them in an African context - or a Greek philosopher and the other would end the quotation. Then Nyerere quoted an American author. Kissinger laughed: Nyerere knew Kissinger had written the words.

Neither man trusted the other. Kissinger wanted the negotiations kept secret. Nyerere, understanding the Americans' duplicity, took the opposite view and as Africa correspondent of the London Sunday newspaper, *The Observer*, I was to become the focal point of the Tanzanians' strategic leaks. That year the newspaper led the front page on an unprecedented 13 occasions on Africa. All the leaks, as Kissinger knew, came from

Nyerere. One political fox had temporarily outwitted the other.

Apart from his simplicity and piercing intellect, one of Nyerere's most endearing traits was his honesty." – (David Martin, "Mwalimu Julius Kambarage Nyerere: Obituary," Southern African Research and Documentation Centre (SARDC). David Martin was a founder-director of the Southern African Research and Documentation Centre of which Nyerere was a patron. He lived in Tanzania for 10 years from 1964 to 1974 and frequently talked with Nyerere through the decades, a period of 35 years, until Nyerere's last days).

His simplicity belied his intellect and leadership potential demonstrated by his meteoric rise to power. He returned to Tanganyika in October 1952 after earning a master's degree from the University of Edinburgh in Scotland. Nine years later, he led his country to independence becoming the youngest national leader in the world. He was 39.

When he was at Edinburgh, no-one thought he would become a titan not only on the African political landscape but on the world stage years later. He did not stand out among other students as a leader or future politician anymore than he did when he was a student at Makerere University College in Uganda before he went to Scotland for further studies.

One of his fellow students from Tanganyika, Abdallah Said Fundikira who was with him at Makerere and who became a cabinet member in the first independence cabinet, said people did not really notice Nyerere. It was when he spoke that others noticed he had leadership qualities in addition to his sharp intellect. As Fundikira put it:

"If you want to know the truth, one did not particularly notice Nyerere." – (Abdallah Said Fundikira, *Africa News*

Online, 8 November 1999).

He had a passionate desire to see his country and Africa as a whole free. Trevor Grundy, who was a critic of Nyerere, stated the following in his review of *Nyerere: The Early Years*, a book written by Thomas Molony, a senior lecturer in African studies at the University of Edinburgh:

"He went on to use his Edinburgh years to great advantage, bewildering – some might say bamboozling – liberal-minded journalists in the 1960s and 1970s with his formidable intellect which was the result of his reading of Jacques Rousseau and John H. Stuart Mill, T. H. Green's *Principles of Political Organization*, Benard Bosanquet's *Philosophical Essay of the State* and Harold Laski, the famous London School of Economics theorist.

He had a blotting paper brain.

Hardly a soul at Edinburgh guessed he would turn into Africa's number one brain box in years to come. As the historian George Shepperson put it in a BBC interview: 'We at Edinburgh were very surprised in mid-1950s when Dr Nyerere's name became widespread throughout the world press. We never felt when he was here that he was going to become a leading politician.'

Statesmen and journalists were amazed at his knowledge....

With his eager tongue, (and) a formidable intellect...he is presented by Commonwealth groupies as the politician who did the most to mastermind the downfall of Portuguese and British/Afrikaner rule in Africa....The Rhodesian leader Ian Smith several times referred to Nyerere as Africa's 'evil genius'....

He did so much to help liberate different parts of Africa from European rule." – Trevor Grundy, "Julius Nyerere Reconsidered," 4 May 2015, africaunauthorised.com).

The years he spent at Edinburgh were some of the most rewarding in terms of intellectual preparation for his role as a national leader after he returned to Tanganyika. He had a passionate desire to see his country and Africa as a whole free.

Nyerere's commitment to the liberation struggle and his uncompromising stand on racial equality was also demonstrated in his negotiations with Kissinger. He did not trust the United States and did not make concessions Kissinger wanted him to make. As James Spain, the American ambassador to Tanzania during that time, stated:

"One of the amusing sidelights of Henry Kissinger's second or third visit was this. He stayed in the Kilimanjaro Hotel. When the party was clearing out to go to the airport, I was told that the Secretary of State wanted me. I went upstairs. People were carrying away files and suitcases.

In the middle of a table there was a 'bug' protector that was still making weird electronic sounds. Henry gets both of us hunched over this thing. He said 'Thank you very much. This visit has been useful. Your arrangements were fine, but I want to warn you about one thing: This fellow Nyerere is not our side.'

This was a pretty accurate reflection of the spirit of the times....

If I did anything useful, it was to convince Washington that Nyerere was not a brutal African dictator and a Communist stooge....

He...loved word play. I never read a book that he hadn't read. He translated Shakespeare into Kiswahili....

He was a hopeless socialist. Still, he was clearly a very sincere and humane man....Most Western development aid to Tanzania came from Scandinavia, particularly the Swedes. They like the intellectual socialist, the benign father of his people who didn't kill or imprison people, while trying to create a new way of life with better prospects....

The fact was that Nyerere certainly wasn't on our side, but he wasn't a tool of the Chinese or the Russians either....

He was a very remarkable man and, I think, a very constructive element in the peaceful solutions to the problems of Southern Africa that eventually emerged." – (James W. S. Spain, interviewed by Charles Stuart Kennedy, 31 October 1995, *The Association for Diplomatic Studies and Training (ADST), Foreign Affairs Oral History Project*, copyright 1998, pp. 36 and 34).

Kissinger's failure to extract concessions from Nyerere prompted American reporters who had accompanied him, as well as other journalists, to conclude that Kissinger's mission was a failure. When Nyerere was asked at a press conference in Dar es Salaam if he considered Kissinger's mission to be a failure, he said in response:

"A mission of clarity is not a mission of failure."

The immediate concern was Rhodesia where guerrilla warfare was most intense during that period. Nyerere played a critical role in helping end white minority rule in that country. Frustrated by Nyerere's intellectual manoeuvres, political skills and determination to remove white minority regimes from power, Rhodesia's prime minister, Ian Smith, called him Africa's "evil genius."

Once Rhodesia was free, Namibia would be next, and finally South Africa. Nyerere was seen as a critical player in all those theatres. Kissinger acknowledged Nyerere's vital role in resolving conflicts in the region, as did others leaders. As Richard N. Viets who served as American ambassador to Tanzania from 1979 to 1981 stated:

"At that time in mid-1979, the so-called front-line states in Southern Africa, I think there were five of them...the organization was chaired by Julius Nyerere, the President of Tanzania, a very remarkable gentleman.

Nyerere really towered over the other four heads of state and this organization in many respects was a one-man operation. Because of his long association with the independence movements in East Africa and throughout Southern Africa he was highly respected.

Nyerere is an intellectual of very considerable dimensions, an extraordinarily articulate person. So the leadership of this group was essentially his without any challenge. He was offering almost daily advise to the Zimbabwean leadership on tactics, strategy, etc. in their negotiations with the British and the Americans and the others involved....

I decided I needed to know more about Julius Nyerere than anybody else on the face of the earth....He is a very shrewd man.

He was...a most remarkable figure in contemporary African political history. I always said, and others who knew him well I think shared this view, that if Nyerere had been born in Western Europe or the Far East or even in North America, he would have been an exceptional figure in public life. He was a superb politician.

He had an acute brain, the memory of an elephant, intellectual horsepower that was second to none.

He was cunning. He could be warm-hearted one moment and cut you off at the legs at the next if it met his political or personal needs.

Nyerere...remains as far as I know the principal translator of Shakespeare from English into Swahili and one of the most gifted orators I have ever heard in English, and a marvelous drafter of the English language." – (Richard N. Viets interviewed by Charles Stuart Kennedy, April 1990, *The Association for Diplomatic Studies and Training, Foreign Affairs (ADST), Oral History Project*, copyright 1998, pp. 56, 58, 59, 61, 67 - 68).

Nyerere was also interviewed in Dar es Salaam in 1976 on an American television programme, ABC's "Issues and

Answers" about the escalating conflict in southern Africa. Her made it clear that the United States and other Western powers were supporting the apartheid regime in South Africa and asked a pointed question:

"Why are Western countries arming South Africa? Why are you arming South Africa? Against what military combination? And you expect us to sit just like that."

His pivotal role in the region also prompted an American journalist on ABC's "Issues and Answers" to ask Nyerere:

"Can you use your influence, which is tremendous influence, and ask Castro to withdraw his troops from Angola?"

Nyerere responded:

"Even if I had that kind of influence, it would be unnecessary. First, you remove the cause...."

He was also asked:

"Will you commit troops (in a war against South Africa)?"

Nyerere:

"Yes, I will commit troops. We would rather hang together than hang separately...".

Nyerere blamed the United States for fomenting trouble and fuelling conflict in Angola. When he was asked on the American television programme, "Issues and Answers," who was causing turmoil in the country, he responded:

"I believe the CIA. Who is doing it? Who else could be doing it? Why do we keep on hearing these whispers coming from Washington, saying, 'Let us create another Vietnam for the Russians in Angola'?...You are causing *us* trouble."

His commitment to the liberation of Africa was clearly evident to the freedom fighters themselves based in Tanzania and even to other people elsewhere. Many Tanzanian soldiers fought and died in the liberation wars in southern Africa and are honoured at a memorial site in Tanzania; so are those who fought and died in the war with Uganda under Idi Amin.

Nyerere's relentless support for the liberation struggle was also underscored by Professor Piero Gleijeses who stated in his book, *Conflicting Missions: Havana, Washington, and Africa, 1959 - 1976*:

"Of all the African leaders who proclaimed their support for the liberation struggle in Africa – Nkrumah, Nasser, Ben Bella, Sekou Toure – he was the most committed. And by the second half of 1964, spurred by events in Zaire and the obvious failure of peaceful attempts to end white rule in southern Africa, this commitment, and his disappointment with Western powers, was increasingly evident.

By the time Che (Guevara) arrived (in Tanzania in 1965), Dar es Salaam had become the Mecca of African liberation movements...Dar es Salaam 'has become a haven for exiles from the rest of Africa,' the CIA lamented in September 1964. 'It is full of frustrated revolutionaries, plotting the overthrow of African governments, both black and white'....

In September 1964, Frelimo, the movement against Portuguese rule in Mozambique, had launched the opening salvo of its guerrilla war from bases in southern Tanzania, its only rear guard.

Following Stanleyville, Nyerere had thrown his full support to the Simbas, and Tanzania had become their main rear guard and the major conduit of Soviet and Chinese weapons for them.

It was also the seat of the Liberation Committee of the OAU. The head offices of Frelimo and a host of other movements struggling against the white regimes in South Africa, Namibia, and Rhodesia were in Dar es Salaam.

The Cuban embassy there was, the CIA reported accurately in March 1965, 'the largest Cuban diplomatic station in sub-Saharan Africa.' The ambassador, Captain Pablo Ribalta, was a close friend of Che Guevara." – (Piero Gleijeses, *Conflicting Missions: Havana, Washington, and Africa, 1959 - 1976*, Chapel Hill, North Carolina, USA: The University of North Carolina Press, 2002, pp. 84 and 85).

About ten years later, Kissinger was in Tanzania trying to find a diplomatic solution to the conflicts in southern Africa, a mission that was somewhat compromised because of American – Western – support for the white minority regimes in the region. As Nyerere stated in his article, "Rhodesia in the Context of Southern Africa" published in *Foreign Affairs* in April 1966:

"The deep and intense anger of Africa on the subject of Rhodesia is by now widely realized. It is not, however, so clearly understood. In consequence the mutual suspicion, which already exists between free African states and nations of the West, is in danger of getting very much worse....

Successive Western governments have declared their hostility to apartheid, and their adherence to the principles of racial equality. They have frequently made verbal declarations of their sympathy with the forces in opposition to South African policies. But they have excused their failure to act in support of their words, on the grounds of South Africa's sovereignty. Africa has shown a great deal of scepticism about this argument, believing that it masked a reluctance to intervene on the side of justice when white privilege was involved. Now, in the case of Southern Rhodesia, legality is on the sde of intervention. What is the West going to do? Will it justify or confound African suspicions?

So far the West has demonstrated its intentions by the gradual increase of voluntary economic sanctions; there has been a refusal even to challenge South African and Portuguese support for Smith by making sanctions mandatory upon all members of the United Nations. And there have been repeated statements by the responsible authority that force will not be used except in case in case of a break-down in law and order - which apparently does not cover the illegal seizure of power! What happens if the economic sanctions fail to bring down the Smith regime is left vague.

The suggestion therefore remains that, despite legality, the domination of a white minority over blacks is acceptable to the West....It is time for...Britain and the United States of America to make clear whether they really believe in the principles they claim to espouse, or whether their policies are governed by considerations of the privileges of their 'kith and kin.'" – (Julius K.Nyerere, "Rhodesia in the Context of Southern Africa," *Foreign Affairs*, New York, April 1966; Julius K. Nyerere, *Freedom and Socialism/Uhuru na Ujamaa: A Selection from Writings and Speeches, 1965 – 1967*, Dar es Salaam, Tanzania: Oxford University Press, 1968, pp. 143, 154 - 155, and 156).

The critical role Nyerere played in finding solutions to the conflicts in southern Africa was also demonstrated by the fact that not only did Kissinger meet with him three times but longer than he did with any other African leader during his mission to the continent in 1976. In acknowledging Nyerere's role, Kissinger wrote the following, "Julius Nyerere and Tanzania: The Ambivalent Intellectual," in his book, *Henry Kissinger: Years of Renewal*:

"Tanzanian President Julius Nyerere proceeded to arrange an official reception that could not have been more cordial. The motive, however, was altogether different from Kenyatta's. Nyerere...was, at heart, deeply suspicious of American society and American intentions.

In international forums, Tanzania's ministers frequently castigated us. Nyerere would not have described friendship with the United States as a national priority; instead, he tended to think of relations with us a necessary evil....

Brilliant and charming, Nyerere had an influence in Africa out of proportion to the resources of his country, proof that power cannot be measured in physical terms alone....Because Tanzania was involved in the armed struggle that was taking place in Rhodesia, and because of Nyerere's intellectual dominance, Nyerere would be a key to any solution....

Many of Nyerere's American admirers thought he and his colleagues were the embodiment of American values and liberal traditions. By contrast, his American critics viewed Nyerere as a spokesman for Communist ideology. Neither view was accurate. Nyerere was his own man. His idiosyncratic blend of Western liberal rhetoric, socialist practice, nonaligned righteousness, and African tribalism was driven, above all, by a passionate desire to free his continent from Western categories of thought, of which Marxism happens to be one. His ideas were emphatically his own....

For our first meeting, Nyerere, a slight, wiry man, invited me to his modest private residence. it was a signal honor, and he introduced me to his mother and several members of his family. He was graceful and elegant, his eyes sparkling, his gestures fluid.

With an awesome command of the English language (he had translated *Julius Caesar* into Swahili), Nyerere could be a seductive interlocutor. But he was also capable of steely hostility. I had the opportunity to see both these sides during my three visits to Dar es Salaam....

Nyerere was the key to the frontline states....

The two most impressive leaders I encountered on this trip, Nyerere and Senghor, were at opposite ends of the African sppectrum. In a sense, they represented metaphors for varying approaches to African identity.

Nyerere was a militant who used ideology as a weapon; Senghor was an intellectual who had taught himself the grammar of power.

Nyerere considered himself as a leader of an Africa that should evolve in a unique way, separate from the currents in the rest of the world which Africa would use without permitting them to contaminate its essence. Senghor saw himself as a participant in an international order in which Africa and *négritude* would play a significant, but not isolated, role.

When all is said and done, Nyerere strove for the victory of black Africa while Senghor sought a reconciliation of cultures within the context of self-determination." – (Henry Kissinger, *Henry Kissinger: Years of Renewal*, New York: Touchstone, 1999, pp. 931 - 932, 936, 949 - 951).

In its assessment of Nyerere, the CIA prepared a report, released in May 1965, about his passionate desire to see Africa free and united and how determined he was to achieve his goal:

"On the question of African liberation, Nyerere is a fanatic. Beneath a charming personality which disarms many Westerners, he is a man of strong conviction, prepared to pay almost any price to achieve a united Africa ruled by black Africans."

Nyerere's commitment to African liberation was indisputable; so was his ambition to see Africa united which even surpassed his desire to achieve socialism. As he stated in an interview in 1998 not long before he died:

"I have always said that I was African first and socialist second. I would rather see a free and united Africa before a fragmented socialist Africa." – (Julius K. Nyerere, in an interview with Ikaweba Bunting, *New Internationalist*, Oxford, UK, December 1998).

And he stated in his speech in Accra on 6 March 1997 on Ghana's 40th independence anniversary:

"Without unity, there is no future for Africa."

It is also true that Nyerere wanted Africa to be ruled by Africans – just as Europe is ruled by Europeans, America by Americans and so on – and wanted Africans to maintain their identity as Africans. As he stated when spoke about the Portuguese colonies in Africa and their policy of assimilation which was actually never implemented as they claimed it was on the basis of racial equality:

"Portugal pretends that her colonies are really part of Europe, and that she abjures racial discrimination. She claims instead to be in the process of making European Gentlemen out of the African inhabitants of those areas, and talks proudly of the policy of equality for the 'assimilado.' But Africans are not European, could not become European, and do not want to become European. They demand instead the right to be Africans in Africa, and to determine their own cultural, economic, and political future. This right is what Portugal denies. The inhabitants of her colonies can certainly be 'African'; but if they are, then they are subjected to special laws, and special taxation and labour levies; their participation in the functions of their own government is ruled out.

In South Africa there is no longer even the pretence that citizens of different races are equal before the law, or in social and economic rights and duties." – (Julius K. Nyerere, "The Honour of Africa," an address to the National Assembly, Dar es Salaam, Tanzania,14 December 1965, before Tanzania broke off diplomatic relations with Britain the following day, the first country to do so – followed by Ghana under Nkrumah and Egypt under Nasser the day after – because of Britain's refusal and unwillingness to use force to remove the white minority government from power in Rhodesia after it unilaterally declared independence on11 November 1965; in Julius K. Nyerere, *Freedom and Socialism/Uhuru na Ujamaa: A Selection from Writings and Speeches 1965 - 1967*, Dar es Salaam, Tanzania: Oxford University Press, 1968, pp. 123 – 124).

Because of the prominent role he played on the political scene in southern Africa, President Nyerere was also invited to Washington by President Jimmy Carter in August 1977 in an attempt to find solutions to the conflicts in the region. He was the first black African leader to be invited by Carter for a state visit.

High on Carter's agenda was Rhodesia, Namibia and the war in Angola and the involvement of Cuban troops in the conflict supporting the MPLA government against South African-backed UNITA forces. As the American ambassador to Tanzania during that time, James Spain, stated in an interview years later:

"Nyerere was the first African chief of state that Carter invited back. I accompanied him. Only twice in my life have I been in substantive sessions in the White House.

I was with Carter and Nyerere, Vance, Moose and Brzezinski for something like five hours. Then too, five or six days are allotted for the distinguished visitor to see the US. We took our own plane out to Chicago, San Francisco and Los Angeles, and the rural Midwest and South. Nyerere didn't play bridge but his foreign minister (Benjamin Mkapa who later became president of Tanzania and was Nyerere's student at St. Francis College, Pugu, on the outskirts of Dar es Salaam) did....

Rhodesia and Namibia were high priority issues at the time. Kissinger had devoted three or four days to them in 1976....David Owen, the British Foreign Secretary, joined him for a couple of his meetings with Nyerere....

Nyerere made no bones that he would give all the support he could, including arms, to the Namibian and Rhodesian rebels. That was to end 'colonialism.' But he saw the situation within South Africa differently. That was a fight between African and Africans. The Boers, as he always called the Afrikaners, were Africans too, bad Africans, but Africans. As he told an American visitor, 'Unlike the British in Rhodesia, they have no place to go home to'....

We were in the middle of the negotiations for an independent Rhodesia.

The personal chemistry between Carter and Nyerere was great. Toward the end of the discussions Carter shuffled his papers and said, 'Well, I think that is all Mr. President. It has been very useful.'

His National Security Adviser who had been sitting down the table and hadn't said a word coughed pointedly.

'Oh, yes,' said Carter. 'There is the matter of the Cubans in Angola.'

'Yes, indeed Mr. President,' Nyerere responded. 'I thought we were going to agree on everything, but that is something that we can disagree on. Let's talk about it.'

Carter didn't seem very eager. He said, 'We feel that's bad.'

Nyerere gave his standard reply: as soon as the South Africans get out of Angola the Cubans will get out.

'How can you guarantee that?'

'Because the president of Angola has promised me and I will see to it that he lives up to his promise.'

There isn't.

Brzezinski broke in. 'Mr. President, are you aware that the number of Cubans in Angola compared to the total population of Angola is larger than the number of Americans who were in Vietnam at the height of our involvement?'

'Oh, really, how interesting,' replied Nyerere.

Carter started folding up his papers.

'And, Mr. President,' asks Brzezinski, 'Are you aware that the number of Cubans in Angola compared to the total population of Cuba is very much larger than the number of Americans in Vietnam at the height of our involvement compared to the total population of the United States?'

This time Nyerere didn't say a word. He waved his hand with a condescending smile.

Carter grabbed his papers, stood up, and announced 'Well, it looks like we are really finished!'" – (James W. Spain, interviewed by Charles Stuart Kennedy, 31 October 1995, *The Association for Diplomatic Studies and Training (ADST), Foreign Affairs Oral History Project*, copyright 1998, p. 41).

On the Rhodesian question, there was hope that the conflict could be resolved diplomatically. But the intransigence of the white minority regime left little room, if any, for a diplomatic solution. As the leader of the white minorities in Rhodesia, Prime Minister Ian Smith, said, there would be no black majority rule in his life time, not even in a thousand years. Africans insisted, there would be, in his lifetime. As he put it:

"'No African rule in my lifetime. The white man is

master of Rhodesia. He has built it, and he intends to keep it.'" – (Ian Smith, in Alan Cowell, "Ian Smith, Defiant Symbol of White Rule in Africa, Is Dead at 88," *The New York Times*, 21 November 2007).

His defiance was even more pronounced in the same year Kissinger went to Africa in his abortive attempt to find a diplomatic solution to the conflict. As the Rhodesian leader bluntly stated in 1976:

"'I don't believe in black majority rule ever in Rhodesia – not in a thousand years.'"

War seemed to be the only solution. As *The New York Times* stated in its report when President Nyerere visited the United States at the invitation of President Carter:

"Other Americans who spoke with Nyerere today (5 August 1977) said that he feared it was too late for a projected new British-American peacekeeping effort in Rhodesia and that the issue between the white minority Government and black nationalist forces would have to be decided by war....
Mr. Nyerere is chairman of a committee of presidents of the so-called 'front-line countries' that lie on or near Rhodesia's borders. The Administration believes he could be the single most influential African leader in getting a fair hearing for the British-American proposals both from the other 'front-line' presidents and from the Patriotic Front, which is waging guerrilla war against Rhodesia's white minority government.
Joshua Nkomo and Robert Mugabe, the leaders of the Patriotic Front coalition, have publicly rejected any further efforts to negotiate a settlement in Rhodesia, a country of 270,000 whites and more than six million blacks, and have said the issue must be resolved by war." – (Graham Hovey, "Nyerere Is Called Hopeful on Rhodesia," *The*

New York Times, 5 August 1977).

Without Nyerere's direct involvement, there was little hope a solution to the conflict could found. President Carter knew that. According to *The Washington Post*:

"Tanzania's President Julius Nyerere, probably black Africa's most widely respected figure, arrives in Washington today (4 August 1977) on his first official trip to the United States since he was President Kennedy's guest 14 years ago. He is the first black African leader invited by President Carter to visit him at the White House.

Since the Vietnam war, the United States and Tanzania have been on opposite sides of almost every major world issue and Tanzania's U.N. ambassador, Salim Salim, has stood out as one of the Third World's most distinguished critics of American policies. Relations between the two countries first soured in 1964 when Tanzania accused the United States of plotting to overthrow the government and they have never been warm since.

Improving bilateral relations is unlikely to be the substance of Nyerere's talks with Carter, however.

Nyerere is chairman of the presidents of the so-called frontline states – Angola, Botswana, Mozambique, Zambia and Tanzania – the independent African countries most directly involved in the southern African drama. This makes him the continent's most influential spokesman on strategies for achieving majority rule in Rhodesia, granting legitimate independence to Namibia (Southwest Africa) and ending apartheid in South Africa.

Nyerere is personally considered to be above reproach. A wealthy Nairobi-based Greek businesswoman, whose family has been involved in Tanzania for two generations, says, 'Nyerere is the only man in East Africa who cannot be bought.' A practicing Roman Catholic of simple tastes, the 55-year old philosopher-president is said to be the lowest paid head of state in Africa.

To much of the continent, the United States...is still regarded as one of the leading collaborators in maintaining white supremacy and black exploitation in southern Africa....

Part of Carter's success in convincing Africans that he is sincere about changing American policy something former Secretary of State Henry Kissinger tried and failed to do, stems from U.N. Ambassador Andrew Young's open identification with the African cause....

Ten months before his 1969 trip to Canada, Nyerere let it be known that he would also like to visit Washington to help improve relations with the United States, but he was told that President Nixon would be too busy.

The following year, when Nyerere came to New York to address the U.N. General Assembly on southern Africa - with a speech that had such an impact on African and black American students that mimeographed copies were passed hand-to-hand throughout American campus communities - no effort was made to see President Nixon.

In 1975, however, Nyerere was invited to deliver the commencement address at Boston University and he asked for a brief meeting with President Ford. He was rebuffed yet by another American President and later declined the Boston invitation." − (Roger Mann, "Nyerere Visit Seen as Symbol of Shift in U.S. Policy on Africa," *The Washington Post*, 4 August 1977).

This deliberate snub of a prominent and highly respected African leader by presidents Nixon and Ford reflected their attitude towards Africa in general as a continent which they saw as a peripheral actor on the global stage and one that could simply be ignored by the United States at will. It is an attitude that was shared by Henry Kissinger who served under both presidents as national security advisor and secretary of state.

It is also a sentiment that was echoed by President

Donald Trump decades later when, on 11 January 2018, he described African countries as "shithole countries." As James K. Bishop, a veteran foreign service officer since the Kennedy Administration who also served as deputy director for West Africa at the State Department and as United States ambassador to Nigeria, Liberia and Somalia among other posts, stated about Nixon and Kissinger:

"For countries I covered, we had a pretty broad spectrum of US interests at a time when the US administration was not particularly concerned about Africa. In addition to other issues that Nixon and Kissinger had to face – Vietnam, China, the Soviet Union, disarmament – they both had also had very disparaging views of Africa.

Nixon told one of our ambassadors – with whom I was working when he made his farewell call on the President at the White House – that Africans were a bunch of children and should be treated as such. Those were the ambassador's marching orders.

Kissinger went to Africa once during my period in Washington when I was the Deputy Office Director for West Africa. Bill Schaufele was the Assistant Secretary at the time; he looked over the manifest for Kissinger's plane and realized that he was the only African expert aboard. He asked whether he could bring an assistant along to help him. I was marched up to Kissinger's office and inspected - as a slave might have been inspected 200 years earlier on a block in Annapolis. He looked at me as if I were a piece of rancid meat.

During the inspection, Kissinger went out of the room to take a telephone call from the President. Winston Lord, who remained with Schaufele and I, was kind enough to tell me not to be offended because Kissinger treated all of his staff the same way.

The bottom line was that I didn't go on the plane; Schaufele went by himself." – (James K. Bishop, Jr., interviewed by Charles S. Kennedy, *The Association for Diplomatic Studies and Training (ADST), Foreign Affairs Oral History Project*, 15 November 1995, p. 30).

Kissinger had a bad reputation as a very arrogant person since his student days at Harvard University and probably even before then.

One of his professors at Harvard, William Yandell Elliott who was his supervisor when he was a doctoral candidate, and who later served in both Democratic and Republican administrations as presidential advisor, told him years later:

"Henry, you're brilliant. But you're arrogant. In fact you're the most arrogant man I've ever met. Mark my words, your arrogance is going to get you in real trouble one day." – (William Yandell Elliott, in Greg Grandin, *Kissinger's Shadow*: *The Long Reach of America's Most Controversial Statesman*, New York: Metropolitan Books, p. 39, 2015).

It was when he served as secretary of state under President Gerald Ford that he had to go to a continent he despised so much and whose leaders he equally despised. The presidents he worked for had no more respect for Africans than he did.

Nixon believed in scientific racism, legitimised by pseudoscience, and expressed extremely racist views. According to *Newsweek*, he described black people in recorded conversations as "Negro bastards" who "live like a bunch of dogs"; "they are not going to make it for 500 years." His predecessor, Lyndon Johnson, routinely called blacks "niggers," civil rights bills "nigger bills."

Blacks were also intellectually "inferior" to whites and members of other races, a belief common among racists.

But when Kissinger went to Tanzania and met with President Nyerere, he met his intellectual equal who was not intimidated by him. And he knew that, despite his arrogance.

It is only when American interests – and the interests of American allies – are at stake that American leaders start to pay attention to African leaders. That was the case with the countries of southern Africa where the white minority rulers, who were allies of the United States, came under increasing pressure from Africans to relinquish power to the indigenous people.

With the war intensifying in Rhodesia, waged by the freedom fighters to end white minority rule in that country, it was clear that Nyerere could no longer be ignored by the United States as a major player on the political scene in southern Africa. It was President Ford who sent Kissinger to Africa to seek a diplomatic solution to the conflict. But Kissinger failed to achieve his goal when he met with Nyerere.

When Carter became president, the new American leader went a step further not only by inviting Nyerere to the White House but by seeking his guidance and support in the quest for an amicable solution to the conflict in Rhodesia and in trying to get Cuban troops out of Angola. He made some progress with Nyerere on the question of Rhodesia but not on the withdrawal of Cuban troops from Angola.

Nyerere's disagreement with the United States on the presence of Cuban troops in Angola sent a clear signal to the Carter administration that Cuban troops were not going to leave Angola, and he would not ask Castro to withdraw his troops, unless South African troops were out of Angola.

President Carter acknowledged Nyerere's role as a major political force in southern Africa and did not want to alienate him by seeking concessions he knew Nyerere would not make. As *The Washington Post* stated about Nyerere's prominence as a leader and as a prime factor and determinant in the calculus of the political events unfolding in southern Africa:

"President Carter asked visiting Tanzanian President Julius K. Nyerere yesterday (4 August 1977) for his crucial support of a new diplomatic attempt to resolve the conflict over majority rule in white-dominated Rhodesia.

The two leaders were said to have agreed there is still 'a possibility' of heading off 'massive bloodshed and civil war' throughout Rhodesia, where black guerrilla spokesmen say the time for diplomacy is gone.

However, 'It cannot be overemphasized,' White House press secretary Jody Powell told reporters after the first Carter-Nyerere meeting, 'that hope for a realization of that [diplomatic] possibility involves an extremely difficult and complex process.'

Nyerere...is a pivotal figure in the Carter administration's African diplomacy in Rhodesia and in South African-ruled Namibia (Southwest Africa).

The United States and Britain are now drafting proposals to try to produce a peaceful transition to majority rule in Rhodesia, where 270,000 whites rule 6 million blacks....

Nyerere...was publicly asked by Carter yesterday for his advice and his counsel and his friendship and his guidance for achieving 'peace with justice' in Africa.

Welcoming Nyerere on the South Lawn of the White House with full military honors, Carter reached back to the memories of the Kennedy administration, when Nyerere last visited the White House, to re-kindle and strengthen the U.S. link with Tanzania.

During the Nixon-Ford years, the relationship was frigid, until 1976 when Secretary of State Henry A. Kissinger suddenly reversed U.S. policy toward black African nationalism, and launched an aborted attempt at a Rhodesian settlement and 'majority rule' in all Africa.

Carter lauded Nyerere yesterday as 'a senior statesman...a scholar, a philosopher, a great writer,' who 'has forgone material wealth and ease in a sacrificial way for his own people.'

The gray-haired Nyerere, whose mild humble appearance conceals the intellect and political skill to bargain shrewdly with the world's Communist and non-Communist leaders responded warmly to the welcome.

There was no allusion on either side yesterday to Nyerere's long-standing complaint about U.S. policy in Africa, that for years it looked at Africa 'through anti-Communist spectacles,' ignoring Africa's basic needs.

Nyerere...has maintained that Africa's nationalists must 'accept help from wherever they can get it' to achieve their own objectives. To achieve black majority rule in Rhodesia and Namibia and South Africa, the stronghold of white-minority rule, Nyerere has said the United States must join in efforts to assure that South Africa is 'isolated economically, politically and socially,' by the rest of the world.

Nyerere...added to his schedule a meeting with members of the Congressional Black Caucus." – (Murray Marder, "President Asks Nyerere for Support on Rhodesia," *The Washington Post*, 5 August 1977).

At the welcoming ceremony after his arrival in Washington, President Nyerere underscored the importance of the United States as a global power exercising economic and military might - including the enormous influence it had on the white minority regimes in southern Africa - when, responding to President Carter who had just welcomed him, he said in his speech:

"We in Tanzania, Mr. President, and in Africa generally, follow American politics with close attention. There is the intrinsic interest of the affairs of the most powerful nation the world has ever known. But more to the point, your politics do affect us. Indeed, we in Tanzania sometimes think that the world should somehow join n the process of electing the American President--[laughter]--for though we realize that the American people do not elect an absolute monarch, the world power structure is such that other peoples in other nations have a vital interest in the person whom the American people choose as their executive head of state." – (The American Presidency Project, University of California, Santa Barbara: Jimmy Carter, XXXIX President of the United States: 1977 – 1981. Visit of President Julius K. Nyerere of Tanzania – Remarks of the President and President Nyerere at the Welcoming Ceremony, 4 August 1977).

After his meetings with President Nyerere, President Carter was asked at a press conference in Washington, D.C.:

Question: "What can you tell us, sir, about the outcome of the visit with President Nyerere?"

Carter: "Well, President Nyerere is a man who has the best insight into African problems of anyone I've ever met. I think he has the trust and confidence of almost all the other nations in Africa and obviously is a natural scholar, student, historian, and political leader.

He and I have reached, I think, almost complete agreement over the goals and purposes of diplomatic efforts relating to Rhodesia and Namibia. And we will try to carry out those purposes, working as closely as we can together, recognizing, of course, that many other nations and leaders will be involved.

But we have, I think, made a great deal of progress in our meetings these last 2 days, and I've developed an increasing respect for him." – (The American Presidency Project, University of California, Santa Barbara: Jimmy Carter, XXXIX President of the United States: 1977 – 1981. Visit of President Nyerere of Tanzania – Remarks to Reporters Following The President's Departure, 5 August

1977).

Pressure exerted on the Rhodesian white minority regime by the freedom fighters and their supporters, who continued to wage war, finally led to a peaceful resolution of the conflict. At a conference at Lancaster House in London in 1979, an agreement was reached for a transition to majority rule through democratic elections. The elections were held in February 1980. Robert Mugabe won. He became prime minister in April. White minority rule had finally ended in Rhodesia which was later renamed Zimbabwe.

Decades later, President Robert Mugabe launched a book, *Julius Nyerere: Asante Sana, Thank You Mwalimu*, a tribute to Nyerere for the major role played in the liberation of the countries of southern Africa. As he stated, the liberation of all the countries in southern Africa was planned in Dar es Salaam under the leadership of Nyerere. He went on to say:

"When we gained our independence in Mozambique and Angola in 1975, in Zimbabwe in 1980, Namibia in 1990, and a new democratic dispensation, in South Africa in 1994, we said – Asante sana, Thank you, Mwalimu....

Mwalimu Nyerere was honoured this year (2015) by the African Union with the naming of the AU Peace and Security headquarters after him....

The time is now to recognise the role played by Julius Nyerere in the political liberation of Africa, and to enshrine his legacy to reside with the present and future generation of Africans." – (Robert Gabriel Mugabe, foreword to *Julius Nyerere: Asante sana, Thank You, Mwalimu*, Harare, Zimbabwe, 2015).

Remembering those days, Philip Ochieng, who worked at the *Daily News* in Dar es Salaam during that period, stated the following:

"Under Julius Kambarage Nyerere, Dar es Salaam served as the external headquarters of practically every one of the nationalist movements fighting to bring down Europe's racially conceited tyrannies all over our continent - all the way from the borders of Egypt in the north to the Cape of Good Hope in the south, including Kenya (Ochieng's home country).

That was how I first met Robert (Bob) Mugabe, a great nationalist, at that time considered as the most redoubtable of all of Southern Africa's campaigners for indigenous self-rule.

For, in the Tanzanian capital, Robert Mugabe was seen then as the topmost and most cherished among Africa's nationalist leaders fighting to bring down European tyranny all over our vast continent, especially in that Southern African colony, and throughout the world.

Power corrupts

Southern Rhodesia, as Ian Smith and other white supremacists conceitedly insisted on calling it, was what Robert Mugabe would soon lead into independence as Zimbabwe – in triumph and to the accompaniment of *vigelegele* all over the continent and the world, especially in Kambarage's Tanzania, where, in Dar es Salaam, I was then working as a weekend newspaper editor and weekly columnist.

Unfortunately, however – as one of Britain's own top political historians had already noticed – power corrupts and absolute power corrupts absolutely.

If anybody doubted it, the Third World's own history since independence, especially Africa's, has powerfully proved the correctness of that dictum by a noted observer of human behaviour.

Corruption is the name of it in all capitals of Africa and the Third World - including ours - and death is frequently the result of all reactions to anybody intrepid enough to criticise and attempt to put paid to it.

In our own country, a number of true fighters for freedom have paid for it with their own personal lives.

However, although Robert Mugabe was initially adored at home and profoundly respected throughout the continent and, indeed, throughout the world, his regime began to be increasingly personified by economic grabbing, political heavy-handedness, social decay and personal arrogance by every one of that country's top leaders.

Independence

Power drunkenness has been the most spectacular characteristic of all leaders in all the countries the world over in which - encouraged by Europe's own economically dominant classes pursuing their own gluttonous self-interests all over the world – 'independence' was granted precisely under that kind of leadership throughout what Europe now contemptuously calls the Third World.

Quiet evidently, nevertheless, times do change. Of all the nationalists fighting to bring down Britain's colonial high-handedness and arrogance, Robert Mugabe was at one time one of Africa's most cherished darlings.

When I worked in Dar es Salaam, I often met and deeply admired the person whom fellow nationalists in exile called 'Dear Bob.'

Time was indeed when I wholeheartedly recommended 'Bob' as the chief spokesman for our continent and for humanity's downtrodden classes all over the world, including even in that same Western Europe which had, for the nonce, assumed the role of model of what was alleged to be 'democracy.'

Specifically, I would wholeheartedly have recommended Robert Mugabe as the future leader of my Zimbabwean cousins.

When I first met face to face and interviewed what was then our 'dear Bob' in an hotel room in Dar es Salaam at some point in the early 1970s, he proved overwhelmingly charming, courteous, captivating in manner, overpowering in intellect and overwhelmingly knowledgeable of history and the modern human world.

Of all the nationalists seeking to defeat Caucasian racist tyranny and conceit in Africa, especially in Namibia and Southern Rhodesia, Robert Mugabe remained what William Shakespeare – the great bard of England's own intellectual and cultural celebration – would have embraced in poetry and drama as 'the nonpareil.'

Quite evidently, it would have been a terrible and embarrassing mistake." – (Philip Ochieng, "The Mugabe We All Adored in Dar Turned Out an Embarrassment," *Daily Nation*, Nairobi, Kenya, 25 November 2017).

Mugabe looked up to Nyerere when he was in prison in Rhodesia for about 11 years for opposing white minority rule and remained close to him from the time he set foot in Dar es Salaam after he was released from confinement.

When Mugabe assumed power in April 1980, Nyerere told him, "You have inherited the jewel of Africa" and advised him to keep it that way. He did for some time and then something went wrong.

Nyerere's influence could not be underestimated. He was an inspiration to freedom fighters throughout the continent as much as Nkrumah was. As Professor Ali Mazrui stated in his lecture at the University of Ghana in 2002:

"The torch of African radicalism, after the coup which overthrew Nkrumah in 1966, was in fact passed to Nyerere. The great voice of African self-reliance, and the most active African head of government in relation to liberation in Southern Africa from 1967 until the 1980s was in fact Julius Nyerere....

On the question of Nyerere's commitment to liberation...Nyerere was second to none in that commitment." – (Ali A. Mazrui in his lecture, "Nkrumahism and The Triple Heritage: Out of the Shadows," University of Ghana-Legon, 2002).

It is an observation shared by others. As Trevor Grundy stated:

"He did so much to help liberate different parts of Africa from European rule while bankrupting Tanzania in the process."

At a meeting of the leaders of the member states of the Southern African Development Community (SADC) in Harare, Zimbabwe, in April 2015 chaired by Robert Mugabe and whose participants included Tanzanian President Jakaya Kikwete, the Zimbabwean leader lamented that Nyerere had not been accorded the respect, recognition and gratitude he deserved for the major and decisive role he played in the liberation of the countries of southern Africa and others elsewhere on the continent. As he stated, among other things:

"The reckonings, the consciousness, of our forefathers, those who formed the Frontline States, we don't have them all now. Only one of them still remains alive, KK.
Mwalimu is gone. Neto of Angola is gone. Machel of Mozambique is gone. Sir Seretse Khama of Botswana is gone. They are the ones who formed the Frontline States which grew and transformed into SADCC, with two Cs, which was a coordinating body at that time; and the coordinating body, on the strength of whose reckonings, much more happened.
Greater freedom came. A new political dispensation later came for South Africa. We got our independence. Namibia got its independence. But must not also be

forgotten that it was the - because of the earlier stand of these founding fathers of our region that the OAU decided that the liberation of the whole of Africa would be done now through a body called the Liberation Committee to be hosted in Tanzania, Mwalimu's country. And all the freedom movements were harboured there; some of them divided, ZANU, ZAPU, we were two. ANC, PAC. SWAPO, SWANU. We were all there.

And the results, of course, were resounding. Africa became free.

So the arm of southern Africa freed, played a great part in freeing the whole of Africa and rendering each independent.

We have not done done much by way of paying tribute to our forefathers. Yes, something has been done to Kwame Nkrumah at the AU, and recently the hall was named after Mandela.

But we forgot, perhaps because we are a new generation, a new generation of leaders, that the greatest burden of freeing Africa was borne by the one country Tanzania, and that one – I am saying the greatest, not that he was alone, Nyerere, Mwalimu.

No mention has been made, no symbol, to remember his part. And I say, no, we must do something, we will do something. Even if Zimbabwe was – we can't be that ungrateful. No. So I would want to say, help us, help me, my thought that we respect Mwalimu at the AU, somehow. N – ("President Robert Mugabe Pays Tribute to Mwalimu," Harare, Zimbabwe, April 2015).

Kwame Nkrumah's eldest son, Gamal Nkrumah, a journalist with a leading Egyptian newspaper *Al Ahram*, who said Nyerere became a father to him after his own father died, also paid tribute to Nyerere when the Tanzanian leader died in October 1999. Coincidentally, both leaders, Nkrumah and Nyerere, died of cancer. Also, both died at hospitals in Europe; Nkrumah in Romania,

Nyerere in Britain. As Gamal stated in his tribute to Nyerere, "The Legacy of a Great African":

"Former Tanzanian President Julius Kambarage Nyerere had the gift of incandescence. Undaunted by the multiplicity and complexity of the development problems his people faced, Nyerere's presence at political rallies, remote poverty-stricken villages, academic conferences and international forums where he pleaded the case of the South always lit up the occasion.

He had a way with words, especially in his native Kiswahili. He was the philosopher-king, intellectual, enlightened, the polar opposite of the despotic ruler so common in the Africa of his day. But he was also a man of the people....

Two years ago, at celebrations marking the 40th anniversary of Ghana's independence, I met and spoke to Nyerere for the last time. I would never have guessed that he was ill. As always, he spoke so eloquently and with such intellectual vigour....

He was not only a man of great integrity, but he also had the courage and modesty to admit to past mistakes. I have heard him speak in London, at the Commonwealth Institute, in several forums in the United States and at the United Nations, as well as in many an African setting. To me personally, Nyerere was always the attentive father figure, never missing an opportunity to remind me that my own father's vision for a united Africa was the only way forward.

With his wit, humour, sharp intellect and disarming sincerity, Nyerere was always a winning personality....

He...continued to champion the liberation movements of southern Africa and provide training camps for their freedom fighters on Tanzanian soil....

However we judge him on particular issues, there is no denying Nyerere's enormous contribution to the post-independence African political scene. His greatest achievement is undoubtedly the successful unification of mainland Tanganyika with the Indian Ocean island of Zanzibar....It was to Nyerere's credit that he managed to unite this most ethnically, linguistically and religiously diverse of nation-states and make it one of Africa's most politically stable countries....

Until his death, Nyerere continued to serve as the Leader and chief spokesman of the Geneva-based South Commission. He also remained actively involved in scores of developmental and peacekeeping missions both in Africa and throughout the developing world....

Nyerere bequeathed his country and Africa a great legacy, that of unity, solidarity with the poor and downtrodden worldwide and political secularism, together with a real pride in the continent's languages and cultural heritage.

He could have chosen an academic career in the West, after graduating from Kampala's celebrated Makerere University, then one of Africa's finest institutions of higher learning, and then again when he left Africa to do postgraduate work at Edinburgh in 1949. He translated two of William Shakespeare's plays into Kiswahili, his namesake *Julius Caesar* and *The Merchant of Venice*. But instead, he wisely chose to return to Africa and lead the anti-colonial struggle. In 1960, he even offered to delay Tanganyika's independence plans if the move would facilitate the creation of an East African Federation of Tanganyika, Kenya and Uganda.

That dream failed, and Nyerere officiated instead over the union of Tanganyika and Zanzibar. It is a union that has lasted long, and there are no signs of cracks in it to this day. That this is so is thanks in large measure to Nyerere's own force of character and vision." – (Gamal Nkrumah, "The Legacy of a Great African," *Al Ahram*, Cairo, Egypt, 21 – 27 October 1999).

Not long before he died, Nyerere had also started

translating Plato's work, *The Republic*, into Kiswahili.

Probably Nyerere's most enduring legacy in a Pan-African context – besides his success in uniting two countries, Tanganyika and Zanzibar, to form Tanzania, the only union of independent states ever formed on the continent and that still exists to day – is the prominent role he played in helping liberate the countries of southern Africa which were still under white minority rule.

He will always be remembered for that as much as Nktumah will always be remembered for his quest for immediate continental unification and his support of liberation movements in Africa.

Nyerere also will be remembered for his approach to continental unity, formation of regional federations as a practical step towards uniting the continent under one government, after he failed to convince the leaders of Kenya and Uganda to form a federation with Tanganyika and achieve independence on the same day as one political entity.

Both leaders shared a vision for a united Africa under one government unlike most of their colleagues with a few exceptions such as Ahmed Sekou Toure of Guinea, Modibo Keita of Mali, Milton Obote of Uganda, Sorou-Migan Apithy of Dahomey, and Kenneth Kaunda of Zambia. As Nyerere stated in his speech in Accra, Ghana, in March 1997:

"Without unity, there is no future for Africa."

In Nkrumah's case, most African leaders ignored him when he exhorted them to unite their countries under one government, immediately, in Addis Ababa, Ethiopia, where they met in May 1963 and formed the Organisation of African Unity (OAU).

Nkrumah's quest for immediate continental unification was sharply contrasted with Nyerere's gradualist approach which was dictated by pragmatic considerations. As

Nyerere stated in an interview with the *New Internationalist* in 1998 not long before he died the following year:

"Kwame Nkrumah and I were committed to the idea of unity. African leaders and heads of state did not take Kwame seriously. However, I did.

I did not believe in these small little nations. Still today I do not believe in them. I tell our people to look at the European Union, at these people who ruled us who are now uniting.

Kwame and I met in 1963 and discussed African unity. We differed on how to achieve a United States of Africa. But we both agreed on a United States of Africa as necessary. Kwame went to Lincoln University, a black college in the US. He perceived things from from the perspective of US history, where 13 colonies that revolted against the British formed a union. That is what he thought the OAU (Organisation of African Unity) should do.

I tried to get East Africa to unite before independence. When we failed in this way, I was wary about Kwame's continental approach. We corresponded profusely on this. Kwame said my idea of 'regionalization' was only balkanization on a larger scale. Later, African historians will have to study our correspondence on this issue of uniting Africa.

Africans who studied in the US like Nkrumah and Azikiwe were more aware of the Diaspora and the global African community than those of us who studied in Britain. They were therefore aware of a wider Pan-Africanism. Theirs was the aggressive Pan-Africanism of W.E.B. Du Bois and Marcus Garvey. The colonialists were against this and frightened of it." – (Julius Nyerere, in an interview with Ikaweba Bunting, "The Heart of Africa: Interview with Julius Nyerere on Anti-Colonialism," in the *New Internationalist*, Oxford, UK, January-February 1999).

He also explained in the same interview what happened when he and Ugandan leader Milton Obote went to see Jomo Kenyatta of Kenya in an attempt to form an East African federation:

"I respected Jomo immensely. It has probably never happened in history. Two heads of state, Milton Obote and I, went to Jomo and said to him: 'Let's unite our countries and you be our head of state.' He said no. I think he said no because it would have put him out of his element as a Kikuyu Elder." – (Nyerere, *New Internationalist*, ibid.).

In an interview with *The New York Times* in his home village of Butiama near the shores of Lake Victoria in 1996, Nyerere said his biggest failure was that he failed to convince the other leaders in East Africa to form an East African federation; his biggest achievement, he said, was forming a united nation out of more than 120 different ethnic groups:

"I felt that these little countries in Africa were really too small, they would not be viable – the Tanganyikas, the Rwandas, the Burundis, the Kenyas. My ambition in East Africa was really never to build a Tanganyika. I wanted an East African federation.
So what did I do in succeeding? My success is building a nation out of this collection of tribes." – (Julius Nyerere in an interview with James C. McKinley Jr., "Many Failures, and One Big Success," *The New York Times*, and in the *International Herald Tribune*, 2 September 1996, p. 2).

In another interview, Nyerere also explained the differences he had with Kwame Nkrumah in an attempt to unite African countries under one continental government:

"My differences with Kwame were that Kwame thought there was somehow a shortcut, and I was saying there was no shortcut. This is what we have inherited, and we'll have to proceed within the limitations that that inheritance has imposed on us.

Kwame thought that somehow you could say, 'Let there be a United States of Africa' and it would happen. I kept saying, 'Kwame, it's a slow process.'

He had tremendous contempt for a large number of leaders of Africa and I said, 'Fine, but they are there. What are you going to do with them? They don't believe as you do - as you and I do - in the need for the unity of Africa. BUT WHAT DO YOU DO? THEY ARE THERE, AND WE HAVE TO PROCEED ALONG WITH EVERYBODY!'

And I said to him in so many words that we're not going to have an African Napoleon, who is going to conquer the continent and put it under one flag. It is not possible.

At the OAU conference in 1963, I was actually trying to defend Kwame. I was the last to speak and Kwame had said this charter has not gone far enough because he thought he would leave Addis with a United States of Africa.

I told him that this was absurd; that it can't happen. This is what we have been able to achieve. No builder, after putting down the foundation, complains that the building is not yet finished. You have to go on building and building until you finish; but he was impatient because he saw the stupidity of the others." – (Julius Nyerere, in an interview with Bill Sutherland in Bill Sutherland and Matt Mayer, eds., *Guns and Gandhi in Africa: Pan African Insight on Nonviolence, Armed Struggle, and Liberation in Africa*, Trenton, New Jersey, USA: Africa World Press, 2000; reproduced by Chambi Chachage, "Excerpt from Interview with Bill Sutherland," Centre for Consciencist Studies and Analyses (CENSCA), 5 September 2008. See also Bill Sutherland in William Minter, Gaily Hovey, and Charles Cobb Jr., eds., *No Easy Victories: African Liberation and American Activists over a Half Century, 1950 - 2000*, Trenton, New Jersey, USA: New Africa Press, 2007).

Prime Minister Abubakar Tafawa Balewa of Nigeria was resolutely opposed to a continental government and bluntly stated in his speech at the OAU summit in Accra, Ghana, in October 1965 that Nigeria would never surrender its sovereignty to a higher authority. As Professor Willard Scott Thompson stated in his book, *Ghana's Foreign Policy, 1957 – 1966: Diplomacy Ideology, and the new State*:

"Sir Abubakar (Tafawa Balewa) let them go no further. An African government was a dream, he said, 'Or a nightmare.' Nigeria, for its part, would never surrender its sovereignty. 'This request, Mr. Chairman, is indirectly a vote of no confidence in the Oirganisation of African Unity. When we started this Organisation only a year ago, we were working, progressing and now we are trying to impose something.' Union government might come, so might world government, he said." – (Willard Scott Thompson, *Ghana's Foreign Policy, 1957 – 1966: Diplomacy Ideology, and the new State*, Princeton, New Jersey, USA: Princeton University Press,1969, p. 355).

And as Nyerere stated in his speech in Accra on Ghana's 40th independence anniversary where he was an official guest invited by President Jerry Rawlings:

"Prior to independence of Tanganyika, I had been advocating that East African countries should federate and then achieve independence as a single political unit. I had said publicly that I was willing to delay Tanganyika's independence in order to enable all three-mainland countries to achieve their independence together as a single federated state.

I made the suggestion because of my fear, proved correct by later events, that it would be very difficult to unite our countries if we let them achieve independence separately.

Once you multiply national anthems, national flags and passports, seats at the United Nations, and individuals entitled to 21-gun salute, not to speak of a host of ministers, prime ministers, and envoys, you will have a whole army of powerful people with vested interests in keeping Africa balkanised. That was what Nkrumah encountered in 1965.

After the failure to establish the union government at the Accra (OAU) summit of 1965, I heard one head of state express with relief that he was happy to be returning home to his country still head of state. To this day I cannot tell whether he was serious or joking. But he may well have been serious, because Kwame Nkrumah was very serious and the fear of a number of us to lose our precious status was quite palpable.

But I never believed that the 1965 Accra summit would have established a union government for Africa. When I say that we failed, that is not what I mean, for that clearly was an unrealistic objective for a single summit. What I mean is that we did not even discuss a mechanism for pursuing the objective of a politically united Africa. We had a Liberation Committee already (based in Dar es Salaam, Tanzania). We should have at least had a Unity Committee or undertaken to establish one. We did not. And after Kwame Nkrumah was removed from the African political scene nobody took up the challenge again." – (Julius K. Nyerere, speech on Ghana's 40th independence anniversary, Accra, March 1997).

The coup against Nkrumah was engineered by the CIA and masterminded by the CIA station chief in Accra,

Howard T. Bane. After he returned to the United States from Ghana, he was quickly promoted and given a senior position at the CIA and the Distinguished Intelligence Medal, the agency's highest award, for his role in overthrowing Nkrumah.

It was an achievement that was well-received by American officials, President Lyndon B. Johnson among them, and was even celebrated in some quarters including the CIA and the State Department. As Robert P. Smith, who once served as United States ambassador to Ghana and was working at the State Department when Nkrumah was overthrown, stated when he explained how Secretary of State Dean Rusk reacted to the news about Nkrumah's downfall:

"I also remember, the morning of the coup, I got the call about 2 a.m. here at the house and went into the Department and immediately set up a little task force in the Operations Center. Later in the same morning, about 8 or 8.30, Secretary Rusk wandered down the hall and came in and said, 'I've seen the early reports, but I just want to hear it firsthand. What's going on in Ghana?' When I related how Nkrumah had landed in Peking and had been informed by his Chinese hosts of what had happened in Ghana, Dean Rusk broke into an ear-splitting grin. I've never seen him look so happy." – (Robert P. Smith, interviewed by Charles Stuart Kennedy, *The Association for Diplomatic Studies and Training (ADST), Foreign Affairs Oral Project,* 28 February 1989, p. 14).

It was also when Dean Rusk was secretary of state that the State Department recommended arming some groups in Tanzania to destabilise the government in an attempt to overthrow President Nyerere. As John Prados states in his book, *Safe for Democracy: The Secret Wars of the CIA:*

"The Special Group (at the CIA) reportedly considered

a State Department proposal to supply arms to certain groups in Tanzania, where secret-war wizards saw President Julius Nyerere as a problem, in the summer of 1964....Like Nyerere, Washington viewed Ghana's leader Kwame Nkrumah as a troublemaker." – (John Prados, Safe for Democracy: The Secret Wars of the CIA, Chicago, Illinois, USA: Ivan R. Dee, Publisher, 2006, p. 328).

Yet the CIA was wary of supporting covert operations against Nyerere to undermine his government in order to overthrow him because he was not corrupt, did not use his position to enrich himself and his family members, and was extremely popular. His commitment to the well-being of the masses and everybody else was beyond question. The CIA knew a coup against him would not have the support of the people, especially the masses who constituted the vast majority of the population and who sincerely believed he cared about them and was doing his best to improve their lives.

Even his opponents who wanted to overthrow him would not have been able to justify his ouster and convince the people that he did not care about them. They included former foreign affairs minister Oscar Kambona who was the mastermind of the 1969 coup attempt.

The coup was exposed by the Tanzanian intelligence service with the assistance of the South African freedom fighters of the Pan-Africanist Congress (PAC) based in Dar es Salaam. The accused started in March 1968 working on plans to overthrow the government. They were arrested in October 1969, the same month they were going to launch the coup.

Kambona sought the assistance of the guerrilla fighters who were being trained in Tanzania but the PAC leader, Potlako Leballo, notified the Tanzanian authorities about that. He continued to cooperate with the coup plotters while working with the Tanzanian intelligence service monitoring the conspirators. Kambona hoped that the guerrilla fighters would team up with some members of the Tanzanian army to overthrow Nyerere.

One colonel, one captain, and one lieutenant of the Tanzanian army were among the leading conspirators who were arrested, tried and convicted of treason. Others were a former cabinet member; the former secretary-general of the only opposition party in the country, the African National Congress (ANC) which died out in the mid-sixties after being overwhelmed at the polls by the ruling Tanganyika African National Union (TANU); a former editor of the ruling party's newspaper; and one woman who was the leader of the women's movement in the country and who played a major role campaigning for independence with Nyerere.

Two of them, the army captain and the former secretary-general of the opposition ANC, were brothers and cousins of Oscar Kambona.

Leballo's testimony proved critical to the outcome of the trial. He was deeply involved in the coup plot in order to provide evidence against the conspirators later during the trial in the high court of Tanzania. He also mentioned the South African minister of foreign affairs, Hilgard Muller, as one of the people Kambona approached to help overthrow Nyerere. According to Colin Legum in *Africa Contemporary Record, 1970 - 1971*:

"The central prosecution witness was Potlako K. Leballo, a founder of the Pan-African Congress (Pan-Africanist Congress) of South Africa (PAC), which had its exile headquarters in Dar es Salaam.

The state maintained that seven defendants attempted to enlist Leballo in the plot but that he informed government officials and only appeared to go along with the plot in order to assist in capturing the conspirators.

Leballo testified that he frequently met with Kambona in London and that Kambona had shown him a cache of $500,000 and told him that he could 'get more where that came from' by contacting a U.S. Information Service 'friend' in London (*The New York Times*, 19 July 1970, 12).

Leballo further testified that Kambona had an agreement with the South African foreign minister, Hilgard Muller, that South Africa would support the coup." – (Colin Legum and John Drsydale, eds., *Africa Contemporary Record: Annual Survey and Documents 1970 – 1971*, London: Africa Rsearch Limited, 1971, pp. 170 – 71).

The coup attempt is covered extensively in Godfrey Mwakikagile's book, *Nyerere and Africa: End of an Era*, in which the author uses transcripts of the court proceedings during the treason trial to document his work. As he stated in his book:

"In spite of his immense popularity, President Nyerere was not immune from subversion. He became a target of a number of attempts, from within and without, to oust him from power. There were also many attempts to destabilize and weaken his government which his enemies and detractors hoped would eventually lead to his downfall.

He was fiercely independent, a stance that rankled Western powers as he went on to forge links with Eastern-bloc countries including the People's Republic of China and the Soviet Union, but especially with China, while maintaining ties with the West in pursuit of his policy of non-alignment. And his strong support for the African liberation movements was not endorsed by Western powers which wanted to perpetuate white minority rule in Africa for hegemonic control of the continent by the West.

So, Western powers wanted him out. Apartheid South Africa and other white minority regimes on the continent including Rhodesia and the Portuguese colonial governments - hence their mother country Portugal - also wanted him out. They did everything they could, including infiltrating and bombing Tanzania, to destabilize his government. One of the attempts to undermine his government involved the United States in the mid-sixties. As Nyerere himself stated in June 1966:

'We have twice quarrelled with the US Government, once when we believed it to be involved in a plot against us, and again when two of its officials misbehaved and were asked to leave Tanzania....The disagreements certainly induced an uncooperative coldness between us.'

Dr. Kwame Nkrumah, in his book *Dark Days in Ghana*, also discusses attempts by the CIA and the American government to undermine and overthrow Nyerere. He himself was ousted from power in a coup engineered and masterminded by the CIA in February 1966.

The most dramatic attempt to overthrow Nyerere came to public attention in October 1969 when the accused conspirators were brought to court in Tanzania's most celebrated treason trial. There was another treason trial in 1983. But it was not as dramatic as the other one mainly because of the people involved, although the plot in 1982 to overthrow the government led to the arrest of 600 soldiers and about 1,000 civilians in January 1983 for their alleged involvement in and support of the coup attempt.

The 1969 treason case involved some of Tanzania's most prominent politicians, including luminaries in the independence movement and two former cabinet members. The leader of the treasonous coterie was Oscar Kambona, Tanzania's former minister of foreign affairs who earlier had also served as minister of home affairs and then as minister of defence. He was also one of the country's three most influential and powerful leaders, together with President Nyerere himself and Vice President Rashidi Kawawa, who spearheaded the independence movement in Tanganyika; Kawawa was vice president of Tanganyika until April 1964 when he became second vice president after Tanganyika united with Zanzibar, and the president of Zanzibar, Abeid Karume, became first vice president under the union constitution.

In July 1967, Kambona left Tanzania and went into self-imposed exile in London, Britain. He continued to exercise some influence on his supporters in Tanzania, disgruntled with Nyerere's socialist policies and one-party rule, but gradually faded into obscurity as a "potent" force on the nation's political scene. His opposition to Nyerere's leadership and socialist policies reached a dramatic point towards the end of January in Arusha just before the adoption of the famous Arusha Declaration which became Tanzania's economic blueprint and political manifesto, covering all aspects of national life across the spectrum including foreign affairs and the liberation of Africa from colonialism and imperialism. Nyerere wrote the Declaration which, even years later just before he died, he said he would not change except for a few words here and there in its Swahili version. As Arthur Wille, a Catholic priest who knew Nyerere well and was close to him since the 1940s, stated:

'When the TANU National Executive Committee met in Arusha January 26 - 29 it turned out to be a stormy session. At this meeting Nyerere proposed that *Ujamaa* become the official policy of the government. Oscar Kambona objected strongly to this policy. Twice during these sessions, the Executive Committee adjourned in order to allow their three leaders, Nyerere, Kambona and Kawawa to go into private session. Each time that they returned to the Executive Committee it was apparent that Kawawa had supported Nyerere to defeat Kambona. The result was that the Arusha Declaration was adopted.'

The Arusha Declaration was adopted on February 5, 1967. It was the most ethical economic and political document ever written by an African leader. As Andrew Nyerere, Mwalimu Julius Nyerere's eldest son with whom I was in regular contact when I worked on the second edition of this book, stated in his comments in August 2003 when he looked at my work in progress:

'The Arusha Declaration forbade leaders to have two salaries. And there is one African businessman who told me that when Nyerere did this, when he restrained his colleagues from becoming rich, that is how we came to prominence; by that, he meant a whole generation of noveau rich people. The man who told me this has since died. He was suffering from a terminal illness. He spoke to me a few months before he died.'

Kambona left Tanzania about five months after the Arusha Declaration was adopted and continued to criticize Nyerere from Britain. And following Tanzania's recognition of Biafra in April 1968, a move that infuriated the Nigerian federal government, Nigerian leaders invited Kambona to Nigeria to lecture. He took this opportunity to denounce Nyerere and pursue his political ambitions. The Nigerian government also immediately broke off diplomatic relations with Tanzania because of her recognition of Biafra as an independent state, the first country to recognize the secessionist region of Eastern Nigeria as a sovereign entity.

Kambona left Tanzania via Kenya where some of his supporters lived and used Kenya's capital Nairobi as one of their operational bases in their conspiracy to overthrow Nyerere. But even in Kenya itself, a neighbouring country whose policies were different from Tanzania's - Kenya was capitalist and pro-Western, Tanzania socialist and non-aligned - there were many people who saw Kambona as a spent force fading into oblivion, although he could not be entirely dismissed as a non-entity. As the *Kenya Weekly News* stated on July 26, 1968, almost exactly one year after Kambona went into voluntary exile in Britain:

'Every lost turning, every sign of human weakness and failing will be exploited by people like Mr. Kambona. While this might be legitimate political opposition at home, it smacks of straw-clutching and opportunism coming from abroad. This is Mr. Kambona's problem; but it is unlikely to dissuade him from seeking to exploit every twist and turn in Tanzania's politics. It is the only way he can remain in business.'

One year and three months later, Kambona was accused of treason. The charges against him and his alleged conspirators were brought before the High Court of Tanzania in Dar es Salaam presided by Chief Justice Philip Telford Georges from Trinidad, who later served in the same capacity in newly independent Zimbabwe under President Robert Mugabe, himself with strong ties to Tanzania before and after he became the leader of his country. The prosecution team was led by Attorney-General Mark Bomani, and later by Senior State Attorney Nathaniel King, also from Trinidad, who almost single-handedly handled the case for the government.

I was a student then, at Tambaza High School in Dar es Salaam, in Form VI, or standard 14, and attended the treason trial with some of my schoolmates; the high court was only within walking distance from our school. I had just reached the age of 20 in October, the same month the treason charges became known to the public in 1969, four months after I was first hired as a reporter by the *Standard*, the country's largest English newspaper, in the nation's capital. But the trial did not start until June 1970. I went to the high court, not as a reporter, but simply as a spectator following the proceedings of the most important case in the history of Tanzania since independence in 1961. It was also the country's first treason trial, but not the last.

Kambona sought help from the CIA to overthrow

Nyerere, just as Simon Kapwepwe did in his attempt to oust Zambian President and his childhood friend Kenneth Kaunda. But neither got the help they needed, at least not enough of it to carry out a coup. The immense popularity of both leaders, their high international stature as highly respected statesmen, and their incorruptible nature, made it highly unlikely that their ouster would be accepted domestically or internationally; thus making it very difficult for their would-be successors to win support and recognition. As Andrew Nyerere stated in his written remarks to me on what I said about the CIA in this chapter when he read my manuscript:

'We were discussing it at Msasani (where President Nyerere and his family lived on the outskirts of Dar es Salaam) one day, the supposed CIA infiltration of our government. We were talking about it with my mother, and Mwalimu Nyerere was present. And my mother said, there was much confusion nowadays. Everyday one hears of more government leaders who are on the payroll of the CIA. And I said that surely there is a misunderstanding concerning this, because the CIA argue with those whom they consider to be the enemies of the United States, and this had nothing to do with us. And I saw that this statement made my mother calm.'

Some observers have emphasized the integrity of the two leaders, as incorruptible individuals, as the prime factor in the refusal or unwillingness of the CIA to support coup attempts against them. As Ben Lawrence, a Nigerian, stated in his article, "Privatization: Nigeria's New Gold Rush":

'The survival of Kenneth Kaunda and Julius Nyerere for so long in power was because of their alliance with the masses. When Oscar Kambona of Tanzania and Kapwepwe of Zambia requested the Central Intelligence

Agency's (CIA) help to overthrow their former friends, they were plainly told that those leaders were impregnable because they were incorruptible and had no loot stashed in foreign vaults.'

But none of this was enough to dissuade Kambona from pursuing his goal of trying to overthrow Nyerere. What I wrote about the CIA in this chapter inspired more remarks from Andrew Nyerere who said the following in his comments to me:

'One day Mwalimu Nyerere was speaking in praise of various US presidents, and then he lowered his voice and spoke in a very hushed tone referring to President Ronald Reagan, saying that, now they have elected this murderer, that is Ronald Reagan. Now that the American people have elected this murderer, there is much chaos in the world. But I do not think that Mwalimu Nyerere meant that he feared his life was in danger. I think he was just wondering how he was going to get aid from the United States now that there was a hostile government in power. Or maybe he was half-hoping that Jimmy Carter would be re-elected and that he would be able to make another visit to the White House. Because he had been very pleased with that visit he made to the White House, he put the picture on the wall at Msasani.'

In the treason trial which began in June 1970 before Chief Justice Philip Telford Georges, a Trinidadian, it was alleged that Kambona was the mastermind behind the coup attempt. The coup was to take place in October 1969. The conspirators wanted not only to overthrow the government but also to assassinate President Nyerere. I was in court and remember during the proceedings when Senior State Attorney Nathaniel King, also a Trinidadian, asked one of the accused, John Lifa Chipaka, what he meant when he said they wanted to 'eliminate' the president. Chipaka responded by saying that they wanted to 'eliminate him politically, not physically.' Nathaniel King looked at Chipaka and laughed when Chipaka said that. Chipaka's denial was not convincing and the evidence presented in court demonstrated otherwise. The plan to overthrow the government included a plot to assassinate the president.

The accused were Colonel William Makori Chacha, a senior army officer in the country's army, the Tanzania People's Defence Forces (TPDF), who, not long before the treason trial, was a military attache at the Tanzania embassy in Peking in the People's Republic of China; John Dustan Lifa Chipaka, 38, former secretary-general of the defunct African National Congress (ANC) led by Zuberi Mtemvu in the 1960s. In the 1990s, after he was released from prison, Chipaka was still active in politics and became one of the opposition leaders in Tanzania and once led a party founded by Oscar Kambona after Kambona returned to Tanzania from Britain where he had lived in self-imposed exile for 25 years.

Others who appeared before the court on treason charges were: Michael Kamaliza, 46, a polio victim and former secretary-general of the National Union of Tanganyika Workers (NUTA) who also once served as minister of labour; Bibi Titi Mohammed, 45, a fiery orator, once a junior minister of labour and community development in the sixties and Tanzania's most prominent female politician who was head of the ruling party's women's movement known in Kiswahili as Umoja wa Wanawake wa Tanzania (UWT), translated as Women's Union of Tanzania; Gray Likungu Mataka, 34, a journalist; Captain Elia Dustan Lifa Chipaka, 32, of the Tanzanian army, the Tanzania People's Defence Forces (TPDF), and younger brother of one of the accused, John Dustan Lifa Chipaka; and Lieutenant Alfred Philip Milinga, 27, also of the Tanzania People's Defence Forces, and the youngest among the accused. They all denied all the charges brought against them.

One of the most remarkable things about this trial was the fact that some of the people involved in the coup attempt were once, or were supposed to be, some of the most loyal to the president. Before his departure from Tanzania in 1967, especially before 1966, the minister for foreign affairs, Oscar Kambona, was one of Nyerere's closest colleagues who even helped quell the army mutiny in 1964 when he went directly to speak to the mutinous soldiers and negotiate with them on their salary demands and insistence that the British army officers should be immediately replaced by indigenous ones. Nyerere also attended Kambona's wedding to Flora Moriyo at St. Paul's Cathedral in London in on 19 November 1960 and gave away the bride. Kambona asked Nyerere to be his best man; they were also very close and worked together campaigning for independence.

Oscar Kambona and Flora Moriyo were the first black couple to be married at the cathedral.

Kambona was also one of the founders of TANU, together with Nyerere and others, a party which led Tanganyika to independence. Another veteran politician and founding member of TANU, Bibi Titi Mohammed, also was known to be a close friend and very loyal supporter of Nyerere; so was former labour minister Michael Kamaliza, even if only by virtue of his position as a cabinet member under Nyerere. Colonel Chacha was also said to be a loyal supporter of President Nyerere.

Yet, they turned out to be the most prominent conspirators against him and his government. Ironically, not long before the treason trial, Nyerere himself had publicly stated in 1966 what turned out to be one of the most "prophetic' statements he had ever made during his presidency, unequivocally saying:

'I've been one of the luckiest presidents in Africa. My colleagues are very loyal to me.'

They proved him wrong; not all, but many of them, including those who lied to him throughout his tenure to promote their own interests. And others, of course, plotted to get rid of him right away, as the treason trial tragically demonstrated.

The most ominous sign of things yet to come was the abrupt resignation of Oscar Kambona from his ministerial post and other positions in June 1967. This came only about four months after the adoption of the Arusha Declaration in February, the country's economic and political manifesto he strongly opposed. In July, he left the country. And within two years or so, he was accused of treason and of being the mastermind behind the coup attempt to overthrow and assassinate Nyerere, his erstwhile compatriot.

His attempts to undermine and oust Nyerere from power gained momentum soon after he settled in London where he launched a blistering attack on the president and his government in a concerted effort to win support and turn the people of Tanzania against him, but to avail. Nyerere's popularity was immense, even if his socialist policies and one-party rule weren't among a significant number of people; a disenchantment Kambona tried to capitalize on and use as a lightning rod to galvanize the opposition against Nyerere within the country.

However, there are different opinions on how much, if any, opposition to Nyerere's economic policies were generated or fuelled by the Arusha Declaration. As Andrew Nyerere stated in some of his comments to me on this second edition which he read when I was working on it:

'No one opposed the Arusha Declaration. There was only one problem in that the young students of primary school accepted it more readily than the older students of secondary school. The young were more idealistic.'

Safe in London, Kambona was not arrested for his involvement in the coup plot. But six of his fellow conspirators were arrested in October 1969. They were all arrested in Tanzania, with the exception of Gray Likungu Mataka who once served as news editor of the TANU ruling party's daily newspaper, *The Nationalist*, a fiercely nationalistic and uncompromising publication whose managing editor, Benjamin Mkapa, became president of Tanzania from 1995 - 2005. Mataka was arrested in Nairobi, Kenya, where he had been acting as a conduit between Kambona and the other conspirators in Tanzania. It was one of the ironies of this trial that Mataka was not only once editor of the ruling party's newspaper but of a paper that was fiercely loyal to the president.

I also remember when I was a news reporter of the *Standard* in Dar es Salaam that we had a sort of an adversarial relationship with *The Nationalist* whose reporters, and sometimes even editorials, now and then lambasted us for working for 'an imperialist newspaper.' The *Standard* was then owned by Lonrho, until it was nationalized in 1970 when it became a state-owned newspaper and rechristened *Daily News*. President Nyerere became editor-in-chief of the *Daily News* but only as a ceremonial head. It was the editor of the paper who exercised power over us. Coincidentally, the treason trial started in the same year in which the paper was nationalized.

And in spite of its reputation as an "imperialist" newspaper before it was nationalized, the *Standard* adhered to the highest journalistic standards in covering the treason trial; so did *The Nationalist,* without slanting facts in favour of the government, despite its strong nationalist bias and unswerving loyalty to President Nyerere.

The first accused was Oscar Kambona. There was speculation that the government would seek extradition of the former foreign affairs minister. But nothing was done, and he was tried in absentia. Andrew Nyerere remembers Oscar Kambona well, as much as he does the early days of independence when our country was still called Tanganyika, and had the following to say in his remarks to me when he read this chapter:

'I remember the day when we went to State House. Mr. Kambona took over the house that we were staying in, the one at Sea View, the residence of the Chief Minister. I gazed at him for a long time as the car sped away. He was taking charge of the house which was to be his new home. It is a pity that he turned out to be such a traitor. If Nyerere knew that he would turn out to be such a heinous traitor, he would not have given him all those responsible positions in government. But I went to his funeral. I felt that all these evils of the past should be forgotten.'

When I asked Andrew what he thought about Kambona since the early days of Tanganyika's independence in the sixties, in terms of what type of person he was, he responded by saying:

'He was a good man. But there was misunderstanding, and what happened, happened. For example, he strongly disagreed with Mwalimu Nyerere about Kassim Hanga, the Zanzibar (cabinet) minister who was sent back and killed. And Kambona was right about this. He did not want Hanga sent back to Zanzibar. And Mwalimu Nyerere said that, concerning Hanga, he sent him back, but he did not know that they were going to kill him.'

During the 1970 treason trial involving Kambona, it was alleged by the prosecution team that the conspirators intended to launch a military coup between October 10 and 15, 1969. During that time, President Nyerere and a large number of high ranking government officials including cabinet members, as well as the head of the Tanzania People's Defence Forces (TPDF), Major-General Mrisho Sarakikya, were out of the country. The plotters felt that this was the perfect time for a coup. Some people in Zanzibar were also implicated in the coup plot.

The director of the Criminal Investigation Department (CID), Geoffrey Sawaya, who was also an intelligence officer, told the high court that Oscar Kambona sent large sums of money to the people in Tanzania who were to take part in the coup; and that all the conspirators used aliases.

One key figure in uncovering the plot was a South African freedom fighter living in exile in Tanzania, Potlako Leballo, the leader of the Pan-Africanist Congress (PAC), a black nationalist group which was formed in 1959 by members who left the African National Congress (ANC) over policy differences. The first leader of the PAC was Robert Mangaliso Sobukwe, a professor at Witwatersrand University and compatriot of Nelson Mandela. Mandela remained in the African National Congress and later became president of the organization which spearheaded the struggle against apartheid.

Leballo became head of the PAC after Sobukwe was sent to prison by the apartheid regime. And his testimony in Tanzania's first treason trial proved to be critical.

The coup plotters approached Leballo and enlisted his help in carrying out the coup, possibly with the help of his guerrilla fighters based in Tanzania, and he went along with the plan to gather intelligence for the government. Leballo met with the conspirators on a number of occasions. He had already informed the government and the conspirators were now under surveillance, with all their meetings being monitored by Tanzania's intelligence officers. Leballo became the government's key witness who unlocked all the secrets of the coup plotters. He also testified in court that Kambona had been given a lot of money to finance the coup.

When Tanzania's Attorney-General Mark Bomani

asked Tanzania's head of the Criminal Investigation Department (CID) how he knew for sure that Leballo met the conspirators, Sawaya said whenever he knew in advance that there would be a meeting, he would assign his intelligence officers to monitor the proceedings in a clandestine operation the coup plotters never knew about. He also testified before the court that Leballo told him, in advance, about a trip to Nairobi, Kenya, on March 25, 1969; and that Leballo did go on that trip and returned to Dar es Salaam on April 1st.

Leballo told the director of the Criminal Investigation Department the purpose of the trip was to meet with Gray Likungu Mataka, who then lived in Nairobi which was one of the operational bases for the coup plotters, to get confirmation of the coup plot as Mataka had explained to him earlier.

awaya went on to say that he already knew that Leballo and Colonel Chacha had a meeting and that Leballo had been introduced to Prisca (one of the code names used by one of the conspirators) and Bibi Titi Mohammed. Chacha and Leballo met at Twiga Hotel in Dar es Salaam. Leballo also met with Bibi Titi Mohammed at an Islamic Centre at Chang'ombe in Dar es Salaam and discussed how President Nyerere and other senior government officials including some cabinet members would be assassinated.

The director of the Criminal Investigation Department further testified that on March 24, 1969, Leballo went to him and told him about the meeting he (Leballo) had with Chacha at Twiga Hotel. When Attorney-General Mark Bomani asked him how he knew the meeting had taken place, Sawaya said he sent his intelligence officers to Twiga Hotel on a surveillance mission after he was told about the meeting in advance. And they observed the meeting taking place.

On the following day, March 25, Leballo left for Nairobi, the intelligence director said, and was 'escorted' by some intelligence officers who had been assigned by the director to accompany him.

Sawaya went on to tell the court that in April 1969, he went on a trip overseas. He said he met again with Leballo on May 2, 1969, and that Leballo told him that the plan for the coup as explained by Gray Mataka in Nairobi was very well received by Colonel Chacha, Michael Kamaliza and Bibi Titi Mohammed in a jovial mood. He also said Mataka had promised to ask for some money from Kambona to facilitate the operation. The intelligence chief further stated that Leballo produced a letter written to Prisca by Mataka, and that Mataka himself copied the letter in his own handwriting and gave the copy to Leballo:

'**Mark Bomani:** Can you recognize the copy of this letter if you see it?
CID director: Yes, I can.
Bomani: How can you recognise this letter?
CID director: I can recognise it by the name of Chaima.
Leballo: He (the CID director) told me that after I met with Mataka for the first time, the accused changed his name and gave himself the code name of Chaima.
Chief Justice: Was the letter translated?
CID director: Soon after the copy of the letter was made, it was translated so that I could understand what it said.
Bomani: Did you know the letter was delivered?
CID director: I was informed that it was being delivered.'

The CID director went on to say that according to the information he got from Leballo, Chipaka, Titi, Kamaliza, Leballo and Prisca were going to have a meeting to discuss what they would be doing when they were waiting for some money from Kambona.

At that meeting, Kamaliza asked Leballo to go to London and ask Kambona to send more money. Kamaliza also asked Chipaka to write Kambona a letter and send him a 10-shilling note for Kambona to sign it. With Kambona's signature on the 10-shilling note, Kamaliza said the note would be passed around to convince some cabinet members and members of parliament to support Kambona in overthrowing the government.

It was also expected that the note would be used to raise more funds for the coup and get support from TANU leaders and workers and from the leaders and members of the country's labour union, the National Union of Tanganyika Workers (NUTA), to oppose the government; thus encouraging others to overthrow it.

Kamaliza told Leballo there was no doubt that the workers of Tanzania would support the coup because the president had removed him (Kamaliza) from the leadership of NUTA against the wishes of the workers.

Geoffrey Sawaya, the CID director, went on to say that Leballo met Titi (Bibi Titi Mohammed) at her house on June 23, 1969. She told him that she had been to Nairobi where she stayed for four days and made a telephone call to Kambona asking him to send one million shillings for overthrowing the government within two weeks.

Titi gave Leballo 400 shillings and said she had received 2,000 shillings, $1,000 for Colonel Chacha, for incidental expenses. Titi told Leballo she would give him 600 shillings in a few days, and did so on June 26. The money was presented in court as evidence.

On June 28, Colonel Chacha made arrangements to meet with Leballo on June 30 in order to introduce him to Major Herman. Chacha and Lieutenant-Colonel Marwa went to Leballo's residence at 3 a.m. on June 30. Chacha and Leballo went into the bedroom, leaving Marwa in the sitting room. There in the bedroom, Chacha told Leballo that he was ready to overthrow the government if he was paid 20 million shillings, and wanted Leballo to tell

Kambona to send the money right away.

On July 3, Chacha and Leballo met again at the army headquarters at Chacha's request. Chacha told Leballo he was disappointed because the money was being delayed. And he wanted Leballo to go to the officers' mess at Lugalo Barracks where Captain Elia Dustan Lifa Chipaka would introduce him to Major Herman.

Leballo went there and found Captain Chipaka waiting for him. Captain Chipaka told Leballo that he did not trust Major Herman as someone who would be involved in overthrowing the government because he was a half-caste from Iringa (in the Southern Highlands of southwestern Tanzania); and that he would give him a list of army officers which would include the name of one officer from Zanzibar. From that list would be chosen a person who would lead the coup.

Afterwards, Captain Chipaka introduced Leballo to Major Herman.

After this meeting, Leballo met with John Chipaka and Michael Kamaliza in the main office of NUTA in Dar es Salaam. They had a discussion and agreed that Leballo should go to London and ask Kambona to send more money.

Around 4.15 p.m. on the same day, Leballo was again asked to go to the same office. He went and found Kamaliza alone in the office. Kamaliza told Leballo that he had sent someone to Kambona to get and bring the money. He also told Leballo that he personally would like Major Herman, and not Colonel Chacha, to lead the coup.

There were conspirators in Zanzibar but, because the former island nation was an autonomous entity with its own legal system even after uniting with Tanganyika to form Tanzania, the authorities in the isles dispensed swift justice against them. So, it was only the ones on the mainland who had to appear before the Tanzania High Court in Dar es Salaam presided over by the Trinidadian jurist Philip Telford Georges.

The head of the Criminal Investigation Department, Geoffrey Sawaya, told the court that the coup did not take place because some of the conspirators were arrested and detained before the scheduled date for the takeover. He said some of them made statements after their arrest admitting most of the allegations about their involvement in the abortive coup attempt. And he produced evidence showing instructions on how strategic locations would be taken over. He also presented to the court lists of prominent people who were to be detained by the coup makers.

There were moonlight trips by dhow between Dar es Salaam and Zanzibar, made by the conspirators and their couriers. Secret meetings were held in expensive hotels in Nairobi, Kenya, in London, and in Dar es Salaam. Nightclubs were another hot spot where the coup plotters met to discuss their nefarious scheme which included a plot to assassinate President Nyerere. There was even a plan, for whatever reason they deemed appropriate, to bomb the University of Dar es Salaam; probably to cause panic while they executed the coup, or simply to wreak havoc and cause mayhem.

One of the most damaging pieces of evidence against the coup plotters presented in court was the 'wedding guest list' found at the residence of Captain Elia Dustan Lifa Chipaka.

All 37 'guests' named on the list were army officers. Captain Chipaka told the court that the names were part of a list of the names of guests he was going to invite to his wedding. But, as Chief Justice Philip Telford Georges said at the end of the trial, the list contained comments which an average person would consider to be totally irrelevant to preparation for a wedding. For example, against the name of one colonel was this comment:

'Dissatisfied, but his stand is not known.'

Other evidence included letters from Oscar Kambona written to the conspirators.

What the coup plotters did not know was that Potlako Leballo, the South African political exile and president of the Pan-Africanist Congress (PAC) was already working for the Tanzania intelligence service but gained their confidence. The outlandish claim by the that Leballo had manufactured the whole thing and was really a spy for the South African apartheid regime was dismissed as nonsense by the court.

In delivering the verdicts, the chief justice denied pleas for clemency made by the defence lawyers and made it clear that overthrowing governments was not an acceptable way to change leadership, emphasizing that the young African nations needed peace and stability to consolidate their independence and serve their people.

The trial lasted 127 days, the longest in the country's history. Chief Justice Philip Telfer Georges did not sentence the conspirators to death as he could have under the law, but nonetheless gave them stiff sentences as follows:

– Bibi Titi Mohammed: life imprisonment for treason.
– Gray Likungu Mataka: life imprisonment for treason.
– Elia Dustan Lifa Chipaka: life imprisonment for treason.
– John Lifa Chipaka: life imprisonment for treason.
– Michael Kamaliza: ten years' imprisonment for misprision of treason.
– William Makori Chacha: ten years' imprisonment for misprision of treason.

Alfred Philip Milinga was acquitted of all charges, but after spending 16 months in detention under the Preventive Detention Act during the investigation and trial of the treason case. The act was passed by parliament to allow the government to detain people if they posed a threat to national security but was criticized by the chief justice during the treason trial for detaining people for too long before they were brought to court.

The ringleader and mastermind of the treasonous coterie, former foreign affairs minister Oscar Kambona, was tried in absentia. Only three years earlier, President Nyerere had said of his cabinet colleague and close political aide:

'Oscar is extremely loyal - to the party, to me, and to the people.'

President Nyerere could be extremely tough when you encroach on his authority. Yet he also had a reputation for being very tolerant, kind, and forgiving. And he lived up to both. About seven years after the treason trial, Bibi Titi Mohammed received a presidential pardon in 1977 and walked out of prison in Dodoma, central Tanzania. She had written the president asking for forgiveness, but had no hope that she would get it.

On 5 February 1978, Otini Kambona, former education and information minister under Nyerere in the first independence cabinet, and Mattiya Kambona, the younger brothers of Oscar Kambona, were released from detention together with 22 other detainees and 7,000 petty criminals. They were all pardoned by President Nyerere. They were freed on the first anniversary of the founding of the ruling Chama Cha Mapinduzi (CMM), formed from a merger of the mainland TANU and its sister counterpart in Zanzibar, the Afro-Shirazi Party (ASP). February 5, 1978, was also the eleventh anniversary of the Arusha Declaration.

Otini and Mattiya Kambona were detained for more than 10 years. They were arrested and detained in December 1967 for supporting their brother's political activities and using a Kiswahili newspaper Otini Kambona published to help further his political ambitions, even if by making oblique references to his brother's agenda.

But more often than not, the newspaper *Ulimwengu* (The World) was explicit in its condemnation of the government. It published articles written by Oscar Kambona highly critical of the government. After the two brothers were arrested, the paper also immediately ceased publication.

Also released in 1972, like Bibi Titi Mohammed, was Eli Anangisye, former secretary-general of the TANU Youth League, who had been detained for his involvement in another plot to overthrow the government by trying to enlist the help of some army officers to carry out the coup. He was the alleged mastermind of the plot.

Why Nyerere freed all these people, despite their attempts to undermine his government, remained a mystery. And he gave no reason for setting them free, in spite of the overwhelming evidence implicating them in the plots. He was not ruthless but took a firm stand against his enemies. And he could have let them rot in prison, instead of pardoning them. Yet, he set them free, demonstrating one of his qualities as a compassionate man.

Kambona, of course, was never arrested. No extradition proceedings took place and he remained in Britain until he willingly returned to Tanzania in April 1992 after the country adopted the multiparty system which enabled him to form a political party and challenge the ruling Chama Cha Mapinduzi (Revolutionary Party) which had been in power since independence, first as TANU. Ironically, multiparty democracy was introduced with the full support of former President Nyerere when he started questioning the functional utility of the one-party state of which he was the architect and which was officially adopted in 1965. But it had become corrupt, he said, and needed to be replaced. Yet his position on the multi-party system was not fully understood. As Andrew Nyerere stated in his written comments on my work in August 2003 when I was writing this expanded edition:

'Mwalimu Nyerere was chairman of the party. And he said, we have been discussing this multi-party democracy at the CCM meeting in Dodoma (Tanzania's new capital). We notice that in many countries there is much talk about the multi-party form of government. After discussing this, we have decided that there is no reason why this country should not follow this kind of multi-party democracy. So we invite everyone to discuss this.

In connection with this, I would like to make a comment about the notes which Mwalimu had been making for a speech which he was going to make, but which he never made, because death overtook him.

He wrote that he hoped he had made a good decision when he spoke in favour of multi-party democracy. This is good, in so far as Mwalimu hoped that all the decisions he had made during his life were good decisions.

But the mere fact that he wrote this meant that he did not see any necessity for a multi-party state, even as he did not see any necessity for a single party state. The only thing that mattered was that the government should serve the people well.'

Twelve years after the treason trial, Oscar Kambona gave an interview in April 1982 in which he explained why he was highly critical of Nyerere, and by implication tried to justify his attempt to overthrow the government, although nothing he said could justify that. As he stated in the interview with *Drum*:

'Nyerere and I go back a long way - we founded TANU. Nyerere was the chairman and I was the secretary-general.

Problems between us began in 1964 during the army mutiny. Nyerere and Kawawa hid themselves in a grass hut while I was left to face the music (Kambona was then minister of defence).

I negotiated with the army and managed to settle the uprising. When Nyerere returned, the army wanted to mutiny again - that was when we asked for military assistance from the British.

After the mutiny, some friends told him that he was losing his grip on the country and I think he believed them.

When Nyerere visited China, he was very impressed with the glorification of Mao Tse-Tung. I think the seeds of a single, all-powerful individual, an autocrat, were sown in him on this trip. And when he came back, he wanted a one-party state.

I sat on the commission that looked at the question of a one-party state and produced a minority report in which I wanted to know what mechanism we had of changing government peacefully.

Nyerere persuaded me not to present my report and said that I should go along with the majority report which was in favour of a one-party state and that at the end of five years, we would review the situation and if we found any weaknesses we could put them right. I agreed, but I refused to sign as a member of the committee.

I think that *Ujamaa* was badly implemented and that is why it has been a failure. The government should have had pilot schemes which were successful so that people could go to see them.

The farmers in Tanzania are very conservative. They want to know what they get from their labour. If a man has a farm and earns 200 British pounds from it, and is then asked to go into an *Ujamaa* village and gets 20 pounds for the same work, he begins to ask: 'How is *Ujamaa* good for me?'

The system in Tanzania is such that Nyerere will continue to remain in power. The president chooses all the candidates for elections. Whichever way you vote, you still vote for his man.

In the presidential elections, there are only two boxes -

one for Nyerere and the other against him. When you go into the polling booth, there is a soldier standing there. He tells you, 'If you want Nyerere, vote there, and if you are an enemy of the people, then vote in the 'no' box.'

Nyerere has been in power for 21 years now. And nowadays he is always saying that he is going to resign. Then the parliamentarians stamp their feet and shout that he is their leader and Nyerere says: 'Well, what can I do? A captain cannot abandon his ship and let it sink.'

But why is it that during all this time he hasn't been able to find anyone who can rule the country besides himself?

I feel very sorry for the person who will take over because the country is bankrupt. If I took over I would change the economic policies and do away with detention for longer than ten days.'

But even after multiparty politics was introduced, Kambona was still not able to get significant support among the people after he returned to Tanzania in April 1992 from 25 years of exile in Britain. Whatever lure and lustre he had before, especially among his admirers, was now gone; having faded after so many years of absence from his country, and tarnished by his treasonous acts of trying to undermine and overthrow an immensely popular president who was also the founding father of the nation. Many people simply saw him as a traitor, and his party, the Tanzania Democratic Alliance (TADEA), never won the support he hoped it would be able to get across the country....

Kambona faded into obscurity and died discredited in his own country he helped lead to independence; yet whose government, of which he once was a prominent member, he tried to overthrow, thus tarnishing his image forever.

Yet, he remained and died a patriot to some people. On his grave, he may have wanted a fitting epitaph written along these lines:

'Here lies Oscar Salathiel Kambona, a leader of the independence movement, and once a prominent cabinet member who tried to change the government by unconstitutional means, and who died a traitor to some, but a patriot to others.'

He was both, at different times, in Tanzania's 'turbulent' history." – (Godfrey Mwakikagile, *Nyerere and Africa: End of an Era*, New Africa Press, 2010, pp. 361 – 375, and 380).

Kambona also attempted to overthrow Nyerere at the wrong time. The Tanzanian leader, who was the father of the nation and was affectionately called Mwalimu, meaning "teacher" because he was once a teacher, was at the peak of his popularity, only a few years after independence. The country had a robust economy and there was no widespread discontent over living conditions. All those factors militated against any attempt to depose him.

He was not infallible. But his integrity was unimpeachable even with all the mistakes he made as a mere mortal with frailties. And the CIA knew that. A coup against him could have resulted in chaos and even retaliation against the coup makers probably in a form of a counter-coup and civil protests and disobedience even if muted. It would have been unpopular.

Resistance to the coup from some segments of the security forces would have made things worse because of Nyerere's popularity across the nation especially among the workers and peasants Even when he made mistakes, they believed he did so with the best of intentions because he had their best interests at heart. It would have been very hard to justify a coup against him.

Also, it would have been hard to justify his ouster even

in a geopolitical context where he was an anchor of stability because of his genuine commitment to non-alignment in the ideological rivalry between the East and the West during the Cold War and because of the enormous influence he had on other leaders in the region.

His popularity and commitment to the well-being of his people was even acknowledged by American diplomats accredited to Tanganyika, later Tanzania, even when they disagreed with on a number of issues including his socialist policies. They still acknowledged that he was a man of high moral integrity, highly principled and selfless. As US Deputy Ambassador Robert Hennemeyer who was in Tanganyika, later Tanzania, from 1961 - 1964, stated:

"(He was) a great leader of his people. I don't believe for a moment that he meant anything but to do the best he could for the wellbeing of his people....He was so revered as the great father." – (Robert Hennemeyer, in Godfrey Mwakikagile, *Why Tanganyika united with Zanzibar to form Tanzania*, New Africa Press, 2014, pp. 56, 113).

But that did not stop the CIA from conducting its espionage activities in Tanzania. It is part of the agency's mandate to have agents in every country. The CIA even recruits foreign students in the United States to work for the agency. For example, there was a report in *The Detroit News* in 1975 stating that the agency was busy on college campuses recruiting foreign students. It named the University of Michigan and Michigan State University as some of the fertile grounds for recruitment by the CIA. The report stated:

"The emphasis is on the emerging nations of Africa."

Even the University of Dar es Salaam in Tanzania was infiltrated by the CIA. One American lecturer, Dr. Stephen Andrew Lucas who taught sociology at the university for seven years in the 1960s, was a CIA agent. He also worked as a CIA agent in Madagascar, Angola and Mozambique. Some students at the university were suspicious of some faculty members from western countries including the United States whom they accused of being spies.

It was a suspicion that could have been misconstrued as a form of xenophobia. But it was subsequently justified, although a blanket condemnation of all Westerners as infiltrators or saboteurs could not be justified and was even criticised by President Nyerere who described the students as "petty nationalists." As Professor Ronald Aminzade states in his book, *Race, Nation, and Citizenship in Postcolonial Africa: The Case of Tanzania*:

"The exclusion of foreigners from university-level education proved more contentious. Marxist-Leninist students at the university, who organized the United African Students Revolutionary Federation (USARF) in 1967 following the Arusha Declaration, regarded the presence of expatriate faculty from Western capitalist countries as imperialist infiltration.

Angered by the presence of U.S. professors in the law school, they occupied the Faculty of Law in March 1969 and demanded the East Africanization of the faculty, the appointment of a Tanzanian to dean of the Faculty of Law, and the hiring of teaching staff from socialist countries.

Radical students claims that some foreign faculty members at the university might be spying on left-wing activists were supported by subsequent revelations, years later, that a visiting U.S. lecturer in sociology, Stephen Lucas, was, in fact, a CIA agent.

When the students confronted President Nyerere, who was also Chancellor of the university, with their demand to remove expatriate faculty from the campus, he responded by asking them where Che Guevara was born (Argentina), where he fought (Cuba), and where he died (Bolivia). He chastised the students for being 'petty nationalists' rather than 'internationalists.'

There were few highly educated Tanzanians to replace the foreign faculty, and the university was necessary for training high-ranking government officials and of, course, future faculty. in this way, foreign faculty remained a vital resource for the socialist project.

Interestingly, government officials were not averse to appealing to antiforeign sentiments to justify their actions in confrontations with Marxist-Leninist students and faculty at the university. They claimed that the Marxist-Leninist rhetoric of radical students was an unwelcome foreign influence in a country trying to build its own distinctive national brand of socialism.

In November 1970, the government banned the USARF and shut down its Marxist-Leninist magazine *Cheche*, which means 'the spark' in Swahili and was a reference to the Leninist journal of the Russian Bolsheviks. In government administrators' view, the organization violated the principle of self-reliance because it was borrowing a foreign ideology and because it gave the false impression that Tanzania was building a 'Russian socialism.'

Student editors Karim Hirji and Naijuka Kasihwaki responded by arguing:

If people think we are building 'Russian Socialism' because of the name *Cheche*, then will they not also think we are building 'American Socialism' since our nationalized institutions get advice from American management consultancy agencies?' – (Ronald Aminzade, *Race, Nation, and Citizenship in Postcolonial Africa: The Case of Tanzania*, New York: Cambridge University Press, 2013, pp. 187 – 188).

But the students were right on target in the case of Dr. Stephen Lucas when they said there were some faculty members who were spying for governments hostile to Tanzania even if they did specifically identify him as an agent or conclusively say he was one but may have suspected that he was. It was years later, after he left the University of Dar es Salaam, that he was identified as a CIA agent. KGB agents in Tanzania probably knew he was one when he was teaching at the university as much as they probably did when he was in Congo-Leopoldville and elsewhere.

Some of the information has come from former CIA agents who have turned against the agency for different reasons and have exposed their colleagues working in different parts of the world.

Before going to Tanzania, Stephen Andrew Lucas was an agent in Congo-Leopoldville and worked under Larry Devlin, the CIA station chief in that country when Patrice Lumumba was arrested and assassinated; so was Frank Carlucci, a senior CIA agent under diplomatic cover, who even befriended Lumumba and was involved in his assassination.

Lumumba's arrest was orchestrated by the CIA, probably by Carlucci himself. Joseph Mobutu who was the head of the army was already on the CIA payroll when he served as Lumumba's secretary before Lumumba promoted him. He ousted Lumumba, in collaboration with the CIA, and sent him to Katanga to be executed. In fact, when Mobutu was president of Zaire (formerly Congo-Leopoldville), the largest CIA station in Africa was in the capital Kinshasa, before then known as Leopoldville.

There were CIA agents in Elisabethville, the capital of Katanga Province, where Lumumba was sent to his arch-enemy, Moise Tshombe, to be assassinated. And there was probably more than one CIA agent on the scene when Lumumba and his colleagues, Joseph Okito and Maurice Mpolo, were shot to death on the outskirts of Elisabethville on 17 January 1961. They were brutally beaten on their flight from Leopoldvile to Elisabethville, and even when they landed at the airport, before they met their fate. Okito, who once served as vice president of the senate, was shot first; he was also the oldest of the three.

Even President Nkrumah blamed Frank Carlucci for being directly responsible for Lumumba's death, as Carlucci himself said then and years later, although he consistently denied any involvement in the assassination of the Congolese leader:

"I arrived (in Congo) 15 days before independence. We had a Consul General who was leaving and an ambassador had been designated, Clare Timberlake. The situation was one of considerable confusion....
I set about to get to know the political figures....I persuaded the DCM (deputy chief of mission), Rob McIlvaine, a marvelous man, to allow me to rent a Volkswagen so I had my own car and didn't go around in an embassy chauffeured car. I then got myself some press credentials because the press moved around more freely than anybody else could. Lumumba tended to hold a press conference a day and I figured it was important to get into those. Then I got myself a pass to the Parliament which was in formation. And basically spent all day outside the embassy. Just floating in from time to time....

We developed a relationship (with Mobutu)....Larry Devlin and I went to see him shortly after he took over....

There wasn't a lot to be obtained in Leopoldville. Most of the action had taken place in Katanga and we had to depend on our consul in Elisabethville to report on what had transpired there. Our best assessment was that he (Lumumba) had been killed after he arrived in Katanga...., probably in the presence of (Godefroid) Munongo....

When this happened, as I recall, I was in Stanleyville. This was shortly after they had arrested all the Europeans in Stanleyville and thrown them out. Timberlake asked me if I'd go up there, back and forth, and act as consul for Stanleyville. They announced on Stanleyville radio that Lumumba had been murdered and that I was the man who had done it. They claimed I was a paratroop captain or colonel, I guess. I had made it up to the rank of colonel. They were going to see that justice was done.

And as I recall, Kwame Nkrumah sent a cable to Dag Hammarskjold about me killing Lumumba and a few other things like that. So we had to worry a little bit about survival. I had to find my way out of Stanleville. I did that by hitchhiking. In fact, I hitchhiked in a UN plane to Bukavu and then to Elisabethville and then back to Leopoldville.

I went back up to Stanleyville a couple of weeks later and they arrested me....They put me under house arrest. They declared me *persona non grata*....It was a breakaway government in Stanleyville, headed by Antoine Gizenga. Kabila was a member of that government. I didn't know him well.

We had Gizenga, Gbenye, Weregemere, and a number of other Lumumba supporters in Stanleyville. They had broken away when - I guess after Lovanium - I can't recall the exact sequence, certainly when Mobutu had taken over. They declared their own government. I had been going back and forth, meeting with them, when they declared me *persona non grata*.

About then, I wanted to introduce my successor, Tom Cassilly, (who later himself got arrested), so I said I'd go up one more time. I flew up and at the airport, they arrested me." – (Ambassador Frank Charles Carlucci III interviewed by Charles Stuart Kennedy, 1 April 1997, *The Association for Diplomatic Studies and Training (ADST), Oral History Project*, copyright 2000, pp. 7, 8, 20 - 21).

Three years after Lumumba's assassination, Carlucci was sent to Zanzibar where he became head of the American consulate. He was there during the revolution in January 1964.

Three months after the revolution, Zanzibar united with Tanganyika to form Tanzania. Carlucci was later expelled from the country. As he himself stated in an interview in 1997:

"I arrived in 1964...in early '64 and...I was expelled in January 1965." – (Ibid., p. 28).

When he was in Zanzibar, he befriended the leader of the new revolutionary government, Abeid Karume, who did not know English and spoke to him in Swahili:

"One of the reasons that I think I got kicked out was that I managed to develop a good relationship with Karume. Karume spoke very little English....I was the only senior diplomat on the island who could converse with him in Swahili and he loved that. So we had a very good relationship....
One of my neighbors, a minister named Jumbe, who later became vice president, had a tendency to drink a bit and one night he came over to my house. No sooner did he come in than the police arrived and essentially told him to get out. We were pretty much isolated. We were socially ostracized. Virtually every Sunday there would be a demonstration against me. I would get my tear gas [mask] and my beer and I'd go to the embassy and watch the demonstrators....
(It was) anti-American. It got serious when the Belgians sent paratroopers into Stanleyville....
The only people at ceremonies I could talk to were the Brit, the Israeli, and the Soviet. I'd have to listen to all the diatribes. In one of the more humorous incidents, I decided to visit the neighboring island of Pemba, which was being run by a Commissar, named Ali Sultan Issa, a man who was trained in Beijing. He was so indoctrinated that he insisted we even share the same bed. 'This is the way we do it in the People's democracy.'
He took me around the island with people chanting and singing since it was in the 'workers' paradise.' Then he had a rally and meeting and I could see during the rally, this

was in the early stages of my stay, that he would point at me and the crowd would applaud and yell and scream. So I asked someone what he was saying and he told me he was saying, 'There's the enemy. Why don't you applaud or don't you think we ought to throw the Americans out?'

Right then and there, I decided that learning Swahili was essential....

There was one other African that I could talk to. He was the Chairman of the Afro-Shirazi Party, Thabit Kombo, who was probably in his 70s or 80s at the time, and was such a revered figure in Zanzibar that he could talk to me without fear of retaliation. He and the President were essentially the only two that I could talk to." – (Ibid., pp. 29, 31, 34, 35).

Carlucci also was the first American diplomat to establish informal ties with the African National Congress (ANC) and the Pan Africanist Congress (PAC) of South Africa.

The CIA had already infiltrated both organisations and other groups in South Africa including the South African Communist Party (SACP). Donald Rickard, a CIA agent working under diplomatic cover in South Africa and who was responsible for Nelson Mandela's arrest when Mandela returned from Tanganyika in 1962 after secretly leaving his home country to seek support for the ANC in the struggle against apartheid, had informers in the upper echelons of the ANC.

They provided him with information on Mandela's return to South Africa and he tipped off the authorities who arrested Mandela on 5 August 1962 when he was driving a car from Durban to Johannesburg disguised as a chauffeur.

But it was Carlucci who openly, even if surreptitiously, interacted with some members and leaders of the ANC and the PAC when it was not official policy of the United States to do so. As he stated in an interview:

"I became personally interested in the evolution of apartheid and while I was a commercial officer in essentially an economic and consulate-post in Johannesburg (1957 - 1959), I undertook on my own initiative to go to a number of ANC [African National Congress] meetings.

They were allowed to meet. There was surveillance on me when I went to the meetings. And after I had gone to a certain number of them, the South African Government complained to our ambassador, Ambassador Byroade, at the time about my activities. So although I wasn't doing anything illegal, they thought it was suspect activity....

I got a sense of what their politics were, how militant they were. Frankly, I felt they were less militant than they'd been described. I got to know some of the splinter groups. I was the first person, for example, to talk to Robert Sobukwe, who founded the Pan Africanist Congress. He later died.

But I got acquainted with the movement, which, interestingly, nobody in Pretoria had been able to do. Our embassy was constrained from attending the meetings. The meetings were in Johannesburg. So I established a relationship, a personal relationship, with some of the political officers in Pretoria and reported to them.

I wrote a number of political – what in those days were airgrams you may recall – political airgrams on these meetings on the ANC. They were well-received in Washington and I think were basically responsible for my subsequent assignment to the Congo as a political officer."
– (Ibid., pp. 5, 6).

Carlucci was adept at forging ties with national leaders, very quickly, wherever he was assigned and was linked to dramatic events which took place when he was there or soon after he left. Whenever he left a station where he was assigned, trouble followed. He said his colleagues even joked about that.

Donald Petterson who was a consular officer in Zanzibar from 1963 to 1965 and once served as United States ambassador to Tanzania (1986 – 1989) had the following to say about Carlucci and some of the experiences he himself had in Zanzibar during and after the revolution:

"A phone call from the rebels finally came. It was from Aboud Jumbe, one of the ministers in the new government, who said he wanted to come over and take Picard to the revolutionary headquarters. In due course he arrived in an open Land Rover with armed people in it. Jumbe himself was heavily armed. Fritz (Frederick "Fritz" Picard, the consul) and I, along with Jim Ruchti and the executive officer, got into the Land Rover and were driven to Raha Leo, the site of the radio station and the African community center.

Raha Leo was now the command headquarters of the revolution. There was electricity in the air when we neared Raha Leo. Hundreds of Africans who were in a very fierce mood ringed the place, many or most armed with everything from sticks to old swords; an occasional rifle was seen. As we approached the headquarters, better-armed revolutionaries came into sight. They carried police rifles, and a few had automatic weapons. We saw Arab prisoners, some of them bloodied, some lying near the entrance to the revolutionary headquarters, all looking despondent. The crowd was so excited because they knew at that moment, or soon thereafter, Ali Muhsin, whom they hated, would be brought in....

The air was so tense as they began to swarm toward the Land Rover that Aboud Jumbe yelled at them in Swahili - he had a bullhorn - to get back or he would open fire. They obliged, and a way was cleared for us. We got out of the Land Rover and waited for somebody to come out of revolutionary headquarters.

After a while, a figure emerged , a man dressed in a semi-military uniform. He had on dark shorts and a dark blue shirt, a peaked cap, knee socks in the British style. He approached us, went up to the executive officer, pulled out a revolver out of his holster, stuck it right at the exec, either in his ribs as I remember it, or in his face as Jim Ruchti remembered it, and said, 'How do you do? I am John Okello.'

With that, he put his revolver back in the holster and said there was going to be some target practice behind revolutionary headquarters. Would we like to join in? Well, figuring that the targets might well be some of the captured Arabs, we declined.

He escorted us into Raha Leo. We went up the stairs into a meeting room, where after another wait we were ushered into the room. Sitting there behind a table with Okello were Abaid Karume, leader of the Afro-Shirazi Party and now president of the new government, Babu, Hanga, and several others....Karume had come back to Zanzibar...from Dar es Salaam...by boat early that morning with Babu and Hanga.

The British high commissioner had met with them just before we did, and as he left we entered. The discussion began. Fritz, first of all, told Okello - who had put his revolver on the table with the barrel pointing at Fritz - that we would not negotiate at gunpoint. Okello made no reply, but picked up and reholstered his weapon. He didn't say much during the ensuing discussion, in which Fritz made the request for an evacuation (of Americans from Zanzibar).

Babu replied angrily, so did Hanga; Karume was uncomfortable. They were angry that the Americans had brought in this warship. And it seemed to us, as we thought about it a bit later, that they didn't know whether the *Manley* might open fire. in any case, they really didn't care for the evacuation. They didn't want to see it happen, but they agreed to it, fearing there might be consequences otherwise.

Finally, Karume indicated that he would not oppose the request. Then he turned to Okello and said, 'It's your decision.'

Okello sort of shrugged and said, 'All right.'

This made it clear to us there that Okello was indeed of great importance. I say this because later on there were those who belittled Okello's role in the revolution. In fact, the official history of the revolution barely mentions him. But he was the force that pulled it off. Weeks later, others with more political sagacity took control....

My Swahili...was very useful. I formed a friendship with Karume as a result, because I was the only American who spoke Swahili and my Swahili was getting better and better all of the time. We carried out our conversations in Swahili. I was very deferential to him; Fritz was not. Fritz, unfortunately, was a bit patronizing with Karume, and that came back to haunt him, as I'll explain.

On the morning of January 16, four days after the revolution...(there) were American, British and Canadian newspapermen - reporters for *Time, Newsweek, The New York Herald Tribune*, a Canadian paper and a British paper - and an Indian photographer for *Life* magazine....They had sailed from in the dhow from the mainland (Tanganyika), arriving in Zanzibar the previous night.

They started asking me questions. Foolishly I answered. At that point a rifle was pointed right in my face, and I was told to 'Shut up!' So I stopped talking, [laughter] the better part of valor! Some authorities from the revolutionary government joined these armed people at the dockside. They said that the men in the boat were spies and we were going to be taken to revolutionary headquarters. Off we went. I tried to explain to the rebels who I was. They couldn't care less, nor did they accept that these were just newspaper people....

I formed a relationship with Karume, and also with Babu, who was a very charming guy, a militant left-winger, to say the least, and very shrewd, very intelligent. Karume was a stolid man, not nearly as bright as Babu, but a man of very real native intelligence. I don't mean to use that term in a derogatory sense at all. He was a very able man in many ways, but impressionable and unsophisticated. As time would go by the results of that would be harmful to Zanzibar....

Frank (Carlucci) was well-regarded by Joe Palmer, the Assistant Secretary of State for African Affairs and by Charlie Whitehouse, and by everybody else. It had been decided that Frank would be the new chargé d'affaires in Zanzibar. He came with a letter from President Johnson that indicated recognition (of the new revolutionary government that had replaced the sultan) would be coming soon.

Frank and Leonhart (the American ambassador to Tanganyika) tried to convince Karume that with recognition just around the corner, it would be much better if he didn't throw me off the island.

By the way, the whole Revolutionary Council, which included all the wild men along with some of the more able and moderate Zanzibari Africans who were in the cabinet, were at this meeting. The discussion went on for a couple of hours, but in the end Karume and the Council rejected the American proposal. Karume, when he said goodbye, said, 'If you come back, if recognition takes place, and you come back, Mr. Carlucci, we'll have a parade in your honor.'

So with that, Frank and Ambassador Leonhart returned to Dar es Salaam.

I went back to the embassy to finish burning the classified materials. I had just started when there was a pounding on the front door. Ali Mahfoudh, the head of the newly created special police force, demanded to come into the embassy. When I refused him entry, he said he would have to take me in custody. He drove me to State House, the seat of the government. An official there told

Mahfoudh to take me back to the embassy and not to interfere with me.

After I did some burning, I went home for a quick lunch. When I returned, the officer in charge of the soldiers who had surrounded the building said I could not reenter it. When I argued with him, he told me a government official wanted to see me and he drove me to a government office. I was taken to the office of Abdul Aziz Twala, one of the more militant members of the cabinet. Unbeknownst to me, an argument had preceded my arrival. some of the people there wanted to kill me.

At least that's what a man named Mohammed Ali Foum, who was there at the time and later became a diplomat in Tanzanian diplomatic service, told me years afterward. We met at the United Nations one day, and he told me this.I don't know if it's true but he swore it was. he said that after some argument, it was decided that killing me would cause too many problems.

At any rate, when I got there, Twala simply me to return to the embassy, then go home and get ready to leave later that day....

Frank had been in the Congo, where he acquired a reputation as an exceptionally able Foreign Service officer. He was the embassy's trouble shooter in the Congo....

He was an excellent reporter. He got out, beat the bushes, met the people. He was charming. He got people to trust him. He dealt with people who were essentially hostile to us at that time, befriended them, and got a lot out of it. He knew what was going on in Zanzibar before he'd been there very long....

He had extraordinary intelligence, coupled with very good common sense, and outgoing nature. He knew how to get along with Africans. He was sensitive to their culture. He had no false pretensions. He was an excellent writer, had superior analytical skills....Somebody who's willing to get out of the office, travel around the country, to do whatever is necessary to get information, to establish rapport with people so they will talk to you. You collect intelligence from people whom you meet and process it through whatever abilities you have. You learn to sift out good information from bad....

Frank set out to meet and establish a relationship with as many people as possible in the government and other areas....(He) worked long, hard hours and gave a great deal of thought to his work....He had all the qualities that would later propel him to high offices in the U.S. government, including secretary of defense." – (Ambassador Donald Petterson interviewed by Charles Stuart Kennedy, 13 December 1996, *The Association for Diplomatic Studies and Training (ADST), Foreign Affairs Oral History Project*, copyright 2002, pp. 37 – 38, 40, 41, 42, 43, 44, 46, 47).

It is those qualities which also helped him pave the way for Lumumba's elimination although he strenuously denied that, in spite of the fact that he served with distinction – in the field, outdoors – as a foreign service officer in Congo during that period and, at the very least, collected invaluable information for the CIA because of the close ties he had with the Congolese leaders including Lumumba's enemies.

He later served as deputy director of the CIA under President Jimmy Carter and as secretary of defence and national security advisor under President Ronald Reagan, among other high-level positions in the federal government through the years.

Stephen Lucas, who like Carlucci learned Swahili in his role as a CIA agent in Congo-Leopoldville and Tanzania, was awarded the Defense Intelligence Director's Award, the Retirement Medallion and Certificate of Distinction from the Central Intelligence Agency after he retired. He went to teach at Louisiana State University where he became head of international programmes. He also founded a Swahili programme at the school and taught Swahili among other subjects including contemporary Africa, intelligence, globalisation and regionalisation as well as others in the area of international studies.

He is still remembered for the role he played as a CIA agent in Africa, working for an agency that has in some ways determined the course of events in many African countries, thus partly determining the destiny of the continent.

Many leaders who led their countries to independence, including Jomo Kenyatta who was revered as one of the fathers of the African independence movement, were on the CIA payroll; so was Kenyatta's heir apparent Tom Mboya.

They were the founding fathers, yet sellouts, bought by the CIA.

Even Emperor Haile Selassie, a revered figure and symbol of African independence and resistance to foreign rule – best exemplified by his dignified resistance to the Italian invasion of Ethiopia – who played a major role in the establishment of the Organisation of African Unity (OAU) in Addis Ababa, Ethiopia, in May 1963 and presided over its formation, was on the CIA payroll.

Those who came after them – not all but most of them – were no better than their predecessors. And that is still the case today.

The CIA operates with impunity in many countries across the continent often in collaboration with the leaders of those countries; so do intelligence services of other powers, as they always have since the sixties when most African countries emerged from colonial rule; only to be ruled again as neo-colonies, controlled and manipulated by their former colonial masters and other powers including the United States, the most powerful country in the world.

But there were exceptions such as Kwame Nkrumah, Julius Nyerere, Ahmed Sekou Toure, Patrice Lumumba, Modibo Keita, Gamal Abdel Nasser, Ahmed Ben Bella,

Milton Obote, Kenneth Kaunda, Muammar Gaddafi and Marien Ngouabi; and later, Robert Mugabe, Samora Machel, Agostinho Neto, Jerry Rawlings, Murtala Mohammed, and Thomas Sankara. They did not succumb to CIA temptations. They were not, and could not, be bought by the CIA and other foreign agencies.

One of the best examples of CIA interference in African affairs to the detriment of Africa's wellbeing was the military coup against President Nkrumah in the sixties.

The coup would not have been carried out when it was, and would not have succeeded, without CIA involvement. The agency had already infiltrated the government and the military as well as security services including the police in preparation for the coup.

The subject has been addressed by Godfrey Mwakikagile in his book, *Western Involvement in Nkrumah's Downfall*. Other researchers and analysts have also written about it.

Before the 1966 military coup, the United States had, at least since 1962 if not 1960, been working on plans to remove Nkrumah from office. His book, *Neo-Colonialism: The Last Stage of Imperialism*, also played a role in his ouster. As Robert P. Smith, former United States ambassador to Ghana, stated in an interview years later:

"While Nkrumah was in the air flying to Red China, he was met on the ground in Peking by his Chinese host and it fell to them to inform him that he was no longer Head of State in the Republic of Ghana. So that was a fascinating time in a fascinating country....

Nkrumah dropped the straw that broke the camel's back, so to speak, in that he published a new book called *Neo-Colonialism (The Last State of Imperialism)*...which was simply outrageous. It accused the United States of every sin imaginable to man. We were blamed for everything in the world.

The book was so bad that I remember the then

Assistant Secretary (of state for African affairs), G. Mennen Williams, called me up and gave me that book and said, 'Bob, I know this is bad. I don't know how bad. I want you to take it home tonight and read it. You're not going to get any sleep and I apologize for that, but on my desk, by eight o'clock tomorrow morning, I've got to have a written summary of this because I have called the Ghanaian ambassador in at ten o'clock tomorrow morning. We're going to protest this book.'

There had already been advance publicity so we knew it was bad, but we hadn't had our hands on a copy. And it was everything we feared it would be. It was awful.

And the next morning – of course, he had me in on this meeting as the note taker – a lovely, old man, Michael Ribiero, was the Ghanaian ambassador. Hated Nkrumah privately, but was a good soldier trying to put the best face on this, a career officer in their foreign service and very respected here and in Ghana.

Governor Williams, of course, was a relatively mild-mannered man. I had never heard Soapy Williams raise his voice until that conversation. Neither have I ever heard an ambassador get a tongue lashing like Ribiero got from Assistant Secretary Williams that morning. He, unfortunately, tried a couple times to interrupt the governor when he was making a point. He had my notes in front of him. And at one point, when Ribiero interrupted him, he said, 'Just a minute, Mr. Ambassador, don't interrupt me. I'm not through.' And he continued to go on.

He was raising his voice. He was shaking his finger in the ambassador's face. And it was a very painful, hour-long interview. To put it mildly, he protested vigorously the contents and publication of this book.

I think the publication of that book might also have contributed in a material way to his overthrow shortly thereafter." – (Ambassador Robert P. Smith, quoted by Godfrey Mwakikagile, *Western Involvement in Nkrumah's Downfall*, New Africa Press, 2015, pp. 134 – 136; Robert

P. Smith, interviewed by Charles Stuart Kennedy, 28 February 1989, *The Association for Diplomatic Studies and Training, Foreign Affairs Oral History Project*, pp. 12 – 15).

Even President Felix Houphouet Boigny of the Ivory Coast who was Nkrumah's political and ideological rival – as well as Sekou Toure's foe – acknowledged that the military coup against Nkrumah was externally engineered. As he stated in an interview with *Jeune Afrique*, 4 February 1981:

"Destabilisation is not a new thing. Did you know why Idi Amin made his coup in 1971? It was not he who did it, but the British. He did not even know what he wanted himself.
It was the same in Ghana when the military overthrew Nkrumah. They [the coup makers] came to see me. I asked them. They replied: 'All is not well anymore.' 'Is that all?' [I asked them]. I also asked them what they were going to do; they did not know. People outside knew it for them."

An indefatigable champion of African unity and independence, Nkrumah was a great inspiration to freedom fighters across the continent. President Nyerere strongly condemned the coup against Nkrumah. As he stated at a press conference in Dar es Salaam soon after Nkrumah was overthrown on 24 February 1966:

"What is happening in Africa? What are the coups about? The last few months have seen changes of governments in many African countries. The latest has been in Ghana. What is behind all this? Are these 'revolutions' intended to remove humiliation and oppresion from Africa?
Let us take the latest in Ghana. The enemies of Africa

are now jubilant. There is jubilation in Salisbury and Johannesburg. Even a fool could begin to wonder whether these 'revolutions' would help Africa.

What was Kwame trying to do? He stood for the liberation of Africa. There is not a single leader in Africa more committed to this than Kwame. Whom did he anger with his commitment to freedom? Certainly not Africa. He was committed to true independence.

He was not merely against ordinary colonialism; he was against neocolonialism – against a colonial power going out through the political door and controlling the country through the e conomic door." – (Julius K. Nyerere, quoted by Kwame Nkrumah, *Dark Days in Ghana*, New York: Monthly Review Press, 1968, p. 137; Opoku Agyeman, *Nkrumah's Ghana and East Africa: Pan-Africanism and Interstate Relations*, Madison, New Jersey, USA: Fairleigh Dickinson University Press, 1992, p. 152).

Nyerere offered Nkrumah asylum. Sekou Toure, Nasser and Modibo Keita also offered Nkrumah asylum. They were ideological compatriots. Nkrumah finally decided to go to Guinea.

A bitter foe of neocolonialism like Nkrumah, Nyerere also maintained until the end of his life that economic inequalities in the international system existed because underdeveloped or developing countries were being treated unfairly; they were at the mercy of the industrialised nations. The poor are poor, and are getting poorer, because they are being exploited by the rich and powerful. Their natural resources do not benefit them but instead benefit powerful nations.

Even racial inequalities and injustices in the countries of southern Africa which were under white minority rule continued to exist because rich and powerful nations – almost all of therm white – supported and sustained white minority regimes for political, economic and racist reasons. leaders of Western countries disagreed with him.

But he continued to maintain his position. As *The Washington Post* reported when he was about to step down as president of Tanzania:

"After 23 years in office, Africa's senior statesman and one of the Third World's most eloquent spokesmen is planning to step down. Tanzanian President Julius Nyerere, 63, says he will retire from office next year, become one of the few rulers in the short history of independent black to relinquish his post voluntarily.

He does not intend to depart quietly. Last month (November 1984) Nyerere accepted the chairmanship of the Organization of African Unity with a blistering attack on U.S. policy toward white-ruled South Africa, and he later urged African nations to withhold payments on their debts to force western governments and financial institutions to negotiate reforms in the international economic order.

The statements were vintage Nyerere, a leader who has forged a reputation as Africa's most vocal critic of the economic inequality between the First World and the Third.

He is also a man of irrepressible intellect and consummate charm who manages to impress even those western diplomats who find his foreign policies unpalatable and his socialist domestic policies unworkable.

'He is a humane, decent person with an extraordinary mind and considerable charm,' said a senior western diplomat here (in Dar es Salaam), 'but he clings to notions that are wrong'....

Nyerere's Tanzania has been...Africa's leader in the struggle for social equity...(and) Nyerere has been sub-Saharan Africa's leading socialist visionary....

anzania boasts black Africa's highest adult literacy rate -- 70 percent -- thanks to his unswerving commitment to public education. Average life expectancy has increased by

10 years during the last generation through improvements in health care and clean water supplies....

He is famous for the learned treatises he has written on underdevelopment and for periodic bursts of self-criticism....

By stressing national institutions and a nationwide public school system, by eschewing favoritism in dealing with Tanzania's 100-plus tribes, and by imposing Swahili as a national language, Nyerere has helped construct one of Africa's rarest entities: a true nation.

By stressing socialist equality, he has given his country a sense of mission, and by invading neighboring Uganda and overthrowing dictator Idi Amin in 1979, he has given Tanzania an epochal moment of moral triumph that may be enshrined in African history as the defeat of Hitler is cherished in Europe.

'For all its problems, this a remarkably stable country, with dignified, intelligent people, a high degree of religious and ethnic tolerance and many of the attributes of nationhood,' said a Western diplomat here.

Nyerere has blamed most of Tanzania's economic woes on outside forces beyond his control. Alternate years of droughts and crippling floods, the 1977 collapse of the East African Community, forcing the country into expensive capital investments for railways and power lines, and the $500 million price tag for the war against Amin are all cited as major contributors to Tanzania's plight.

Most of all, Nyerere see inequities in a world trade system in which exportable commodities of poor nations such as Tanzania have steadily lost value during the past decade while oil, and vital imports from the industrial West, have increased sharply.

In 1972, Tanzania spent 5 percent of its foreign exchange earnings on imported oil. Last year (1983) it spent nearly 60 percent, even though it has cut oil consumption by nearly one-third.

'It is as if we had been robbed,' Nyerere has said. 'To buy a seven-ton truck in 1981, we had to produce and sell abroad about four times as much cotton, or three times as much cashew, or three times as much coffee, or 10 times as much tobacco as we had to produce and sell in 1976.'

He has also said,' It it true internationally that the rich are rich because the poor are poor. The inevitable oversimplification of that statement does not invalidate it.'

Nyerere's supporters dismiss the idea that his socialist policies have contributed to Tanzania's problems, pointing out that capitalist countries such as Kenya and the Ivory Coast are also suffering from extreme economic shocks.

'Other countries don't have our policies and they are suffering too,' said a top presidential aide....

Nyerere's relations with the United States, which improved dramatically during the Carter administration, have deteriorated under President Reagan. Nyerere has been harshly critical of U.S. support for South Africa and has accused the Reagan administration of encouraging South African aggression against its black-ruled neighbors.

Some of his top aides say that they believe that the United States is encouraging the International Monetary Fund (IMF) to coerce Tanzania into politically risky austerity measures and that the Americans are quietly gloating over the failure of Nyerere's socialist experiment.

American officials have insisted that such views are mistaken....

'Julius has been in charge for too long, but people love him...,' said a senior diplomat." – (Glenn Frankel, "Nyerere Resignation to End 23-Year Era in East Africa," *The Washington Post*, 9 December 1984).

He stepped down from the presidency in November 1985 when white minority rule was coming to an end in southern Africa. Only apartheid South Africa, and Namibia which was ruled by South Africa, remained under white minority governments.

He was one of the greatest leaders Africa has ever produced. As Ugandan President Yoweri Museveni said when assessing Nyerere' role in the liberation of Africa:

"He was the greatest black man that ever lived. There are other black men such as Nelson Mandela and Kwame Nkrumah, but Nyerere was the greatest. – (Yoweri Museveni, *New Vision*, Kampala, Uganda, 4 April 2012).

They all will be remembered for the role they played in liberating Africa from colonial rule and racial oppression. However, unity on a continental scale has remained elusive as much as it was in the sixties when most African countries won independence. But as Nyerere warned in his Accra speech, "Without unity, there is no future for Africa."

And in what amounted to a farewell speech to Africa not long before he died, Nyerere said the following at a conference at the University of Dar es Salaam - the speech was informal and conversational in style, sprinkled with personal anecdotes, and was given before a diverse audience of politicians, academicians, students and diplomats:

"You wanted me to reflect. I told you I had very little time to reflect. I am not an engineer (reference to the vice-chancellor of the University of Dar es Salaam who identified himself as an engineer in his introductory remarks) and therefore what I am going to say might sound messy, unstructured and possibly irrelevant to what you intend to do; but I thought that if by reflecting, you wanted me to go back and relive the political life that I have lived for the last 30, 40 years, that I cannot do.

And in any case, in spite of the fact that it's useful to go back in history, what you are talking about is what might be of use to Africa in the 21st century. History's important, obviously, but I think we should concentrate and see what might be of use to our continent in the coming century.

What I want to do is share with you some thoughts on two issues concerning Africa. One, an obvious one; when I speak, you will realise how obvious it is. Another one, less obvious, and I'll spend a little more time on the less obvious one, because I think this will put Africa in what is going to be Africa's context in the 21st century. And the new leadership of Africa will have to concern itself with the situation in which it finds itself in the world tomorrow - in the world of the 21st century. And the Africa I'm going to be talking about, is Africa south of the Sahara, sub-Saharan Africa. I'll explain later the reason why I chose to concentrate on Africa south of the Sahara. It is because of the point I want to emphasise.

It appears today that in the world tomorrow, there are going to be three centres of power: some, political power; some, economic power, but three centres of real power in the world. One centre is the United States of America and Canada; what you call North America. That is going to be a huge economic power, and probably for a long time the only military power, but a huge economic power. The other one is going to be Western Europe, another huge economic power. I think Europe is choosing deliberately not to be a military power. I think they deliberately want to leave that to the United States. The other one is Japan. Japan is in a different category but it is better to say Japan, because the power of Japan is quite clear, the economic power of Japan is obvious.

The three powers are going to affect the countries near them. I was speaking in South Africa recently and I referred to Mexico. A former president of Mexico, I think it must have been after the revolution in 1935, no, after the revolution; a former president of Mexico is reported to have complained about his country or lamented about his country. 'Poor Mexico,' said the president, 'so far from God yet so near the United States.' He was complaining about the disadvantages of being a neighbour of a giant.

Today, Mexico has decided not simply to suffer the disadvantages of being so close to the United States. And the United States itself has realised the importance of trying to accommodate Mexico. In the past there were huge attempts by the United States to prevent people from moving from Mexico *into* the United States; people seeking work, seeking jobs. So you had police, a border very well policed in order to prevent Mexicans who *seek*, who *look* for jobs, to *move* into the United States. The United States discovered that it was not working. It *can't* work.

There is a kind of economic osmosis where whatever you do, if you are rich, you are attractive to the poor. They will come, they'll even *risk* their own lives in order to come. So the United States tried very hard to prevent Mexicans going into the United States; they've given up, and the result was NAFTA. It is in the interest of the United States to try and create jobs in Mexico because, if you don't, the Mexicans will simply come, to the United States; so they're doing that.

Europe, Western Europe, is very wealthy. It has two Mexicos. One is Eastern Europe. If you want to prevent those Eastern Europeans to come to Western Europe, you jolly will have to create jobs in *Eastern* Europe, and Western Europe is actually *doing* that. They are *doing* that. They'll help Eastern Europe to develop. The whole of Western Europe will be doing it, the Germans are doing it. The Germans basically started first of all with the East Germans but they are spending lots of money also helping the other countries of Eastern Europe to develop, including unfortunately, or *fortunately* for them, including Russia. Because they realise, Europeans realise including the Germans, if you don't help *Russia* to develop, one of these days you are going to be in trouble. So it is in the interest of Western Europe, to help Eastern Europe including Russia. They are pouring a lot of money in that part of the world, in that part of Europe, to try and help it to develop.

I said Western Europe has two Mexicos. I have mentioned one. I'll jump the other. I jump Europe's second Mexico. I'll go to Asia. I'll go to Japan. Japan - a wealthy island, *very* wealthy indeed, but an *island*. I don't think they're very keen on the unemployed of Asia to go to Japan. They'd rather help them where they are, and Japan is spending a lot of money in Asia, to help create jobs *in* Asia, prevent those Asians dreaming about going to Japan to look for jobs. In any case, Japan is too small, they can't find wealth there.

But apart from what Japan is doing, of course Asia *is* Asia; Asia has *China!* Asia has *India*, and the small countries of Asia are not very small. The population of Indonesia is twice the population of Nigeria, your biggest. So Asia is virtually in a category, of the Third World countries, of the Southern countries; Asia is almost in a category of its own. It is developing as a power, and Europe knows it, and the United States knows it. And in spite of the *huge* Atlantic, now they are talking about the Atlantic *Rim*. That is in recognition of the importance of Asia.

I go back to Europe. Europe has a second Mexico. And Europe's second Mexico is North Africa. North Africa is to Europe what Mexico is to the United States. North Africans who have no jobs will not go to Nigeria; they'll be thinking of Europe or the Middle East, because of the imperatives of geography and history and religion and language. North Africa is part of Europe and the Middle East.

Nasser was a great leader and a great *African* leader. I got on extremely well with him. Once he sent me a minister, and I had a long discussion with his minister at the State House here, and in the course of the discussion, the minister says to me, 'Mr. President, this is my first visit to Africa.' North Africa, because of the pull of the

Mediterranean, and I say, history and culture, and religion, North Africa is pulled towards the North. When North Africans look for jobs, they go to Western Europe and southern Western Europe, or they go to the Middle East. And Europe has a specific policy for North Africa, specific policy for North Africa. It's not only about development; it's also about security. Because of you don't do something about North Africa, they'll come.

Africa, south of the Sahara, is different; *totally* different. If you have no jobs here in Tanzania, where do you go? The Japanese have no fear that you people will flock to Japan. The North Americans have no fear that you people will flock to North America. Not even from West Africa. The Atlantic, the Atlantic as an ocean, like the Mediterranean, it has its own logic. But links North America and Western Europe, not North America and West Africa.

Africa south of the Sahara is isolated. That is the first point I want to make. South of the Sahara is totally isolated in terms of that configuration of developing power in the world in the 21st century - on its own. There is no centre of power in whose self-interest it's important to develop Africa, *no* centre. Not North America, not Japan, not Western Europe. There's no self-interest to bother about Africa south of the Sahara. Africa south of the Sahara is on its own. *Na sijambo baya.* Those of you who don't know Kiswahili, I just whispered, 'Not necessarily bad.'

That's the first thing I wanted to say about Africa south of the Sahara. African leadership, the coming African leadership, will have to bear that in mind. You are on your own, Mr. Vice President. You mentioned, you know, in the past, there was some Cold War competition in Africa and some Africans may have exploited it. I never did. I never succeeded in exploiting the Cold War in Africa. We suffered, we suffered through the Cold War. Look at Africa south of the Sahara. I'll be talking about it later. Southern

Africa, I mean, look at southern Africa; devastated because of the combination of the Cold War and apartheid. Devastated part of Africa. It could have been *very* different. But the Cold War is gone, thank God. But thank God the Cold War is gone, the chances of the Mobutus also is gone.

So that's the first thing I wanted to say about Africa south of the Sahara. Africa south of the Sahara in those terms is isolated. That is the point I said was not obvious and I had to explain it in terms in which I have tried to explain it. The other one, the second point I want to raise is completely obvious. Africa has 53 nation-states, most of them in Africa south of the Sahara. If numbers were power, Africa would be the most powerful continent on earth. It is the weakest; so it's obvious numbers are not power.

So the second point about Africa, and again I am talking about Africa south of the Sahara; it is fragmented, fragmented. From the very beginning of independence 40 years ago, we were against that idea, that the continent is so fragmented. We called it the Balkanisation of Africa. Today, I think the Balkans are talking about the Africanisation of Europe. Africa's states are too many, too small, some make no logic, whether political logic or ethnic logic or anything. They are non-viable. It is not a confession.

The OAU was founded in 1963. In 1964 we went to Cairo to hold, in a sense, our first summit after the inaugural summit. I was responsible for moving that resolution that Africa must accept the borders, which we inherited from colonialism; accept them as they are. That resolution was passed by the organisation (OAU) with two reservations: one from Morocco, another from Somalia. Let me say why I moved that resolution.

In 1960, just before this country became independent, I think I was then chief minister; I received a delegation of Masai elders from Kenya, led by an American missionary.

And they came to persuade me to let the Masai invoke something called the Anglo-Masai Agreement so that that section of the Masai in Kenya should become part of Tanganyika; so that when Tanganyika becomes independent, it includes part of Masai, from Kenya. I suspected the American missionary was responsible for that idea. I don't remember that I was particularly polite to him. Kenyatta was then in detention, and here somebody comes to me, that we should break up Kenya and make part of Kenya part of Tanganyika. But why shouldn't Kenyatta demand that the Masai part of Tanganyika should become Masai of Kenya? It's the same logic. That was in 1960.

In 1961 we became independent. In 1962, early 1962, I resigned as prime minister and then a few weeks later I received Dr. Banda. *Mungu amuweke mahali pema* (May God rest his soul in peace). I received Dr. Banda. We had just, FRELIMO had just been established here and we were now in the process of starting the armed struggle.

So Banda comes to me with a big old book, with lots and lots of maps in it, and tells me, 'Mwalimu, what is this, what is Mozambique? There is no such thing as Mozambique.' I said, 'What do you mean there is no such thing as Mozambique?' So he showed me this map, and he said: 'That part is part of Nyasaland (it was still Nyasaland, not Malawi, at that time). That part is part of Southern Rhodesia, That part is Swaziland, and this part, which is the northern part, Makonde part, that is *your* part.'

So Banda disposed of Mozambique just like that. I ridiculed the idea, and Banda never liked anybody to ridicule his ideas. So he left and went to Lisbon to talk to Salazar about this wonderful idea. I don't know what Salazar told him. That was '62.

In '63 we go to Addis Ababa for the inauguration of the OAU, and Ethiopia and Somalia are at war over the Ogaden. We had to send a special delegation to bring the president of Somalia to attend that inaugural summit, because the two countries were at *war*. Why? Because Somalia wanted the Ogaden, a *whole* province of Ethiopia, saying, 'That is part of Somalia.' And Ethiopia was quietly, the Emperor quietly saying to us that 'the whole of Somalia is part of Ethiopia.'

So those three, the delegation of the Masai, led by the American missionary; Banda's old book of maps; and the Ogaden, caused me to move that resolution, in Cairo 1964. And I say, the resolution was accepted, two countries with reservations, and one was Somalia because Somalia wanted the Ogaden; Somalia wanted northern Kenya; Somalia wanted Djibouti.

Throw away all our ideas about socialism. Throw them away, give them to the Americans, give them to the Japanese, give them, so that they can, I don't know, they can do whatever they like with them. *Embrace* capitalism, fine! But you *have* to be self-reliant. You here in Tanzania don't dream that if you privatise every blessed thing, including the prison, then foreign investors will come rushing. No! No! Your are dreaming! *Hawaji*! They won't come! (*hawaji*!). You just try it.

There is more to privatise in Eastern Europe than here. Norman Manley, the Prime Minister of Jamaica, in those days the vogue was nationalisation, not privatisation. In those days the vogue was *nationalisation*. So Norman Manley was asked as Jamaica was moving towards independence: 'Mr. Prime Minister, are you going to nationalise the economy?' His answer was: 'You can't nationalise *nothing*.'

You people here are busy privatising not *nothing*, we did *build* something, we built *something* to privatise. But quite frankly, for the appetite of Europe, and the appetite of North America, this is privatising nothing. The people with a really good appetite will go to Eastern Europe, they'll go to Russia, they'll not come rushing to Tanzania! Your blessed National Bank of Commerce, it's a branch of some major bank somewhere, and in Tanzania you say,

'It's so big we must divide it into pieces,' which is *nonsense*.

Africa south of the Sahara is isolated. Therefore, to develop, it will have to depend upon its own resources basically. Internal resources, nationally; and Africa will have to depend upon Africa. The leadership of the future will have to devise, try to carry out policies of *maximum* national self-reliance and *maximum* collective self-reliance. They have no other choice. *Hamna*! (You don't have it!) And this, this need to organise collective self-reliance is what moves me to the second part.

The small countries in Africa must move towards either unity or co-operation, unity of Africa. The leadership of the future, of the 21st century, should have less respect, less respect for this thing called 'national sovereignty.' I'm not saying take up arms and destroy the state, no! This idea that we must *preserve* the Tanganyika, then *preserve* the Kenya as they *are*, is nonsensical!

The nation-states we in Africa, have inherited from Europe. They are the builders of the nation-states par excellence. For centuries they fought wars! The history of Europe, the history of the *building* of Europe is a history of war. And sometimes their wars when they get hotter although they're European wars, they call them *world wars*. And we all get involved. We fight even in Tanganyika here, we *fought* here, one world war.

These Europeans, powerful, where little Belgium is more powerful than the whole of Africa south of the Sahara put together; these *powerful* European states are moving towards unity, and you people are talking about the atavism of the tribe, this is nonsense! I am telling *you* people. How can anybody think of the tribe as the unity of the future? *Hakuna!* (There's nothing!).

Europe now, you can take it almost as God-given, Europe is not going to fight with Europe anymore. The Europeans are not going to take up arms against Europeans. They are moving towards unity - even the little, the little countries of the Balkans which are breaking up, Yugoslavia breaking up, but they are breaking up at the same time the building up is taking place. They break up and say we want to come into the *bigger* unity.

So there's a *building* movement, there's a *building* of Europe. These countries which have old, old sovereignties, countries of hundreds of years old; they are forgetting this, they are *moving* towards unity. And you people, you think Tanzania is sacred? What is Tanzania!

You *have* to move towards unity. If these powerful countries see that they have no future in the nation-states - *ninyi mnafikiri mna future katika nini*? (what future do you think you have?). So, if we can't *move*, if our leadership, our future leadership cannot move us to bigger nation-states, which I *hope* they are going to try; we tried and failed. I tried and failed. One of my biggest failures was actually that. I tried in East Africa and failed.

But don't give up because we, the first leadership, failed, no! *Unajaribu tena*! (You try again!). We failed, but the idea is a good idea. That these countries should come together. Don't leave Rwanda and Burundi on their own. *Hawawezi kusurvive* (They cannot survive). They can't. They're locked up into a form of prejudice. If we can't move towards bigger nation-states, at least let's move towards greater co-operation. This is beginning to happen. And the new leadership in Africa should encourage it.

I want to say only one or two things about what is happening in southern Africa. Please accept the logic of coming together. South Africa, small; South Africa is very small. Their per capita income now is, I think $2,000 a year or something around that. Compared with Tanzanians, of course, it is very big, but it's poor. If South Africa begins to tackle the problems of the legacy of apartheid, they have no money!

But compared with the rest of us, they are rich. And so, in southern Africa, there, there is also a kind of osmosis, also an economic osmosis. South Africa's neighbours send their job seekers *into* South Africa. And South Africa will simply have to accept the logic of that, that they are big, they are attractive. They attract the unemployed from Mozambique, and from Lesotho and from the rest. They have to accept that fact of life. It's a problem, but they have to accept it.

South Africa, and I am talking about post-apartheid South Africa. Post-apartheid South Africa has the most developed and the most dynamic private sector on the continent. It is white, so what? So forget it is white. It is South African, dynamic, highly developed. If the investors of South Africa begin a new form of trekking, you *have* to accept it.

It will be ridiculous, absolutely ridiculous, for Africans to go out seeking investment from North America, from Japan, from Europe, from Russia, and then, when these investors come from South Africa to invest in your own country, you say, 'a! a! These fellows now want to take over our economy' - this is nonsense. You can't have it both ways. You want foreign investors or you don't want foreign investors. Now, the most available foreign investors for you are those from South Africa.

And let me tell you, when Europe think in terms of investing, they *might* go to South Africa. When North America think in terms of investing, they *might* go to South Africa. Even Asia, if they want to invest, the first country they may think of in Africa *may* be South Africa. So, if *your* South Africa is going to be *your* engine of development, accept the reality, accept the reality. Don't accept this sovereignty, South Africa will reduce your sovereignty. What sovereignty do you have?

Many of these debt-ridden countries in Africa now have no sovereignty, they've lost it. *Imekwenda* (It's gone). *Iko mikononi mwa IMF na World Bank* (It's in the hands of the IMF and the World Bank). *Unafikiri kuna sovereignty gani*? (What kind of sovereignty do you think there is?)

So, southern Africa has an opportunity, southern Africa, the SADC group, *because* of South Africa.

Because South Africa now is no longer a destabiliser of the region, but a partner in development, southern Africa has a tremendous opportunity. But you need leadership, because if you get proper leadership there, within the next 10, 15 years, that region is going to be the ASEAN (Association of South-East Asian Nations) of Africa. And it is possible. But forget the protection of your sovereignties. I believe the South Africans will be sensitive enough to know that if they are not careful, there is going to be this resentment of big brother, but that big brother, frankly, is not very big.

West Africa. Another bloc is developing there, but that depends very much upon Nigeria my brother (looking at the Nigerian High Commissioner - Ambassador), very much so. Without Nigeria, the future of West Africa is a problem. West Africa is more balkanised than Eastern Africa. More balkanised, tiny little states.

The leadership will have to come from Nigeria. It came from Nigeria in Liberia; it has come from Nigeria in the case of Sierra Leone; it will have to come from Nigeria in galvanising ECOWAS.

But the military in Nigeria must allow the Nigerians to exercise that vitality in freedom. And it is my hope that they will do it.

I told you I was going to ramble and it was going to be messy, but thank you very much." – (Julius K. Nyerere in Godfrey Mwakikagile, *Nyerere and Africa: End of an Era*, New Africa Press, 2010, pp. 553 - 560. Source: Mwalimu Nyerere Memorial Site: Written Speeches, South Centre, Geneva, Switzerland, 2001. This is an abridged version of Nyerere's speech at an international conference at the University of Dar es Salaam, Tanzania, December 15, 1997. The transcription of the non-written speech came from Mrs. Magombe of the Nyerere Foundation, Dar es

Salaam. Translation of Swahili words, phrases and sentences in Nyerere's speech into English in the preceding text, done by the author, Godfrey Mwakikagile).

Professor Haroub Othman of the University of Dar es Salaam said that was Nyerere at his best; it was one of his best speeches if not the best, he said.

It was a fitting farewell to Africa. Nyerere died almost two years later after warning his fellow Africans as an elder statesman in that speech: "Africa south of the Sahara is on its own."

And as Nkrumah stated years earlier in the sixties: "Africa Must Unite." That was also the title of his book published to coincide with the first meeting of the 32 African heads of state and government who met in Addis Ababa, Ethiopia, from 22 – 25 May 1963 and formed the Organisation of African Unity (OAU) on the last day of the conference.

The countries which were the founding members of the OAU were Algeria, Burundi, Cameroun, Central African republic, Chad, Congo-Brazzaville, Congo-Leopoldville, Dahomey, Ethiopia, Gabon, Ghana, Guinea, Ivory Coast, Liberia, Libya, Madagascar, Mali, Mauritania, Morocco, Niger, Nigeria, Rwanda, Senegal, Sierra Leone, Somalia, Sudan, Tanganyika, Togo, Tunisia, Uganda, United Arab Republic, and Upper Volta.

The rest joined in the following years after they became independent.

Although African leaders failed to unite their countries under one government in the sixties, as urged by Nkrumah, they were at least united in their goal to liberate the countries which were still under white minority rule and eventually succeeded in doing so.

In his seminal work, *Nyerere and Africa: End of an Era*, Godfrey Mwakikagile has written extensively about the liberation struggle, and the liberation movements, in Southern Africa in what is probably one of the best accounts of that critical phase in the history of Africa. He has also, in the same book, written an excellent analysis of the Congo Crisis during the turbulent sixties.

Another major book he has written on struggle for freedom and independence in the countries of southern Africa is *The African Liberation Struggle: Reflections*.

Godfrey Mwakikagile has also written a book about the struggle against apartheid and the end of white minority rule in South Africa and on the prospects and challenges the country faces in the post-apartheid era. The work is entitled, *South Africa in Contemporary Times*.

The years he spent on the editorial staff at the *Standard* and the *Daily News* were critical to his future career as a writer. Those were his formative years, and had he not become a news reporter, his life, and his career as an author, might have taken a different turn. As he states in *Nyerere and Africa: End of an Era*, he was first hired by renowned British journalist David Martin who was the deputy managing and news editor of the Tanganyika *Standard*. The managing editor was Brendon Grimshaw, also British who, in the seventies, bought Moyenne Island in the Seychelles and became its only permanent inhabitant. Brendon Grimshaw also played a major role in recruiting Godfrey Mwakikagile as a member of the editorial staff at the *Standard*.[32]

It was a turning point in Godfrey Mwakikagile's life.

That was in June 1969 when he was a student at Tambaza High School in Dar es Salaam. He was 19 years old and probably the youngest reporter on the editorial staff at the *Standard* during that time.

The *Standard* which was renamed *Daily News* in 1972 was the largest English newspaper in Tanzania and one of the largest and most influential in East Africa. And it served Godfrey Mwakikagile well, not only in terms of providing him with an opportunity to sharpen his writing skills but also – after it became the *Daily News* – in helping him to go to school in the United States where he became an author many years after he graduated from college.

David Martin, when he worked at the Tanganyika *Standard* and at the *Daily News*, and thereafter, was the most prominent foreign journalist in Eastern and Southern Africa in the sixties and seventies. And he wrote extensively about the liberation struggle in the region for the London *Observer* and for BBC.

He went to the combat zone with FRELIMO guerrilla fighters in Mozambique and also covered the Angolan civil war for BBC and for CBC (Canadian Broadcasting Corporation).

He knew and worked closely with all the leaders of the liberation movements including Robert Mugabe, Dr. Eduardo Mondlane, president of FRELIMO, who was assassinated in Dar es Salaam, Tanzania, in February 1969; and Mondlane's successor Samora Machel who died in a "mysterious" plane crash in 1986 when he was president of Mozambique.

The plane crashed on the South African side of the border with Mozambique and the apartheid regime was suspected of having caused the "accident." He was succeeded by Mozambique's foreign affairs minister, Joaquim Chissano, as president.

David Martin was also very close to many Tanzanian leaders including President Julius Nyerere, and President Benjamin Mkapa who was also his close friend for many years since the sixties when they worked together in the media.

He also interviewed President Kenneth Kaunda of Zambia during the liberation struggle when many freedom fighters were based in that country and used it as an operational base as they did Tanzania.

He wrote more than 20 books. He died at his home in Harare, Zimbabwe, in August 2007, where he went to live after Zimbabwe won independence in April 1980.

President Mugabe delivered an official condolence

message and David Martin was accorded a state-assisted funeral in recognition of his works exposing apartheid South Africa's destabalisation campaign in neighbouring countries, racial brutalities and injustices under white minority regimes throughout Southern Africa and for his outstanding role as a champion of racial equality.

The report of his death which included President Robert Mugabe's long message of condolence on behalf of the government and the ruling party ZANU-PF was published in the Zimbabwean government-owned newspaper, *The Herald*, 22 August 2007, headlined, "President Mourns David Martin."[33]

Another report on David Martin's contributions as a journalist when he reported extensively on the liberation struggle in Southern Africa, and on his support for regional integration of the countries in that part of the continent after the end of white minority rule, was published in the same paper on August 24, headlined, "Martin – Man of Many Talents."[34]

He was buried in Harare, the capital of Zimbabwe. Mozambican President Armando Guebuza and former Tanzanian President Benjamin Mkapa were some of the African leaders who sent condolence messages.

Zimbabwean government leaders including cabinet members, Tanzanian officials, war veterans who fought for Zimbabwe's independence during the liberation struggle in the sixties and seventies, and diplomats, attended the funeral, according to *The Herald*, Harare, Zimbabwe, 25 August 2007, in a report headlined, "Martin Laid to Rest."[35]

David Martin often said he credited his education to the 10 years he spent working as a journalist in Tanzania and was inspired by President Nyerere and by the liberation leaders and movements based there. He interviewed many of those leaders many times during the liberation struggle and thereafter.

In his book *Nyerere and Africa: End of an Era*,

Godfrey Mwakikagile has written about David Martin and the role he played as a journalist during the liberation struggle in Southern Africa. But David Martin was also instrumental in opening the door for Godfrey Mwakikagile into the world of journalism, writing everyday, after which both became successful writers.[36]

Godfrey Mwakikagile himself has stated in his books – *Nyerere and Africa: End of an Era*, *Africa after Independence: Realities of Nationhood*, *The Modern African State: Quest for Transformation*, *Military Coups in West Africa Since The Sixties* and in *Africa is in A Mess: What Went Wrong and What Should Be Done* – that his background as a news reporter which included meeting deadlines when writing news articles prepared him for the rigorous task of writing books.[37]

Criticism of post-colonial Africa

Godfrey Mwakikagile lived and grew up under the leadership of Tanzanian President Julius Nyerere, a legendary figure, liberation icon and staunch Pan-Africanist and one of the most influential and most respected leaders Africa has ever produced, whose socialist policies he has also defended in his writings because of the egalitarian ideals they instilled in the people of Tanzania enabling them to build a peaceful, cohesive nation in which they saw themselves as one people and equal in terms of rights and dignity as fellow human beings in spite of the poverty they endured under ujamaa, Nyerere's African version of socialism.

Yet, in spite of his admiration for liberation icons, he also is highly critical of African leaders from the same generation who led their countries to independence, contending that most of them did not care about the well-being of their people; a position he forcefully articulates in his writings.[38]

He gives them a lot of credit for leading the struggle for independence and contends that they were very successful in mobilising the masses and the elite and in fuelling nationalist sentiments to end colonial rule. But he also bluntly states that they were, in most cases, a tragic failure in terms of nation building and national development during the post-colonial era.

They fostered divided loyalties along ethnic and regional lines, practised tribalism, and pursued wrong policies. They embraced and adopted imported -isms especially Marxism and other alien ideologies while ignoring indigenous knowledge, institutions and systems of thought – which are relevant to African conditions, local circumstances and historical experience – in the quest for development.

They formulated unrealistic development plans and programmes, launched unnecessary capital-intensive projects just for demonstration effect, and underutilised human capital including abundant labour for labour-intensive projects.

They mismanaged the economy, squandered resources, stole from the people, raided national coffers, bankrupted the treasury, enriched themselves, institutionalised corruption, instituted the highly centralised state as an oppressive apparatus for mass regimentation although it also served as an effective instrument of mobilisation of resources and manpower that was unfortunately misused or wasted in most cases.

And they tortured, imprisoned and killed their critics and opponents, muzzled the opposition and stifled dissent instead of encouraging cross-fertilisation of ideas across the spectrum which could have led to formulation of better policies critical to nation building and economic development, as he clearly states in his books, *Economic Development in Africa, Africa After Independence: Realities of Nationhood, The Modern African State: Quest for Transformation,* and *Africa is in A Mess: What Went*

Wrong and What Should Be Done.

It is an assessment, and a disillusionment with African leadership, that is shared by his fellow Africans. As Wole Soyinka stated when he saw Nigerian leaders assume power in October 1960 after the end of colonial rule, with pomp and ceremony, he became apprehensive about the future and knew, from then onwards, the enemy was now within, not without. The enemy was the new African leaders who went against everything they had fought for, totally ignoring the wellbeing of their people. Assumption of power was only a means to enrich themselves and trample on the rights of their fellow countrymen.

Godfrey Mwakikagile belongs to a generation that preceded independence and was partly brought up under colonial rule. He even wrote a book, *Life in Tanganyika in The Fifties*, about those years.

Independence meant a lot to him as much as it did to his fellow Africans. He even attended the independence celebrations when Tanganyika attained sovereign status under the leadership of Julius Nyerere.

He witnessed the flags changing at midnight when the Union Jack was lowered and the flag of the newly independent nation of Tanganyika went up. As he states in his autobiographical writings, he vividly remembers attending the independence celebrations with his uncle Johan Chonde Mwambapa, popularly known as Chonde, in the town of Tukuyu. His uncle took him on a bicycle to Tukuyu, four miles north of their home area, to witness the historic occasion. The celebrations were held on a football (soccer) field. He was 12 years old.

Early in his life when he was a teenager, he developed strong Pan-Africanist views under the influence of Julius Nyerere and other Pan-Africanist leaders such as Kwame Nkrumah and Ahmed Sekou Toure. He still holds those views today, crystallised into an ideology for a new African liberation and forcefully articulated in his writings.

He writes as an African more than anything else, not just as a Tanzanian. As Professor Guy Martin states in his book *African Political Thought* about Godfrey Mwakikagile and other Pan-Africanist theorists and thinkers, their individual national identities are secondary to their primary identity as Africans and even irrelevant when they articulate their position from a Pan-African perspective:

"Note that all these scholars are dedicated Pan-Africanists and many would shun the reference to their nationality, preferring to be simply called 'Africans'.... Some of the most prominent Africanist-populist scholars include... Godfrey Mwakikagile....

Chapter 4 is a survey of Pan-Africanism as a political and cultural ideal and movement eventually leading to African unity.... The chapter first shows how the Pan-Africanist leaders' dream for immediate political and economic integration in the form of a 'United States of Africa' was deferred in favor of a gradualist-functionalist approach....

The chapter then analyzes the reasons for the failure of the Pan-Africanist leaders' dream of unity... and surveys past and current proposals for a revision of the map of Africa and a reconfiguration of the African states put forward by various authors such as Cheikh Anta Diop, Marc-Louis Ropivia, Makau wa Mutua, Arthur Gakwandi, Joseph Ki-Zerbo, Daniel Osabu-Kle, Godfrey Mwakikagile, Pelle Danabo, and Mueni wa Muiu....

Chapter eight reviews the ideas and values for a new, free, and self-reliant Africa put forth by African academics who have the best interest of the people at heart and thus advocate a popular type of democracy and development. However, unlike the populist-socialist scholars, these African-populist scholars refuse to operate within the parameters of Western ideologies – whether of the socialist, Marxist-Leninist, or liberal-democratic persuasion – and call on Africans to get rid of their economic, technological, and cultural dependency syndrome.

These scholars are also convinced that the solutions to African problems lie within Africans themselves. Thus they refuse to remain passive victims of a perceived or preordained fate and call on all Africans to become the initiators and agents of their own development.... For the reasons stated previously, the chapter will focus exclusively on the last four scholars mentioned: namely, Osabu-Kle, Ake, Mwakikagile, and Muiu." – Guy Martin, *African Political Thought*, New York: Palgrave Macmillan, 2012, pp. 8, 6).

One of Godfrey Mwakikagile's critics has described him as "a shrewd intellectual in defence of liberation icons" and accuses him of not being intellectually honest about leaders such as Nyerere, Nkrumah and Sekou Toure for not criticising them harshly for their failures because he admires them so much as staunch Pan-Africanists.[39]

In a way, some people may see him as a complex character not always easy to understand, although he articulates his position clearly and forcefully.

Some of the confusion among his readers about his position on African leaders of the independence generation has to do with his own background since he was an integral part of that generation in the sense that he witnessed the end of colonial rule and the emergence of the newly independent African states although he was not old enough to have participated in the independence struggle himself.[40]

He admires the leaders who led their countries to independence, yet he is highly critical of them in most cases for their failures during the post-colonial period. He became disillusioned with the leadership on the continent through the years, filled with broken promises, and not long after the countries won independence. He admires many aspects of Nyerere's socialist policies in Tanzania, yet concedes the policies were also a failure in many cases. And he strongly favours fundamental change in African countries, yet he is nostalgic about the past.[41]

His advocacy for fundamental change is articulated in many of his writings including *The Modern African State: Quest for Transformation*, which was published in 2001 and which is also one of his most well-known books.

In his review of the book, Ronald Taylor-Lewis [born of a Sierra Leonean father], editor of *Mano Vision* magazine, London, described it as "a masterpiece of fact and analysis."[42]

The book has also been reviewed in other publications. Tana Worku Anglana reviewed Godfrey Mwakikagile's *Modern African State: Quest for Transformation* in *Articolo* and described it as "unbiased literature."[43]

Other people have also cited the book in their different analyses of the African condition. They include Dr. Elavie Ndura, a professor at George Mason University in Virginia, USA, who used Godfrey Mwakikagile's book, *The Modern African State: Quest for Transformation*, among other works, in supporting her central thesis in her study, "Transcending The Majority Rights and Minority Protection Dichotomy Through Multicultural Reflective Citizenship in The African Great Lakes Region," in *Intercultural Education*, Vol. 17, No. 2, published by Routledge, Taylor & Francis Group, in May 2006.

Professor Elavie Ndura, a Hutu from Burundi where her family experienced genocide, taught for many years at a number of schools in the United States, including the University of Nevada-Reno and George Mason University.

Others who have used Godfrey Mwakikagile's book, *The Modern African State: Quest for Transformation*, together with the works of other scholars, in their academic pursuits include Ole Frahm when he wrote his dissertation to earn a Ph.D. from The Humbold University of Berlin in Germany. His doctoral thesis was "How a state is made: Statebuilding and nationbuilding in South Sudan in the light of its African peers," in which he quotes Mwakikagile stating:

"Godfrey Mwakikagile delivers a harsh indictment of colonial boundary-making in the case of Sudan: 'The creation of Sudan from colonial boundaries arbitrarily drawn by the imperial powers was a colossal mistake, and a monstrosity, considering what it has spawned: a cauldron of intense racial hatred which has led to genocide against blacks.' - Mwakikagile (2001), p. 215."

Ethnic conflicts in Rwanda and Burundi between the Hutu and the Tutsi is one of the subjects Godfrey Mwakikagile has addressed extensively in his books, *The Modern African State: Quest for Transformation, Identity Politics and Ethnic Conflicts in Rwanda and Burundi: A Comparative Study, Burundi: The Hutu and the Tutsi: Cauldron of Conflict and Quest for Dynamic Compromise, Peace and Stability in Rwanda and Burundi: The Road Not Taken*, and *Civil Wars in Rwanda and Burundi: Conflict Resolution in Africa.*

In many of his writings, Godfrey Mwakikagile focuses on internal factors – including corruption, tribalism and tyranny by African leaders – as the main cause of Africa's predicament, but not to the total exclusion of external forces.

And the position he articulates in his writings on many issues is cited by other people to support their arguments in their works.

One of the works in which Godfrey Mwakikagile is cited and quoted is a compiled study by Professor Robert H. Bates of Harvard University, *When Things Fell Apart: State Failure in Late-Century Africa: Cambridge Studies in Comparative Politics*, published by Cambridge University Press in February 2008.

Godfrey Mwakikagile is also quoted by Professors Robert Elgie and Sophie Moestrup in their book, *Semi-*

Presidentialism Outside Europe: A Comparative Study – Routledge Research in Comparative Politics, Routledge, 2007; Mueni wa Muiu and Guy Martin in *A New Paradigm of the African State: Fundi wa Afrika*, Palgrave Macmillan, 2009; Minabere Ibelema, *The African Press, Civic Cynicism, and Democracy - The PalgraveMacmillan Series in International Political Communication*, Palgrave Macmillan, 2007; James Crawford and Vaughan Lowe in *British Yearbook of International Law 2005: Volume 76*, Oxford University Press, 2007, and in other works.

Others who have cited Godfrey Mwakikagile and his works include Professor Robert I. Rotberg, director at Harvard University's John F. Kennedy School of Government and president emeritus of the World Peace Foundation. He used Godfrey Mwakikagle's book *Ethnic Politics in Kenya and Nigeria*, among other works, to document his study, *Crafting The New Nigeria: Confronting The Challenges*, a book that was published in 2004.

Other researchers and scholars who have cited and quoted Godfrey Mwakikagile in their works include Gabi Hesselbein, Frederick Golooba-Mutebi, and James Putzel,James in their study, "Economic and Political Foundations of State-making in Africa: Understanding State Reconstruction", Crisis States Research Centre, London School of Economics and Political Science, London, UK, 2006; E.M. Poff, "Liberal Democracy and Multiethnic States: A Case Study of Ethnic Politics in Kenya," Ohio University, 2008; PJ McGowan, "Coups and Conflict in West Africa, 1955 - 2004: Part II, Empirical Findings," Armed Forces and Society, Sage Publications, 2006.

Others are Martin P. Mathews, in his book, *Nigeria: Current Issues and Historical Background*, Nova Science Publishers, New York, 2002; Isidore Okpewho and N Nzegwu, in their book, *The New African Diaspora*, Indiana University Press, 2009; C.M. Brown, S. Reader and G. Lober, "US National Security Interests in Africa and The Future Global War on Terrorism (GWOT)," Naval Postgraduate School, Monterey, California, USA, 2005.

Nigerian scholar Adaobi Chiamaka Iheduru of Wright State University also used Godfrey Mwakikagile's books, *Relations between Africans and African Americans: Misconceptions, Myths and Realities*, and *Africans and African Americans: Complex Relations, Prospects and Challenges*, to complement her research for her doctorate in psychology. Her dissertation was "Examining the Social Distance between Africans and African Americans: The Role of Internalized Racism."

Another Nigerian scholar, Rotimi T. Suberu, a political science lecturer at the University of Ibadan, Nigeria, used Godfrey Mwakikagile's book *Ethnic Politics in Kenya and Nigeria*, among different works by other scholars, in his analysis, "Federalism and Ethnic Conflict in Nigeria," published in the *African Studies Review 46, No. 2*, September 2003, pp. 93–98.

Godfrey Mwakikagile's book *Ethnic Politics in Kenya and Nigeria* was also used by Dickson Onwuka Uduma, a Nigerian, who earned a master's degree in development and international relations from Aalborg University in Denmark. He wrote a thesis on Nigerian federalism and how it attempts to accommodate ethnicity and nationalism, at the same time, entitled, "Ethnic Identity Politics: Nigeria as a Case Study," and drew on the work of Godfrey Mwakikagile and other scholars.

Joseph Kuria Nyiri, a Kenyan, also used *Ethnic Politics in Kenya and Nigeria* by Godfrey Mwakikagile, together with other works by different scholars, to document his thesis and earn a master's degree in international studies when he submitted it to The Institute of Diplomacy and International Studies at the University of Nairobi in Kenya. His thesis was "The Impact of Ethnic Conflict on Economic Development: The Case of Post-Election Violence in Kenya, 2007 – 2008."

Jimmy Ssentongo, a Ugandan, used Godfrey Mwakikagile's book, *Ethnicity and National Identity in Uganda*, among other works by other scholars, to write his doctoral dissertation, "Ethnicity and Socio-Economic Exclusion in Uganda: Perceptions, Indicators and Spaces for Pluralism with Specific Reference to Cosmopolitan Kampala," which he completed at the University of Humanistic Studies, Utrecht, Netherlands.

Professor Michael Vickers, University of Oxford, in his book *Ethnicity and Sub-Nationalism in Nigeria: Movement for a Mid-West State* (Oxford, UK: WorldView Publishing, 2001), also cited Godfrey Mwakikagile, among other scholars, to document and support the central thesis of his book.

Gerald Anietie Ignatius Akata, a Nigerian, used Godfrey Mwakikagile's book, *Military Coups in West Africa Since the Sixties*, together with the works of other scholars, to complete his PhD dissertation in education, "Leadership in the Niger Delta Region of Nigeria: A Study of the Perceptions of Its Impact on the Acquired Leadership Skills of Expatriate Nigerian Postgraduates," at East Tennessee State University.

Michael Kweku Addison also used Godfrey Mwakikagile's work, *Military Coups in West Africa Since the Sixties*, together with others, to write his thesis and earn a master's degree from the Naval Postgraduate School, Monterey, California. His thesis was "Preventing military intervention in West Africa: A case study of Ghana."

Joakim Kreutz used the same book by Mwakikagile, *Military Coups in West Africa Since the Sixties*, together with other works, to support his thesis for a doctoral degree from Uppsala University in Sweden. His dissertation was "Dismantling the Conflict Trap: Essays on Civil War Resolution and Relapse."

Daniel Eric Esser also used *Military Coups in West Africa Africa Since the Sixties* by Godfrey Mwakikagile, and other works by other scholars, to complete his dissertation and earn a Ph.D. from the London School of Economics and Political Science. His dissertation was "How Local is Urban Governance in Fragile States? Theory and Practice of Capital City Politics in Sierra Leone and Afghanistan."

Nathan Wolcott Black also used Mwakikagile's *Military Coups in West Africa Africa Since the Sixties*, among other works, to write his PhD thesis in political science at the Massachusetts Institute of Technology (MIT). His dissertation was "The Spread of Violent Civil Conflict: Rare, State-Driven, and Preventable."

Another scholar, Paul K. Bjerk, an American, used some of Godfrey Mwakikagile's works, including *Nyerere and Africa: End of an Era*, in his research for his doctoral dissertation at the University of Wisconsin-Madison. His dissertation was "Julius Nyerere and the Establishment of Sovereignty in Tanganyika." Professor Bjerk also taught at Tumaini University in Tanzania for three years before he went to teach at Texas Tech University.

Thomas Molony, a lecturer in African studies at the University of Edinburgh in Scotland and author of *Nyerere: The Early Years*, also used Godfrey Mwakikagile's work, *Nyerere and Africa: End of an Era*, among others, to complement his research.

Katrina Demulling of Boston University also relied on Godfrey Mwakikagile's work, *Nyerere and Africa: End of an Era*, together with the works of other scholars, to write her doctoral thesis, "We are One: The Emergence and Development of National Consciousness in Tanzania." As she stated:

"The primary works included in this discussion are: Godfrey Mwakikagile's *Nyerere and Africa: End of an Era*, William Smith's *We Must run While Others Walk: A Portrait of Africa's Julius Nyerere*, A.B. Assensoh's *African Political Leadership: Jomo Kenyatta, Kwame*

Nkrumah, and Julius Nyerere, Juma Aley's *Twenty One Years of Leadership Contrasts and Similarities*, and John Charles Hatch's *Two African Statesmen: Kaunda of Zambia and Nyerere of Tanzania*. A number of other articles and books will also be referenced. – (Katrina Demulling, "We are One: The Emergence and Development of National Consciousness in Tanzania," Boston University Theses and Dissertations, 2015, p. 212).

Prince Kwasi Bediako Frimpong, a Ghanaian, also used Godfrey Mwakikagile's book, *Nyerere and Africa: End of an Era*, to complement his research for his thesis, "Nrumahism and Neo-Nkrumahism," to earn an M.A. degree from the University of Louisville, Kentucky, USA.

Christopher Richard Kilford used Godfrey Mwakikagile's works, *Nyerere and Africa: End of an Era* and *Military Coups in West Africa since the Sixties*, together with the works of others scholars, to complete his dissertation and earn a doctoral degree from Queen's University in Canada. His doctoral thesis was "The Other Cold War: Canadian Military Assistance in the Developing World."

Professor Ronald Aminzade of the University of Minnesota also used Godfrey Mwakikagile's books, *Nyerere and Africa: End of an Era*, and *The Union of Tanganyika and Zanzibar: Product of The Cold War?*, among other works by other scholars, in his research for his book, *Race, Nation and Citizenship in Post-Colonial Africa: The Case of Tanzania*, Cambridge University Press, New York, 2013. As he states in his book concerning the union of Tanganyika and Zanzibar which Godfrey Mwakikagile has addressed extensively and which is also one of the subjects he has tackled in his work *Race, Nation and Citizenship in Post-Colonial Africa: The Case of Tanzania*:

"There is considerable disagreement among scholars

about why Tanganyika chose to unite with the residents of a relatively small island off its coast. One compelling account highlights the role of foreign powers, especially the United States, which was worried about communists in Zanzibar's government and feared a 'Cuba off the coast of Africa' would spread revolution throughout the African continent. The Union did take place at the height of the Cold War, amid rumors of a Cuban presence on Zanzibar....

An alternative account of the creation of the Union was that it was a victory for African unity and pan-African solidarity. This view is forcefully argued by Godfrey Mwakikagile, who contends that the Union was an African initiative and an expression of Nyerere's pan-African commitment rather than a product of Cold War pressures....When Nyerere urged the Tanganyikan Parliament to approve the Union, he emphasized it was a first step toward a united Africa. It demonstrated that 'a single Government in Africa is not an impossible dream, but something which can be realized....If two countries can unite, then three can; if three can, then thirty can' (Nyerere, "The Union of Tanganyika and Zanzibar," *Freedom and Unity*, p 292).

In justifying the Union as part of an effort to promote Pan-Africanism, Nyerere emphasized the commonalities between the mainland and the islands, including a common language and historical and cultural ties.... Nyerere further portrayed the Union as a product of 'the overall desire for African unity,' arguing that 'those who welcome unity on our continent must welcome this small move toward it.' 'It is an insult to Africa,' he said, 'to read cold war politics into every move toward African unity' (ibid)....

Support for the merger with the mainland from Abdulrahman Babu and Kassim Hanga, the two Marxist-Leninists who generated the most concern on the part of Western governments, suggests that the union was also not simply the product of a Western anticommunist conspiracy engineered by the United States and Great Britain. (Ronald Aminzade, *Race, Nation and Citizenship in Post-Colonial Africa: The Case of Tanzania*, pp. 99 – 100, 101, 102).

Godfrey Mwakikagile's book, *The Union of Tanganyika and Zanzibar: Product of the Cold War?* cited by Professor Ronald Aminzade, is a strong rebuttal to the argument that Cold War politics provided probably the only context in which the merger of the two East African countries took – and could have taken – place as if union of African countries is impossible unless it is externally engineered.

The union of Tanganyika and Zanzibar and the Zanzibar revolution are subjects Godfrey Mwakikagile has also addressed in detail in two of his other books:*Why Tanganyika united with Zanzibar to form Tanzania* and *Africa in The Sixties*.

Mwakikagile's books have been used by other scholars in their research in different academic disciplines.

German scholar Christa Deiwiks of ETH Zurich, a university in Zurich, Switzerland, where she also earned a master's degree in comparative and international studies, used Godfrey Mwakikagile's book, *Ethnic Politics in Kenya and Nigeria*, a comparative study, in her research for her doctoral degree which she obtained from the same university. Her dissertation was "Ethnofederalism – A Slippery Slope Towards Secessionist Conflict?"

Godfrey Mwakikagile is also cited in the work of Dr. Stephen Macharia Magu, *Political Economy, Social Development and Conflict in Africa*.

Richard L. Whitehead used Godfrey Mwakikagile's book, *Tanzania under Mwalimu Nyerere: Reflections on an African Statesman*, together with the works of other scholars, to write a dissertation for his PhD at Temple University, USA. His dissertation was "Single-Party Rule in a Multiparty Age: Tanzania in Comparative Perspective."

Another book by Godfrey Mwakikagile that has been used extensively in post-graduate studies is *Uganda: A Nation in Transition: Post-colonial Analysis*.

Scholars who have used the book, among many other works by other researchers, include Hannah Marie Vidmar when she wrote her thesis, "The East African Community: Questions of Sovereignty, Regionalism, and Identity," to earn her master's degree from Ohio State University; Kevin Keasbey Frank who used the same book, as well as others, to earn his Ph.D. from the University of Southern Mississippi when he wrote his dissertation, "Strategic Culture in Sub-Saharan Africa: The Divergent Paths of Uganda and Tanzania."

David O. Munyua also used the same book, *Uganda: A Nation in Transition: Post-colonial Analysis*, when he wrote his thesis, "Evading the Endgame in an Insurgency Undertaking: The Case of the Lord's Resistance Army and Beyond," to earn his master's degree from the Naval Postgraduate School, Monterey, California; so did Vick Lukwago Ssali when he wrote his dissertation, "Ethnicity and Federalism in Uganda: Grassroots Perceptions," to earn a Ph.D. from Doshisha University in Japan.

Jane Ayeko-Kummeth also used the same work by Mwakikagile, *Uganda: A Nation in Transition: Post-colonial Analysis*, when she wrote her doctoral thesis, "The Politics of Public Policy Decisions in Local Government in Uganda," to earn her degree from the University of Bayreuth in Germany; so did Bryn Higgs for his dissertation, "The International Criminal Court's Intervention in the Lord's Resistance Army war: impacts and Implications," to earn his doctorate from the University of Bradford in England.

Many others have used Godfrey Mwakikagile's book, *Uganda: A Nation in Transition: Post-colonial Analysis*, to complete their studies.

Other scholars have also used other works by Godfrey Mwakikagile to pursue their studies in different fields. They include Andrew C. Dickens who used Godfrey Mwakikagile's book, *Ethnic Diversity and Integration in The Gambia*, together with other works by other scholars, to earn his Ph.D. in economics from York University, Toronto, Canada, when he wrote his dissertation, "Essays on the Economics of Ethnolinguistic Differences"; so did Chutima Tontarawongsa who used Mwakikagile's work, *The Gambia and Its People: Ethnic Identities and Cultural Integration in Africa*, among others by other scholars, to write her dissertation and earn a doctorate in economics from Duke University in North Carolina, USA. Her doctoral thesis was "Essays on Social Networks in Development."

Another book by Godfrey Mwakikagile, *Burundi: The Hutu and the Tutsi: Cauldron of Conflict and Quest for Dynamic Compromise*, was used by Emily Katherine Maiden, together with other works, to earn her master's degree from the University of Louisville in Kentucky, USA. Her thesis was "Girls with Guns: The Disamarment and Demobilization of Female Ex-combatants in Africa."

Dickson Kanakulya, a Ugandan scholar, used several of Mwakikagile's works, together with others by other scholars, to earn his Ph.D. from Linkoping University in Sweden.

Mwakikagile's books which Kanakulya used were *Tanzania under Mwalimu Nyerere: Reflections on an African Statesman*, *Ethnicity and National Identity in Uganda: The Land and its People*, *My Life as an African: Autobiographical Writings*, *Why Tanganyika united with Zanzibar to form Tanzania*, and *Restructing the African State and Quest for Regional Integration: New Approaches*.

His doctoral thesis was "Governance and Development of the East African Community: The Ethical Sustainability Framework."

In pursuit of his doctoral degree at the University of Cape Town, Peter Haussler used one of Mwakikagile's works, *Nyerere and Africa: End of an Era*, among others by other scholars, to write his dissertation, "Leadership in Africa: A Hermeneutic Dialogue with Kwame Nkrumah and Julius Nyerere on Equality and Human Development."

Chandra R. Dunn earned a doctorate from The American University in Washington, D.C., after completing a dissertation based on the works of many scholars including Mwakikagile's *Africa and America in The Sixties: A Decade that Changed the Nation and the Destiny of a Continent*.

Dunn's doctoral thesis was "Africa and Liberia in World Politics: An Analysis of Liberian Foreign Policy During the 20th Century."

Other people, not just academicians and students, have cited Godfrey Mwakikagile's works in different analyses across the ideological spectrum. They include Tom Hayden, a prominent American radical of the sixties who wrote the *Port Huron Statement* – he was a strong opponent of the Vietnam War, a leading supporter of the civil rights movement and a relentless social activist for decades. He used Godfrey Mwakikagile's works including *Congo in The Sixties*, among others by different scholars and political analysts, when he wrote his book, *Listen, Yankee!: Why Cuba Matters*.

Others who also have cited Godfrey Mwakikagile in their studies in different analytical contexts include Rajend Methrie, "South Africa: The Rocky Road to National Building," in a book, Andrew Simpson,*Language and National Identity in Africa*, Oxford University Press, 2008; Valéria Cristina Salles, "Social Representations Informing Discourse of Young Leaders: A Case Study of Tanzania," University of Cape Town, 2005; L.B. Inniss, "A Domestic Right of Return? Race, Rights, and Residency in New Orleans in the Aftermath of Katrina," in the *Boston College Third World Law Journal*, Boston, Massachusetts,

USA, 2007.

Others scholars who have used Mwakikagile's works include Eric M. Edi, in his book, *Globalization and Politics in the Economic Community of West African States (Carolina Academic Press Studies on Globalization and Society)*, Carolina Academic Press, 2007; James John Chikago, in his book, *Crossing Cultural Frontiers: Analysis and Solutions to Poverty Reduction*, 2003; James Kwesi Anquandah, Naana Jane Opoku-Agyemang, and Michel R. Doortmont, in their book, *The Transatlantic Slave Trade: Landmarks, Legacies, Expectations*, Sub-Saharan Publishers, Accra, Ghana, 2007; Luciana Ricciutelli, Angela Rose Miles, Margaret McFadden in their book, *Feminist Politics, Activism and Vision: Local and Global Challenges*, Zed Books, London, 2005; Emmanuel Ike Udogu, in his book, *African Renaissance in the Millennium: The Political, Social, and Economic Discourses on the Way Forward*, Lexington Books, New York, 2007; and others.

Godfrey Mwakikagile's books have been used by many other scholars in different analytical contexts in a number of countries in the Third World and in industrialised nations.

And his diagnosis of – and prescription for – Africa's ailments has also been cited by scholars and other people for its relevance in other parts of the Third World. As Dr. Hengene Payani, a political scientist at the University of Papua New Guinea in Port Moresby, Papua New Guinea, stated in his review of Godfrey Mwakikagile's book *Africa is in A Mess* on amazon.com:

"The book is excellent, honest and thought-provoking and is relevant even in the context of Papua New Guinea, a country which has been ruined by greedy politicians."

He also contacted Godfrey Mwakikagile to congratulate him for his work.

Although he has written mostly about Africa, and as a political scientist or as a political analyst, his works cover a wide range of scholarship including American studies.

One of Godfrey Mwakikagile's books, *Black Conservatives in The United States*, was cited by Christopher Alan Bracey, a professor of law and African-American Studies at Washington University in St. Louis, Missouri, USA, in support of his research when he also wrote a book about black conservatives entitled *Saviors or Sellouts: The Promise and Peril of Black Conservatism, from Booker T. Washington to Condoleezza Rice*, published in February 2008.

Dr. Michael L. Ondaatje, a lecturer at The University of New Castle, Australia, also used Godfrey Mwakikagile's book on black conservatives, among other works by other scholars, for his doctoral dissertation on the rise of black conservative intellectuals in the United States. He earned his PhD from the University of Western Australia and wrote a book, *Black Conservative Intellectuals in Modern America* (University of Pennsylvania Press 2009) in which he cited Godfrey Mwakikagile's work to complement his research. The book is based on his doctoral dissertation.

Others who have used the same book, *Black Conservatives in The United States* by Godfrey Mwakikagile to complement their research include Professor Angela Lewis of the University of Alabama when she wrote her book, *Conservatism in the Black Community: To the Right and Misunderstood*; Robbin Shipp and Nicole Chiles in their work, *Justice While Black: Helping African-American Families Navigate and Survive the Criminal Justice System*, and Professor Cathy Schlund-Vials of the University of Connecticut in her book, *Modeling Citizenship*, among other scholars and researchers.

But there are limitations to the role played by people like Godfrey Mwakikagile in their quest for fundamental change in African countries. Their contribution is limited in one fundamental respect: They are not actively involved with the masses at the grassroots level precisely because of what they are. They belong to an elite class, and the concepts they expound as well as the solutions they propose are discussed mainly by fellow elites but rarely implemented.

This should not be misconstrued as unwarranted criticism of Godfrey Mwakikagile's writings or the role he plays in the quest for fundamental change in Africa. It is mere acknowledgement of the limitations he faces in his attempt to accomplish this task in conjunction with his brethren across the continent.

Still, there is no question that in many cases, only a few members of the African elite have played and continue to play the role of intellectual activists like Dr. Walter Rodney who wrote his best-selling book, *How Europe Underdeveloped Africa*, in the early 1970s when he was teaching at the University of Dar es Salaam in Tanzania; coincidentally during the same period when Godfrey Mwakikagile was a member of the editorial staff at the *Daily News* in Tanzania's capital Dar es Salaam.

In fact, it was one of his colleagues at the *Daily News*, renowned Kenyan journalist and socio-political analyst Philip Ochieng, who edited Walter Rodney's book, *How Europe Underdeveloped Africa*.

The book was published by Tanzania Publishing House (TPH), Dar es Salaam, in 1973. Ochieng also wrote a feature article, "How Africa Developed Europe," in the *Daily News* in 1972, about Rodney's book, not long before the book was first published by Bogle-L'Ouverture Publications, London, that year.

In an interview with one of Kenya's leading newspapers, the *Daily Nation*, Nairobi, on 6 July 2013, where he worked as an editor and columnist, Philip Ochieng, who coincidentally was also a close friend of Barack Obama Sr., the father of US President Barack

Obama, stated that it was he who edited Rodney's book when he was working at the *Daily News* in Dar es Salaam in 1972. As he stated:

"Walter Rodney was my friend and I even edited his seminal work *How Europe Underdeveloped Africa*. Dar es Salaam was the world headquarters of intellectual debate those days."

One of the revolutionary thinkers who was drawn to Tanzania was Che Guevara who, a few years earlier, stayed in Dar es Salaam for many months from October 1965 to the end of February 1966 after his attempts to help Lumumba's followers fight Western-backed forces in the former Belgian Congo failed. He also wrote his famous book, *The African Dream: The Diaries of the Revolutionary War in the Congo*, when he was staying in Dar es Salaam during those months.

It was also in the same year Che Guevara left Tanzania that Walter Rodney, who strongly admired Che, first arrived in Dar es Salaam to teach at the University of Dar es Salaam. He taught there from 1966 to 1967. He then left Dar es Salaam and went to teach at his alma mater, the University of the West Indies, Mona campus, Kingston, Jamaica.

In October 1968, the Jamaican government banned Rodney from teaching at the university. He was declared *persona non grata* and returned to Tanzania to teach at the University of Dar es Salaam from 1969 to 1974 before going back to Guyana, his home country, in the same year. He was actively involved in intellectual debates in Dar es Salaam, and at Makerere University, Kampala, Uganda, where he famously debated renowned Kenyan academic, Professor Ali Mazrui, whose ideological orientation sharply differed from Rodney's. Mazrui was teaching at Makerere during that period. He was the head of the political science department and dean of the faculty of arts and social sciences.

Walter Rodney also founded and led a discussion group at the University of Dar es Salaam whose members included Yoweri Museveni who was a student at the university during that period and who later became president of Uganda. Museveni was also one of Rodney's students.

Before returning to Tanzania from Jamaica in 1969, Walter Rodney was actively involved with the masses when he taught at the University of the West Indies in Kingston. He was expelled from Jamaica because of his political and intellectual activism and went to teach at the University of Dar es Salaam in a country where his views and his role as an activist intellectual found acceptance under the leadership of President Julius Nyerere who was a superb intellectual himself and who was acknowledged as one even by some of his critics such as Professor Ali Mazrui.

In his book, *On Heroes and Uhuru-Worship: Essays on Independent Africa*, and in some of his other writings, Professor Mazrui described Nyerere as "the most original thinker" among all the leaders in Anglophone Africa, and Senegalese President Leopold Sedar Senghor in Francophone Africa.

Mazrui also described Nyerere as the most intellectual of the East African presidents, an attribute which enabled Walter Rodney to thrive in Tanzania as an intellectual activist. As he stated in his lecture at the University of Nairobi, "Towards Re-Africanizing African Universities: Who Killed Intellectualism in Post-Colonial Africa?," in September 2003:

"The most intellectual of East Africa's Heads of State at the time was Julius K. Nyerere of Tanzania – a true philosopher, president and original thinker."

And in an interview with *The Gambia Echo* in

February 2008, Professor Mazrui also stated:

"The fact that Nkrumah had a greater positive impact on me than has any other leader does not necessarily mean that I admire Nkrumah the most. Intellectually, I admired Julius K. Nyerere of Tanzania higher than most politicians anywhere in the world. Nyerere and I also met more often over the years from 1967 to 1997 approximately. I am also a great fan of Nelson Mandela. By ethical standards Mandela is greater than Nyerere; but by intellectual standards Nyerere is greater than Mandela."

Years before then, Professor Mazrui also stated the following:

"Julius Nyerere is the most enterprising of African political philosophers. He has philosophized extensively in both English and Kiswahili.

He has tried to tear down the language barriers between ancestral cultural philosophy and the new ideological tendency of the post-colonial era.

Nyerere is superbly eloquent in both English and Kiswahili. He has allowed the two languages to enrich each other as their ideas have passed through his intellect.

His concept of *ujamaa* as a basis of African socialism was itself a brilliant cross-cultural transition. *Ujamaa* traditionally implied *ethnic* solidarity. But Nyerere transformed it from a dangerous principle of ethnic nepotism into more than a mere equivalent of the European word 'socialism.'

In practice his socialist policies did not work – as much for global reasons as for domestic. But in intellectual terms Nyerere is a more original thinker than Kwame Nkrumah – and linguistically much more innovative.

Nkrumah tried to update Lenin – from Lenin's *Imperialism: The Highest Stage of Capitalism* to Nkrumah's *Neo-Colonialism: The Last Stage of*

Imperialism. Nyerere translated Shakespeare into Kiswahili instead – both *Julius Caesar* and *The Merchant of Venice*.

Nkrumah's exercise in Leninism was a less impressive cross-cultural achievement than Nyerere's translation of Shakespeare into an African language.

Yet both these African thinkers will remain among the towering figures of the twentieth century in politics and thought." – (Ali A. Mazrui in Ali. A. Mazrui, ed., *General History of Africa VIII: Africa Since 1935*, Berkeley, California, USA: University of California Press, 1993, p. 674; Ali A. Mazrui, *African Thought in Comparative Perspective*, Newcastle upon Tyne: Cambridge Scholars Publishing, 2014, p. 22).

Jonathan Power, a British conservative who described Nyerere as "independent Africa's greatest leader" but who was critical of his socialist policies and one-party rule, stated the following in his article, "Lament for Independent Africa's Greatest Leader":

"Tanzania in East Africa has long been one of the 25 poorest countries in the world. But there was a time when it was described, in terms of its political influence, as one of the top 25. It puched far abovoe its weight. That formidable achievement was the work of one man (Julius Nyerere), now lying close to death in a London hospital....

His extraordinary intelligence, verbal and literary originality...and apparent commitment to non-violence made him not just an icon in his own country but of a large part of the activist sixties' generation in the white world who, not all persuaded of the heroic virtues of Fidel Castro and Che Guevara, desperately looked for a more sympathetic role model.

Measured against most of his peers, Jomo Kenyatta of Kenya, Kwame Nkrumah of Ghana, Ahmed Sekou Toure of Guinea, he towered above them. On the intellectual plane only the rather remote president of Senegal, the great poet and author of Negritude, Leopold Senghor, came close to him.

Not only was Nyerere financially open, modest and honest, he was uncorrupted by fame and position. He remained, throughout his life, self-effacing and unpretentious. Above all, he inspired his own people to resist the tugs of tribalism and pull together as one people. To this day Tanzania remains one of the very few African countries that has not experienced serious tribal division....

He was to become the eminence grise of the southern African liberation movements in Angola, Zimbabwe, Namibia and South Africa extending a wide open embrace to their operations. For this his country paid a heavy price, both in material terms but also because of Nyerere's role as interlocutur with the West demanded enormous amounts of time and energy." – (Jonathan Power, "Lament for Independent Africa's Greatest Leader," TFF Jonathan Power Columns, London, 6 October 1999).

Professor Ali Mazrui also paid glowing tribute to Nyerere when Nyerere died in October 1999. As he stated in his article "Nyerere and I":

"He was one of the giants of the 20th century.... He did bestride this narrow world like an African colossus....

'The two top Swahili-speaking intellectuals of the second half of the 20th century are Julius Nyerere and Ali Mazrui.' That is how I was introduced to an Africanist audience in 1986 when I was on a lecture-tour of the United States to promote my television series: *The Africans: A Triple Heritage* (BBC-PBS). I regarded the tribute as one of the best compliments I had ever been paid. In reality, Mwalimu Nyerere was much more eloquent as a Swahili orator than I although Kiswahili is my mother tongue and not his.

In the month of Nyerere's death (14 October 1999), the

comparison between the Mwalimu and I took a sadder form. A number of organisations in South Africa had united to celebrate Africa's Human Rights Day on October 22. Long before he was admitted to hospital, they had invited him to be their high-profile banquet speaker.

When Nyerere was incapacitated with illness, and seemed to be terminally ill, the South Africans turned to Ali Mazrui as his replacement. I was again flattered to have been regarded as Nyerere's replacement. However, the notice was too short, and I was not able to accept the South African invitation....

Let me also refer to Walter Rodney. He was a Guyanese scholar who taught at the University of Dar es Salaam and became one of the most eloquent voices of the left on the campus in Tanzania. When Walter Rodney returned to Guyana, he was assassinated.

Chedi Jagan, on being elected president of Guyana, created a special chair in honour of Walter Rodney. Eventually I was offered the chair and became its first incumbent. My inaugural lecture was on the following topic: 'Comparative Leadership: Walter Rodney, Julius K. Nyerere and Martin Luther King Jr.'

After delivering the lecture, I subsequently met Nyerere one evening in Pennsylvania, USA. I gave him my Walter Rodney lecture. He read it overnight and commented on it the next morning at breakfast. He promised to send me a proper critique of my Rodney lecture on his return to Dar es Salaam. He never lived long enough to send me the critique....

Julius Nyerere was my Mwalimu too. It was a privilege to learn so much from so great a man." – (Ali A. Mazrui, "Nyerere and I," Africa Resource Center, October 1999; *Daily Nation*, Nairobi Kenya, 26 December 1999).

Professor Walter Rodney himself was a great admirer of Nyerere as a leader and as an intellectual even before he went to Tanzania to teach at the University of Dar es

Salaam.

After Rodney left Tanzania in 1974 and returned to Guyana, he continued to be actively involved with the workers at the grassroots level until he was assassinated in June 1980 by a government agent when Guyana was under the leadership of Prime Minister Forbes Burnham.

Most African intellectuals don't do that. They don't work with the masses at the grassroots level. And that severely limits their role as agents of dynamic and fundamental change in Africa.[44]

African writers like Godfrey Mwakikagile and other intellectuals are also severely compromised in their mission because most African leaders don't want to change. Therefore they don't listen to them—in many cases the entire state apparatus needs to be dismantled to bring about meaningful change.[45]

But, in spite of the limitations and the obstacles they face, many African writers and other intellectuals still play a very important role in articulating a clear vision for the future of Africa. And Godfrey Mwakikagile's writings definitely fit this category because of his analysis of the African condition and the solutions he proposes, although he is not a political activist like other African writers such as Ngũgĩ wa Thiong'o in neighbouring Kenya or Wole Soyinka in Nigeria.

But even they had to flee their homelands, at different times, for their own safety, in spite of the courage they had to contend with the political establishment in their home countries, and sought sanctuary overseas although that has not been the case with Godfrey Mwakikagile and many other Africans who once lived, have lived or continue to live in other countries or outside Africa for different reasons.

Writers like Godfrey Mwakikagile and other members of the African elite have a major role to play in the development of Africa.[46]

They do have an impact on constructive dialogue

involving national issues. But it is not the kind of impact that reverberates across the spectrum all the way down to the grassroots level precisely because they are not an integral part of the masses, and also because they are not actively involved with the masses to transform society.

So, while they generate ideas, they have not been able to effectively transmit those ideas to the masses without whose involvement fundamental change in Africa is impossible, except at the top, recycling the elite. And while they identify with the masses in terms of suffering and as fellow Africans, many of them - not all but many of them - have not and still don't make enough sacrifices in their quest for social and political transformation of African countries. And Godfrey Mwakikagile is fully aware of these shortcomings, and apparent contradictions, in the role played by the African elite. He's one himself.

Yet, he has not explicitly stated so in his writings concerning this problem of African intellectuals; a dilemma similar to the one faced by the black intelligentsia in the United States and which was addressed by Harold Cruse, an internationally renowned black American professor who taught at the University of Michigan for many years, in his monumental study, *The Crisis of The Negro Intellectual*. The book was first published in 1967 at the peak of the civil rights movement, five years before Godfrey Mwakikagile went to the United States for the first time as a student.

But that does not really explain why Godfrey Mwakikagile has not fully addressed the subject, the dilemma African intellectuals face in their quest for fundamental change, especially in his books – *The Modern African State: Quest for Transformation*, *Africa is in A Mess: What Went Wrong and What Should Done*, and *Africa After Independence: Realities of Nationhood* – which are almost exclusively devoted to such transformation in Africa in the post-colonial era.

African leaders have failed Africa. But African

intellectuals themselves have not done enough to help transform Africa into a better society.

Still, Godfrey Mwakikagile belongs to a group of African writers and the African elite who believe that the primary responsibility of transforming Africa lies in the hands of the Africans themselves, and not foreigners, and that acknowledgement of mistakes by African leaders is one of the first steps towards bringing about much-needed change in African countries; a position he forcefully articulates in his writings.

Political Science Professor Claude E. Welch of the State University of New York-Buffalo, in his review of one of Godfrey Mwakikagile's books – *Military Coups in West Africa Since The Sixties* – published in the *African Studies Review* (Vol. 45, No. 3, December 2002, p.114) – described the author as merciless in his condemnation of African tyrants.

The same book was also cited by James C. Owens of the University of Virginia in his article, "Government Failure in Sub-Saharan Africa: The International Community's Response," in the *Virginia Journal of International Law*, 2002. He used Godfrey Mwakikagile's book, *Military Coups in West Africa Since The Sixties*, among other works, to document the failure of leadership in many African countries in the post-colonial era.

And that is valid criticism of African leadership in post-colonial Africa by Godfrey Mwakikagile and others. Corrupt and despotic rulers don't deserve mercy. They don't deserve sympathy. They are not entitled to it. They have destroyed Africa.

Vision for an African Federal Government

Mwakikagile advocates for a closer union within Africa in the form of an African confederation or African federal government starting with economic integration, leading to an African common market, and eventually, resulting in a political union. Concretely, he proposed the following plan for a Union of African states:

"If the future of Africa lies in federation, that federation could even be a giant federation of numerous autonomous units which have replaced the modern African state in order to build, on a continental or sub-continental scale, a common market, establish a common currency, a common defense and maybe even pursue a common foreign policy under some kind of central authority – including collective leadership on rotational basis – which Africans think is best for them."

Mwakikagile identifies the type of government best suited for the African situation as a *democracy by consensus,* which, in his view, would allow all social, ethnic and regional factions to freely express themselves. Such a democracy should take the form of a government of national unity, inclusive of both the winners and the losers in the electoral process, and would entail a multiparty system approved by national referendum; it should also be based on extreme decentralization down to the lowest grassroots level to enable the masses, not just the leaders and the elite, to participate in formulating policies and making decisions which affect their lives. That is the only way it can be a people's government and federation that belongs to the masses and ordinary citizens instead of being a government and federation of only the elite and professional politicians. Let the people decide. He has elaborated on that in his other books, *Africa at the End of the Twentieth Century: What Lies Ahead* and *Restructuring The African State and Quest for Regional Integration: New Approaches.*

He also believes that in this democratic system the tenure of the president must be limited to one term (preferably five to six years), and the tenure of the members of the national legislatures to two three-year terms.

Controversy

In what is probably his most controversial book, *Africa is in A Mess: What Went Wrong and What Should Be Done*, Godfrey Mwakikagile strongly criticises most of the leaders of post-colonial Africa for tyranny and corruption, and for practising tribalism, a common theme in the works of many African writers and other people including well-known ones and many African scholars in and outside Africa. But his book stands out as one of the most blunt ever written about Africa's rotten leadership.

Unfortunately, because of its vitriolic condemnation of most African leaders during the post-colonial era, the book has been cited by some people, who obviously have not read it well if at all, as a clarion call for the re-colonisation of Africa (because things are so bad, colonial rule was better) although the author says exactly the opposite in his work.[47]

One of the people he has quoted in his book articulating a similar position is Moeletsi Mbeki, the younger brother of former South African President Thabo Mbeki and head of the South African Institute of International Affairs, who said in September 2004 that Africans were better off under colonial rule than they are today under African leadership in the post-colonial period.

Mbeki also said African leaders and bureaucrats were busy stealing money and keeping it in foreign countries while colonial rulers built and maintained the infrastructure and ran their African colonies efficiently. He was quoted by BBC in a report entitled "Africa 'Better

Colonial Times" published on 22 September 2004:

"The average African is worse off now than during the colonial era, the brother of South Africa's President Thabo Mbeki has said. Moeletsi Mbeki accused African elites of stealing money and keeping it abroad, while colonial rulers planted crops and built roads and cities. 'This is one of the depressing features of Africa, he said....

'The average African is poorer than during the age of colonialism. In the 1960s African elites/rulers, instead of focusing on development, took surplus for their own enormous entourages of civil servants without ploughing anything back into the country,' he said.

In July, a United Nations report said that Africa was the only continent where poverty had increased in the past 20 years.

Moeletsi Mbeki was addressing a meeting of the South African Institute of International Affairs, which he heads." ("Africa 'Better in Colonial Times,'" BBC, 22 September 2004).

Yet in spite of all that, Godfrey Mwakikagile unequivocally states in his book, *Africa is in A Mess*, that he does not support any attempt or scheme, by anybody, to recolonise Africa, but also bluntly states that African countries have lost their sovereignty to donor nations and multilateral institutions such as the World Bank and the International Monetary Fund (IMF) dominated by Western powers including those who once colonised Africa and are therefore virtual colonies already.

He also contends that African countries have really never been free in spite of the instruments of sovereignty they are supposed to have. He also warns about the dangers of the Second Scramble for Africa by the industrialised nations which are busy exploiting Africa's resources for their own benefit and contends that globalisation is in many ways a new form of imperialism.

Yet he has wrongly been portrayed, along with some prominent African and European scholars including Professor Ali Mazrui, Christoph Blocher, Mahmood Mamdani, Peter Niggli, and R. W. Johnson as someone who advocates the recolonisation of Africa.[48]

Godfrey Mwakikagile states exactly the opposite in his book *Africa is in A Mess*.

The premier of Western Cape province in South Africa, Helen Zille of the Democratic Alliance (DA), the main opposition party in the country, also cited Godfrey Mwakikagile in her speech in parliament on 28 March 2017 in defence of what she wrote about colonialism in her Tweets. She also cited Nelson Mandela, Professor Ali Mazrui, Nigerian author Chinua Achebe and former prime minister of India, Manmohan Singh, saying they articulated the same position she did on the impact of colonialism on the colonised.

The tweets caused a political firestorm in South Africa where her critics contended that she defended colonial rule – she clearly did not – and called for her resignation as premier of Western Cape, although she also had a lot of support across racial lines for what she said; probably more support than criticism as was demonstrated by the comments on social media including South African newspapers and Al Jazeera. Her Tweets were also covered by BBC. Her speech was also posted on Tanzania's leading social media outlet, Jamiiforums.

Helen Zille was a leading political activist during the apartheid era and campaigned against racial oppression and discrimination, incurring the wrath of the white minority regime. She was the first news reporter to report that South African leading political activist, Steve Biko, had been killed in police custody. According to a report by BBC, "Helen Zille of South Africa's Democratic Alliance - A Profile," 25 April 2014:

"Long before pursuing a career in politics, Ms Zille

was a journalist with the now-defunct liberal *Rand Daily Mail* newspaper. Her greatest scoop as a political reporter came in 1977 when she uncovered how Black Consciousness activist Steve Biko – Ms Ramphele's partner - had been tortured to death while in police custody."

And as she stated in her speech in the Western Cape parliament, which was reprinted in some South African newspapers including the *Daily Maverick* under the title "From the Inside: A debate of national importance" and on *Times Live*, "Why I raised the subject of colonialism on Twitter":

"There is no question that colonialism was driven by greed and oppressive intent. The question for countries today is whether they are able, like Singapore, to leverage aspects of the legacy of an oppressive past to their advantage....

In online conversations I wanted to raise this question in a South African context. As we all now know, this caused a volcanic political eruption. In the process many untruths and fabrications were disseminated including false allegations that I defended, justified or praised colonialism or apartheid; failure to distinguish between an evil system and the question of what can be re-purposed from its legacy; outright fabrications that I have been charged 'over racism'; no such charge exists.

If anyone genuinely (i.e., without animus or a private agenda) thought I was actually defending, justifying or praising colonialism, I apologised unreservedly and stressed that this was not so. Many prominent people have repeatedly made the same point as I, including Nelson Mandela, Chinua Achebe, Ali Mazrui, Godfrey Mwakikagile and even a current matric history text book.

So why the mass hysteria when I made exactly the same point?...

I am glad we are having this debate today because South Africa needs it. Debate requires rational argument. I have no intention of settling scores, only setting out facts.

This debate is about a series of tweets relating to lessons learnt from my recent visit to Singapore and Japan.

None of them defended, justified or praised colonialism or apartheid. I can factually say that few in this house have put as much on the line to fight apartheid as I did.

Of course, colonialism had a diabolical impact worldwide, including South Africa. That was the very premise of my tweets. Anyone who read them without a personal or political agenda would have understood that. If you say the consequences of something were not ONLY negative, you are saying most WERE negative.

But if there was anyone who genuinely thought I was praising, defending or justifying colonialism, I apologised unreservedly and stressed that this was not so. I do so again.

In South Africa, colonialism and apartheid subjugated and oppressed a majority, and benefitted a minority, on the basis of race. This is indeed indefensible, and I have never supported, justified, praised or promoted it, as my life story attests.

My visit to Japan and Singapore, one a coloniser, the other colonised, was eye-opening. It seemed to me that the colonised has overtaken the coloniser on the world stage, and I thought it worthwhile asking why.

Let's start with another question. If I were to state that a worldwide legacy of colonialism was causing on average 3,287 human deaths daily, people would justifiably be outraged if anyone suggested the benefits might outweigh the cost. I am talking about the motorcar. Today in South Africa, this colonial left-over is not only a means of transport but the ultimate status symbol.

Of course, you may argue that the intention of the motorcar was not conquest. It was convenience; People wanted cars.

Fair point.

So let me look at another example: if I said that zealots with a mission using colonialism's methods of conflict and conquest had killed countless millions of people to impose their ideas on others, you would be appalled if anyone suggested the consequences were not only negative.

Of course, I am talking about most of the world's dominant religions, Speaker.

To be consistent on the principle, if people believe the price was too high to acknowledge any advantage, then they mustn't drive a car, or visit most houses of religious worship.

According to modern definitions, there are only 10 countries in the world that have never been colonised. And Africans have not only been the victims of conquest and genocide. They have also been its perpetrators.

Some countries that were brutally colonised in living memory have been spectacularly successful; many that have been free for decades, have not; the same can be said about the handful of countries that have never been colonised. Whether or not a country was colonised is not a predictor of success in the 21st century. In Singapore, they have discussed for decades what factors lead to their economic transformation. I wanted my series of tweets to initiate that debate here.

Many much more famous people have already expressed themselves on the subject and reached the same conclusions I did.

I have written before about how our own former President Nelson Mandela repeatedly discussed this issue. Today I quote from a speech he gave at Magdalene College, Cambridge, on 2 May 2001:

'Britain,' he said, 'was the main colonial power in our history, with all of the attendant problems and consequences of such a relationship.

Much of our traditional systems and institutions still carry the scars of the distortions inflicted by colonial rule. At the same time, so much of what we have to build on in the competitive modern world is also the result of what we could gain from that interaction and engagement with Britain.

Our indigenous understanding of the rule of law, viz that not kings or chiefs but the institutions of law and democracy are supreme, was strengthened and enhanced by our reference to the British understanding of that concept.

If there were one single positive aspect that I had to identify from the history of colonial contact between our two countries, it would be that of the educational benefits our country derived from it.'

Time does not permit me to quote so many others. Nigerian Nobel laureate Chinua Achebe's later work, Ali Mazrui, Godfrey Mwakikagile, Manmohan Singh. I could go on and on.

But more than that, Speaker: we continue to teach exactly the same lesson to our own schoolchildren every day.

I have brought to this house today, Speaker, a history textbook, written in the 21st century, and used in our schools from 2004 to the present. Its lead author is prominent academic historian, Dr Maanda Mulaudzi. For 13 years, Speaker, many thousands of born-free South Africans have studied from this book, maybe even some honourable members here today.

It devotes a significant section to the devastating effects of colonialism in Africa and South Africa. And rightly so.

And then, it asks an interesting question:

'Did colonisation have any positive effects?'

And I quote:

'Although most historians emphasise the negative effects that colonisation had on Africa, some also show that it did have some positive effects. For example, the colonisation of East Africa at last put an end to the slave trade there, which had continued to exist long after it had come to an end in West Africa.

Colonisation also brought with it Western education, medicine and technology as well as language, cultural, and sporting links that have enabled Africa to interact with the rest of the world.

Part of the legacy of colonisation has been the development of Africa into a network of modern, independent states.' (*In Search of History*, sixth impression 2005, page 182).

Why have we tolerated this textbook in our schools for so long? Will we demand that Dr Mulaudzi be fired?

Of course not. So why the political tsunami over what I said?"

In his speech on the Motion for Ghana's Independence to the Gold Coast Legislative Assembly on 10 July 1953, Kwame Nkrumah stated:

"The strands of history have brought our two countries together. We have provided much material benefit to the British people, and they in turn have taught us many good things. We want to continue to learn from them the best they can give us and we hope that they will find in us qualities worthy of emulation." – (Kwame Nkrumah, in George Padmore, *Pan-Africanism or Communism? The Coming Struggle for Africa*, London: Dennis Dobson, 1956, p. 412).

Yet he was not accused of defending colonialism when he said the British had taught Africans many good things and Africans would continue to learn from them after the end of colonial rule. That is because he did not defend colonialism when he said that. It was a historical fact.

Nkrumah was an uncompromising foe of colonialism who also had fierce pride in his African heritage and identity. He once said: "I am not African because I was born in Africa but because Africa was born in me."

He would be the last person to be accused of being an apologist for colonial rule because of what he said in his speech to the Gold Coast Legislative Assembly about four years before he led his country to independence as the new nation of Ghana.

He blazed the trail for the African independence movement when he led his country to become the first in sub-Saharan Africa to emerge from colonial rule and is sometimes acknowledged as the father of African independence.

Yet that did not stop him from assessing the impact of colonial rule in its proper historical context even if some people thought he was glorifying the colonial rulers when he said the British had taught Africans many good things.

An article about Helen Zille in Wikipedia provides the following details about her and her critics:

"In March 2017, after a trip to Singapore and Japan..., Zille commented on Twitter that the legacy of colonialism was not all bad because it had left a legacy of infrastructure and institutions, which South Africa could build upon....

Following accusations that she was defending colonialism, Zille noted that her views had been misconstrued....

Among those who disagreed with her were other DA (Democratic Alliance) members, such as Mbali Ntuli, who stated that colonialism was 'only' negative, and who herself faces a disciplinary hearing in 2017 for 'liking' in December 2016 a Facebook comment that characterised Zille as racist; Phumzile van Damme, who stated that there was not 'a single aspect of [colonialism] that can be said to be positive or beneficial to Africans'; and party leader Mmusi Maimane, who stated 'Colonialism, like Apartheid, was a system of oppression and subjugation. It can never be justified', but also said in the aftermath that Zille was not a racist and that she had 'consistently fought oppression.'

DA MP Ghaleb Cachalia defended Zille as well-intentioned. He agreed with her that colonialism was not solely negative, and noted that many prominent intellectuals, including Chinua Achebe, Ali Mazrui, Godfrey Mwakikagile and Manmohan Singh, have expressed similar sentiments.

Kwame Nkrumah, who led the Gold Coast, renamed Ghana, to become the first country in sub-Saharan Africa to win independence, expressed similar sentiments in his speech on the Motion for Ghana's Independence to the Gold Coast Legislative Assembly on 10 July 1953....

Nkrumah was an anti-colonialist of immense stature and was never accused of being an apologist for colonial rule. He was never subjected to vitriolic condemnation the way Helen Zille was when she articulated the same position he did; nor was Nelson Mandela who expressed the same view. Chinua Achebe and other African scholars, Ali Mazrui and Godfrey Mwakikagile, expressed similar views without incurring the wrath of other Africans the way Helen Zille did.

Moeletsi Mbeki, the younger brother of former South African President Thabo Mbeki and head of the South African Institute of International Affairs, made similar remarks without causing a political firestorm when he said life for Africans was better during colonial times in terms of how governments discharged their responsibilities, according to a BBC report,'Africa 'better in colonial times", 22 September 2004....Yet his remarks did not draw public condemnation as an endorsement of colonial rule the way Zille's comments did.

The ANC and Economic Freedom Fighters (EFF) both demanded that Zille be removed from her position as Western Cape Premier.

As a result of her online comments, Zille was referred to the DA's federal legal commission for a disciplinary hearing on charges of bringing the party into disrepute and damaging the party. Following this news, Zille further defended herself by noting that Nelson Mandela had held the same opinion about colonialism." – (Helen Zille, Wikipedia, 17 September 2017).

Godfrey Mwakikagile has articulated the same position – Nkrumah, Helen Zille, Mandela, Ali Mazrui, Chinua Achebe and others have on the legacy of colonialism – in his book, *Africa is in A Mess* and in his other works including *Africa After Independence: Realities of Nationhood*.

In fact, the title of his book *Africa is in A Mess*, although not the sub-title, comes from President Julius Nyerere who said exactly the same words in 1985: "Africa is in a mess."

Godfrey Mwakikagile explicitly states that in his book, saying he got the title from Nyerere's statement and felt it was appropriate for his work, although the tone and content might be disturbing to some people. He is brutally frank about the continent's deplorable condition.

But the book echoes the sentiments of tens of millions of Africans across the continent who live in misery and those who are frustrated by lack of fundamental change in African leadership notorious for corruption and other vices including tribalism and tyranny as Godfrey Mwakikagile bluntly states in his work.

His fellow Africans who have reviewed the book amazon.com and elsewhere in different publications and on the Internet strongly support the author and share his concerns about Africa's plight and the misguided leadership the continent has had to endure for decades since independence.[49]

One African reviewer, Khadija Mona Kabba, a member of Sierra Leonean President Ahmed Tejan Kabba's family, also contacted the author to congratulate him for writing such an honest book, as she stated in her review of the book on amazon.com. And she provided an additional perspective, as an insider, that shed more light on Africa's predicament in her review of Godfrey Mwakikagile's book, *Africa is in A Mess*, and said she was going to work with him on a joint project about Africa.

And in the same book, *Africa is in A Mess*, Godfrey Mwakikagile is also highly critical of Western powers for ruthlessly exploiting Africa even today in collusion with many African leaders.

His harsh criticism of bad leadership on the African continent prompted Ghanaian columnist and political analyst Francis Kwarteng to put him in the same category with George Ayittey, a Ghanaian professor of economics at The American University, Washington, D.C., and author of *Africa Betrayed* and *Africa in Chaos*, among other books. As he stated in his article, "Great Lessons From Dr. Yaw Nyarko's Work," GhanaWeb, 8 January 2014:

"Prof. Ayittey's intellectual assault on Africa is, probably, no different from Godfrey Mwakikagile's."

Yet there is a clear distinction between the two African scholars, reinforced by Godfrey Mwakikagile's ideological orientation and strong Pan-Africanist views which separate him from Professor George Ayittey who does not share the philosophical conceptions, in a Pan-African context, of prominent Pan-Africanist leaders such as Nkrumah and Nyerere the way Mwakikagile does.

Academic reviews

Godfrey Mwakikagile's books have also been reviewed in a number of academic publications, including the highly prestigious academic journal, *African Studies Review*, by leading scholars in their fields.

They include *Military Coups in West Africa Since The Sixties* which was reviewed in that journal by Professor Claude E. Welch of the Department of Political Science at the State University of New York, Buffalo; and *Ethnic Politics in Kenya and Nigeria* reviewed by Nigerian Professor Khadijat K. Rashid of Gallaudet University, Washington, D.C.[50]

His other books have also been reviewed in the *African Studies Review* and in the *Journal of Contemporary African Studies*. They include *Nyerere and Africa: End of an Era* and *The Modern African State: Quest for Transformation* which were reviewed in the *African Studies Review*; and *Nyerere and Africa: End of an Era* which was also reviewed in the *Journal of Contemporary African Studies*.

Another one of his books, *Western Involvement in Nkrumah's Downfall*, was reviewed by Professor E. Ofori Bekoe in *Africa Today*, Vol. 62, no. 4, Summer 2016, an academic journal published by Indiana University Press.

See also an analysis of Godfrey Mwakikagile's book, *Ethnic Politics in Kenya and Nigeria*, in A. Simpson and B. Akintunde Oyetade, "Nigeria: Ethno-linguistic Competition in the Giant of Africa," published in *Language and National Identity in Africa*, Oxford University Press, 2007, pp. 172–198; and Godfrey Mwakikagile's *Military Coups in West Africa Since The Sixties* in P.J. McGowan, "Coups and Conflict in West Africa, 1955 - 2004: Part II, Empirical Findings," in *Armed Forces & Society*, Sage Publications, in 2006.

For more reviews of his books, see also *Expo Times*, Sierra Leone; *The Mirror*, Zimbabwe, and other publications including those featured on the Internet.[51]

He has also written about race relations in the United

States and relations between continental Africans and people of African descent in the diaspora. His titles in these areas include *Black Conservatives in The United States*; *Relations Between Africans and African Americans*; and *Relations Between Africans, African Americans and Afro-Caribbeans*.

Professor Kwame Essien of Gettysburg College, later Lehigh University, a Ghanaian, reviewed Godfrey Mwakikagile's book, *Relations Between Africans and African Americans: Misconceptions, Myths and Realities*, in *Souls: A Critical Journal of Black Politics, Culture, and Society, Volume 13, Issue 2, 2011*, an academic journal of Columbia University, New York, and described it as an "insightful and voluminous" work covering a wide range of subjects from a historical and contemporary perspective, addressing some of the most controversial issues in relations between the two. It is also one of the most important books on the subject of relations between Africans and African Americans.

The book has also been discussed on different forums on the Internet. It was also the subject of a radio talk show in the United States when it was first published. The talk show was on WCLM, Richmond, Virginia, and the book was discussed three different times in April and May 2006. It was the station's Book Club Choice and generated a lot of interest.

The show was broadcast nationwide and could be heard on the Internet worldwide. Listeners were invited to call in and participate in the discussion. The main guests who discussed the book were Professor Adisa A. Alkebulan, an African American, of San Diego State University, and Professor Albion Mends, a Ghanaian, of Central Missouri State University, also known as the University of Central Missouri. The host of the show said she received hundreds of emails from different parts of the United States and other countries on the subject of relations between Africans and African Americans when the book was being discussed.

Godfrey Mwakikagile's books are found in public and university libraries around the world and have been adopted for class use at many colleges and universities in the United States and other countries. Most college and university libraries in the United States have his books.

Selected publications

Titles by Godfrey Mwakikagile

- *Economic Development in Africa*, 1999
- *Africa and The West*, 2000
- *The Modern African State: Quest for Transformation*, 2001
- *Military Coups in West Africa Since The Sixties*, 2001
- *Ethnic Politics in Kenya and Nigeria*, 2001
- *Nyerere and Africa: End of an Era*, 2002
- *Africa is in A Mess: What Went Wrong and What Should Be Done*, 2004
- *Tanzania under Mwalimu Nyerere: Reflections on an African Statesman*, 2004
- *Black Conservatives: Are They Right or Wrong?*, 2004
- *Nyerere and Africa: End of an Era: Expanded Edition with Photos*, 2005
- *Relations Between Africans and African Americans: Misconceptions, Myths and Realities*, 2005
- *Life in Tanganyika in The Fifties: My Reflections and Narratives from The White Settler Community and Others*, 2006
- *African Countries: An Introduction*, 2006
- *Africa After Independence: Realities of Nationhood*, 2006
- *Life under Nyerere*, 2006
- *Black Conservatives in The United States*, 2006
- *Africa and America in The Sixties: A Decade That Changed The Nation and The Destiny of A Continent*,

2006
- *Relations Between Africans, African Americans and Afro-Caribbeans: Tensions, Indifference and Harmony*, 2007
- *Investment Opportunities and Private Sector Growth in Africa*, 2007
- *Kenya: Identity of A Nation*, 2007
- *South Africa in Contemporary Times*, 2008
- *South Africa and Its People*, 2008
- *African Immigrants in South Africa*, 2008
- *The Union of Tanganyika and Zanzibar: Product of The Cold War?*, 2008
- *Ethnicity and National Identity in Uganda: The Land and Its People*, 2009
- *My Life as an African: Autobiographical Writings*, 2009
- *Uganda: The Land and Its People*, 2009
- *Botswana Since Independence*, 2009
- *Congo in The Sixties*, 2009
- *A Profile of African Countries*, 2009
- *Africans and African Americans: Complex Relations - Prospects and Challenges*, 2009
- *Africa 1960 - 1970: Chronicle and Analysis*, 2009
- *Nyerere and Africa: End of an Era,* Fifth Edition, 2010
- *Zambia: Life in an African Country*, 2010
- *Belize and Its Identity: A Multicultural Perspective*, 2010
- *Ethnic Diversity and Integration in The Gambia: The Land, The People and The Culture*, 2010
- *Zambia: The Land and Its People*, 2010
- *Belize and Its People: Life in A Multicultural Society*, 2010
- *The Gambia and Its People: Ethnic Identities and Cultural Integration in Africa*, 2010
- *South Africa as a Multi-Ethnic Society*, 2010
- *Life in Kenya: The Land and The People, Modern and Traditional Ways*, 2010
- *Botswana: Profile of A Nation*, 2010
- *Uganda: Cultures and Customs and National Identity*, 2011
- *Burundi: The Hutu and The Tutsi: Cauldron of Conflict*

and Quest for Dynamic Compromise, 2012
- *Identity Politics and Ethnic Conflicts in Rwanda and Burundi: A Comparative Study*, 2012
- *The People of Uganda: A Social Perspective*, 2012
- *Uganda: A Nation in Transition: Post-colonial Analysis*, 2012
- *Obote to Museveni: Political Transformation in Uganda Since Independence*, 2012
- *Uganda Since The Seventies*, 2012
- *Civil Wars in Rwanda and Burundi: Conflict Resolution in Africa*, 2013
- *Peace and Stability in Rwanda and Burundi: The Road Not Taken*, 2013
- *Africa at the End of the Twentieth Century: What Lies Ahead*, 2013
- *Statecraft and Nation Building in Africa: A Post-colonial Study*, 2014
- *Africa in The Sixties*, 2014
- *Remembering The Sixties: A Look at Africa*, 2014
- *Restructuring The African State and Quest for Regional Integration: New Approaches*, 2014
- *Africa 1960 – 1970: Chronicle and Analysis*, Revised Edition, 2014
- *Post-colonial Africa: A General Study*, 2014
- *British Honduras to Belize: Transformation of a Nation*, 2014
- *Why Tanganyika united with Zanzibar to form Tanzania*, 2014
- *Congo in The Sixties*, Revised Edition, 2014
- *The People of Kenya and Uganda*, 2014
- *Namibia: Conquest to Independence: Formation of a Nation*, 2015
- *Western Involvement in Nkrumah's Downfall*, 2015
- *Africa: Dawn of a New Era*, 2015
- *The Union of Tanganyika and Zanzibar: Formation of Tanzania and its Challenges*, 2016
- *The People of Ghana: Ethnic Diversity and National*

Unity, 2017
Africa in Transition: Witness to Change, 2018
The African Liberation Struggle: Reflections, 2018
Life under British Colonial Rule: Recollections of an African and a British Administrator in Tanganyika and Southern Rhodesia, 2018

References

1. Godfrey Mwakikagile, *Life in Tanganyika in The Fifties*, ISBN 9789987160129, New Africa Press, Dar es Salaam, Tanzania, 2009, p. 19. See also, G. Mwakikagile, *My Life as an African: Autobiographical Writings*, ISBN 9789987160051, New Africa Press, Dar es Salaam, Tanzania, 2009, p. 21.

2. *Life in Tanganyika in The Fifties*, p. 20; *My Life as an African*, p. 367; *The London Review of Politics, Society, Literature, Art & Science, Volume 9*, 24 September 1864, p. 341: "To open up this central African plateau to a legitimate and profitable trade with England and to European colonization is the leading feature of Dr. Livingstone's scheme." See also Philemon A.K. Mushi, *History and Development of Education in Tanzania*, ISBN 9789976604948, Dar es Salaam University Press, Dar es Salaam, Tanzania, 2009, p. 64; Bella Walters, *Zambia in Pictures*, Lerner Publishing Group, September 2008, p. 77; Joseph F. Conley, *Drumbeats That Changed The World: A History of The Regions and Beyond Missionary Union and the West Indies Mission, 1873 – 1999*, ISBN 087808603-X, William Carey Library, Pasadena, California, 2000, p. 60; A. T. Dalfovo, et al.,eds., *The Foundations of Social Life: Ugandan Philosophical Studies*, ISBN 1565180070, The Council for Research in Values and Philosophy, Washington, D.C., 1992, p. 110.

3. *Life in Tanganyika in The Fifties*, p. 21-22. See also *My Life as an African*, p. 23; *Life in Tanganyika in The Fifties*,

p. 58.
4. *My Life as an African*, p. 87.
5. *Life in Tanganyika in The Fifties*, pp. 44, 77, 122; *My Life as an African*, pp. 47, 48, 78, 89, 92, 117, 119, 138, 154, 172, 175; *Tanzania under Mwalimu Nyerere: Reflections on an African Statesman*, ISBN 9780980253498, New Africa Press, Pretoria, South Africa, 2006, pp. 15 – 16.
6. "Newsman Leaves for America," *Daily News*, Dar es Salaam, Tanzania, 7 November 1972, p. 3; *Life in Tanganyika in The Fifties*, pp. 122 – 123; *My Life as an African*, p. 176.
7. *My Life as an African*, pp 89 – 90; "Newsman Leaves for America," *Daily News*, Dar es Salaam, Tanzania, 7 November 1972, p. 3; *Life in Tanganyika in The Fifties*, p. 56.
8. "Newsman Leaves for America," *Daily News*, Dar es Salaam, Tanzania, 7 November 1972, p. 3; *Life in Tanganyika in The Fifties*, p. 123; *My Life as an African*, p. 90.
9. Wayne State University Alumni, 1975; *My Life as an African*, pp. 76, 86, 120, 140, 164, 188, 190, 192, 246, 250, 266, 281; Godfrey Mwakikagile, *Nyerere and Africa: End of an Era*, ISBN 0980253411, Fifth Edition, New Africa Press, 2010, Pretoria, South Africa, pp. 86, 491, 509-511, 658, 664-665.
10. *My Life as an African*, pp. 306, 328; *Nyerere and Africa*, p. 649.
11. "Former CUNA (Credit Union National Association) chairman Ken Marin dies," *Credit Union Times*, Hoboken, New Jersey, January 8, 2008. See also *My Life as an African*, p. 306; *Nyerere and Africa*, p. 649, 664.
12. *My Life as an African*, p. 328. *Nyerere and Africa*, p. 664; "Former CUNA (Credit Union National Association) chairman Ken Marin dies," *Credit Union Times*, Hoboken, New Jersey, January 8, 2008;*Credit Union Times*, December 4, 2012.

13. Godfrey Mwakikagile, *Economic Development in Africa*, ISBN 978-1560727088, Nova Science Publishers, Inc. Huntington, New York, June 1999.

14. Godfrey Mwakikagile, *Nyerere and Africa: End of an Era*, Fifth Edition, ISBN 0980253411, New Africa Press, Pretoria, South Africa, 2010; Fumbuka Ng'wanakilala, "Three Years After Mwalimu Nyerere: Nyerere: True Pan-Africanist, Advocate of Unity," *Daily News*, Special Edition, Dar es Salaam, Tanzania, Monday, October 14, 2002, p. 19.

15. F. Ng'wanakilala, "Three Years After Mwalimu Nyerere: Nyerere: True Pan-Africanist, Advocate of Unity," *Daily News*, Special Edition, Dar es Salaam, Tanzania, Monday, October 14, 2002, p. 19; A.B. Assensoh, review of *Nyerere and Africa: End of an Era*, in *African Studies Review*, Journal of African Studies Association; Kofi Akosah-Sarpong, "Nyerere's Vision," in *West Africa*, 25 November - 1 December 2002, p. 41.

16. David Simon, ed., *Fifty Key Thinkers on Development: Routledge Key Guides*, Routledge, Taylor & Francis Group, London, New York, 2005.

17. amazon.com, Barnes & Noble and other book sellers.

18. Kofi Akosah-Sarpong, "Nyerere's Vision," in *West Africa*, 25 November - 1 December 2002, p. 41; K. Akosah-Sarpong, "Back to The Roots," in *West Africa*, 21–27 January 2002, p. 43.

19. F. Ng'wanakilala, "Nyerere: True pan-Africanist, advocate of unity," in "Three Years After Mwalimu Nyerere, " in the *Daily News*, Dar es Salaam, Tanzania, Monday, October 14, 2002, p. 19.

20. Godfrey Mwakikagile quoted by South African Deputy President Phumzile Mlambo-Ngcuka in "Address Delivered by the Deputy President, Ms. Phumzile Mlambo-Ngcuka at the Third Annual Julius Nyerere Memorial Lecture at the University of the Western Cape, South Africa." Issued by the Presidency through the Ministry of Foreign Affairs, Pretoria, South Africa, 6

September 2006.
21. Kofi Akosah-Sarpong, "Back to The Roots," in *West Africa*, 21–27 January 2002, p. 43.
22. Godfrey Mwakikagile, *Africa and The West*, ISBN 9781560728405, Huntington, New York, 2001, pp. 1–46, and 201-218.
23. Godfrey Mwakikagile, *Nyerere and Africa: End of an Era*, ISBN 0980253411, Fifth Edition, New Africa Press, 2010, Pretoria, South Africa. For Mwakikagile's Pan-Africanist views and perspectives, see also Professor Eric Edi of Temple University, in his paper, "Pan-West Africanism and Political Instability: Perspectives and Reflections," in which he cites Godfrey Mwakikagile's books, *Military Coups in West Africa Since The Sixties* and *The Modern African State: Quest for Transformation*.
24. Kwesi Johnson-Taylor, "Author, a shrewd intellectual in defence of liberation icons," book review of *Nyerere and Africa: End of an Era*, amazon.com, February 21, 2006.
25. *Nyerere and Africa: End of an Era*.
26. Godfrey Mwakikagile, *Africa After Independence: Realities of Nationhood*, ISBN 9789987160143, New Africa Press, Dar es Salaam, Tanzania, 2006, pp. 86, 91, 168-171; Godfrey Mwakikagile, *Africa 1960 - 1970: Chronicle and Analysis*, ISBN 9789987160075, New Africa Press, Dar es Salaam, Tanzania,2009, p. 510; Roger Pfister, *Apartheid South Africa and African States: From Pariah to Middle Power, 1961 – 1994*, ISBN 1850436258, International Library of African Studies 14, Tauris Academic Studies, an imprint of I.B. Tauris & Co. Ltd., London, New York, 2005, p. 40; Joseph Hanlon, *Beggar Your Neighbours: Apartheid Power in Southern Africa*, ISBN 0852553072, James Currey Ltd., London, UK, and Indiana University Press, Bloomington, Indiana, USA, 1986, p. 237; Mwesiga Baregu and Christopher Landsberg, eds., *From Cape to Congo: Southern Africa's Evolving Security Challenges*, ISBN 1588261026; ISBN

1588261271, Lynne Rienner Publishers, Inc., London, UK, and Boulder, Colorado, USA, 2003.

27. Jorge Castaneda, *Companero: The Life and Death of Che Guevara*, ISBN 9780679759409, Alfred A. Knopf, Inc., New York, 1998, p. 277; *Nyerere and Africa: End of an Era*, pp. 156, 158, 737.

28. In May 1963, the Organisation of African Unity (OAU) was founded in Addis Ababa, Ethiopia. The OAU chose Tanzania to be the headquarters of the African liberation movements under the auspices of the OAU Liberation Committee which was based in Tanzania's capital Dar es Salaam.

29. *Nyerere and Africa: End of an Era*, pp. 209, 223, 224, 252, 254, 255, 404, 487-489, 503.

30. *Life in Tanganyika in The Fifties*, pp. 92 – 93. See also *Nyerere and Africa: End of an Era*, pp. 10 – 12, 65, 314, 363, 375, 484.

31. *Nyerere and Africa: End of an Era*, pp. 224, 487-488; "Newsman Leaves for America," *Daily News*, Dar es Salaam, Tanzania, 7 November 1972, p. 3.

32. *Nyerere and Africa: End of an Era*, pp. 360, 486. See also, "Brendon Grimshaw Dead," *Seychelles Nation*, Victoria, Seychelles, Thursday, 7 July 2012; "Brendon Grimshaw is dead," *Daily News*, Dar es Salaam, Tanzania, 7 July 2012.

33. "President Mourns David Martin," *The Herald*, Harare, Zimbabwe, 22 August 2007; "David Martin (April 1936 - August 2007) – 40 years of service to African liberation," Southern African Research and Documentation Centre (SARDC), Harare, Zimbabwe.

34. "Martin - Man of Many Talents," *The Herald*, Harare, Zimbabwe, 24 August 2007.

35. "Martin Laid to Rest," *The Herald*, Harare, Zimbabwe, 25 August 2007.

36. *Nyerere and Africa: End of an Era*, pp. 486, 500, 569; *My Life as an African: Autobiographical Writings*, pp. 89, 156, 176, 375-376, 378.

37. *Nyerere and Africa: End of an Era*; Godfrey Mwakikagile, *Africa after Independence: Realities of Nationhood*, ISBN 9789987160143, New Africa Press, Dar es Salaam, Tanzania, 2006; *The Modern African State: Quest for Transformation*, ISBN 9781560729365, Nova Science Publishers, Inc., Huntington, New York, 2001; *Military Coups in West Africa Since The Sixties*, ISBN 9781560729457, Nova Science Publishers, Inc., Huntington, New York, 2001; *Africa is in A Mess: What Went Wrong and What Should Be Done*, ISBN 0980253470, New Africa Press, Dar es Salaam, Tanzania, 2006.

38. *Africa is in A Mess: What Went Wrong and What Should Be Done*, ISBN 0980253470, New Africa Press, Dar es Salaam, Tanzania, 2006; *Africa After Independence: Realities of Nationhood*, ISBN 9789987160143, New Africa Press, Dar es Salaam, Tanzania, 2006; *The Modern African State: Quest for Transformation*, ISBN 9781560729365, Nova Science Publishers, Inc., Huntington, New York, 2001;*Military Coups in West Africa Since the Sixties*, ISBN 9781560729457, Huntington, New York, 2001; *Military Coups in West Africa Since the Sixties*, ISBN 9781560729457, Huntington, New York, 2001. George B. N. Ayittey, *Africa Betrayed*, Palgrave Macmillan, New York, ISBN 9780312104009, 1993, p. 294.

39. Kwesi Johnson-Taylor, "Author, a shrewd intellectual in defence of liberation icons," in his review of Godfrey Mwakikagile's book, Nyerere and Africa: End of an Era, on amazon.com, February 21, 2006.

40. *Life in Tanganyika in The Fifties*, pp. 7 – 8.

41. *Life in Tanganyika in The Fifties*, pp. 31 – 32. See also *Africa is in A Mess* and *Africa and The West*.

42. Ronald Taylor-Lewis, in his review of Godfrey Mwakikagile, *The Modern African State: Quest for Transformation*, in *Mano Vision*, London, Issue 23, October 2001, pp. 34 – 35. See also Professor Catherine

S.M. Duggan, Department of Political Science, Stanford University, in her paper, "Do Different Coups Have Different Implications for Investment? Some Intuitions and A Test With A New Set of Data," in which she cites Godfrey Mwakikagile on fundamental changes in African countries. See also Godfrey Mwakikagile, cited in Christopher E. Miller, *A Glossary of Terms and Concepts in Peace and Conflict Studies*, p. 87; and in Gabi Hesselbein, Frederick Golooba-Mutebi, and James Putzel, "Economic and Political Foundations of State-Making in Africa: Understanding State Reconstruction," *Working Paper No. 3*, 2006.

43. *The Modern African State: Quest for Transformation*, op.cit.; Wole Soyinka, *The Open Sore of a Continent: A Personal Narrative of The Nigerian Crisis*, Oxford University Press, 1997; Chinua Achebe, *The Trouble with Nigeria*, Fourth Dimension Publishing Co., Enugu, Nigeria, 2000.

44. Henry Augustine Brown-Acquaye, *African Developments in Doldrums*, ArtHouse, 2008, p. 81; M.I.S. Gassama, in *West Africa*, March 21–27, 1994; G. B.N. Ayittey, *Africa Betrayed*, p. 295; Peter Anassi,*Corruption in Africa: The Kenyan Experience*, Trafford Publishing, Victoria, British Columbia, Canada, 2006, p. 209.

45. Ibid. See also Ismail Rashid, a Sierra Leonian in exile in Canada, in the *New African*, London, May 1992, p. 10; Rashid Ismail in G.B.N. Ayittey, *Africa Betrayed*, op.cit., p. 295. See also George B.N. Ayittey, *Africa in Chaos: A Comparative History*, Palgrave Macmillan, 1997; Wole Soyinka, in a speech at Wellesley College, Massachusetts, quoted by Zia Jaffrey, "The Writer in Exile as 'Opposition Diplomat,'" in the *International Herald Tribune*, May 2, 1997, p. 24; *Africa is in A Mess*, pp. 63 – 64; Peter Anassi, *Corruption in Africa: The Kenyan Experience*, p. 209; Peter Anyang' Nyong'o, in *Popular Struggles for Democracy in Africa* (London: Zed Books, 1987), pp. 14 – 25.

46. Ibid. Alfred A.R. Latigo, *The Best Options for Africa: 11 Political, Economic and Divine Principles*, Trafford Publishing, Victoria, BC, Canada, 2010, pp. 114 – 115; Senyo B-S.K. Adjibolosoo, *The Human Factor in Developing Africa*, Praeger Publishers, Westport, Connecticut, USA, 1995, p. 64; John Mukum Mbaku, *Institutions and Development in Africa*, Africa World Press, 2004. p. 236.

47. Dr. Kenday Samuel Kamara of Walden University in his abstract, "Considering the Enormity of Africa's Problems, is Re-Colonization an Option?" in which he cites Godfrey Mwakikagile's *Africa is in A Mess* and related works by other African leading academic authors including Professor Ali Mazrui, and Professor George Ayittey's *Africa in Chaos*. See Mwakikagile's book on the subject, *Africa is in A Mess: What Went Wrong and What Should Be Done*. See also Tunde Obadina, "The Myth of Neo-Colonialism," in *Africa Economic Analysis*, 2000; and Timothy Murithi, in his book, *The African Union: Pan-Africanism, Peacebuilding and Development*.

48. Professor Sabelo J. Ndlovu-Gatsheni, a Zimbambwean teaching international studies at Monash University, South Africa campus, in his abstract, "Gods of Development, Demons of Underdevelopment and Western Salvation: A Critique of Development Discourse as a Sequel to the CODESRIA and OSSREA International Conferences on Development in Africa," June 2006. Professor Ndlovu-Gatsheni advances the same argument Godfrey Mwakikagile does and cites Mwakikagile's work, *Africa is in A Mess*, to support his thesis. See also Floyd Shivambu, "Floyd's Perspectives: Societal Tribalism in South Africa," September 1, 2005, who cites Godfrey Mwakikagile's *Ethnic Politics in Kenya and Nigeria*, in his condemnation of tribalism in post-apartheid South Africa; Mary Elizabeth Flournoy of Agnes Scott College, in her paper, "Nigeria: Bounded by Ropes of Oil," citing Godfrey Mwakikagile's writings including *Ethnic Politics in Kenya*

and Nigeria; Professor Eric Edi of Temple University, in his paper, "Pan West Africanism and Political Instability: Perspectives and Reflections," in which he cites Godfrey Mwakikagile's books, *Military Coups in West Africa Since The Sixties* and *The Modern African State: Quest for Transformation*.

49. Professor Claude E. Welch, Jr., in *African Studies Review*, Vol. 45, No. 3, December 2002, pp. 124–125; and *Ethnic Politics in Kenya and Nigeria*, reviewed by Nigerian Professor Khadijat K. Rashid of Gallaudet University, Washington, D.C. In *African Studies Review*, Vol. 46, No. 2, September 2003, pp. 92 – 98).

50. Ibid.

51. Godfrey Mwakikagile in *Expo Times*, Freetown, Sierra Leone, and in *The Mirror*, Harare, Zimbabwe, 2002.

Africa in The Sixties

THE SIXTIES changed the destiny of the African continent and its people in many fundamental respects.

It was a period marked by the end of colonial rule as one country after another won independence. Coincidentally, it was during the same period that the civil rights movement in the United States gained momentum and reached its peak.

The victory of Africans in their struggle for independence in most countries on the African continent also inspired black Americans in their struggle for racial equality. They not only drew inspiration from this victory but felt proud because of the common African heritage they shared with their brethren on the continent.

At no other time in American history did such pride among blacks manifest itself as it did in the sixties. Even without the victories in Africa, African Americans, galvanised by the civil rights movement, found a renewed sense of purpose in their lives as a distinct group proud of their identity and forcefully proclaimed their pride as black people. As Eldridge Cleaver, the minister of information of the militant Black Panther Party, said:

"They have seized on their blackness and rallied around it."

Stokely Carmichael, who later changed his name to Kwame Ture after he moved to Africa and who probably was the most prominent advocate of Black Power, had this to say:

"It is time to stop being ashamed of being black – time to stop trying to be white. When you see your daughter playing in the fields, with her nappy hair, her wide nose and her thick lips, tell her she is beautiful. *Tell your daughter she is beautiful.*" – (Stokely Carmichael, *This Fabulous Century: 1960 – 1970,* New York: Time-Life Books, 1988, p. 32).

And as James Brown proudly said in one of his songs with the same title:

"I'm black and I'm proud."

It was a pride they shared with Africans in Africa. And it was a pride that went beyond slavery all the way back to Africa's ancient kingdoms and to the newly independent nations. It was also a pride that embraced African culture as a way of life and bond of unity between Africa and the African diaspora.

Many African Americans took African names and began to learn African languages, especially Kiswahili (popularly known as Swahili), which got its biggest boost in 1966 when Maulana Karenga, one of the most prominent black militants in the sixties, started the Kwanzaa festival based on Nguzo Saba (a Swahili term meaning Seven Principles) and encouraged other blacks to learn the language which transcends ethnic identity as a Pan-African language.

No single African ethnic group can claim Kiswahili as its own language like Yoruba, Zulu, Kikuyu or any of the other African languages. It evolved from many African languages and is older than modern English.

Not only did many black Americans – officially known as African Americans since 1988 – start to learn Kiswahili in the sixties; they adopted African life styles, wearing African clothes, eating African foods, dancing to African music and singing African songs. They also embraced African traditional beliefs and religions; and started buying, promoting and producing African art, and decorating their homes with African carvings, paintings and other items. And they proudly wore the Afro hair style and braids and called themselves Afro-Americans.

They were no longer Negroes. As Malcolm X said in one of his speeches: "Where is Negroland?" He emphatically stated that black people in the United States were Africans: "You are nothing but Africans" born in America.

All that racial pride and identification with their ancestral motherland strengthened their ties to Africa.

The manifestation of black pride and admiration of the African heritage among black Americans was also expressed in another very significant way: demand for the establishment of Black or Afro-American studies departments in colleges and universities across the United States.

It was in the sixties, especially from the mid-sixties, that Afro-American and African studies became an integral part of the curriculum in institutions of higher learning across the nation. And the introduction of these studies, after persistent demands by black students and faculty members including some of their white supporters, had a profound impact in transforming education in the United States and in projecting a positive image of black Americans and the continent of Africa and its people.

The transformation coincided with, and was partly reinforced by, the emergence of African countries from colonial rule as independent nations.

It was in the sixties when, for the first time, Africans emerged on the international scene not only as free people but as a people who spoke for themselves, and defined themselves, and were no longer defined and dominated by the imperial powers who had exploited them and muzzled them for so long when they were colonial subjects.

Before the sixties, no black African countries were represented in international forums as independent nations except Liberia and Ethiopia.

Tragically, the sixties were also years of conflict. It was a period that witnessed some of the most violent conflicts in the history of Africa, most notably in Congo and Nigeria, two black nations which had the potential to be the best hope for Black Africa because of their wealth and size.

The Nigerian civil war from 1967 – 1970 was the bloodiest conflict in modern African history up to that time and remained one for decades until it was surpassed by the death toll in the Sudanese civil war and by the carnage in the Great Lakes region of east-central Africa where the death toll from the late nineties to the early part of the twentieth-first century reached 5 million.

Almost 1 million people, mostly Tutsi, were massacred in Rwanda during the 1994 genocide. More than 200,000 Hutus were killed – in eastern Congo where they had sought refuge – in retaliatory violence at the hands of the the Tutsi-dominated Rwandan Patriotic Army (RPA) to avenge the massacre of the Tutsi by Hutu extremists during the genocide. And about 4 million people perished since August 1998 in the Democratic Republic of Congo, mostly in the eastern part of the country.

At least 300,000 people, mostly Hutu, were killed in the civil war in Burundi in 10 years since October 1993 when Melchior Ndadaye, the country's first democratically elected president in the country's history since independence in 1962, was assassinated by Tutsi soldiers after being in office only for about three months.

All these conflicts had their genesis in the turbulent sixties and in the flawed nature of the institutions of authority Africans inherited at independence which did not reflect or accommodate African realities.

The conflicts also had their origin in the way power was transferred to the new African rulers without taking into account conflicting ethno-regional interests and the asymmetrical relationship between different ethnic and regional groups in the allocation of power and distribution of resources; and in the way the colonial rulers themselves exacerbated tensions and helped ignite and fuel conflicts by transferring power to members of some ethnic groups and excluding others. For example, in Nigeria the Hausa-Fulani assumed power at the expense of the Yoruba, the Igbo and other ethnic groups.

That was one of the main causes of the Nigerian civil war – the structural imbalance of the Nigerian federation with power concentrated in the hands of northerners, especially the dominant Hausa-Fulani.

In Burundi the Tutsi, although a very small minority, assumed power at the expense of the Hutu who constitute the vast majority of the population in both Rwanda and Burundi, two states in the Great Lakes region which are almost a mirror image of each other in terms of ethnic composition and inequity of power between the two ethnic groups.

Besides all these conflicts, the sixties were also the years which witnessed the consolidation of the nation-states across the continent and the emergence of authoritarian rule which in many cases amounted to dictatorship and tyranny as many African leaders justified curtailment of freedom and suffocation of dissent on grounds of national unity; contending that if the people were allowed "too much freedom" – a relative term depending on the context in which it is used – and the right to form opposition parties, the countries would break up since those parties would most likely be formed on ethnic and regional basis, fueling ethno-regional rivalries leading to conflict. And there were cases in which this was a rational fear.

One of the most effective ways to avert such catastrophe, hence neutralise dissent, was by encouraging and sometimes forcing people to support or join the ruling party which usually was the party that led the struggle for independence. Thus, the emergence of authoritarian rule, therefore dictatorship – with the leaders invoking the spectre of national disintegration to mobilise the masses and rally support – led to the introduction and institutionalisation of one-party rule which became one of the most prominent features of the political landscape and national life in most countries across the continent for decades.

All that had its beginning in the sixties. But as African leaders assumed more power and worked hard to strengthen the one-party system, another phenomenon came to affect national life and profoundly changed the way African countries were governed. This new phenomenon was military coups which led to the introduction of military rule in many parts of the continent. It was the era of militocracy.

After the first military coup took place in Togo in January 1963, many others followed in different parts of the continent, including the one in Nigeria in January 1966, a seminal event which led to a series of catastrophes including the Nigerian civil war.

Another major coup took place in Ghana with the help of the CIA and led to the ouster of Dr. Kwame Nkrumah in February 1966.

In addition to military intervention in government, a phenomenal event in those years and in the following decades, there were other important events and developments which took place in the sixties and changed the course of African history. One of those events was the formation of the Organisation of African Unity (OAU) in

Addis Ababa, Ethiopia, in May 1963.

Although the OAU did not achieve many of its goals and became no more than a debating and social club for corrupt and despotic rulers – what Julius Nyerere called "a trade union of tyrants" – it did play a major role in supporting liberation movements on the continent, especially in southern Africa and in the Portuguese colony of Guinea-Bissau in West Africa. That was undoubtedly its biggest achievement; and the OAU will always be remembered for that.

Another major event in the sixties was the unilateral declaration of independence by the white minority regime in Rhodesia under the leadership of Ian Smith in November 1965, two-and-a-half years after the OAU was formed.

It was an act of ultimate defiance by the white settlers and a major challenge to the black African majority in that country and the rest of Africa.

African countries were too weak to bring down the Smith regime, although Nkrumah wanted to send troops to topple Smith; one of the reasons Akwasi Afrifa in his book *The Ghana Coup* – as well as other Ghanaian army officers – gave to explain why they overthrew Nkrumah. Afrifa also stated that Nkrumah wanted to send Ghanaian soldiers to fight in a country that was so far away and in a war they had nothing to do with; a sentiment that could be expressed only by someone who did not care about the freedom and wellbeing of fellow Africans and who did not see them as his brothers and sisters.

The unilateral declaration of independence by the white minorities in Rhodesia – which came to be known as UDI – only helped to intensify the liberation struggle on the continent and was one of the main factors that led to the adoption of guerrilla tactics which became the main feature of the liberation wars not only in Rhodesia but throughout southern Africa.

In fact, the freedom fighters had already started waging

guerrilla warfare in some of the colonies even before the white settlers in Rhodesia declared independence.

In Angola, the Popular Movement for the Liberation of Angola (MPLA) launched the armed struggle against the Portuguese colonial rulers in 1961.

In Portuguese Guinea in West Africa, the independence struggle began even earlier, in 1959.

And in Mozambique, another Portuguese colony, the Front for the Liberation of Mozambique (FRELIMO) started waging guerrilla warfare in 1964.

But the illegal seizure of power by the white settlers in Rhodesia gave impetus to all those struggles and in Rhodesia itself where guerrilla warfare by the nationalist forces of the Zimbabwe African People's Union (ZAPU) and the Zimbabwe African National Union (ZANU) started a few years later in 1974; coincidentally, in the same year Guinea-Bissau won independence after waging an armed struggle for 15 years against the Portuguese colonial forces, becoming the first Portuguese African colony to win independence after more than 500 years of colonial rule.

While the liberation struggle was an African phenomenon, and an African initiative as well an indigenous military expression of political aspirations, it also entailed foreign involvement and became very much a part of the Cold War between the East and the West as the two ideological camps competed for control of the Third World of which Africa was an integral part and one of the main theatres of conflict.

Thus, as the liberation wars started in earnest, the Cold War also came to Africa in the sixties with a fury. It had a profound effect on the course of events in different countries and influenced the course of African history. As independent nations, Africans were no longer mere spectators as they once were during colonial rule. They became active participants in the international arena sometimes in a way that offended big powers even though they played only a peripheral role because of their weakness.

But it was precisely their weakness that was also their strength as world powers in the East and the West competed for ideological allies among them, hoping to turn them into what Dr. Nkrumah described as "client states." As Nyerere warned: "We are not going to allow our friends to choose our enemies for us."

Some of them became client states of Western or Eastern powers, as Africa got caught between the two ideological camps contending for hegemonic control of the Third World.

It was not until after the collapse of the Soviet Union and her satellites in the late 1980s and early 1990s that African countries escaped the scourge of the Cold War, but only to come under domination of the industrial West, the driving force behind globalisation in the post-Cold War era in this unipolar world dominated by the United States.

All this has echoes from the sixties when the United States was also the world's undisputed industrial and economic giant enjoying enormous prosperity despite the challenge to its military might by the Soviet Union.

The United States also projected its image in Africa and other parts of the Third World in the sixties with the establishment of the Peace Corps. As John F. Kennedy stated in his inaugural address on 20 January 1960 when he again spoke about the need for the Peace Corps:

"To those people in the huts and villages of half the globe struggling to break the bonds of mass misery, we pledge our best efforts to help them help themselves, for whatever period is required – not because the communists may be doing it, not because we seek their votes, but because it is right. If a free society cannot help the many who are poor, it cannot save the few who are rich."

The Peace Corps became a reality less than two months

later when President Kennedy issued an executive order establishing it.

Under the peace Corps, many young American men and women, mostly fresh out of college, were sent to many parts of the Third World to help the people in developing countries meet their own needs. One of those areas was education, and many Peace Corp volunteers went to teach in African countries and elsewhere in the developing parts of the world.

When I was a teenager in Tanzania in the sixties, some of my teachers were American Peace Corps.

I remember very well what one of our first Peace Corp teachers said when he introduced himself to us in class at Mpuguso Middle School in Rungwe District in the Southern Highlands one morning in the early part of 1964 when I was in Standard Eight, what Americans call the eighth grade. He said: "My name is Leonard Levitt. I am a Jew from New York City."

I also remember that he followed the news very closely including the conflict in Congo and pronounced African names well. He had quite a way of saying "Antoine Gizenga," "Christophe Gbenye."

More than 40 years later, Gizenga, an enduring political phenomenon who also served as deputy prime minister of Congo under Lumumba, again emerged on the political scene when he ran for president in 2006. He won a respectable 13 per cent of the vote in the first round in August in a field of about 20 presidential candidates.

The leading contender, President Joseph Kabila won 45 per cent of the vote, and his most serious rival, Jean-Pierre Mbemba won 20 per cent. Nzanga Mobutu, the son of former president, Mobutu Sese Seko, won 5 per cent, and another candidate Oscar Kashala won 4 per cent.

Both Gizenga and Nzanga Mobutu later endorsed Kabila against Mbemba in order to keep the country united.

Probably many people in the 1960s did not think

Gizenga would still be on the political scene more than 40 years later. But there he was again, in 2006, as a serious contender for president. However, his political fortunes were greatest in the sixties when he was Lumumba's deputy and later one of the main leaders of the pro-Lumumbist nationalist forces fighting the Western-installed government in Leopoldville during those turbulent years.

The year 1964, one year after Leonard Levitt became our teacher, was one of the worst in Congo's history. I remember the Simba rebellion and the battle for Stanleyville very well and Levitt liked to talk a lot about that and other events in Congo.

Our country was still called Tanganyika. Just a few months later, it united with Zanzibar on 26 April the same year to form Tanzania. The new country was simply known as the United Republic of Tanganyika and Zanzibar until October 29th when it was renamed Tanzania.

I was 14 years old in 1964 at that boarding school for boys where Leonard Levitt taught us math and English, together with another Peace Corp teacher we simply called Mr. Wayne from Colorado. They arrived at our school in 1963.

Little did I know that I myself would end up in the United States only eight years after I left Mpuguso Middle School in 1964.

When Levitt returned to the United States in 1965, he wrote a book, *An African Season*, about his experiences at our school and in Tanganyika in general. He also wrote about his trips to Rhodesia and South Africa during those days.

His book was one of the most well-read about the experiences of American Peace Corps around the world. He later became a news reporter. He worked for *Newsday* in Long Island, New York. He was also a reporter for the *Detroit News* and the Associated Press and served as an editor of the *New York Post*. He also wrote for other newspapers and magazines, including *The New York Times*.

He became a successful author and wrote a number of non-fiction books besides *An African Season*.

After Mpuguso Middle School, I went to Songea Secondary School where I was also taught by some American Peace Corps. But most of our teachers were African and British.

The Peace Corps made a great contribution to education and in other fields not only in Africa but in other parts of the Third World. That is one of the most important legacies of the sixties and President Kennedy's policies.

It was a decade that changed the destiny of Africa. Africa has never been the same since then because of what happened in the sixties.

Probably more than anything else, the sixties was a decade of excitement as Africans celebrated the end of colonial rule in most countries across the continent.

The people had indeed regained their dignity and the right to rule themselves. And they were highly optimistic of the future, riding on a wave of excitement and high expectations for the fruits of independence although they did not see any tangible benefits right away.

The excitement did not last long. When they woke up the next day, things were the same. Little had changed. Even years later, nothing much had changed.

The only major change they witnessed, or were aware of, was the transfer of power from Europeans to Africans. And the most obvious difference was in the race and skin colour of the rulers. In most cases, white rulers relinquished power to blacks and in some cases to other non-whites as well. They were the people who led the struggle for independence and were an integral part of the indigenous elite that assumed the leadership of the newly independent countries.

But in terms of power and institutional arrangements, and the relationship between the leaders and the led, things remained almost the same as they were under colonial rule. The power structure instituted by the colonialists remained intact; only that this time it had new masters: the indigenous elite. To the new rulers, one of the most attractive features of the colonial power structure was centralisation or concentration of power in the hands of a few people at the centre under a unitary state.

In a very disturbing way, the departing colonial rulers found many comfortable allies among the indigenous elite who admired European ways of life and institutions far more than they did their own. Many of them were even ashamed of their African way of life.

It was clear where they got this influence. Almost all the new African leaders were educated in schools which had been established by the missionaries or by the colonial governments.

Like the colonial rulers, the missionaries themselves came from Western countries. The education they provided, as did the colonial authorities, was based on the Western intellectual tradition. And the values they instilled in their African students were also Western.

Many educated Africans became carbon copies of Europeans, although poor copies. They could never be the same as the original.

Yet, in spite of all that, they still and quite often tried to be more European than the Europeans themselves. Among them were dedicated "nationalists" who led the struggle for independence.

Some of the best examples of this abjectly servile and despicable imitation of the imperial masters were the leaders of Francophone Africa who after independence remained beholden to France and were unabashedly Francophile. There were only a few exceptions, notably Sekou Toure of Guinea and Modibo Keita of Mali.

Another good example of imperial devotion among African leaders was Dr. Hastings Kamuzu Banda of Malawi who was very British in his manners, values and attire. He even established a school in Malawi named after him, Kamuzu Academy, where he allowed only whites to teach in order to produce a generation of African Anglophiles who would follow in his steps to spread Western education and "civilization" in Malawi and, hopefully, in other African countries as well.

He also ended up being one of the most brutal dictators Africa has ever produced. Soon after independence, he turned against his colleagues such as Kanyama Chiume and Henry Chipembere, the very same people who had invited him to return to Nyasaland from Britain to lead the struggle for independence.

By the time he was invited, he had lived in the United States and Britain for 40 years, mostly in Britain. He also spent some time in Ghana after his friend Kwame Nkrumah became prime minister of that country, only to become a tyrant soon after he led Nyasaland to independence.

His former colleagues were forced to flee their homeland and sought refuge in neighbouring countries, especially Tanzania and Zambia.

Banda was just one among many African leaders who went on to establish authoritarian or despotic regimes soon after independence.

Therefore, while independence was supposed to have ushered in a new era of freedom, the people soon learned that the freedom they had been promised was more apparent than real. Yet, one of the most attractive slogans African leaders used in their campaign for independence was that they would establish democracy the people had been denied under colonial rule. But when independence came, it was an entirely different story.

In almost all African countries, the new African rulers had little respect for freedom. They justified curtailment of freedom on grounds of nation unity and security, contending that they could not afford the luxury of freedom which entails the establishment of opposition parties in pursuit of partisan interests to the detriment of national unity and wellbeing.

Therefore multiparty democracy was out of the question, not only for the sake of national unity but for other reasons as well: nation building and consolidation of independence could not be achieved without mass regimentation.

Freedom of speech was curtailed and opposition parties were strongly discouraged or banned, ushering in what became a new era of one-party rule and dictatorship on a continent where the people had been promised freedom during the struggle for independence.

There were only a few exceptions in countries such as Nigeria with its regionally entrenched parties dominated by the country's three main ethnic groups – the Hausa-Fulani in the north, the Yoruba in the southwest and the Igbo in the southeast; Botswana, Gambia, and Senegal; also Zambia but where the ruling party (UNIP – United National Independence Party) remained dominant at the expense of two opposition parties which, unfortunately, thrived on ethnoregional loyalties in the western and southern provinces.

Kenya is another example. The ruling party, KANU (Kenya African National Union), wanted a strong central government under a unitary state but virtually as an ethnocracy dominated by Kikuyu.

Soon after independence, Jomo Kenyatta and other KANU leaders neutralised KADU (Kenya African Democratic Unity), the opposition party in parliament which wanted a federal constitution under which there would be devolution of power to the regions to safeguard the interests of smaller ethnic groups which were afraid of being dominated by the country's main ones: the Kikuyu and the Luo.

The situation was the same in the other countries which had opposition parties. The parties were neutralised or simply withered soon after independence. In many cases, they were banned right away.

Even in countries such as Tanganyika where the opposition party, the African National Congress (ANC), was simply overwhelmed at the polls by the ruling party, TANU (Tanganyika African National Union), and thus died a natural death in the early sixties, laws were passed to give legal status to one-party rule leading to the establishment of the one-party system. Tanganyika became a *de jure* one-party state in 1965. That was only within five years after independence when it was a *de facto* one-party state like most were across the continent.

One-party states became the dominant feature of the African political landscape at the expense of freedom soon after independence. Tolerance of dissent was equated with weakness and abdication of responsibility by the leaders.

Some people still spoke up, but at their own risk. They knew that criticism of government was tantamount to treason. And the authorities left no doubt in any one's mind how they would respond. They were ruthless in their suppression of dissent.

Thus, paradoxically, the new era of freedom led to denial of freedom. If the new nations could not be built into cohesive units because the people had the freedom to disagree on how to build those nations, then freedom had to go.

Therefore in most African countries, freedom became the first casualty under the new African leaders who felt that it was only they who knew what was best for the people and not the people themselves. It was a betrayal of trust and the people became increasingly distrustful of their own leaders who not too long ago had led them to independence and promised them freedom.

But freedom was not the only casualty. Nation building, which the new leaders argued could not be achieved if opposition parties were allowed to exist and if criticism of government even by individuals was allowed as well, also suffered because the people were not given the opportunity to examine and challenge government decisions and policies.

Had they been allowed to do so, and had opposition parties which were truly national in character been allowed to exist, African countries would have had the chance to pursue alternative policies which in many cases would probably have been better than the policies pursued by the government.

But the people were not allowed to do that. They could not even freely discuss government policies and offer constructive criticism even among themselves without fear of being arrested. They were muzzled.

All that led to apathy with dire consequences for the new nations in terms of nation building and national development. For, without the people's involvement in decision making all the way down to the grassroots level, meaningful change including development is virtually impossible. It is the people themselves who know what is best for them. Yet the leaders turned a deaf ear to what they had to say except in a few cases. The result was formulation and implementation of wrong policies leading to stunted economic growth.

This was compounded by a lack of high-level manpower and necessary skills needed in many areas to implement development projects and provide efficient administration throughout the country.

At independence, almost all African countries lacked a critical mass of educated people and professionals as well as administrative skills not only in technical fields but in almost all the other areas as well. For example, when my home country, Tanganyika, won independence from Britain in December 1961, it had only two engineers and 12 doctors.

The situation was the same in most countries across the continent except in countries such as Ghana and Nigeria which had a significant number of educated people compared with other African countries.

Without trained workers and high skills, it was obvious the young African nations would not be able to develop. The only place they could turn to for help to meet their needs was foreign countries including their former colonial masters.

But foreign aid, which included financial and technical assistance, did not solve Africa's problems. In most cases, there were no trained people or well-established institutions to use aid effectively and on the right projects. In some cases, the wrong kind of aid was sought or provided, sadly demonstrated by rusted machinery which one could see in many countries on the continent. The equipment could not be used and was simply left out there to rust.

In other cases, when the equipment arrived, there were no skilled people to use it; or there were no spare parts or someone to fix it when it broke down. Sometimes it was the wrong kind of machinery that was sent; for example, snow ploughs, instead of tractors, sent to Guinea from the Soviet Union.

Also, because the new governments lacked accountability since there was no organised or formal opposition to act as a watchdog over those in power, mismanagement of resources including outright theft became a major problem in the early days of independence.

Ethnic loyalties was also a major factor in the allocation of power and resources and, most of the time, those in power usually came from one or only a handful of ethnic groups, thus accentuating ethnic cleavages in multiethnic societies. People sought power to help themselves and "their people," members of their own tribes, in many cases to the total exclusion of other ethnic groups.

Thus, while the leaders who led the struggle for independence also campaigned against tribalism and regionalism, contending that the colonial rulers had used divide-and-rule tactics by keeping tribes separate from each other and sometimes even turning some against others, they did exactly the same thing when they assumed power.

They used ethnic and regional loyalties to perpetuate themselves in power by keeping their opponents divided. They also outlawed opposition parties even if there were some prospects that some of those parties could have become truly national in character, transcending ethnic loyalties, regionalism and other forms of partisanship militating against national unity.

Yet, there were some leaders who made genuine attempts to achieve national unity on the basis of equality for all regardless of race, class, ethnicity, national origin or religious affiliation: Nkrumah, Nyerere, Sekou Toure, Obote, and Kaunda among others. They were also some of the most prominent Pan-Africanists and among the strongest advocates of African unity on a continental scale and on regional basis.

Nkrumah stood out alone among them as an opponent of regional federations or formation of any regional blocs which he described as "balkanization on a grand scale" and an obstacle to continental unification.

But in spite of genuine attempts by a number of African leaders to create a sense of national unity and identity among their citizens, ethnoregional loyalties remained strong and an intractable problem in most countries; it was also one of the most devastating. And it was only one among many problems the young nations faced in their early days of independence in spite of the optimism the leaders and the people had for the future free from colonial rule.

Therefore, in the initial euphoria after independence, even the leaders themselves did not realise the scope and magnitude of the task that lay ahead especially in terms of nation building. And in many cases, it is a task that has yet to be accomplished.

A large number of countries across the continent remain fractured along ethnic and regional lines. And most of them are still trapped in poverty more than 50 years after independence.

The struggle for power among different ethnic and regional groups, mainly because many of them have been excluded from the decision-making process and allocation of resources, is a perennial problem. And it has been one of the major causes of conflict on the continent since independence.

But that and other subjects are the focus of another study exclusively devoted to the post-colonial era since the sixties.

The sixties is indeed a decade to remember. For those of us who grew up in the sixties, and witnessed what happened in the sixties, we will always remember the sixties. Always.

Critical Phase of the Liberation Struggle

As the sixties were coming to an end, another phenomenal event was taking place on the continent. It was a movement. It gained momentum in the last years of the decade far more than it did in any other period. It was the liberation movement.

So, while the civil war was still going on Nigeria in 1969, another war was also going on in another part of Africa. It was a different kind of war but not quite in terms of fighting for freedom just as the Biafrans did.

The other war was in southern Africa where the freedom fighters were waging guerrilla warfare against the white minority regimes in one of the most protracted conflicts in the history of the continent since the advent of colonial rule. The end of the sixties turned out to be some of the most critical years in the conflict, especially in terms of escalation.

It was mainly horizontal escalation covering a war front of more than 2,000 miles stretching from the east cost of southern Africa to the western part of the continent in Portuguese Guinea, now Guinea-Bissau. But there was also vertical escalation in this conflict in terms of weaponry and intensity of warfare as the freedom fighters gained more experience and got more weapons from their allies especially countries in the Eastern bloc.

The Soviet Union, the People's Republic of China and other Eastern countries were willing to supply them with whatever weapons they needed to fight the white minority regimes which were being armed by the West. It was an ideological war between two camps – East versus West – but one of freedom and survival for Africans who accepted weapons from anyone who was willing to help them.

In 1968, President Kenneth Kaunda of Zambia warned the world of an impending war between Black Africa and White Africa along the banks of the Zambezi River which served as a demarcation line between the two in a large area of southern Africa.

Other African leaders had issued similar warnings around the same time and even before then in the case of President Julius Nyerere of Tanzania. One of Nyerere's warnings was in an article he wrote, "Rhodesia in the Context of Southern Africa," published in *Foreign Affairs* in April 1966 not long after the white minority regime in Rhodesia unilaterally declared independence on 11 November 1965.

By the late 1960s, especially by 1969, the danger these leaders had warned about had not only materialised but got worse. The fighting was already taking place in the form of guerrilla warfare; and it was escalating.

The confrontation was costing hundreds of lives and millions of pounds (£) or dollars every year; and the war was being fought not just along the Zambezi. As John Parker stated in "Expanding Guerilla Warfare":

"Africans are fighting white men along a 'front' that stretches more than 2,000 miles from the Atlantic to the Indian Ocean.

The battle has been going on for nearly seven years, ever since African nationalists took up arms against the Portuguese authorities in Angola; but in 1968, for the first time, a 'grand purpose' began to emerge and the issues started to crystallize into recognizable shape.

The 'battle areas' are fairly clearly defined....Active fighting is going on in Angola, Mozambique and Portuguese Guinea (in West Africa). Periodic battles are occurring along the northern border of Rhodesia. And on both ocean flanks persistent...attempts are being made to infiltrate armed insurgents into South and South-West Africa.

So far, the 'purified white tip' of Africa has not yet announced a defence treaty between South Africa, Rhodesia and the Portuguese territories in Africa. Such a treaty has been urged by Afrikaner and Portuguese strategists from time to time, and there is no doubt that the South African Government has gone a good part of the way to taking the practical steps necessary to turn the idea into reality.

The reason for this reluctance is certainly political. While South Africa can maintain reasonable relations with her African neighbours she will do so, and there is no doubt that a 'White Defence Pact' would immediately focus strongly adverse world attention onto a situation which South Africa prefers brushed under the carpet.

But the military to-ing and fro-ing between Pretoria, Salisbury, Lourenco Marques and Luanda is hard to keep secret; and only recently South Africa admitted for the first time that 300 'police' are now on regular duty in Rhodesia.

There can be no doubt that a co-ordinated policy exists for the defence of South Africa; even if it exists only in the minds of the South Africans who...are pragmatically willing to use the territories to the north of her as buffer zones toward off any form of attack – military, political, economic and ideological.

South Africa is currently spending £147m. a year on her defence forces and a further £42m.on the para-military police force. Her armaments are the most sophisticated on the continent of Africa, and her forces the most highly trained.

Portugal maintains 115,000 troops in Africa - 55,000 in Angola, 40,000 in Mozambique and 20,000 in Guinea-Bissau according to the Institute of Strategic Studies in London. Military expenditure in Portugal absorbs nearly half the entire budget.

In Rhodesia, expenditure has just increased by 10 per cent on both defence and police forces to a total of nearly £14m. a year – a very heavy strain on a budget already stretched tight by sanctions.

On the African side, details of expenditure are very hazy and deliberately obscured by the Organization of African Unity (OAU). But there is increasing evidence now that the African liberation effort, more and more co-ordinated by the African Liberation Committee of the OAU, is finding direction, purpose, training - and funds.

Already the Organization itself is voting an annual sum – undisclosed, but running into several millions of pounds – for the support of the various liberation movements. This figure is probably doubled by the communist sources of arms and training, both of which seem to be provided without cost to the guerilla movements which avail themselves freely of the services offered to them.

Although the struggle has been going on for some years in the Portuguese territories, it is the sudden sharpening up of guerilla activities in Rhodesia which has brought the future into focus during 1968. Because of Mr. Ian Smith's Unilateral Declaration of Independence (UDI) in 1965, the eyes and ears of the world press have been trained on Rhodesia, and in spite of every effort to minimize 'adverse' publicity, details of the battles fought along the Zambesi escarpment have managed to filter out.

The casualty figures speak for themselves. The Rhodesians claim to have killed 20 guerillas in 1966, 25 in 1967; and so far in 1968 more than 100 have been killed and nearly as many captured. Hardly a day passes without another African being tried and sentenced in Salisbury for subversion and terrorism.

With one lull for the rains in 1967 and another for the downpours in 1968, fighting has been going on sporadically for more than 18 months. It shows no sign of diminishing.

By early December (1968), news came from Rhodesia that the Salisbury authorities have word of up to 1,000 insurgents preparing to cross the Zambesi Valley from base camps in Zambia.

There is no knowing how correct the figures issued by the Rhodesians are; and indeed the rival African nationalist movements in Rhodesia – n the Zimbabwe African National Union (ZANU) and the Zimbabwe African People's Union (ZAPU) - have from time to time claimed to have killed scores of white Rhodesians and South Africans. In some cases, they have 'substantiated' their claims by quoting names and service numbers (of the soldiers killed).

At first, the little bands of men who tried to take on the trained professionals of the Rhodesian army and the paramilitary police forces were badly armed, ill-equipped and inexperienced.

Some were killed, some were captured and some escaped to Botswana. More still died of thirst and starvation in the bush, and others just gave themselves up.

But now things have changed. The rivals ZANU and ZAPU are reported to be considering coming together as the Zimbabwe African Liberation Army, financed by the African Liberation Committee of the OAU. The men who now cross the Zambesi by boat have had months - and sometimes years - of training in bush fighting, endurance and personal survival in China, Cuba, Russia, Algeria and even North Korea.

They are well-armed with weapons they know how to use, including the highly efficient Chinese Kalashinkov A.K. 47 automatic rifles. They carry 100-lb. packs of grenades, land mines, first aid kits and iron rations, and use short-wave radios to communicate with each other and their bases. Headquarters is in Dar es Salaam, where the former Rhodesian lawyer, Herber Chitepo - who was also Tanzania's first Solicitor-General - is responsible for much of the co-ordination work.

There are two main routes of entry across the Zambesi from the base camps (in Zambia)....

The first is to the West of Lake Kariba – in some cases using the smooth waters of the head of the lake itself. This is the route used by ZAPU, in conjunction with the African National Congress (ANC) men from South Africa. ZAPU and ANC have struck up a useful collaboration.

The second route, used mainly by ZANU forces, strikes across the river more than 250 miles to the east – below the Kariba Dam itself in the Chirundu area and as far east as Tete.

On the western front, the guerillas fan out west and south into the Wankie area – where Rhodesia's coal is mined - and towards the Kalahari and South West Africa. So intensive has been the fighting here that there are stories that the game has started to move from the Wankie National Park because it is continually disturbed by the firing and the air strikes.

On the Chirundu front, the guerillas form a potential threat to the rich farming areas of Karoi and Sinoia, while at the same time pointing a warning spearhead at Salisbury itself. Some of the farmers in the area have moved their families to Salisbury for safety....

The overall objective of the African nationalists is long term....Their achievements in the face of a well-armed, sophisticated army and police force should not be underestimated. As one senior ZANU official told me: 'For two years we have kept the Rhodesian army and police at full stretch. They've had to send for help to South Africa, and their losses are far higher that they admit (including helicopters shot down by the guerilla fighters).'

He agreed that guerilla losses had been heavy, and with Rhodesian claims that the security forces have captured large quantities of weapons and ammunition. 'There's plenty more where that came from,' he said. 'And it doesn't cost us anything.'" – (John Parker, *Africa Contemporary Record*, op. cit., .pp. 53, 55 – 56).

The guerrilla strategy employed by the freedom fighters enabled them to mingle with the local population in the rural areas without being detected by the Rhodesian security forces. They also won sympathy and support from the people in the villages, many of whom provided them with food and shelter and even joined the liberation movement. When some of the guerrilla fighters were killed by the members of the Rhodesian army and the para-military police, the freedom fighters got even more support from the local population.

Also, the freedom fighters showed not only courage but competence on the battlefield when they fought the enemy. Before then, they had been dismissed as inept and inexperienced; no more than a ragtag army of rebels incapable of engaging even raw recruits of the white Rhodesian army. But that was no longer the case by the end of the sixties. They had become a credible fighting force.

The backbone of their support was the local population, in addition to the help they were getting from their supporters and allies in other African countries such as Tanzania, Zambia, Uganda, Nigeria, Algeria, Ethiopia, Ghana, Egypt, Guinea, Congo-Brazzaville, and others elsewhere, especially in the Eastern bloc:

"The (ZANU) official claimed significant advances in winning support from the local population. The Rhodesians claim their security is among the best in the world, and they are adept and experienced in the use of informers in the kraals in the bush....

The Rhodesian Air Force has become expert in winkling out guerilla strongholds. Their obsolescent Hunters, Vampires and Canberras, plus the Alouette helicopters they have acquired from France, are ideally suited to this type of 'search and destroy' operation, although at least one Alouette has been shot down by the guerillas....

But 'even the loss of our men has helped us,' said the ZANU official. 'Relatives and friends soon get to know about someone being killed or captured. And their attitude changes from apathy to military overnight.'

As the bushcraft of the security forces has improved along with that of the invaders, so the white troops and police have reluctantly grown to respect the African guerillas for their fighting qualities. True, the pictures fed to the Press by the Rhodesian authorities show tough, Afrika-Korps-type whites interrogating at gunpoint a grovelling captive who, they say, has 'spilled the beans.'

But the image is not borne out by facts. When they have met the white troops on an equal footing the guerillas have stood their ground and fought bravely; and their spirit of defiance has shone through even in the courts where they have faced mandatory death sentences." – (Ibid., pp. 57, and 56).

By the late sixties, the battle lines had not only been drawn but sometimes shifted because of the intensity of warfare and the increasing ability of the freedom fighters to win battles and hold the territory they had captured or reclaimed from the whites.

In southern Africa, Mozambique and Angola provided the best examples of this kind of success by the guerrillas.

The freedom fighters in Zimbabwe were headed in the same direction; it would be only a matter of time before they also would claim major victories.

African journalists and others from elsewhere were some of the people who witnessed the major advances made by the freedom fighters in Mozambique and in Angola by the late sixties.

By 1969, large parts of Angola and Mozambique were liberated zones, protected and administered by the liberation movements in both countries – the MPLA (Popular Movement for the Liberation of Angola), and FRELIMO (Front for the Liberation of Mozambique).

The liberation wars had not yet been won by 1968 or 1969, and it would be a few more years before those countries would be finally free. But by the end of the sixties, there was no question that the guerrillas were not only competent fighters; they were also capable of defending the territories they had captured even when they were faced with massive attacks by the colonial forces which had been forced to depend on reinforcements from the mother country, Portugal, to continue fighting effectively.

Yet, even these reinforcements were not enough to neutralise let along dislodge the guerrilla fighters from the liberated zones. Even in Zimbabwe, the guerrillas were more than just a nuisance, in spite of the help the Rhodesian security forces got from apartheid South Africa, the country with the strongest army on the continent:

"The Zimbabwe freedom fighters have not yet matched the exploits of their brothers-in-arms in Mozambique and Angola, who claim effective control over large tracts of their respective countries in spite of the huge forces ranged against them. Recent accounts by journalists who have made hazardous and often uncomfortable trips into the territories confirm the claims.

One journalist, Basil Davidson, went with Frelimo (the

Mozambique Liberation Front) across the Ruvuma River which is technically the border between Tanzania and Mozambique and marched in daylight without any hindrance from Portuguese troops, to an astonishing congress in the bush. He wrote:

'At a place where newly-built huts stood within the cover of a wood, about 150 political and military leaders were assembled. They had come from all parts of a colony that is one-and-a-half times as big as France.

They began fighting the Portuguese in 1964. Since then they have cleared the Portuguese out of most of the rural country of Cabo Delgado and Niassa, a region not much smaller than the British isles. In this liberated zone they have set up schools and clinics and introduced their own economic system.

The congress I attended was the first since the fighting started. It was called to discuss how they could push farther to the south and extend the war. Present were the whole central committee of the Liberation Front, including its president 48-year-old Eduardo Mondhlane, once a Doctor of Sociology at Syracuse University, New York State....'

Just as astonishing is an account of a young Zambian journalist Tommy Chibaye, who only recently returned from six weeks spent with the African nationalist forces in Angola.

He attended a similar congress, headed by the poet, Dr. Agostinho Neto (he was a medical doctor by training), of the MPLA. He reports that the Africans claim considerable control in at least 10 of Angola's 15 provinces, with continuous fighting over the past seven years (since 1961):

'We passed many wrecked shops and villages razed to the ground by the Portuguese soldiers. Despite their having had their homes burned, the villagers had happily settled down in temporary camps under the supervision of the guerillas.

There they have established co-operative gardens to feed themselves and the guerilla forces, growing cassava, rice, tomatoes, onions and other vegetables.'

Not once in his six weeks, although he lived rough, did Tommy Chibaye go hungry. He found the MPLA providing schooling and instruction to Angolan Africans of all ages in a three-pronged drive. They set up a Post Command for military instruction, a Medical Assistance Service to look after health, particularly of war victims, and a Revolutionary Instruction Centre, where academic and political instruction is given.

From the centres, trained activists moved throughout the country raising more volunteers for the guerilla forces; in giving effect to a new policy for some time now all guerilla volunteers have been trained within Angola. Chibaye reports that the Portuguese have now taken to travelling everywhere in convoys of not less than 50 vehicles in the Moxico Province, covered by helicopters the whole time.

With the evidence at his fingertips, it is not surprising that Dr. Kaunda is apprehensive about the future. His country is already at the heart of the guerilla activity....

He has already complained that Zambian villages have been the subject of attack by Angolan Air Forces and commando raids; and he is worried by the constant threat the strong South African and Rhodesian Air Forces pose from the south." – (Ibid., pp. 57 – 58).

Although Zambia was highly vulnerable to attack from two fronts – the Angolan-Zambian and the Rhodesian-Zambian borders – the longest attack came from Angola because the war in that Portuguese colony had been going on for a number of years, thus for a longer period than the conflict in Rhodesia.

The liberation war in Angola started in 1961. In January of that year, there was a revolt on the cotton plantations in Malange. In February police stations and prisons in Luanda were attacked by the MPLA, and in March full-scale war broke out in the northern part of the country.

The MPLA was formed in December 1956 from a number of clandestine groups which first began to emerge in the capital, Luanda, in 1953. It underwent a series of initial crises between 1961 and 1965 when it began to consolidate itself under the leadership of Dr. Agostinho Neto.

Although a number of Angolan nationalist organisations were based in neighbouring countries and had offices elsewhere, one of them stood out. That was the MPLA. It was the best organised and most nationalist-oriented, transcending racial and ethnic differences.

When the MPLA was first formed and launched guerrilla attacks, it operated mainly from Congo-Brazzaville and Zambia. Shortly thereafter, it also had an office and training facilities in Tanzania which, in 1963, was chosen by the OAU as the headquarters of all the African liberation movements. The MPLA launched guerrilla operations in Cabinda, the Dembo region, and southeast Angola.

Another group was the UPA which was later renamed the FNLA (National Front for the Liberation of Angola). The UPA was formed in 1954 mainly with the support of the Bakongo and other ethnic groups in Northern Angola. It initially provided the main challenge to the Portuguese colonial rulers at the beginning of the insurrection in 1961 and was even recognised by the OAU. Under the leadership of Dr. Holden Roberto, the UPA and its affiliated groups formed the Government-in-Exile of Angola (GRAE) in 1963 with the blessings of the OAU but later lost its legitimacy.

In February 1968, OAU Secretary-General Diallo Telli

announced that a recommendation by the OAU Liberation Committee based in Dar es Salaam, Tanzania, had advised OAU member-states to re-examine and change their attitude towards GRAE. The report said investigations had shown that GRAE was more concerned with intrigue and personality conflicts than it was with the liberation struggle in Angola. GRAE, like its successor the FNLA under the same leadership of Roberto Holden, was also severely compromised by its ethnic base and bias.

Although other ethnic groups were involved in the formation of the FNLA as they were in GRAE's, the FNLA was still mainly Bakongo and was based in the Congo Democratic Republic (renamed Zaire); and its limited operations also had a strong ethnic base mainly in northern and northwestern Angola.

In 1964, another group emerged on the scene. It was UNITA (National Union for the Total Liberation of Angola) led by Dr. Jonas Savimbi. It was based in eastern Angola. UNITA was formed as a breakaway from UPA. Until 1967, UNITA had its headquarters in Lusaka, Zambia, but Savimbi was expelled by President Kaunda. After spending some time in Egypt and Guinea, Savimbi and his cadres moved to eastern Angola.

But like the UPA and later the FNLA, UNITA was also limited in its membership and support because of ethnicity. It drew its strongest support from the Ovimbundu in eastern and central Angola. Savimbi himself was a member of this ethnic group.

There were a number of smaller groups based mainly in the Congo Democratic Republic, pursuing a nationalist agenda in varying degrees. But none equalled the MPLA, the FNLA or UNITA – especially the MPLA – in stature, influence and support.

They were the largest Angolan nationalist organisations and even fought among themselves just before and after independence until the MPLA emerged victorious.

In fact, by the late sixties, the MPLA was the most

effective nationalist organisation in Angola and fought the most, enabling it to capture most of the territory before the decade came to an end.

Even the bastion of white minority rule on the continent, apartheid South Africa, was apprehensive about its future as it came under increasing threat from the African nationalist forces supported by the independent African countries and other allies. The leaders of the apartheid regime made it clear that they took the threat seriously. As South African Defence Minister P.W. Botha, who later became one of the last two presidents of apartheid South Africa, warned in November 1968:

"We must realise once and for all that we will live in danger for many years to come, and we must realise that not only our soldiers, but all our people must be prepared to fight for all we hold dear." – (P.W. Botha, *Africa Contemporary Record*, p. 287).

He was definitely addressing whites, not blacks and other non-whites. As victims of officially-sanctioned racial oppression and exploitation, apartheid was not something they cherished or were prepared to die for.

Also, apartheid was not supported by all whites in South Africa. There were those who were strongly opposed to all other forms of racial discrimination, oppression and exploitation. Some of them were members and leaders of the largest anti-apartheid organisation, the African National Congress (ANC).

Yet, the clock was ticking, and time was running out for the architects and supporters of that abominable institution. Racial confrontation and violence was looming on the horizon and prospects for guerrilla warfare in South Africa itself were real.

There was mounting concern among all sectors of the white society about the country's security which had never been expressed before since apartheid was instituted in

1948.

The sixties, especially the late sixties, were years of reckoning for many whites. Their future was uncertain. As one leading Afrikaner industrialist, Dr. Anton Rupert, told the Public Relations Institute in April 1968:

"Do we all realise that we nearly had a potential Cuba in our midst in Lesotho?

I have been studying the possible reply to this insidious revolutionary warfare for some years now. In the course of my travels I have spoken to many famous generals about this problem.

One of the most knowledgeable of them all warned me three years ago that within a decade at the utmost we would be faced with an Algerian-type situation in Southern Africa.

Yet, a revolutionary war is mainly a political action, for the final outcome depends on the support of the masses. It is, therefore, important to offer the masses hope for the future. It is essential that our own people of various races know that they are better off than the masses of Africa and Asia, and that this condition will improve even further.

It is essential that we work with our own and neighbouring peoples, who believe with us that terrorising, rioting and revolution is no way to improve the estate of man." – (Anton Rupert, ibid., p. 290).

The general who warned Dr. Rupert in 1965 that southern African would be faced with a situation similar to what happened in Algeria against the French in the fifties was right in his prediction. Within ten years, virtually the entire region of southern Africa was engulfed in guerrilla warfare.

All the countries bordering apartheid South Africa were at war. The freedom fighters were busy fighting the colonialist forces. Even Botswana, which became independent in 1966, was involved because it supported the freedom fighters. Its territory became a sanctuary for the freedom fighters including those from South Africa who posed an increasing threat to the apartheid regime.

In fact, within that ten-year period from 1965 to 1975, two colonies, Mozambique and Angola, won independence after 500 years of Portuguese colonial rule in the oldest colonies on the continent together with Portuguese Guinea in West Africa which won independence as Guinea-Bissau in 1974. And within five years after Mozambique and Angola became independent, Rhodesia also became independent. It won independence in April 1980 and was renamed Zimbabwe.

Only South Africa and South West Africa, both ruled by the same apartheid regime, remained under white minority rule.

The dagger was now pointed at the apartheid regime itself, the bastion of white supremacy on the African continent. In fact, the situation in South Africa had been deteriorating for quite some time.

The biggest change was caused by the regime itself as a repressive apparatus when it refused to negotiate with the African nationalist leaders and instead cracked down on them, forcing them to abandon non-violence and go underground and into exile to seek support for a violent confrontation with their oppressors. But the transformation came slowly. It was not until the Sharpeville massacre in March 1960 that African leaders and their supporters finally decided to embrace armed struggle as a complementary strategy in their quest for freedom and racial equality. They did not give up negotiations if the apartheid regime was willing to talk to them seriously

Still, it was a turning point in the liberation struggle and in the history of South Africa when leaders such as Nelson Mandela, Robert Mangaliso Sobukwe, Oliver Tambo and Walter Sisulu decided to use violence to end apartheid.

Their decision formally marked the end of an era; an

era of conciliatory politics dominated by stalwarts of the freedom struggle such as Chief Albert Luthuli who was the national chairman of the African National Congress (ANC) during that time. As Oliver Tambo stated in the official publication of the African National Congress in exile, *Sechaba*, in 1968:

"For a long time the ANC has been conducting militant struggle relying on non-violent methods. This became particularly intense during the '50s and gradually led to a stage at which the Movement switched over from nonviolence to the phase of armed struggle.

During 1967 the first armed clashes occurred between, on the one hand, the combined forces of the Smith and Vorster regimes, and on the other, the united guerillas of the ANC (African National Congress) and ZAPU (Zimbabwe African People's Union).

It can be said that for the ANC this is the beginning of the armed struggle for which we have been preparing since the early '60s.

It is a phase in which we can rightly claim to have scored victories by virtue of the superiority which our fighters demonstrated over the racist forces sending a wave of panic throughout the area dominated by the racist regimes and arousing the masses to a new revolutionary mood.

This is, however, only a small beginning in terms of the bitterness and magnitude of the revolution which is unfolding and which embraces the whole of Southern Africa. But it is an impressive and effective beginning providing what I consider a guarantee for the success of our armed struggle." – (Oliver Tambo, *Africa Contemporary Record*, ibid.).

The freedom fighters first surfaced on South Africa's horizon in 1966. That was when they entered South West Africa which was virtually an integral part – a province –

of South Africa.

It was also in the same year, in October 1966, that the United Nations passed a resolution to revoke South Africa's mandate over South West Africa (Namibia). But the apartheid regime remained defiant until 1988.

The guerrillas who entered South West Africa were members of the South West African People's Organisation (SWAPO) led by Sam Nujoma. They entered from Zambia and Botswana through Caprivi Strip which is a part of South West Africa.

Another guerrilla threat so close to South Africa came in 1967 from the guerrillas of the African National Congress (ANC) who forged links with the forces of the Zimbabwe African People's Union (ZAPU) in Rhodesia. They were right across the border and ready to enter South Africa itself.

The citadel of white power on the continent was not as secure as it seemed to be. As Colin Legum, writing during that period, stated:

"By 1968 the potential threat of escalating guerilla attacks became elevated to a top priority of the South African regime, in stark contrast to its claims in 1948 that its policies would increase the country's state of security.

Late in 1967 the Government appointed an expert in counter-insurgency, Lieutenant-General C.A. Fraser, as General Officer Commanding Joint Combat Forces.

This threat was taken a stage further on April 24 (1968) by Commandant-General S.A. Melville, former head of the South African Defence Force, who said that South Africa already had sufficient justification and provocation for retaliation against countries which 'harboured' and encouraged terrorists whose only intention was to penetrate South Africa or South West Africa.

He supported the Minister of Defence's (P.W.Botha's) view that such countries should receive a 'sudden hard knock.'" – (Colin Legum, ibid., p. 291).

It was clear which countries they had in mind: Tanzania and Zambia. They were the only countries, together with Botswana, which were independent during that period in the region and close to South Africa. They were also the only ones in the region which offered sanctuary to the people who fled from oppression and persecution under the apartheid regime and the colonial governments in Angola and Mozambique.

Unlike Botswana, Tanzania and Zambia also provided military training for the freedom fighters from South Africa, South West Africa, and Rhodesia; and in 1968, Tanzania also built a powerful radio transmitter for the external service of Radio Tanzania, Dar es Salaam (RTD), to help the freedom fighters broadcast their message worldwide.

The two countries were clearly seen as enemies of South Africa. The threat by South Africa's Defence Minister P.W. Botha that countries which harbour and support terrorists – freedom fighters in the lexicon of Africans – should receive a "sudden hard knock" was, without question, a pointed reference to Tanzania and Zambia.

I remember some of the first "sudden hard knocks" Tanzania received in the late sixties when I was a student at Songea Secondary School in Ruvuma Region in the southern part of the country. They came from the Portuguese forces across the border in Mozambique who were getting a lot of help from the South African Defence Force.

The apartheid regime also had agents who infiltrated Tanzania and Zambia. Many of them went to those countries ostensibly as political refugees or freedom fighters to undergo military training in guerrilla camps.

They were engaged in subversive activities and did everything they could to weaken and undermine the liberation movements. The infiltrators were also a strain on the Tanzanian and Zambian intelligence services which had to track them down. The liberation movements themselves did a very good job identifying those enemies.

All that was a part of a grand strategy by the apartheid regime to neutralise the freedom fighters.

Although the Portuguese may have been capable of penetrating our air space during those years, the aerial bombing of southern Tanzania, especially Mtwara Region, including the use of napalm was facilitated by the assistance the colonial forces got from South Africa, the United States and other Western allies of Portugal. In fact, some of the weapons including bombs which were used by the Portuguese in Mozambique came from the United States; so did the ones used in Angola.

The United States collaborated with the South African apartheid regime, the white minority government in Rhodesia and with the Portuguese authorities in Angola and Mozambique to contain and neutralise what they perceived to be a threat to white and Western interests in Africa.

They had a number of people, including some leaders in the liberation movements, on the CIA payroll. For example, in the case of Angola, the Americans felt that the leader of the FNLA, Dr. Holden Roberto, was someone they could easily buy and manipulate at will and went on to put him on the CIA payroll around 1961 or 1962. Yet, at the same time, they continued to support the colonial regime while pretending to be sympathetic towards the freedom fighters, especially Holden Roberto his colleagues in the FNLA.

Even some of Africa's eminent leaders, Jomo Kenyatta and Emperor Haile Selassie, were on the CIA payroll. The CIA also had a large staff in Nairobi including a number of Kenyan government officials besides Kenyatta himself who worked for the spy agency. In fact Nairobi has always been one of the CIA's main stations on the continent and the largest in East Africa..

In neighbouring Ethiopia, the United States had a large secret military base in the southern part of the country since the early sixties. But the largest CIA station in Africa was in Kinshasa when Mobutu was in power.

Therefore it was not just Holden Roberto and Joseph Mobutu (as Mobutu Sese Seko was then known before he changed his name) who were on the CIA payroll since the sixties among Africa's political figures. But they were among the most prominent together with Kenyatta and Haile Selassie.

In the following years after the early sixties when Dr. Holden Roberto was put on the CIA payroll, the United States provided weapons and ammunition, and counter-insurgency training the Portuguese colonial rulers needed to contain and if possible neutralise the nationalist forces of the MPLA and the FNLA.

The devastation caused by American-supplied weapons used by the Portuguese against Africans including innocent civilians – women and children being among the biggest victims – was extensive. As John Marcum, an American scholar who walked 800 miles through Angola and visited FNLA training camps in the early sixties, wrote:

"By January 1962 outside observers could watch Portuguese planes bomb and strafe African villages, visit the charred remains of towns like Mbanza M'Pangu and M'Pangala, and copy the data from 750-point napalm bomb casings from which the Portuguese had not removed the labels marked 'Property U.S. Air Force.'" – (John Marcum, quoted by William Blum, "Angola 1975 to 1980s: The Great Powers Poker Game," in W. Blum, *Killing Hope: U.S. Military and CIA Interventions since World War II* (London: Zed Books Ltd., 2003, p. 250).

It was the same case in Mozambique. American assistance to the colonial forces in Mozambique was just as critical in their war against the freedom fighters; so was the assistance they got from South Africa.

The apartheid regime was also using the Portuguese colonies of Angola and Mozambique and the British colony of Rhodesia as buffer zones. But that was not enough to insulate white South Africa from the nationalist forces; a concession made by the government itself:

"On April 25 (1968), the Deputy Minister of Police, Mr. S.L. Muller, informed parliament on information about fresh groups of 'terrorists' gathering in Zambia.

The Prime Minister said in the same debate that while conditions were quiet inside the Republic he did not want to give an assurance that everything would always be like that. The ANC, he added, was still active (although it had been outlawed in 1960); but the Pan-Africanist Congress (PAC) was finding things more difficult.

The figures he gave of ANC casualties in Rhodesia were: in 1967, 29 killed, 17 wounded and 34 fled to Botswana; in 1968, of 30 ANC guerillas who entered Rhodesia, 'a number' was killed. He added: 'The combating of terrorism had advanced as well as could be expected under the circumstances.'

On May 17, Mr. Vorster, speaking at the National Party's 'twenty years of Nationalist rule festival,' said that slowly but surely an army would be built up in certain Central African States for an eventual 'now or never' attack on South Africa." – (Colin Legum, *Africa Contemporary Record*, op. cit., p. 291).

He was not far from the truth, as the independent African countries and other allies especially in the Eastern bloc as well as the People's Republic of China, Cuba and North Korea, kept on supporting the freedom fighters, providing them with military assistance in their struggle against the apartheid regime.

Two days before Prime Minister Vorster issued that

warning, a summit meeting of 14 East and Central African leaders was held in Dar es Salaam, Tanzania, on 15 May 1968. The leaders promised full support to the freedom fighters in all the countries in southern Africa still under white minority rule.

A number of African countries, not just those in East and Central Africa, were ready to mobilise forces to help the freedom fighters.

The independent countries close to white-ruled southern Africa – not just South Africa – were the frontline states in the struggle against white minority rule in the region; the exception was Malawi under Dr. Hastings Kamuzu Banda who had cordial relations with the apartheid regime and the Portuguese colonial rulers in Mozambique. And they were ready to support the freedom fighters. When Nyerere was asked in interview on an American television programme ABC's "Issues and Answers" in July 1977 if he would commit troops to help the freedom fighters if they went to war against apartheid South Africa, he answered: "Yes, I will commit troops. We would rather hang together than hang separately."

The apartheid regime introduced several measures in the late sixties to counter the "terrorist" threat, as the freedom fighters continued to mobilise forces in their struggle against white minority rule. On 2 June 1968, the South African minister of justice, P.C. Pelser, introduced the Terrorism Bill and announced that there was every reason to believe that South Africa had not "seen the last of the terrorists."

The bill sought extensive powers to detain indefinitely anybody suspected of being engaged in subversive activities or of withholding information about terrorist threats or activities. It also demanded the death penalty for the crime of terrorism. As he stated in parliament in Cape Town:

"The Bill should be judged against the whole

background of internal onslaughts on the legal order since 1960.

The terrorists who are now returning are largely the harvest of the subversive activities of the ANC, PAC, SWAPO and the Communists.

It is largely their trained, so-called freedom fighters who are now returning." – (P.C. Pelser, *Africa Contemporary Record*, p. 292).

Nothing the apartheid regime did was able to deter the freedom fighters from pursuing their goal.

On 11 June 1968, the Portuguese colonial authorities in Mozambique announced that they had foiled an attempt by the Pan-Africanist Congress (PAC) to establish a new route to South Africa through that country. They claimed that four guerrillas were killed in a fight with the Portuguese forces near Vila Pery, 50 miles from the border with Rhodesia.

In July the same year, SWAPO claimed to have inflicted heavy damage on strategic places maintained by the apartheid regime in South West Africa. They included the airfield at Katima Mulilo in Caprivi Strip along the Botswana-South West African (Namibian) border. The guerrilla fighters claimed the South Africans lost some lives in the fiery exchange. At first, the South African authorities denied reports of any guerrilla activities in Caprivi Strip but later confirmed the existence of considerable activity by the freedom fighters in that area.

It was obvious that the threat to the apartheid regime was real; a point underscored by the Commandant-General of the South African Defence Force, General Hiemstra, on 8 August 1968 when he was answering a question about increasing guerrilla activity – whether or not he thought guerrilla fighting in neighbouring Rhodesia could one day develop into a full-scale war as in Vietnam. He said:

"Most certainly yes. This is the technique the

communists used in Vietnam. This technique involves the gradual building up of terrorism until it eventually becomes conventional warfare." – (Hiemstra, *Africa Contemporary Record*, Ibid.).

Towards the end of the year in October 1968, South Africa's Commissioner of Police, Major-General J.P. Gouws, also admitted that there was increasing guerrilla activity in South West Africa in Caprivi Strip by the SWAPO freedom fighters whom he also called "terrorists," a term in the lexicon of the white minority rulers used to tarnish the image of the freedom fighters.

He said after the guerrillas fighters failed to penetrate by using force, they were now concentrating on slipping into South West Africa to recruit people from the local population for the insurgency. He knew the freedom fighters had adopted the right strategy since local support was critical to the success of any guerrilla warfare; and that worried the apartheid regime.

He went on to say that "terrorists" were moving from village to village in an attempt to recruit chiefs who would in turn mobilise local support for the liberation struggle, and conceded that they had had some success in this effort. He said five chiefs had recently been arrested in Caprivi Strip for supporting the guerrillas. Other people were also arrested in connection with the campaign to help SWAPO and recruit fighters. Although he said some arrests had been made, he still admitted that it was impossible to fully secure a border stretching 5,000 miles to protect South Africa:

"Some terrorists may have avoided security forces and be working much further inland. We have much more than 50,000 illegal immigrants in this country, and some of them could well be Communist-trained guerillas." – (J.P. Gouws, ibid., p. 293).

The Minister of the Interior, Mr. L. Muller, denied SWAPO reports that 63 Africans were "publicly slaughtered" after attacks in Caprivi Strip on 13 October 1968. However, South African intelligence officers admitted that there were signs of fresh attacks from "across the Rhodesian frontier soon." They claimed that the guerrilla offensive would be launched by 2,000 Africans who had left South Africa "under the pretence of studying abroad."

There was every indication that the end of the sixties, especially 1968 and 1969, was a time of intensified guerrilla activity in southern Africa, with the apartheid regime being one of the primary targets, unlike before when the South African authorities felt more secure.

The warning of an impending attack by the African nationalist forces in the form of a guerrilla insurgency was also issued by the Minister of Police and Interior, Mr. Muller, on October 13th who said, far from having receded, the danger of guerrilla attacks had become much more serious. As he put it:

"In actual fact the forces against South Africa are now stronger than ever before." – (L. Muller, *Africa Contemporary Record*, p. 293).

He also admitted that in some of the areas where guerrillas had been successful in getting support, not all Africans were well-disposed towards whites. That is something that should not have been difficult for him to understand. But, instead, he attributed that to illiteracy and poverty; implying that had those Africans not been poor, and had they been educated, they would not have been hostile towards or suspicious of whites – as if they did not suffer from racial oppression under apartheid.

The deteriorating situation in southern Africa also came into sharp focus when the apartheid regime sent its forces into Rhodesia to help neutralise guerrilla fighters who – as white rulers and their supporters felt – threatened the entire region and the well-being of white minorities. In November 1968, the United Nations discussed a resolution condemning the presence of South Africa's military forces in Rhodesia.

The UN also said South Africa's military involvement in Rhodesia aggravated the situation and constituted a threat to the sovereignty and territorial integrity of the independent African states. The South African delegate to the UN, Carl von Hirschberg, was defiant and had this to say in response to that:

"The South African police are in Rhodesia exclusively for the purpose of dealing with terrorists en route to South Africa for the purpose of committing acts of terrorism and subversion, and they will remain there for as long as this threat to the security of South Africa persists, for it is the duty of the South African government, no less than any other government, to resist with all means at their disposal, any and every attempt to endanger the safety and security of South Africa and her peoples.

Thus, those States which object to the presence of South African Police in Rhodesia and who, at the same time, train, equip or harbour these terrorists, need only to stop these unjustified and illegitimate practices and the need to have South African Police in Rhodesia will fall away." - (Carl von Hirschberg, ibid., pp. 293 - 294).

By the end of the sixties, the apartheid regime had more than enough warning about the perils it faced once sucked into guerrilla warfare, fighting virtually an invisible enemy hardly distinguishable from the local population. It was an outcome the white minority government and its supporters wanted to avoid, but chose the wrong approach, confrontation, when they refused to make meaningful concessions to the black African majority and other non-whites.

Yet, in spite of such defiance, the white rulers of South Africa conceded that they were facing a new enemy they had never fought before in terms of strategy and tactics.

At the end of August 1968, in the same month Defence Minister Pieter W. Botha made a threat against Tanzania and Zambia that the two countries should received a "sudden hard knock" for harbouring and training "terrorists," the South African General Officer Commanding Joint Combat Forces, General C.A. Fraser, gave a military appraisal of the nature of the guerrilla threat to South Africa at a symposium held in Potchefstrom and, in an ominous warning, had this to say:

"For 50 years, the world has seen widespread and virtually continuous political revolution. Probably more governments have come into being, passed through drastic change, or ceased to exist, than in any comparable period of history.

These changes in regime have been brought about, in the main, by a new kind of warfare, now widely termed revolutionary warfare. It has crystalised rapidly since the end of the Second World War. It differs fundamentally from the wars of the past in that victory does not come from the clash of two armies on a field of battle. Revolutionary wars are conducted as a carefully co-ordinated system of actions, political, economic, administrative, psychological, police and military.

The insurgent will use any means to overthrow the established regime, including ruthless force. His primary task is to gain support of the population. Without the consent and active aid of the people, the guerilla would be merely a bandit and could not long survive.

From the point of view of the insurgents, perhaps the basic ingredients of successful revolution are a popular cause, trained, efficient and dedicated leadership, support of the population, outside support and a firm base or sanctuary. It has been said that a revolutionary war is 20 per cent military action and 80 per cent political. The failure to recognise this is bound to lead ultimately to failure in countering and defeating the insurgency.

The basic tenet of the exercise of political power is that there is always an active minority for the cause, an uncommitted majority and an active minority against the cause. For ultimate victory it is necessary to gain support of the neutral majority. The objective for both sides in a revolutionary war is thus the population itself.

The operations designed to win the population, either by the insurgents or by the government, are essentially of a political nature. It is important to realise that adequate support for a guerilla movement does not necessarily mean the enthusiastic, voluntary backing of a large majority of the population. The active participation of a small number of people, or the general apathy of the majority, often provide all the popular support necessary to make a successful revolution.

The support of the population for a government is gained through the favourable minority. Every operation, whether in the military field or in the political, social economic or psychological fields, must be geared to this end.

Staying power is an attribute that is vital for eventual government success. Operations in Malaya took 12 years, and in Algeria eight years to be concluded. Mao-Tse-tung took 35 years to get China. The communists think they have a monopoly on patience.

We made a study of all this. We know what to do. May I assure that we will win." – (C.A. Fraser, ibid., p. 294).

History proved him wrong, although it was not until 26 years later – a time span almost equal to the number of years Nelson Mandela spent in prison – that the walls of that abominable institution, the edifice of apartheid, finally came tumbling down when the first multiracial democratic elections in the nation's history were held in 1994 and

Mandela was elected president.

But even as far back as 1968 and 1969, as the sixties were coming to an end, it was clear to some people that mounting opposition to apartheid would finally prevail over racial oppression, ushering in a dawn of a new era when everybody would be free. The apartheid regime showed every sign of being under siege or felt that it was in imminent danger of attack, as it dramatically increased defence expenditure. The government was preoccupied with security more than anything else.

Procurement of weapons for armed forces went up; expenditure on police forces and on the intelligence services also went up as never before. For example, expenditure on secret services was increased by R640,000 to R2,342,000 for 1968/69. Fortunately for the regime, the rand was still very strong during those critical years.

South Africa also improved its capability to manufacture its own weapons to complement purchases from other countries such as Britain, France, the United States and Germany which were the biggest sources of arms for the apartheid regime; and in October 1968, the apartheid regime established its first missile base on the east coast of Natal Province. The first guided missile was launched from the site in December the same year.

The country was already building its own submarines, aircraft, and a number of war ships; making rifles, mortars, ammunition, grenades, bombs including napalm, mines and other weapons.

Its armaments industry was under the management of the Armaments Development and Production Corporation (ARMSCOR) whose first chairman was Professor H.J. Samuels. But all those weapons were useless against guerrilla warfare and the strategy employed by the liberation movements to make the country ungovernable until apartheid was abolished.

Compounding the problem was the deteriorating situation in Rhodesia, a more vulnerable outpost of white tyranny over blacks where the freedom fighters from South Africa and Rhodesia itself coordinated their activities.

On 30 July – 31 July 1967, the Luthuli Combat Detachment – named in honour of Chief Albert Luthuli who was the president of the ANC – comprising ZAPU and ANC guerrillas, crossed the Zambezi River into Rhodesia. That was the beginning of guerrilla warfare in Rhodesia, South Africa's neighbour. And on 18 August 1967, ANC and ZAPU formally announced that they had formed a military alliance.

They clashed with Rhodesian and South African forces in Wankie and Sipolilo in Rhodesia and demonstrated their fighting ability in a way their enemies never expected. The conflict lasted until late 1968, sending a strong warning to the white minority government in Rhodesia and the apartheid regime in South Africa that guerrilla warfare would soon engulf the region.

The apartheid regime was fully aware of the danger although it claimed it would be able to contain it. But to show that it took the danger seriously, it increased its military preparedness and passed a law to achieve that goal.

On 4 August 1967, the Defence Amendment Act came into force. Every young white male would be liable for military service.

The amendments were also intended to make all medically fit citizens liable for military training – except those who join the permanent force, the South African police, and the railways or prison services.

Expenditure on citizen forces and commando training was increased by almost R1m in 1968 to an estimated R30m.

In fact, many ordinary whites felt they were under siege. They already had a fortress mentality, further fortified by their fear of what they perceived to be an impending guerrilla war waged by freedom fighters trained in Tanzania and Zambia and other countries.

On 8 September 1967, it was officially disclosed by the apartheid regime that South African police were in Rhodesia actively helping Rhodesian armed forces in their fight against nationalist guerrillas. The South African government claimed it had been forced to intervene in Rhodesia because of an attempt by several hundred guerrillas to invade South Africa and South West Africa from Zambia at the urging of the OAU Liberation Committee.

It was also during the same time that Prime Minister B.J. Vorster announced the arrest of what he said was a fully trained KGB agent, Yuri N. Loginov, in Johannesburg, while on a special mission to South Africa. His arrest aroused widespread interest among Western intelligence services.

The arrest was deliberately timed to coincide with the announcement that African guerrillas were getting ready to invade South Africa and South West Africa (Namibia) from Zambia. And since one of their biggest supporters was the Soviet Union, providing them with arms, the implication of Loginov's presence in South Africa around the same time was obvious: He was sent there not only to spy on the apartheid regime but to coordinate guerrilla activities and collect information that would help the freedom fighters and their supporters in the Soviet Union.

That may have been the interpretation of the apartheid regime; if it was, it did not resonate well in African nationalist circles.

Tensions between South Africa and the independent African countries were heightened just a few months later on 5 April 1968, when Defence Minister P. W. Botha issued his first warning to them when he told the House of Assembly (Parliament) that countries aiding and inciting terrorism and guerrilla warfare against South Africa could provoke retaliation against them. It was interpreted as a warning to Zambia and Tanzania that guerrilla bases in those two countries could be attacked by South Africa. He issued the same warning again later in August the same year. But the two countries and the rest except Malawi and a few others continued to support the freedom fighters in spite of the threats by the apartheid regime that it would launch retaliatory strikes and engage in hot pursuit of the guerrilla fighters – chase them all the way back to where they were trained.

What this showed, however, was that in spite of the threats by the apartheid regime and its ability to defend South Africa, the situation was not getting any better; it was getting worse and neither side was willing to compromise.

Their differences were irreconcilable and inexorably led to conflict involving guerrilla warfare and other forms of confrontation including sustained strikes and total non-cooperation with the authorities to force the racist regime to capitulate and help pave the way for multiracial democracy. But the apartheid regime was still defiant even when the guerrilla threat got worse towards the end of the sixties.

Some of the South African freedom fighters formed a new nationalist party in Dar-es-Salaam, Tanzania, on 9 September 1968 to direct the freedom struggle inside South Africa. The party was named the National Liberation Front of South Africa (NALFSA) and applied for recognition by the OAU Liberation Committee.

As the apartheid regime continued to defy international opinion and the wishes of the non-white majority in its own country, Prime Minister Vorster announced in April 1969 that members of the South African Police Force would remain in Rhodesia as long as it was necessary to protect South Africa from "terrorist" attacks. In the following month, the African National Congress (ANC) at its conference in Morogoro, Tanzania, called for a full-scale offensive against apartheid using a multi-pronged approach.

It also said both armed struggle and mass political struggle must be used to defeat the enemy. But the ANC also emphasised that the armed struggle and the involvement of the masses in the liberation struggle depended on building ANC underground structures within South Africa to mobilise the people and ultimately weaken and end apartheid. It was a complementary strategy that was bound to succeed.

The Morogoro conference focused on bringing about a qualitative change in the organisational structure of the liberation movement in keeping with the new situation to launch a revolutionary people's war. It was one of the most successful conferences in the history of the ANC.

As the year 1969 came to an end, marking the end of the decade, guerrilla activity had intensified in southern Africa; and the apartheid regime was deeply involved in the neighbouring countries of Rhodesia, Angola and Mozambique where it had sent its armed forces and intelligence agents to help thwart guerrilla advances.

On 21 November 1969, the UN General Assembly condemned South Africa for its apartheid policies and for its collaboration with Portugal and Rhodesia; and also for intervening in Angola and Mozambique to help the colonial forces suppress Africans in their quest for freedom. But all that fell on deaf ears, as the regime defiantly continued to enforce apartheid and help the governments of Rhodesia, Angola and Mozambique fight the guerrillas.

In Rhodesia, the end of the sixties were some of the most critical years in the country's history. It was the first time that the Rhodesian army and security forces came face to face with the enemy on the battlefield. It was also the first time South Africans entered Rhodesia to launch preemptive strikes against the guerrillas in an attempt to stop them from moving south across the border into South Africa.

It was also the first time that the white settlers in

Rhodesia became aware of the danger they faced from guerrilla war. It was also during that period that the Organisation of African Unity (OAU) launched a concerted effort to support the freedom fighters in their military campaign against the white minority regime in Salisbury.

The Rhodesian government was fully aware of the danger it faced. It was fighting a new war: guerrilla war. And it was fighting a new enemy who was as elusive as he was resilient, with an indispensable operational base in the local population of which he was an integral part. But without external support in the form of military training and provision of weapons and other necessities, he would not have been as effective as he was.

Underscoring the importance of such support, the rebel prime minister of Rhodesia, Ian Smith, described President Julius Nyerere of Tanzania, whose country was the headquarters of all the African liberation movements, as "the evil genius on the Rhodesian scene" who was also behind all the guerrilla wars in southern Africa.

As the decade came to an end, Rhodesia witnessed its first major conflict in March 1968 when guerrilla fighters who entered the British colony from Zambia clashed with the security forces. Clashes on this scale were unheard of before the white minorities unilaterally declared independence from Britain in November 1965.

Before the March 1968 military engagement, there had been other clashes on a smaller scale. One of those clashes took place in April 1966 in which seven seven guerrilla fighters who were members of the Zimbabwe African National Union (ZANU) crossed the Zambezi River from Zambia and entered Rhodesia. They were shot in running battles with the security forces in the Sinoia area 85 miles north of the capital Salisbury.

By 1967, the guerrilla fighters were better organised, mainly because of the cooperation between the forces of ZAPU and the ANC. In the first military engagement with the security forces in August that year in Matebeleland in southwestern Rhodesia, 31 guerrilla fighters were killed and the security forces lost seven members. So serious was this incursion that the Rhodesian government immediately sought help from South Africa. The apartheid regime responded favourably and sent troops, so-called police, early in September.

But it was the fighting in March 1968 that marked a turning point in the history of armed conflict between the freedom fighters and the security forces in Rhodesia:

"The fighting in March continued intermittently for over a month; it was reported by Security Force headquarters in Salisbury on 25 April (1968) that the number of guerillas killed had reached 55.

Two members of the Security Forces were also reported killed, and quantities of arms, ammunitions and equipment captured.

A view of the seriousness of the unrest can be formed from the fact that additional Territorial Force personnel had to be called up at the end of March for 'base duties'; while the South African Minister of Defence, Mr. P.W. Botha, warned on 5 April that countries aiding and inciting terrorism and guerila warfare against South Africa could eventually provoke South Africa into 'hitting back hard.'"
– (*Africa Contemporary Record*, pp. 373 - 374).

Another clash occurred in July 1968 when Rhodesia's minister of law and order, Lardner Burke, announced that "terrorist" groups had crossed into Rhodesia from Zambia.

It was also during the same time that it was announced that the first South African "policeman" had been killed when a South African-Rhodesian patrol was ambushed by the freedom fighters near the Zambezi River.

Three other South Africans and two Rhodesians were wounded in the same incident; and 10 guerrilla fighters were reported killed.

Fighting continued for another week during which, according to Radio Salisbury, at least two members of the Security Forces and 18 more guerrillas were killed. The fighting was intense enough to force the Rhodesians to resort to other means to contain the guerrillas. Fighter jets of the Rhodesian Air Force were brought in to support the ground forces.

A joint communique issued by ZAPU and the ANC in Lusaka, Zambia, on 25 July 1968, claimed that 33 members of the Rhodesian Security Forces were killed in the conflict in the Zambezi Valley. Confirmation of the improved capacity of the guerrilla fighters came from the annual report of the Rhodesian Commissioner of Police published in July in which he said:

"It would be wrong to minimise the dangers which Rhodesia faces from terrorist infiltrators; these are now employing more sophisticated tactics and are well armed."

Rhodesia had been in a state of emergency for quite some time because of increasing guerrilla activity and the government was compelled to extend it to cope with the crisis and assure the white minority that they would be protected by the security forces.

There was also apprehension in official circles in Salisbury that the assistance the guerrilla fighters were getting from other countries such as Tanzania and Zambia was a critical factor in the conflict and could even tip scales in their favour, even if not necessarily on long-term basis. But it was a problem the white minority government had to contend with; a concession that was made by the minister of law and order in the rebel colony:

"The Rhodesia rebel Minister of Law and Order, Mr. Lardner Burke, extending the state of emergency at the beginning of 1968, said that the number of 'terrorists' waiting in Zambia and Tanzania to cross the Rhodesian border continued to mount.

The South African Deputy-Minister of Police, Mr. S.L. Muller, said Tanzania posed 'the greatest potential threat to the Republic.' He claimed there were '40 camps in Tanzania for the training of terrorists and all the offices of subversive organisations.' In Zambia, he said, there were '19 training and transit camps.'

A new external service of Radio Tanzania was inaugurated in 1968 to assist in 'propagating the ideological principles of the liberation movements in Tanzania.'" – (Ibid., p. 220).

The guerrilla camps in Tanzania and Zambia were not only for the freedom fighters from South Africa and Rhodesia but also for those from Mozambique, Angola, and South West Africa.

Among all the white minority regimes in southern Africa, the Portuguese were the most vulnerable and came under sustained attack. As President Nyerere said at the OAU summit in Cairo on 20 July 1964, African countries were strong enough to expel Portugal from Africa. He was right. The problem was the powers behind her. As he stated at the conference:

"I am convinced that the finer the words the greater the harm they do to the prestige of Africa if they are not followed by action ...

Africa is strong enough to drive Portugal from our continent. Let us resolve at this conference to take the necessary action." – (Nyerere, quoted by Ali A. Mazrui in his lecture "Nkrumahism and The Triple Heritage: Out of the Shadows" at the University of Ghana-Legon in 2002).

By 1969, the Portuguese had 130,000 troops tied down mostly in Angola and Mozambique, with a smaller number in Guinea-Bissau. But they were fighting a losing battle. Portugal was the poorest and weakest country in Western

Europe. It could not have been able to maintain her colonies without support from other Western countries which was critical in fighting the guerillas. As Dr. Eduardo Mondlane, the leader of FRELIMO, said about the armed struggle in Mozambique – which started on 25 September 1964 – in an interview with the Tanzanian daily newspaper, *The Nationalist*, on 30 July 1968:

"The meaning of the protracted struggle is more clear now and the combatants have redoubled their determination to fight to the bitter end until they destroy the enemy.

The situation of the war now inside Mozambique is more favourable to us as the Portuguese are in a stalemate and the only active force of the enemy is the Air Force.

We have now moved from the phase of ambushes and we are concentrating on attacking the enemy in his own territory, that is in garrisons, bases, posts and isolating the towns where he is hiding.

The enemy is completely isolated and the revolutionary enthusiasm of the masses is very high. We have actually more people ready in technical warfare training than we can provide the arms for fighting. All ages are involved and now we have formed the women's fighting detachment.

The prospects of crossing the Zambezi River and carrying the struggle farther south are very bright and no matter what the Portuguese do the war rages on and it is a fierce one.

We know that they are increasing their forces of white soldiers and they have intensified in Mozambique the forced conscription of Africans. They get a lot of technical aid from NATO countries, and the apartheid regime of South Africa is deeply involved – it has many of its military officers fighting in Mozambique.

Countries like West Germany, it is well-known to us, are training white Portuguese soldiers in Portugal in counter-insurgence techniques. In short, we are fighting Portugal and all her NATO allies."

Six months later, they killed him. A bomb was hidden in a book of Russian essays mailed to him from Japan. It exploded when he opened the package, killing him in Oyster Bay, Dar es Salaam. It was the work of the Portuguese secret service.

But Mondlane's assassination on 3 February 1969 did not stop the people of Mozambique from fighting for their independence. In fact, they expected such setbacks as a part of the struggle.

So, the struggle continued even after Mondlane was killed. His assassination was a big tragedy as the sixties came to an end. But it was also a moment of reflection on the liberation struggle and the problems that lay ahead, as the war became more intense. For example, on 25 September 1968, which was the fourth anniversary of the armed conflict, FRELIMO said that during the past year (1967), its forces had killed more than 1,000 Portuguese soldiers, shot down 20 aircraft, and destroyed more than a hundred military vehicles; a claim that was later confirmed by some journalists and other observers; and by September 1968, more than 100 Portuguese soldiers were killed and hundreds injured within that year alone.

The sixties ended with the death toll mounting in all the liberation wars throughout southern Africa, as the freedom fighters intensified the struggle and scored bigger victories they never had won before. It was the dawn of a new era.

Thus, while the early and mid-sixties were years of celebration, as one African country after another won independence from colonial rule, the late sixties witnessed another phenomenon in the liberation struggle. And it had an equally profound impact on the destiny of the continent.

Africa entered a new phase. It was the phase of the

armed struggle. And it proved to be the most difficult phase in the history of African liberation until the rest of the continent was finally free many years later.

The end of the sixties, or the year 1969 in particular, was also significant in another important respect. The bleeding heart of Africa, Congo, had finally stopped bleeding; at least not as profusely as it did in the first years of the decade and even as late as 1965 and 1966, although the pro-Lumumbist nationalist forces never gave up until Mobutu was finally ousted from power about 30 years later in May 1997. But as the decade came to an end, so did the life of one man who wreaked so much havoc across the Congo during the turbulent sixties. The man was Moise Tshombe.

In June 1967, his plane flying from Spain en route to Congo where he intended to cause more mischief was hijacked and forced to land in Algiers, Algeria. After it landed, Tshombe was arrested and kept under house arrest. He died in the same month, reportedly of heart failure. He was 49, a few months before his 50th birthday on November 10th.

His death also marked the end of an era. At least 100,000 Congolese died in the sixties when the country became the bleeding heart of Africa.

Dr. Walter Rodney who wrote *How Europe Underdeveloped Africa* when he was teaching at the University of Dar es Salaam in Tanzania arrived at the same conclusion in his research – 100,000 people killed during the Congo crisis – as he stated in his book *The Groundings with My Brothers*.

Not long after Tshombe died, another personality emerged on the African political scene. That was Colonel Muammar Qadhafi.

On 1 September 1969, Qadhafi overthrew 79-year-old King Idris of Libya in a bloodless military coup. He was 28 and became one of the youngest heads of state in the world.

He instituted a controversial regime which became one of the most prominent in Africa and the rest of the Third World for decades.

So much for Africa, as the sixties came to an end. It is, indeed, a decade to remember.

The Struggle for Mozambique

THE STRUGGLE for the liberation of Mozambique was led by FRELIMO, a Portuguese acronym for *Frente de Libertacao de Mocambique*, meaning Front for the Liberation of Mozambique.

FRELIMO was founded in Dar es Salaam, the capital of Tanganyika, now Tanzania, in May 1962, just a few months after Tanganyika won independence from Britain on 9 December 1961. But it was not officially launched until June the same year, and in the same city, under the leadership of Dr. Eduardo Chivambo Mondlane.

President Julius Nyerere played a critical role in uniting various Mozambican nationalist groups that led to the establishment of FRELIMO, one of the most successful liberation movements in colonial history. That was only about two years before he was to accomplish another memorable feat, uniting two independent countries, Tanganyika and Zanzibar, in April 1964 to form Tanzania; the first such union in Africa, and the only one that exists today. No other independent countries on the continent have united to form one country or have even seriously attempted to do so.

And no other major liberation groups in any of the other white-ruled countries in southern Africa ever successfully united to form a single nationalist movement as the Mozambican nationalist organisations did in

Tanzania under the aegis of Julius Nyerere. Instead, the trend was the opposite among a number of them.

In South Africa, the Pan-Africanist Congress (PAC) was established under the leadership of Robert Mangaliso Sobukwe by members who left the African National Congress (ANC) in 1959. In Zimbabwe, the Zimbabwe African National Union (ZANU) was formed as a breakaway group from the Zimbabwe African People's Union (ZAPU) in 1963, first under the leadership of Reverend Ndabaningi Sithole, and then Robert Mugabe. And in Angola the three main nationalist groups, the Popular Movement for the Liberation of Angola (MPLA) led by Dr. Agostinho Neto, the Front for the National Liberation of Angola (FNLA) led by Dr. Holden Roberto, and the Union for the Total Independence of Angola (UNITA) led by Dr. Jonas Savimbi, went to war against each other.

It was only in Mozambique that the various nationalist groups united to form a single nationalist movement, FRELIMO. Mozambique also had the distinction of being the first country in southern Africa - where liberation wars were fought - to win independence after waging an intense guerrilla campaign against the Portuguese colonial rulers for 10 years.

The groups which united to form FRELIMO in Tanzania in 1962 were an assorted lot, and themselves products of coalitions of even smaller groups, most of them without a clear ideological line. And not all of them were formed in Mozambique. But it was the conditions in Mozambique which were responsible for this political awakening among the Africans as a nationalist response to Portuguese oppression.

One of the first nationalist groups to be formed was the Mozambican African National Union (MANU) . It was formed in Mombasa, Kenya, by the leaders from the Makonde tribe in northern Mozambique, an ethnic group that straddles the Tanzanian-Mozambican border, in preparation for an armed struggle against the Portuguese colonial rulers. Because of their proximity to Tanzania, which served as a rear base, the Makonde regions in northern Mozambique - with an excellent terrain for insurgency operations - proved to be critical to the liberation struggle after guerrilla warfare started. MANU became one of the most important groups in the coalition that led to the establishment of FRELIMO in Tanzania the following year.

The liberation struggle in Mozambique was from the beginning and in subsequent years influenced by a number of factors at different times throughout that period and even after Mozambique won independence after 500 years of Portuguese colonial rule.

One of the primary factors was the nature of the liberation organisations which were regionally entrenched and fostered ethno-regional rivalries. They were fractured along ethnic lines. Another factor was the ideological orientation of the organisations. Then there was the involvement of some African leaders in independent Africa, especially Kwame Nkrumah and Julius Nyerere.

The involvement of the two leaders in the liberation struggle was also shaped by rivalry between them. Kwame Nkrumah, who was seen by many people as the father of the African independence movement, wanted to chart the course of the liberation struggle not only in Mozambique but also in South Africa and in other countries in the region still under white minority rule.

Nkrumah's involvement was clearly demonstrated as far back as 1959 when Robert Mangaliso Sobukwe and his colleagues in South Africa left the African National Congress (ANC) to form their own organisation, the Pan-Africanist Congress (PAC). Nkrumah immediately embraced them and supported the organisation against the African National Congress whose most prominent leaders were Chief Albert Luthuli and Nelson Mandela. Even when Mandela secretly left South Africa for the first time in 1962 to seek support from other African countries for the liberation struggle against apartheid in South Africa, the reception he got, or didn't get, depended on the leaders of the countries he visited.

The first African country he visited was Tanganyika under the leadership of Julius Nyerere who agreed to support the liberation struggle in South Africa. Tanganyika was the first country in the region to win independence. Mandela went to other African countries. One of them was Ghana. But he did not get the support he needed because Nkrumah had taken sides with the Pan-Africanist Congress of Robert Sobukwe whom he supported against Mandela's African National Congress.

The involvement by Nkrumah in the liberation struggle in the countries of southern Africa was also clearly evident in the case of Mozambique where he wanted to direct the liberation struggle according to his wishes and ideological dictates. This was seen as an inteference in the region by the leaders of Tanganyika who strenuously resisted the move. They saw it as an attempt by Nkrumah to diminish the role of Nyerere and overshadow him when he was, clearly, already the biggest supporter - in the entire region - of the liberation struggle in Mozambique and even helped to unite rival Mozambican organisations to enable them to present a united front against Portuguese colonial rule. In fact, it was Nyerere who persuaded Eduardo Mondlane, who became the leader of the independence struggle in Mozambique, to return to Africa from the United States and establish a base in Dar es Salaam, Tanzania's capital, for the Mozambican liberation movement.

The involvement of Nkrumah in Mozambique's liberation struggle, and the rivalry among the Mozambican political organisations, are some of the subjects which have been addressed by a number of people, including Mozambican author Joao Manuel Cabrita in his book, *Mozambique: The Tortuous Road to Democracy*.

Ghana's involvement was clearly demonstrated from the beginning when FRELIMO was formed. Although the organisation was formed in Dar es Salaam, Tanzania, some of the leaders of this coalition organisation who were pro-Nkrumah decided to announce in Ghana's capital, Accra, the formation of FRELIMO, far away from where it was formed, Tanzania, which was also its base and headquarters. As Cabrita states in his book:

"The formation of Frelimo was announced for the first time in Accra on 29 May 1962 by the União Democrática Nacional de Moçambique (MANU). For several months, the two organizations of exiled Mozambicans had been holding talks in their Tanzania base.

A third organization, Uniao Nacional Democratica de Moçambique Independente (Unami), joined before Frelimo's official debut in Dar es Salaam in June 1962.

It was more a marriage of convenience imposed on the Mozambicans than a genuine united front against Portuguese colonialism, ultimately contributing to divisions within the colony's independence movement. Interference by African governments with different agendas for continental issues had been a determining factor in the marriage.

Formed in Rhodesia in November 1960, Udenamo was the first of the three Mozambican independence movement to advocate violence to bring about independence. Udenamo was influenced by Zimbabwean politics, and its members had a history of involvement with Joshua Nkomo's National Democratic Party. Adelino Gwambe, a 20-year-old Mozambican from Inhambane, led the organization.

As a campaign for the independence of Mozambique could not be waged from white-ruled Rhodesia, Gwambe and his followers left for Tanzania, where, in view of its forthcoming independence, Udenamo would be better positioned to wage an armed campaign against the

Portuguese.

Once based in Dar es Salaam, Udenamo continued to attract Mozambicans. In April 1961, Udenamo's vice-president, Fanuel Mahluza, wrote to Eduardo Mondlane, a U.S. educated Mozambican anthropologist working for the UN Trusteeship Council in New York, inviting him to join the organization. Mondlane did not accept the invitation. he had his own agenda, which did not conform to Udenamo's."[1]

It was not until Nyerere convinced Mondlane to leave New York and go to Tanzania and help unite rival nationalist organisations that serious attempts were made by the rival groups to forge a united front against the Portuguese colonial rulers in Mozambique. The groups did not have much in common besides their desire to end colonial rule in their home country. They had many differences among themselves, including political - how the struggle should be conduted and along what lines. Therefore their differences were also ideological even though some of them did not have clear ideological preferences.

In addition to ideological differences, and even conflict among them, there was also personal rivalry. Personal rivalry among the nationalist leaders was one of the major factors which influenced the tempo and direction of the Mozambican liberation movement. There was not enough will and commitment among many leaders to transcend such rivalry.

The rivalry among the leaders was also acknowledged by Dr. Eduardo Mondlane himself, who was the main leader, in his conversation with Bill Sutherland, a black American who went to live in Tanganyika (later Tanzania) in 1963 and became a close friend of President Julius Nyerere. Before then, Sutherland had lived in Ghana and was close to Nkrumah but fell out with him and left, settling in Tanzania where he lived for more than 30 years.

He died on 2 January 2010. He was 91.

In an interview with Prexy Nesbitt and Mimi Edmunds on 19 July 2003 published in a book, *No Easy Victories: African Liberation and American Activists over a Half Century, 1950 -2000* - which is a collection of interviews with a number of people compiled by William Minter, Gail Hovey and Charles Cobbs Jr. - Sutherland had the following to say about the Mozambican leaders he had known in Dar es Salaam, Tanzania, where he lived:

"NESBITT: You knew Samora?

SUTHERLAND: Yes.

NESBITT You knew people like Marcelino do Santos?

SUTHERLAND: I knew Marcelino very well. And it was —Marcelino would have been —he would have put me right in the line with Eduardo. Eduardo, at one time, this was—

EDMUNDS: Eduardo Mondlane?

MONDLANE: Mondlane. He told me one time, he says, I know they're going to try to push me aside as this thing goes on. I don't represent the true Marxist position, he said. And I'm ready for that. I know it.

NESBITT: Eduardo said that to you?

SUTHERLAND: Oh, yes. He said it to me right on my own porch, that he realized that they would probably do that to him.

NESBITT: 'They' would be? Meaning the rest of FRELIMO?

SUTHERLAND: Well, the Marxists, the Marxist element there. And that they thought he was useful at the stage that the revolution was, but they would not consider him the most reliable person to be head of the state.

NESBITT: I often think Eduardo must be rolling over in his grave about what is happening in today's Mozambique.

SUTHERLAND: Well, I think Eduardo would. I think a lot of people would. I think Nyerere would be very disappointed. Oh, a lot of people would be, because the whole continent has not meant a change for the ordinary people. The ordinary people have not benefited. You know it's an unfinished revolution, that's what it is, throughout. But I have the faith that the revolution will continue.

EDMUNDS: If you could say who you think has been the longest-lasting or most impressive leaders of the continent today, who would you give that to?

SUTHERLAND: I think that Nyerere and, of course, Nkrumah had his vision of a united Africa. But I think Nyerere and Mandela probably to me are the two outstanding people."[2]

The largest organisation among the different nationalist groups was UDENAMO. And its most influential leader and ideological thinker was Marcelino dos Santos. As Cabrita states in his book, *Mozambique: The Tortuous Road to Democracy*:

"Gwambe's decision to appoint Marcelino dos Santos...as Udenamo's deputy secretary general undoubtedly provided the organization with its most capable intellectual and organizer, but also with a dedicated Stalinist.
His appointment was to have far-reaching

consequences not only in the subsequent armed struggle against the Portuguese, but also in independent Mozambique. It was Marcelino dos Santos who drafted Udenamo's constitution, structuring it under the principles of of 'democratic centralism.'

As Udenamo expanded its links further afield, its leaders saw signs of uneaseness on the part of their hosts. Tanzania's Julius Nyerere government was concerned over the organization's links with Ghana, established through the Ghana Bureau of African Affairs when Udenamo operated from Rhodesia.

Ghana, the first country to assist Udenamo financially, extended regular invitations for the organization's senior officials to visit Accra. it funded Gwambe's visit to Conakry and Helsinki, and provided an office for the Udenamo representative in Accra.

The Tanzanians viewed Ghana's Kwame Nkrumah as too radical for their taste. They resented what they believed to be Nkrumah's blatant effort to bring the Mozambican nationalists under his sphere of influence. Fearing that he could in fact pose a threat to Nyerere's desire to become the champion of southern Africa's nationalist cause, the Tanzanians took action.

The Nyerere government opted for MANU, essentially an organization of makonde people with roots in Mozambique's Cabo Delgado province, bordering Tanzania. Some of its members had been born and reared in Tanzania, others in Zanzibar and Kenya. In the early 1960s, there were an estimated 250000 Mozambicans, notably Makonde, living in Tanzania. They worked primarily in plantations, but were also involved in trade union and political activities.

Rashidi Kawawa, who became secretary general of the Tanzanian ruling party, TANU, was a Makonde from Mozambique (he was a Ngoni, not a Makonde, born and brought up in Songea, Ruvuma Region, southern Tanzania, and later became prime minister and vice president of

Tanzania under Nyerere – correction by Godfrey Mwakikagile).

Oscar Kambona, the Tanzania home affairs and foreign minister, was another Makonde (he was a Nyasa, not a Makonde, also born and brought up in Ruvuma Region (in Mbinga Disitrict), Tanzania – correction by Godfrey Mwakikagile)....

In January 1961, the MAA - Makonde African Association - branches in Dar es Salaam, Mombasa and Zanzibar, led respectively by Matthew Mmole, Samuly Diankali and Ali Madebe, merged as MANU. The presidency and vice-presidency of the new party were given to Mmole and Lawrence Malinga Milinga, both born in Tanzania.

The similarities between MANU and TANU were not only in the name. some in MANU aimed at the unification of Cabo Delgado with Tanzania for a greater Makonde homeland.

Udenamo felt that the prospect of an armed struggle looked unlikely. The Tanzanian government discontinued food supplies and other assistance that it had been giving Udenamo. Tanzania declared Adelino Gwambe persona non grata (italicised) for stating at a news conference on the eve of that country's independence that arrangements had been made for Udenamo to start the armed struggle in Mozambique. He was allowed to leave for Accra, but was allowed to return to Tanzania soon afterwards.

When Ghana invited Udenamo to attend the May-June 1962 African Freedom Fighters Conference in Accra, the Tanzanians refused to issue travel documents to the Udenamo delegation. These had to be organised by the Ghanaian Commission in Dar es Salaam.

It was not only the Tanzania government that had grown distrustful of Nkrumah. Marcelino dos Santos was not at all impressed with Nkrumah for regarding him as not truly representative of the black people of Mozambique since he was a mulatto.

To prevent a worsening of relations with Tanzania, and bearing in mind that the strategic importance of that country for the attainment of Mozambique's independence, Marcelino dos Santos advised his fellow leaders to merge with MANU. Gwambe rejected the idea outright; Marcelino dos Santos reacted by threatening to leave Udenamo and join MANU. But at several meetings of Udenamo's Executive Commitee held throughout October 1961, it was decided that, in order to overcome the prevailing situation, Udenamo and MANU should unite.

In order to gain MANU's sympathy, Udenamo officials made use of their financial resources to virtually bribe members of the Makonde organization to join them. in another move, Udenamo included MANU leaders in its delegation to the African Freedom Fighters Conference in Accra.

At a ceremony held under the auspices of the Tanzanian government in Dar es Salaam on 24 May 1962, Udenamo and MANU finally 'decided to bring unity of all the patriotic forces of Mozambique by means of forming a common front,' pending the return of the respective leaders from Accra.

Much to the irritation of the Tanzanians, Gwambe told a news conference in Accra five days later that the decision to merge was in response to Nkrumah's call for the closing of ranks for the liberation of Africa. As proposed by Mahluza, the front was to be known as the Frente de Libertação de Moçambique."[3]

The unification of the different nationalist organisations did not necessarily make things easy for Mondlane, the leader of FRELIMO. There were some people who were opposed to his leadership. As he once told Bill Sutherland, he knew that others in FRELIMO saw him only as a temporary leader who should occupy that position only as a matter of expediency. They needed him then. But he would have to go some day.

In fact, he felt the same way even before he talked to Bill Sutherland about that. Bill Sutherland went to Tanzania in 1963 for the first time. Mondlane had already faced opposition from his colleagues before 1963. Also, the involvement of Ghana continued to cause some problems for some of the nationalist leaders, including bad relations with the Tanzanian government. As Cabrita states:

"In Dar es Salaam, Mondlane encountered strong resistance...among the Udenamo and MANU leaders. Gwambe was committed t taking upon himself the leadership of Frelimo and soon starting the war of independence with the backing of Ghana where Mozambicans had reportedly undergone military training. For Mondlane, time was running out. He had to be back at Syracuse before the end of June.

On 18 June, a despondent Mondlane called in Thomas Byrne, the acting American chargé d'affaires in Dar es Salaam, to report his dismay at Gwambe's complete commitment to Nkrumah and to cummunist blco countries. Mondlane alleged that the Udenamo leader was a regular recipient of substantial funds from Ghana and the USSR, and that he had recently received $14000 from the Ghanaians. Mondlane was also disturbed to learn that Mmole and his lieutenants were in Gwambe's pay.

Mondlane realized that there was a degree of discontent among Udenamo's rank and file over the tight control that Gwambe had over the organisation's financial resources. Mondlane informed the chargé d'affaires that he had raised the issue with Kambona, pointing out to him that a continuation of the existing arrangement, whereby Gwambe had ample resources while both Udenamo and MANU treasuries were empty, meant that the Mozambique nationalist movement belonged to Gwambe and h in turn could deliver it to his Ghanaian and Russian paymasters. Mondlane urged Kambona to consider the advantage of securing funds from Western sources n order to free the Mozambique movement from Gwambe.

Mondlane's recommendations were music to the Tanzanians' ears in view of their reluctance to have an organization based in their country, but under Ghanaian influence. Moreover, by this time the Tanzanians realized that of all the Mozambicans who had flocked to Dar es Salaam, Mondlane was the one who possessed the best qualities to head an independence movement: mature, well-educated, articulate, able to move in diplomatic circles, and committed to a negotiated settlement with Portugal, an option they initially preferred for Tanzania felt impotent to deal with possible Portuguese military retaliation."[4]

Mondlane was finally able to secure the leadership of the Mozambican nationalist movement under the umbrella of FRELIMO.

His position was further strengthened by the close relationship he had with Nyerere, a leader who played a key role in the liberation struggle in southern Africa.

It was Nyerere who invited Mozambican and other African nationalist groups to establish bases in Tanganyika soon after the country won independence from Britain in December 1961. That was before the Organization of African Unity (OAU) was founded in May 1963 to support such groups, among other goals. It was also Nyerere who urged the Mozambican liberation groups to form a united front. And it was he who asked Dr. Eduardo Mondlane - back in the late 1950s when the two met at the United Nations in New York - to return to Africa and unite the Mozambican nationalist groups. He also asked him to establish a base in Dar es Salaam for Mozambique's liberation movement and promised him full support to liberate Mozambique from Portuguese colonial rule. And it was Nyerere who also helped rival nationalist groups to form a cohesive bloc in preparation for the armed struggle against the Portuguese colonialist forces in Mozambique.

The Makonde territory in Cabo Delgado Province in northern Mozambique was later to prove critical to the armed struggle when the war was launched only two years later after FRELIMO was formed. Members of the Makonde tribe themselves were a major component of FRELIMO when the organisation was formed. And they went on to play an even bigger role when their territory in northern Mozambique became the launching pad for other attacks by FRELIMO in different parts of the country farther south and west. In fact, the liberation war by FRELIMO started in Cabo Delgado Province, the Makonde territory.

Historically and politically, Tanzania and Mozambique have also been equally linked by the Makonde and other ethnic groups such as the Yao and the Makua who, like the Makonde, also straddle the Tanzanian-Mozambican border forming insoluble bonds between the two countries. In fact, some tribes in Tanzania migrated from Mozambique.

Also highly significant was the involvement of the Mozambican Makonde in the struggle for Tanganyika's independence. Their political activism became critical to the rise of Mozambican nationalism in their home country as a whole, not just in Cabo Delgado Province, their traditional homeland and stronghold in northern Mozambique.

But although the different nationalist organisations did indeed - with the help of the Tanzanian government - succeed in coming together under one umbrella unlike other organisations in southern Africa, there is no question that divisions remained within between and among them. FRELIMO was an umbrella organisation, more than anything else, whose members - from different political groups - were united only by a common desire to win independence. But nothing else united them. They were still divided and weakened by rivalries within.

In fact, such rivalry even erupted into violence

involving gunfire at the FRELIMO headquarters on Nkrumah Street in Dar es Salaam when I lived in that city. And, coincidentally, just across the street from FRELIMO's office, only a few buildings up the same Nkrumah Street, was the office of the African National Congress (ANC) of South Africa.

The rivalries among the nationalist leaders of Mozambique within FRELIMO continued until and after Mondlane's assassination in Dar es Salaam, Tanzania, on 3 February 1969. He was killed when he opened a parcel at his house.

The parcel was a book of Russian essays which contained a bomb. Some pages had been cut out to conceal the bomb between the pages. The bomb exploded and killed him instantly when he opened the parcel on a table at his house in Oyster Bay, a suburb of Dar es Salaam which was home to high-ranking government officials and diplomats as well as a number of leaders of the liberation movements based in Dar es Salaam.

The parcel was mailed to him from Japan by the Portuguese secret police. They mailed it from Japan as a diversionary tactic to make it difficult for investigators to trace it and find out who sent it or exactly where it came from. It somehow eluded the attention of Tanzania's intelligence service which was considered to be one of the best in Africa during that period of the liberation wars in southern Africa against the white minority regimes.

Mondlane was buried at Kinondoni Cemetery in Dar es Salaam. I remember the day. I was a student in Form V (Standard 13) at Tambaza High School which was not far from the cemetery. Some of us walked from our school and went to Kinondoni Cemetery to attend the funeral. Uria Simango, the vice president of FRELIMO, was the main speaker. Mondlane's wife, Janet, and their two children were at the grave site and witnessed the burial. President Nyerere, cabinet members, diplomats and members of the liberation movements based in Dar es

Salaam were among the people who attended the funeral.

Mondlane's assassination intensified the power struggle within FRELIMO between the supporters of Uria Simango and those who were opposed to his leadership. After Mondlane was killed, Uria Simango was one of the three top leaders of FRELIMO together with Samora Machel and Marcelino dos Santos. Finally, Samora Machel emerged as the leader of FRELIMO, succeeding Mondlane. And dos Santos became FRELIMO's vice president.

Initially, Uria Simango was suspected of being involved in Mondlane's assassination. He was FRELIMO's vice president, under Mondlane, and had ambitions of his own. It was believed that he wanted to remove Mondlane from office and replace him as the leader of the nationalist organisation. And he did, in fact, serve in that capacity for some time as FRELIMO's president after Mondlane was killed until it was agreed to form a triumvirate - comprising Simango, Machel and Marcelino dos Santos - to lead the organisation during that period.

And for the rest of his life, Uria Simango lived with the lingering suspicion hanging over his head that he was involved in Mondlane's assassination. Coincidentally, he was expelled from FRELIMO in the same year Mondlane was assassinated and went to Egypt where he formed a rival organisation, further fuelling speculation and suspicion about his involvement in Mondlane's assassination and about his true ambitions. He was later killed by FRELIMO probably in Nachingwea in southern Tanzania where FRELIMO had a base. And he was probably buried there. His wife was executed later and may also be buried in Nachingwea.

The year of Mondlane's assassination also witnessed a number of events and developments in the liberation struggle in Mozambique by FRELIMO from their bases in Mtwara Region in southern Tanzania.

I attended secondary school in southern Tanzania, in

Ruvuma Region which together with Mtwara Region borders Mozambique, from 1965 to 1968 (Form I or Standard 9 to Form IV or Standard 12) and I remember that Portuguese forces sometimes launched attacks on the region. But most of the attacks including aerial bombings were directed at Mtwara Region which was the main operational base for the FRELIMO guerrilla fighters in their war against the Portuguese colonial forces in Mozambique. Among the casualties were civilians - Tanzanian and Mozambican - including some who were killed or maimed by napalm bombs dropped by the Portuguese air force. The colonial forces in Mozambique were also supported by apartheid South Africa and their NATO allies.

But the liberation war continued against formidable odds. And the year 1969 in which Mondlane was assassinated was one of the most important in the struggle for the liberation of Mozambique.

The war in Mozambique was preceded by an armed struggle in Angola, another Portuguese colony, where nationalist forces set the stage for what was to come not only in Angola but in other parts of southern Africa. It was a part of a wider struggle co-ordinated against colonial forces and white minority regimes in southern Africa, and the liberation movement in Mozambique benefited from this concerted effort.

About a year before FRELIMO was established, African nationalists in Angola had just launched an armed struggle against their colonial masters in 1961, prompting the authorities in Mozambique to intensify their campaign of terror and intimidation against black dissidents and agitators. But the crackdown had unintended consequences. It fuelled and intensified nationalist sentiments among the Africans and triggered an outflow of even more refugees into neighbouring countries, especially Tanganyika whose 500-mile border with Mozambique made it very easy for them to cross and seek asylum in that country.

The long border also proved to be critical to the liberation of Mozambique when the guerrilla campaign started, enabling the freedom fighters to move back and forth at will and maintain secure supply lines for weapons and other material from their bases in what became Tanzania. Without such access, provision of weapons and other items to the guerrilla fighters would have been a logistical nightmare. And FRELIMO leaders were fully aware of that.

One of the first leaders of FRELIMO was David Mabunda who was elected secretary-general when the oganisation was formed in Dar es Salaam, Tanzania.

Years later, he ended up in Grand Rapids, Michigan, in the United States, where he taught at Grand Rapids Junior College, and later at Muskegon Community College in Muskegon about 30 miles from Grand Rapids. I was living in Grand Rapids in those days and I had the chance to talk to him in 1977.

When I told him I was a Tanzanian, he said he had close ties to Tanzania and that his wife came from Moshi, which is a district in the northeastern part of the country where Mount Kilimanjaro is located.

He was one of the early luminaries in the Mozambican liberation movement. He left Muskegon College in 1994 and moved to South Africa where he became director of Kruger National Parks.

Like all the other Mozambican nationalist leaders, he was fully aware of the critical role Tanzania would play, and later played, in the liberation of Mozambique.

Any leader who did not fully comprehend or appreciate how indispensable Tanzania was to the liberation struggle in Mozambique risked alienation and even total isolation.

Tanzania was the only country in the region which could function as a full operational base for the freedom fighters in Mozambique. It shared a long border with Mozambique, hundreds of miles long. Tanzania also had access to the sea, critical to bringing in weapons the freedom fighters needed. It served as a conduit, the only independent country in the region which was in a strategic position to do so. Tanzania also had leaders who were fully committed to the liberation struggle in Mozambique. The freedom fighters needed such a country in order to be fully operational, and successful, in their struggle against the colonial forces in Mozambique.

FRELIMO guerrilla fighters waged war against formidable odds. But they remained undaunted, in spite of the setbacks they had suffered including the assassination of their leader, Dr. Eduardo Mondlane, in 1969. While they continued to mourn him that year, they also continued to fight. Nobody, of course, knew that independence was only six years away.

And just the year before Mondlane was killed, there was plenty of evidence showing that the freedom fighters had made great progress in their war against the Portuguese colonial forces, a point underscored in a report by John Parker, "Expanding Guerilla Warfare," in *Africa Contemporary Record: Annual Survey and Documents 1968 - 1969*:

"The Zimbabwe freedom fighters have not yet matched the exploits of their brothers-in-arms in Mozambique and Angola, who claim effective control over large tracts of their respective countries in spite of the huge forces ranged against them.

Recent accounts by journalists who have made hazardous and often uncomfortable trips into the territories confirm the claims.

One journalist, Basil Davidson, went with Frelimo - the Mozambique Liberation Front - across the Ruvuma River which is technically the border between Tanzania and Mozambique and marched in daylight without any hindrance from Portuguese troops, to an astounding congress in the bush. He wrote:

'At a place where newly-built huts stood within the cover of a wood, about 150 political and military leaders were assembled. They had come from all parts of a colony that is one-and-a-half times as big as France.

They began fighting the Portuguese in 1964. Since then they have cleared the Portuguese out of most of the rural country of Cabo Delgado and Niassa, a region not much smaller than the British Isles. In this liberated zone they have set up schools and clinics and introduced their own economic system.

The congress I attended was the first since the fighting started. It was called to discuss how they could push farther to the south and extend the war.

Present were the whole central committee of the Liberation Front, including its president, forty-eight-year-old Eduardo Mondhlane, once a Doctor of Sociology at Syracuse University, New York State....'

As this article was going to Press, Dr. Mondhlane was assassinated at his desk in a quiet suburb of Dar es Salaam. How this will affect FRELIMO remains to be seen. What is certain is that the freedom movements will not be deterred from their final objectives by this type of action. Indeed, they expect it."[5]

The assassination of Dr. Mondlane only fuelled the liberation struggle.

And there is no question that Tanzania played one of the biggest roles in the Mozambican war of independence. Without Tanzania operating as a rear base for the freedom fighters, Mozambique would not have won independence as soon as it did, although it took more than 10 years of guerrilla warfare to liberate the country. But it would have taken much longer if Tanzania was also still a colony, therefore equally hostile to the freedom fighters; was led by someone like Mobutu Sese Seko or Kamuzu Banda who did not want to support freedom fighters anywhere in Africa; or did not commit as much resources and provide logistical support to the guerrilla fighters as it did under the leadership of Julius Nyerere.

And if Kenya - another East African country like Tanzania and Mozambique - under the leadership of Jomo Kenyatta bordered Mozambique, or if Kenyatta was president of Tanzania, FRELIMO freedom fighters would not have been able to get as much support, if any, as they did from Tanzania under Nyerere. Kenyatta did nothing to support the African liberation movements despite his image - highly inflated - as the embodiment of Mau Mau. The true leader of Mau Mau was Dedan Kimathi, not Jomo Kenyatta. Kenyatta did not even talk about the liberation struggle in southern Africa, except in a perfunctory manner, and only on very few occasions.

Nyerere was exactly the opposite and helped change the course of African history, especially in southern Africa, because of his uncompromising support for the liberation movements. And probably nowhere else did he have such a direct impact as he did on Mozambique because of the common border between Tanzania and Mozambique, providing direct, unimpeded access to the battlefield for the freedom fighters from their bases in Tanzania.

Tanzania's support for the liberation struggle in Mozambique and other countries in southern Africa also involved committing troops to the battlefield.

By the time Mozambique won independence from Portugal on 25 June 1975 on the 13th anniversary of the official launching of FRELIMO in Dar es Salaam on 25 June 1962 - it was "granted" provisional government on 20 September 1974 - after waging guerrilla war since 25 September 1964 in which about 70,000 Portuguese troops fought against the freedom fighters, a significant number of Tanzanian soldiers had fought and died in Mozambique, together with FRELIMO guerrillas, fighting to end the oldest and last colonial empire in Africa: Portuguese. Thousands of people died in this conflict, mostly in Mozambique itself.

In addition to Tanzanian soldiers who died together with FRELIMO guerrilla fighters in the war against the Portuguese colonial forces, Tanzanian civilians and Mozambican refugees living in southern Tanzania also died in the attacks which included aerial bombings by the Portuguese backed by their Western allies such as the United States and apartheid South Africa. As a member of NATO, Portugal was free to use weapons obtained from the United States and other Western powers in her wars against the freedom fighters and civilians in her African colonies and neighbouring countries supporting the liberation movements.

Tanzanian soldiers also fought and died in other liberation wars in southern Africa, including Zimbabwe and Angola; also an entire battalion of Nigerian soldiers fought in Angola in the seventies on the side of the MPLA against South African troops who invaded the country and attempted to capture the capital Luanda to install a puppet regime in place of the staunchly anti-colonial MPLA government. At least 5,000 Nigerian soldiers went into combat against the South African invaders. And as Tanzanian Minister of Defence and National Service, Philemon Sarungi, stated in Tanzania's parliament on 11 July 2002, the bodies of Tanzanian soldiers who died in other African countries during the liberation struggle would be returned home for reburial. According to a report in the *Daily News*, Dar es Salaam, Tanzania:

"The government plans to return home remains of bodies of those who fought, died and were buried outside the country during the liberation wars of southern Africa and accord them a heroes' funeral in a heroes' square.... The Minister for Defence and National Service, Professor Philemon Sarungi,... told the National Assembly that Tanzanian soldiers were buried in countries including Mozambique and Zimbabwe where they fought in the liberation wars for these countries.

Professor Sarungi also told the House that his ministry was planning to erect a monument where Tanzanian soldiers died in the Kagera War (in Kagera Region in northwestern Tanzania) against Uganda's dictator Idi Amin. 'Those who have died in other places during wars will have their names listed on the monument in order to keep the records for future reference of the country's history in the liberation of the continent,' he said.... Sarungi said July 25 every year has been earmarked as the day for remembrance of national heroes at Mnazi Mmoja in Dar es Salaam."[6]

Without Julius Nyerere, or another leader of his calibre and depth of commitment, it is highly unlikely that Tanzania would have played such a critical role in the liberation of Africa. And without good leadership, even a country with enormous wealth and potential amounts to nothing, as has been tragically demonstrated in the case of Congo, the bleeding heart of Africa, since independence in 1960.

No one knows what Lumumba would have done had he lived and continued to lead Congo for a number of years. But he showed a lot of promise and left his people with a sense of national identity and pride that is still sustained by his memory. Even a traitor like Mobutu invoked Lumumba's name to burnish his image. But everybody knows what Mobutu and his Western backers and masters did to Congo and to Africa as a whole. And the world knows what Nyerere did for Africa. As the Zambian ambassador to the United Nations, Mwelwa C. Musambachime, stated:

"To Zambians, Mwalimu Nyerere holds an exalted place in the history of our country. He had a direct and personal contribution to our political independence and economic development.

The Tanzania-Zambia Railway (TAZARA) and the Tanzania-Zambia Pipeline (TAZAMA) linking Ndola with Dar es Salaam, are some of the features that are closely linked to Mwalimu. Above all, every Zambian knows how close he was to our first President, Dr. Kenneth Kaunda. They were like twin brothers. To show the depth of their friendship, President Kaunda gave Mwalimu's middle name Kambarage to one of his sons....

Rarely is a person given the praises and high marks that Mwalimu received from people from all walks of life when still alive. In life, he was lionized by the people of Africa. He was given high accolade and status as one of the giants of a generation of leaders that has disappeared. That generation, sacrificed itself to the cause of the liberation of the African continent....

Mwalimu was not only a believer in Pan-Africanism; he was an actor who took very difficult steps to fulfill his total commitment to the liberation of Africa from colonialism and apartheid. Even though Tanganyika was not rich, Mwalimu readily shared the little that country had with the liberation struggle. All political parties in Central and Southern Africa received direct monetary and material support from Nyerere and the Tanganyika African National Union (TANU). This included vehicles, office equipment, housing, food, clothes, training and diplomatic passports and air tickets.

Soon after independence, Mwalimu opened up his country to the freedom fighters, a move that brought an end to racism and colonialism in South Africa, in Zimbabwe, Mozambique and Angola. For Nyerere, the move marked the beginning of an effective commitment to African liberation movements; later, he played host to the African National Congress (ANC) and the Pan-Africanist Congress (PAC) of South Africa, to Samora Machel's FRELIMO - battling against the Portuguese in Mozambique, Joshua Nkomo's ZIPRA (Zimbabwe People's Revolutionary Army) and later Robert Mugabe's

ZANLA (Zimbabwe African National Liberation Army) forces, which opposed colonial rule in the then Southern Rhodesia.

He did this fully knowing the risks involved. He was resolute and undeterred. He was, as Smith described him later, the initial 'evil genius' behind the liberation struggle and the guerrilla wars, which followed. The freedom fighters were trained not only in the military sphere. Many pursued academic studies that took them to various parts of the world to attain professional qualifications. Today many of these are holding very senior positions in government.

Thousands of political exiles swarmed the country.... There was always trouble in their ranks. Add to this, the dangers and actual infiltration by agents of hostile countries into their ranks, management problems, frustrations, challenges to the party leaderships, enemy attacks, and also the resentment that some Tanzanians began to cultivate for the exiles. Mwalimu and his countrymen overcame these problems and moved on.

Practically for its entire life, the Liberation Committee, an organ of the Organization of African Unity (OAU), charged with the responsibility of co-ordinating the liberation struggle, was based in Dar es Salaam, under a Tanzanian military officer, Colonel (later Major-General) Hashim Mbita. Tanzania's ability to continue to host it year after year was a great credit to the inspiration provided by Mwalimu. With his guidance, the Committee was able to register success after success as the countries of Southern Africa were liberated one after another.

Through his leadership style, dress, speeches and writings as well as personal discussion, Mwalimu was able to exert a lot of influence on many African leaders in Southern Africa. These included Kaunda and Chiluba of Zambia, Marcel and Chissano of Mozambique, Robert Mugabe of Zimbabwe, Sam Nujoma of Namibia, Thabo Mbeki of South Africa and Uganda's Yoweri Museveni as well as the new breed of African leaders. He played an 'enormous' role in the fight for independence and the liberation of Southern African countries.

As a Pan-Africanist, he could not be faulted for putting his country in the forefront of the frontline states against white minority rule in Africa. He took a principled stand at a great loss to his country. Credit should be given to the people of Tanzania, for in spite of the problems this sacrifice brought, they never really complained. Tanzania became a home for exiled freedom fighters who are now the leaders and civil servants in a number of Southern African states. A few of them have become international civil servants in many multilateral organizations.

Mwalimu was an African leader who outgrew his country and his continent. He was an influential figure on the international scene and one of Africa's most respected elder statesmen.... Mwalimu was also a strong believer in African Unity. He was one of the founders of the Organization of African Unity (OAU) in 1963 and was one of the 32 signatories to the Charter of the Organization of African Unity. Later he served as chairman of the Organization of African Unity in 1984/85 and piloted the discussions on the independence of Namibia and the end to apartheid in South Africa.

He left an indelible mark on the social and political history of the continent. He was an architect of the East African Community (EAC) and the Southern African Coordination Council now the Southern African Development Community (SADC).... He was also involved in seeking solutions to the many conflicts that raged in Africa. In 1995, the OAU asked him to devote his efforts to bringing peace in the troubled country of Burundi. Sadly, he was taken away without concluding his mission.

Aside from politics, Nyerere was a scholar with a formidable intellect of the highest repute. He contributed immensely to the area of education reforms and coined the term 'education for self-reliance' which found wide acceptance and currency all over the world. He was a poet of modest pretensions. His translation of Shakespeare's *Julius Caesar* (and *Merchant of Venice*) into Kiswahili, a regional lingua franca, was brilliant. He has left us with brilliant essays on political theory and political thought that have a great impact and influence on us....

Mwalimu was not only a Zanaki from Butiama, Musoma, a Tanzanian and an African, he was an internationalist.... We thank Mwalimu for teaching us the true meaning of being the servant of the people."[7]

The liberation of Mozambique, masterminded from Tanzania's capital Dar es Salaam where FRELIMO was founded in 1962, was but one example of the historic role Tanzania under the leadership of Julius Nyerere played in the liberation of Africa, and in the global context in general, especially with regard to North-South relations, protecting and promoting the interests of the Third World.

One of the poorest countries in the world became one of the world's most significant players in international affairs. It was one of the world's 25 poorest, yet in political terms was described as one of the top 25. An economic featherweight, it became a political heavyweight in the international arena dominated by the big powers. As *The Washington Post* put it, Tanzania punched far above its weight.

And it did so, with a megaton punch, because of Julius Nyerere.

Chapter notes

1. João Manuel Cabrita, "Marriage of Convenience," in his book, *Mozambique: The Tortuous Road to Democracy*, Palgrave Macmillan, 21 March 2001, p. 5. See also http://www.palgrave.com/pdfs/0333920015.pdf. In my previous edition of *Nyerere and Africa: End of an*

Era, I used some material from João Manuel Cabrita's book reproduced in the pdf file cited here and have used some of the same material in this edition. I have re-written this chapter on Mozambique to include other details from other sources including myself which were not in the previous edition and it is not necessary to include all the material from Cabrita's book I used in that edition. The material I used then from his book was pertinent to the chapter on Mozambique in the previous edition of my work. But some of it is not relevant to the current chapter the way it has been re-written.

2. Bill Sutherland in an interview published in William Minter, Gail Hovey and Charles Cobbs Jr., ed., *No Easy Victories: African Liberation and American Activists over a Half Century, 1950 - 2000*, Lawrenceville, New Jersey, USA: Africa World Press, 5 November 2007.

See also Bill Sutherland, "No Easy Victories: African Liberation and American Activists over a Half Century, 1950 – 2000" at: http://www.noeasyvictories.org/interviews/int01_sutherland.php, retrieved on 25 February 2010.

3. Joao Manuel Cabrita, *Mozambique: The Tortuous Road to Democracy*, op. cit., pp. 7 - 9.

4. Ibid., p. 10 - 11.

5. John Parker, "Expanding Guerilla War," in Colin Legum and John Drysdale, ed., *Africa Contemporary Record: Annual Survey and Documents 1968 - 1969*, London: Africa Research Limited, 1969, pp. 57 and 58.

6. Philemon Sarungi, in "Remains of Fallen Heroes to be Returned," in *Daily News*, Dar es Salaam, Tanzania, 12 July 2002.

7. Mwelwa C. Musambachime, Permanent Mission of the Republic of Zambia to the United Nations, "Memorial to Mwalimu Nyerere on his 80th Birthday," April 15, 2002. See also Barbara Cornwall, *The Bush Rebels: A Personal Account of Black Revolt in Africa* (New York: Henry Holt & Co., 1972); Luis B. Serapiao, *Mozambique*

in the Twentieth Century: From Colonialism to Independence (Maryland: University Press of America, 1979); M.D.D. Newitt, *A History of Mozambique* (Bloomington, Indiana: Indiana University Press, 1995).

The Rhodesian Crisis:
The Struggle for Zimbabwe

TANZANIA was the first African country to break off diplomatic relations with Britain because of the refusal of the British government to intervene in Rhodesia to end the illegal seizure of power by the white minority regime which unilaterally declared independence in that British colony.

The unilateral declaration of independence (UDI) by whites on November 11, 1965, under the leadership of Prime Minister Ian Smith, was a flagrant violation of the rights of the black majority who were denied racial equality and excluded from the government of their country. And it was strongly condemned by African countries which demanded immediate action by Britain to end the rebellion in her colony.

When Britain failed to do so by December 15, 1965, most African countries severed diplomatic ties with her in protest and in fulfillment of a resolution adopted by the Organization of African Unity (OAU) requiring all African countries to take such action.

President Julius Nyerere set the tone for Africa's collective response to the crisis by being the most relentless and outspoken champion of black majority rule in Rhodesia among the leaders of the frontline states which included Tanzania, Zambia, Botswana, Mozambique, and Angola. He was also chairman of the leaders of the frontline states, and Tanzania the headquarters of all the African liberation movements. As he stated in an interview with *Time*, 9 October 1978:

"We will win in Rhodesia. But you can help us shorten the war....We are left only with the fighting. We will back the nationalists and fight to the end. We have no choice."

Tanzania was also the first country in the region to win independence, as Tanganyika in 1961, and immediately offered sanctuary to the freedom fighters and refugees from countries still under white minority rule. A large number of the freedom fighters and refugees who sought asylum in Tanzania came from Rhodesia.

Rhodesia's road to independence was filled with minefields, in the literal sense as well, and presented Britain with one of her most vexing problems mainly because of the pressure exerted on her by African countries - most of them independent by then - to end the rebellion by the white minority regime. But Britain was unwilling to take action due to a number of factors: economic interests, East-West ideological rivalry, security of the West, and racial considerations; with the vast majority of the whites in Rhodesia being British themselves.

South Africa was Britain's third largest export market and the recipient of one third of British overseas investment in the 1960s. And the vast majority of whites in South Africa, including the apartheid regime itself, were overwhelmingly in favour of UDI.

The opposition leader in the South African parliament, Sir de Villiers Graaff, went so far as to say that the government of Prime Minister Hendrik Verwoerd was not giving enough help to Rhodesia; Verwoerd himself being a fierce proponent of white supremacy. And because of her vested interests in South Africa, Britain was reluctant to support full mandatory sanctions - endorsed by the United Nations - against Rhodesia because she feared that this would generate momentum for a comprehensive embargo against South Africa as well. As Professor Richard Coggins of Oxford University states:

"Southern Rhodesia's Unilateral Declaration of Independence in November 1965 created arguably the most intractable problem in British foreign and colonial policy in the post-war period. For 15 years successive UK governments sought to end the rebellion by the white settler regime entrenched in Salisbury. Economic sanctions and political initiatives failed to convince the regime of Ian Smith to agree to concede power to the black majority in the country now known as Zimbabwe....

Rhodesian independence raised several conflicting problems for Harold Wilson's Labour government.... Beset by ongoing economic crisis, the government had to reconcile backbench opinion, sceptical - if not hostile - criticism from the African Commonwealth, and pressure at the United Nations, with the need to dispose of the problem in a practicable way, taking into account essential economic interests in South Africa and Zambia. The principal dilemma for British policy makers was a classic one: balancing considerations of Realpolitik against fundamental principles of democracy for the black majority in Rhodesia."[1]

Besides South Africa, Britain also had significant economic interests in Zambia on whose copper supplies - at least 40 percent - British manufacturers and other businesses were heavily dependent. Therefore, ignoring Zambian demands over Rhodesia and her security concerns would have jeopardized relations between the two countries and could even have led to curtailment of copper supplies to Britain.

One of the considerations of Realpolitik which clashed with the fundamental principles of democracy for the black majority in Rhodesia was Britain's desire to neutralize Soviet and Chinese influence in Africa which was gaining ground because of Russian and Chinese support for the liberation movements across the continent, especially in southern Africa.

Yet, Britain's unwillingness to end the Smith rebellion, by force if necessary as circumstances seemed to dictate, could not be reconciled with her desire to contain or neutralize Eastern-bloc influence in Africa, or with the universal assumption that race-neutral democratic principles were the accepted norm in international relations; at least in theory even if not in practice in all cases, and as an ideal to be attained.

Britain's failure to aggressively advance the cause of freedom for the black majority in Rhodesia not only undermined British interests in independent Africa but enhanced the image of the Russians and the Chinese as well as their communist allies - the Cubans, the East Germans and others - as "true friends" of the Africans in the liberation struggle against white minority rule. It also provided the communists with ample ammunition to attack and portray Britain and other Western countries as racist (the same way the Soviet Union did to the United States when black Americans in the southern states were being attacked during the civil rights movement in the fifties and sixties) because of their friendly policies towards white minority regimes in Africa - including apartheid South Africa, the bastion of white supremacy - and their refusal even to help bring about fundamental change in white-dominated countries on the continent.

Therefore, the issue of racial equality in Rhodesia was not of paramount importance to Britain and her Western allies; nor was it to the Russians and the Chinese, although they used it effectively as a propaganda weapon against the West in their ideological rivalry at the height of the Cold War.

But it was of utmost importance to Africa. And Smith's unilateral declaration of independence was an act of ultimate defiance of fundamental human rights, and of the wishes of the African majority, that could not go unchallenged by the independent African states. It was in this context that President Nyerere articulated his position on the Rhodesian crisis, one of the most urgent problems ever confronted by independent Africa.

And the refusal by Britain to use military force to end the rebellion was hypocritical. Britain herself used military force to expand and maintain her colonial empire. And that included Rhodesia itself in the 1890s, besides Ghana against the Ashanti, the Mau Mau in Kenya in the 1950s, and even the military campaigns against Germany in Africa and Asia in World I and World II. Yet, the British government refused to use force to end the Smith rebellion even though that would have been the only and most effective way to do so, as clearly demonstrated 15 years later when a sustained military campaign by the freedom fighters compelled Smith to capitulate and relinquish power to the black majority.

Even in the 1960s, when the white minority regime illegally seized power in Rhodesia, Britain did not refrain from using military force in other parts of the Commonwealth to protect and promote her interests. She did so in Malaysia, Aden, South Arabia, and even in Tanganyika in January 1964 when President Nyerere requested British assistance to suppress the army mutiny as we learned earlier. And she almost did so in Zanzibar in January 1964 to reinstate the Arab regime that had been overthrown in the revolution and would have done so had it not been for the intervention by Kenyan Foreign Affairs Minister Joseph Murumbi who refused to allow British troops in Kenya to go to Zanzibar at the request of the sultan to put him back in power.

So why not in Rhodesia?

The argument that Britain did not militarily intervene in Rhodesia because dislodging Smith from power and ending his rebellion would have required a large military operation and troop commitment, is not supported by facts. Britain used massive military force in previous wars - in World War II and even in the Boer War in South Africa - yet refused to do so against Rhodesia.

It seemed obvious that Britain did not want to intervene militarily because the intervention would have been directed against fellow whites and would have ended white privilege enjoyed at the expense of blacks; an interpretation given validity by Britain's strong denunciations of President Robert Mugabe in the nineties and beyond against his seizure of white-owned land to correct historical injustices perpetrated against the African majority during British colonial rule, while maintaining virtual silence on despotic rule and other injustices committed by black leaders against blacks elsewhere on the continent if Britain's concern in the case of Zimbabwe was, indeed, simply a matter of justice and not racially motivated.

Even the intelligence services of Britain, Rhodesia, and apartheid South Africa - the British M15, the Rhodesian Central Intelligence Organization (CIO), and the South African Bureau of State Security (BOSS) - worked very closely; a concession also made by the head of the Rhodesian Central Intelligence Organization (CIO), Ken Flower, in his book, *Serving Secretly: Rhodesia's CIO Chief on Record.*[2] It was a tripartite alliance which amounted to a security pact of kinsmen to protect white interests in Africa.

There was no other explanation - besides race, why Britain did not intervene militarily in Rhodesia - that would have convinced Africans otherwise, including those in other countries across the continent. And that was the only plausible and credible explanation. Britain was stronger than Rhodesia. Therefore ending the rebellion by military force was a practical proposition. But Britain chose not to do so, thus incurring the wrath of African countries.

Dr. Kwame Nkrumah was one of the strongest proponents of military intervention in Rhodesia and strongly urged Britain to exercise this option. He even proposed mobilizing a Pan-African force to intervene in Rhodesia and oust Smith, thus paving the way to black majority rule, but was overthrown in February 1966 in a coup engineered and masterminded by the CIA, three months after Rhodesia illegally declared independence. In fact, Akwasi A. Afrifa, who led the coup, stated in his book, *The Ghana Coup*,[3] that one of the reasons why he and his fellow soldiers overthrew Nkrumah was that he was getting ready to send them to fight a war they had nothing to do with, and in a faraway country they knew nothing about; an inexplicable statement coming from an African.

Yet, the collective sentiment articulated across the continent was exactly the opposite of how Afrifa and his treasonous coterie felt. Military force was the only viable option in the Rhodesian context. Smith could not be ousted any other way, as African countries clearly showed when they gave full support to the freedom fighters, training and arming them. In the Commonwealth, the strongest exponents of military intervention to end the rebellion in Rhodesia were presidents Nkrumah, Nyerere, Obote, and Kaunda.

These leaders also knew that race was a factor in Britain's refusal or unwillingness to use military force in Rhodesia. In fact, it was highly unlikely that British soldiers would have obeyed orders to go and fight their "kith and kin." And there was a strong possibility that South Africa would have intervened on Rhodesia's side for the same reason, racial solidarity, a point underscored by Colin Legum in "Witness Seminar on Rhodesian UDI":

"The heated early arguments over whether Britain should have intervened militarily to stifle UDI at the beginning ignored two political factors as well as assumptions about the willingness of the army to obey an order to go to Rhodesia, and possible South African reactions.... Another political factor was that a military decision would not only have divided parliament between Labour and Conservatives but would also have polarised the British electorate over 'kith and kin' sentiments. (And) the anti-military interventionist made an issue about the possibility that South Africa would intervene militarily, directly or indirectly.

Much was made of the assumption that the army would refuse to fight against 'kith and kin.' At the time I was engaged in lecturing at the four UK regional commands. At the Southern Command, the commanding officer at a mess lunch said emphatically that most of his senior officers would resign rather than accept an order to go to Rhodesia.

On the other hand, the commanding officer at Scottish command was equally emphatict hat it was unthinkable that the British Army would refuse a legal command. General Henry Alexander, who had experience in Ghana, Nigeria and the Congo, told me that he was prepared personally to take a brigade to Salisbury to take over and establish control over the international airport which would give the British Government a bargaining position to discuss terms with Smith.

Contrary to official denials that a contingency plan for military intervention was ever prepared, I met an army team in Southern Command who had worked on a contingency plan, the outline of which was given to me."[4]

The fact that the British military, on orders from the government, worked on a contingency plan for military intervention in Rhodesia is indisputable evidence showing that the British government and armed forces believed that a military operation was a feasible undertaking; thus invalidating the argument that Britain did not intervene because the mission would have failed. It also lends credibility to the contention that the main reason why the British government refused to use military force against the white minority regime in Rhodesia was race.

Preparation for the contingency plan also showed that logistical problems were not an insurmountable obstacle to military intervention, had Britain decided to launch an operation.

British officers who went to Zambia to assess the country's defence needs, because of the potential threat from neighbouring Rhodesia, conceded that a large military intervention, including large-scale bombing to destroy the Rhodesian Royal Air Force (RRAF), would be necessary; so would a deployment of considerable military force of divisional strength. Zambian airfields would have to be used to launch an operation of such magnitude against Rhodesia, but the airfields' capacity was limited; and military helicopters taking off from an aircraft carrier in the Madagascar Strait would have had enough fuel to fly British soldiers to Rhodesia, but not to get them out if things went wrong - did anyone ever ask Tanzania, which is not very far from Rhodesia, if the helicopters en route to Rhodesia from the Madagascar Strait in the Indian Ocean could use her facilities to re-fuel to make sure they had enough fuel to fly back?

But in spite of all those obstacles mentioned here, British military planners concluded that they would be able to launch a successful military operation against Rhodesia. That is why they drew up a contingency plan for military intervention, thus vindicating the position taken by African countries that the white minority regime in

Salisbury could indeed be removed by force.

Even South African intervention on Rhodesia's side, however massive, could not have prevented the British military from carrying out a successful military operation against the Smith regime. Advanced as South Africa is, by African and Third World standards, her armed forces would still have been no match for British military might, had the British government been fully committed to its mission of ousting Smith by force. But it never embarked on this mission, triggering a sharp response from African countries and intensifying pressure on Britain to end the rebellion by any means possible. The military option remained one such possibility and the most effective one, if economic sanctions failed as they were bound to, because of sanctions-busting by a number of countries including South Africa, France, the United States (buying chrome and engaging in other anti-embargo activities), Portugal, Spain, Japan, Taiwan, Israel and others.

In the Commonwealth, the number of countries which took the most uncompromising stand on the Rhodesian crisis dropped to three after Ghana left the ranks following the ouster of Dr. Nkrumah. They were Tanzania, Zambia, and Uganda. But they were soon joined by Nigeria when a military regime came to power and took a more militant stand on Rhodesia, including a threat to nationalize a major British oil company if Britain kept on dragging her feet over the Rhodesian crisis. The threat caused great concern on Britain. And pressure intensified on the British government to resolve the crisis:

"After 1970, Commonwealth summit conferences began to focus increasingly on the Rhodesian issue. Criticism, led by Tanzania's President Julius Nyerere, Sierra Leone President Albert Margai, and Uganda's President Milton Obote, condemned (British Prime Minister Harold) Wilson's negotiations with Smith on board Tiger and Fearless, fearing a sell-out. They invented the slogan NIBMAR - No Independence Before Majority Rule.

The Commonwealth factor became increasingly important to the point where, under a Nigerian threat, Wilson's Foreign Secretary, James Callaghan, flew to Nigeria for a meeting, the result of which was Wilson's astonishing statement that sanctions would succeed in a 'matter of weeks.' At the time I was in close touch with W.A.W. Clarke, the official in the Commonwealth Office responsible for monitoring the progress of the sanctions programme; he told me that Wilson's statement disregarded all reports submitted to him and was devoid of reality."[5]

It was clear to African leaders that British Prime Minister Harold Wilson was not serious about ending the rebellion in Rhodesia, leaving them with only one option: supporting guerrilla warfare against the minority regime. President Nyerere was the most outspoken supporter of the freedom fighters and established military training camps for them in Tanzania, prompting rebel Prime Minister Ian Smith to describe him "the evil genius on the the Rhodesian scene" and behind all the liberation movements in Africa.

He equally incurred the wrath of apartheid South Africa, first by threatening in August 1961 that Tanganyika would not join the Commonwealth - after attaining sovereign status on December 9, 1961 - if South Africa remained a member. As he bluntly put it: "To vote South Africa in, is to vote us out." The threat was taken seriously by Britain and other countries and forced the apartheid regime to withdraw. Nigeria also played a major role in forcing South Africa out of the Commonwealth.

Nyerere also launched a sustained campaign to stop Britain from arming South Africa; opened up military training camps in Tanzania for freedom fighters from the land of apartheid and other countries under white minority rule; and provided the freedom fighters with an external service at Radio Tanzania, Dar es Salaam (RTD), which became very effective in mobilizing forces and support against the white racist regimes on the continent. According to *Africa Contemporary Record*:

"The Rhodesian rebel Minister of Law and Order, Mr. Lardner Burke, extending the state of emergency at the beginning of 1968, said that the number of 'terrorists' waiting in Zambia and Tanzania to cross the Rhodesian border continued to mount. The South African Deputy-Minister of Police, Mr. S.L. Muller, said Tanzania posed 'the greatest potential threat to the Republic.' He claimed there were '40 camps in Tanzania for the training of terrorists and all the offices of subversive organisations.' In Zambia, he said, there were '19 training and transit camps.'

An external service of Radio Tanzania was inaugurated in 1968 to assist in 'propagating the ideological principles of the liberation movements in Tanzania.'"[6]

Tanzania's and Zambia's uncompromising stand and strong support for the freedom fighters triggered a sharp response from South Africa. On April 24, 1968, the former head of the South African Defence Force, Commandant-General S.A. Melville, threatened the two countries, contending that South Africa already had sufficient justification and provocation for retaliation against countries which "harboured" and encouraged "terrorists" to penetrate South Africa and South West Africa.[7] South West Africa, now Namibia, was a German colony the Germans lost in World War I. It was taken over by South Africa - under the League of Nations mandate - which continued to rule the former German colony in defiance of the United Nations which terminated its mandate in 1966.

The threat by Commandant-General S.A. Melville included South West Africa because it was a virtual colony, or province, of apartheid South Africa. The Minister of Defence P.W. Botha, who later became president, used even more blunt language to threaten Tanzania and Zambia, saying countries which harbor and train "terrorists" should receive a "sudden hard knock."[8] Rhodesia itself, although weaker, was equally committed to the same policy of hot pursuit of the "terrorists" all the way back to the countries where they were based and trained.

South Africa and Rhodesia invoked sovereign rights to justify their position and even their diabolical policies. It is true that South Africa, even under apartheid, was a legal sovereign entity and recognized as one by the international community. But Rhodesia was not, and only claimed to be a legally constituted state; its "legitimacy" derived from usurpation of power under the Crown, which was tantamount to treason since it was legally *still* a British colony. Yet, for all practical purposes, it functioned as an independent state in spite of its dubious credentials; a matter that was also addressed by the Rhodesian High Court but to the satisfaction of no one in the African nationalist movement. According to *Africa Research Bulletin*:

"The five judges of the Appellate Division of the Rhodesian High Court, hearing the constitution test case appeal, ruled on January 29th, 1968, by a majority of 3 to 2 that the Rhodesian Government was not yet a *de jure* government. But four of the judges agreed that it was in effective control of the country and therefore the *de facto* government. A minority of two of the judges found that the Government had acquired *de jure* status and one judge considered that Rhodesia was already a *de facto* republic."[9]

Although the Rhodesian High Court conferred legitimacy on the Smith regime despite its treasonous acts, the fundamental problem that there shall be no independence before majority rule - a position maintained by African nationalists and other Africans across the continent - was not even addressed by the court. Therefore, what came to be known as the NIBMAR principle - No Independence Before Majority Rule - articulated by President Julius Nyerere and others - was collectively invoked by African countries under the auspices of the Organization of African Unity (OAU) as the rationale for armed struggle. And it became the cornerstone of all the negotiations conducted through the years to resolve the Rhodesian crisis, while the liberation war was being prosecuted at the same time and used as a bargaining tool to extract meaningful concessions from the white minority regime in Salisbury.

The Rhodesian crisis became a test case for independent Africa, and was the most urgent issue confronting the continent since the chaos in the Congo. But the Rhodesian impasse was also a test case for Britain to live up to her commitments. As Nyerere stated on December 14, 1965 - before severing diplomatic ties with Britain the next day over the Rhodesian crisis - in his speech to the Tanzania National Assembly, aptly entitled, "The Honour of Africa":

"The policies of Tanzania, and of Africa, in relation to Southern Rhodesia, have always had one object, and one object only. That was, and is, to secure a rapid transition to independence on the basis of majority rule....

Africa maintains that Southern Rhodesia is at present a colony of the United Kingdom, and that ultimate responsibility for events there resides, in consequence, with the Government of the united Kingdom in London.... (But) Britain has not shown serious determination either to get rid of those in Southern Rhodesia who have usurped British power, or to replace them with representatives of the people. For it is not the independence of Rhodesia that Africa is complaining about; it is independence under a racialist minority government....

Southern Rhodesia is a British colony; its constitution is subject to the will of the British Parliament. As an international entity Southern Rhodesia does not exist. Internationally, by both law and custom, there exists only Britain and its colony.

The colony of Southern Rhodesia has been self-governing since 1923; for 43 years increasing *de facto* power has been exerted by a government based in Salisbury. But the constitution under which that government operated reserved certain powers to the British Government and Parliament in London. The fact that successive British Governments did not use their powers to prevent acts which were contrary to the interests of the African people does not alter the existence of these 'Reserved Powers'; nor the ultimate responsibility of the British Government for the actions of the Southern Rhodesian government.

In saying this there is no need to argue abstract cases of law. Britain herself accepts responsibility for Southern Rhodesia. More, she claims that responsibility. Britain claims that she, and she alone, can decide what is to be done about Southern Rhodesia. The only time she has ever used her veto in the United Nations was when Ghana proposed a resolution which would have blocked the transfer to the Southern Rhodesian government of the Air Force which had been built up by the defunct Federation of Rhodesia and Nyasaland. In the Commonwealth Conferences of 1964 and 1965, the Government of Britain maintained this stand, and it was conceded by the rest of the Commonwealth - including the African members. And just over a week ago - on 6 December 1965 - Mr. Wilson, the Prime Minister of Britain, is reported to have said once again, 'Rhodesia is Britain's responsibility.'

There is thus no dispute between Britain and Africa about the British responsibility. What then of the manner in which that responsibility has been, and is being, exercised?

I do not propose to go back further than October 1964 in an examination of the British record. The record before that date is a shameful one; time after time the interests of the African majority were subjected to the selfish power hunger of the settler minority.

Even after 1947, when other colonies in Africa began to feel some hope of ultimate freedom, the settlers of Southern Rhodesia were able to extend their sway. In return for some concessions on the periphery of power, some verbal acceptance of the theory of 'partnership,' they were able to secure dominance in a federation of Rhodesia with the countries, which are now Zambia and Malawi.

In 1961, with the tide running hard against them, and when they were concerned to try and save their federation, they still managed to secure a constitution for Southern Rhodesia, which entrenched minority power while only appearing to make some concessions to the African population. And in 1963, at the break-up of the federation (which was established in 1953), they secured into their own hands the real instruments of power - the aeroplanes, the equipment, and the administration of the Army and the Air Force.

For the settler government of Southern Rhodesia even this was not enough. In 1963, and even more in 1964, they began to demand independence for themselves.

That was the position in October 1964....

On 27 October 1964, the Prime Minister of Britain said openly to Mr. Smith, the Prime Minister in the British colony, that a unilateral 'declaration of independence would be an open act of defiance and rebellion, and it would be treasonable to take steps to give effect to it.' These strong words meant that Africa was heartened despite the fact that the statement went on to speak only of economic consequences of such a declaration.

In November, however, the Smith government called for a referendum in support of independence for Southern Rhodesia under the 1961 constitution. He received 58,000 votes in support. I ask that this House should take particular note of that number; it is less than the total registered voters in the Dar es Salaam South constituency of Tanzania. And even that vote was only obtained after Mr. Smith had said that he was not asking for a vote in support of an illegal declaration of independence!

Threats of illegal action nonetheless continued to come from Salisbury, and apart from warnings about what would happen if they were carried out, nothing was done to those who made the threats. Indeed, by the end of the year there were indications from London that independence might be granted without majority rule. Mr. Bottomley, the British Commonwealth Secretary, was reported as saying , 'We must be satisfied that the basis on which independence is to be granted is acceptable to the people as a whole.' This ambiguous statement was clearly deliberate, and it succeeded in one of its designs. Africa thought that this was merely a tactical move, an endeavour to avoid provoking Smith before Britain was ready to deal with him....

Although UDI was declared to be an act of rebellion there was a studious avoidance by British Ministers of the statement that the rebellion would be brought down by all necessary means, including the use of force. The Smith group were never faced with that prospect. On several occasions British Ministers said, 'We shall not use force to impose a constitutional solution' to the Rhodesian situation. They never went further. Africa worried, and waited.

Even more serious for Africa was the deliberate vagueness about the ultimate objective of the negotiations (between Smith and the British government) and the opposition to UDI....

Britain's 'five principles' which had to be met before independence would be granted by the British Government did not specify the existence of majority rule. On the contrary, they clearly showed that if certain 'safeguards' were enshrined in a document, then majority rule would not be insisted upon. There was only one ambiguous statement in principle five, which many genuine people - including African leaders - believed provided a safeguard. Principle five stated that 'any basis proposed for independence must be acceptable to the people of Rhodesia as a whole.' Many of our friends said that the people of that colony could not possibly agree on an independence without majority rule, and that therefore, so long as this principle was maintained, Rhodesia would not become completely a second South Africa without hope of peaceful progress.

Tanzania was less sanguine; in the Commonwealth Conference I therefore demanded that the words *'independence on the basis of majority rule'* be included in the final communique. They were not included; and in consequence Tanzania disassociated itself from the Southern Rhodesia section of the communique. Our friends thought us needlessly suspicious. But it was quite clear to us that the British Government was willing to grant independence on the basis of minority rule.

Now it is one month after the minority government of Rhodesia has seized power.... Have we yet had the assurance (of independence on the basis of majority rule), which Tanzania sought in June? The answer is no. The 1961 constitution remains in being, with some few powers having been resumed by the Government in London. This resumption having been forced upon Britain by Smith! Let me quote Mr. Wilson, the Prime Minister of the United Kingdom, speaking in the House of Commons, London, on 23 November 1965 - 12 days after the rebellion. He said - as reported in the *Times*:

'While we have power to revoke or amend sections of the 1961 constitution we have said we have no present intention of revoking it as a whole, and I cannot at this stage foresee circumstances in which we would do so.'

Mr. Wilson went on to deal with the role of this constitution in what he calls 'the resettlement period.' He said:

'When the Governor is able to report that the people of Rhodesia are willing and able to work on constitutional paths, we are prepared to work together with their leaders to make a new start. For this purpose the 1961 constitution remains in being, though the House will realize the need for those amendments which are required to prevent its perversion and misuse such as we have seen in the last fortnight, and those amendments, too, which are needed to give effect to the five principles to which all parties in this House have subscribed'....

Later in the same speech Mr. Wilson said:

'All along we have made it plain - we did all throughout the negotiations - that while guaranteed and unimpeded progress to majority rule is the policy of all of us, we dot believe it can be immediate.... But all of us are committed to an early attempt by the Rhodesian people to pronounce on their own future. That was the reason for the suggested referendum and for the Royal Commission.'

The thing, which I notice in the last statement, Mr. Speaker, is that this was not an assurance about majority rule; it was an assurance against majority rule.

At the end of last week the British Broadcasting Corporation (BBC) news service reported that Mr. Wilson had suggested that after all, when British authority was re-established in Southern Rhodesia, there might be a period of direct rule by the Governor with advisers from all races. As this would mean the end of the 1961 constitution I had a moment of hope; we would begin over again. But the report went on to say that Mr. Wilson stressed that majority rule could not come for a very long time - and still there was no suggestion that independence would be held up until this majority rule had finally been attained....

It is not the timing, which is causing Africa to become so angry; we could argue about time. Our anger and suspicion arise from the fact that Britain is not even now - 14 December 1965 - committed to the principle of 'independence only on the basis of majority rule.'

I must, however, now move to the question of whether Britain has shown serious determination to get rid of those in Southern Rhodesia who have usurped her power. Africa maintains that she has not....

What has Britain done since 11 November?

On that date Mr. Wilson used some strong words: he said, 'It is an illegal act, ineffective in law; an act of rebellion against the Crown and against the constitution as by law established.' But he then went on to instruct the civil servants of Southern Rhodesia to 'stay at their posts but not assist in any illegal acts.' He was unable to explain how they could do that when they were serving an illegal government.

As regards the use of force Mr. Wilson repeated his stock phrase despite the changed circumstances. Britain would not use force to impose a constitutional settlement he said, but he went on to say that the British Government 'would give full consideration to any appeal from the Governor for help to restore law and order.' Mr. Wilson refrained from explaining how the law could be more broken than it had been by the usurpation of power, that is to say, by treason. He refrained later from explaining how the Governor was to transmit his appeal once the telephone had been taken from him as well as all the furniture of his office, his staff and his transport.

Instead, Mr. Wilson obtained the approval of the British Parliament for economic action against the regime. Capital exports to southern Rhodesia were stopped; exchange restrictions were imposed; Commonwealth preference was suspended, and a ban was imposed on the

British import of Rhodesian tobacco and sugar. The British Foreign Secretary was sent to the United Nations to secure international support for these actions.

The United Nations was highly critical: it demanded further action. Finally, on 20 November Britain accepted a Security Council resolution which included this phrase: 'Calls upon all states...to do their utmost in order to break all economic relations with Southern Rhodesia, including an embargo on oil and petroleum products'....

On 23 November Mr. Wilson spoke to the House of Commons, saying, 'We are going to study all aspects of trade and oil.... We are not going in for a trade embargo or oil embargo alone.' And in explanation of this, he said that there are many difficulties and 'there is the position of Zambia to be considered'! That Zambia had supported the resolution appeared irrelevant to the British Prime Minister, who clearly thought he knew the business of that independent African state better than President Kaunda. On 1 December Mr. Wilson again said, 'We are not contemplating an embargo immediately.'

What is Africa expected to think of this mockery of a UN resolution which was already - at Britain's insistence - less than a firm, binding declaration of determination to defeat Smith?

On 1 December, however, Mr. Wilson announced new and much sterner economic measures against Rhodesia. Ninety-five per cent of Rhodesia's exports to Britain were then blocked, and financial measures taken which could have had a fairly quick and fairly severe effect on the economy of that colony. But Mr. Smith of Rhodesia was yesterday reported to have said that these have come too late to affect Rhodesia's economy. I do not believe that he is bluffing. He has had weeks in which to prepare for these measures. But the timing is not my only criticism. I have argued that economic sanctions against Rhodesia will not work as long as South Africa is allowed to trade freely with the rebel colony. And it is Britain, which has blocked obligatory sanctions under Chapter 7 of the UN Charter....

The British Government has not shown serious determination either to get rid of those in Southern Rhodesia who have usurped British power, or to replace them with representatives of the people.... Britain... has failed to live up to the responsibilities she has claimed, and she has failed to protect...an independent state (Zambia) which is threatened because of her failure to immediately overthrow the rebel regime."[10]

On the next day, December 15, Tanzania broke off diplomatic relations with Britain because of Britain's unwillingness to end the rebellion in Rhodesia. The British government did not even ask for a multilateral force under UN auspices to intervene if she did not want to do so alone and commit only British troops to combat. Nyerere became the first African leader to sever diplomatic ties with Britain in compliance with the OAU resolution adopted on December 2, 1965, in Addis Ababa, Ethiopia, by all independent African countries except two, including Malawi under Dr. Hastings Kamuzu Banda, a perennial opponent of OAU policies towards white minority regimes on the continent.

Tanzania was followed by Ghana under Dr. Nkrumah, and Egypt under Gamal Abdel Nasser, some of the strongest supporters of the African nationalist groups in Rhodesia and other white-ruled countries in Africa. They were also some of Lumumba's uncompromising supporters during the Congo crisis and sent troops to the Congo under UN command to help save his government. Nkrumah was also the first African leader to propose sending a Pan-African force to Rhodesia and offered Ghanaian troops for combat in the rebel colony to oust Smith from power.

Even before illegally declaring independence, Smith was confident of success. His confidence could largely be attributed to the fact that he did not believe Britain would send troops to Rhodesia to kill their "kith and kin"; also to the fact that no all countries around the world would abandon Rhodesia or enforce economic sanctions against his regime even if they publicly condemned the unilateral declaration of independence (UDI). He calculated well, and was right on both counts.

And after winning what came to be known as the "Constitution Test Case" before the Appellate Division of the Rhodesian High Court which conferred legitimacy on Rhodesia as an independent state, Smith felt vindicated in his claim that he had the electoral mandate to declare Rhodesia a sovereign entity; although only 58,000 voters, all white - out of a population of about 250,000 whites and more than 4 million Africans - endorsed his move, and only when he told them that it would not be illegal, although he knew full well that it was; since Rhodesia was still legally a British colony - therefore could not legally become independent without the approval of the British parliament. He totally ignored the wishes of the vast majority, the 4 million Africans who constituted more than 95 percent of the total population.

Zambian Minister of Foreign Affairs Reuben Kamanga expressed his government's "utter disgust" with the way the British government had handled the situation in Rhodesia "by resorting to ineffective means instead of bringing down the rebellion by force."[11]

But demands in the UN Security Council by African countries that Britain should use force against the white minority regime in Rhodesia were rejected by British Prime Minister Harold Wilson on March 14, 1966. Lack of such action or any other effective measures to end the rebellion emboldened Rhodesian Prime Minister Ian Smith to say in a broadcast on March 24, 1966, that any personal doubts he had about Rhodesia becoming a republic had been "wiped out completely by the antics of Harold

Wilson and his socialist Government." He went on to say that recent attempts by the British to interfere with the maintenance of law and order in Rhodesia, openly or by hiding behind the skirts of their Queen, were "one of the most despicable acts ever committed by a Government in Britain"; and defiantly added that things "are going well in Rhodesia and according to plan."[12]

But the "Constitution Test Case" won in Rhodesia had a different outcome in Britain where in July 1966 the Privy Council ruled that the emergency regulations passed by the Rhodesian government - and used to detain people - had no legal validity; and that the "usurping Government now in control (in Rhodesia) could not be regarded as the lawful Government."[13]

However, the Rhodesian authorities dismissed the ruling as irrelevant, since their own high court had already ruled that Rhodesia was a legal sovereign entity and therefore no longer subject to British law. Yet, despite its status as a pariah in the international arena where, at least officially, no country recognized this British colony as an independent nation, it continued to function as a *de facto* independent state and got a lot of support from apartheid South Africa which refused to enforce economic sanctions imposed by the United Nations on the white minority regime in Salisbury.

South Africa also sent police and military reinforcements to Rhodesia to help the regime fight African nationalists and flatly refused to withdraw them when Britain asked the apartheid government to do so. Containing or neutralizing the nationalist insurgency in Rhodesia, with the help of South African forces, was also considered by the South African government to be in the best security interests of the apartheid state.

Emboldened by this crucial assistance from South Africa, Rhodesian Prime Minister Ian Smith became even more defiant in his public pronouncements, virtually daring African countries to go after him, as he continued to emphasize that there shall be no black majority rule in Rhodesia. Because of this unholy alliance between the two white-dominated countries - together with the Portuguese in their colonies of Angola, Mozambique and Portuguese Guinea (Guinea-Bissau) - African countries were confronted with what was essentially the same problem, only in different territories.

Therefore, although the Rhodesian crisis was serious enough by itself, it could not be separated from the other crises in the region. And the destiny of all the countries in southern Africa became inextricably linked with that of the rest of the continent; as had indeed always been the case, only in a more pronounced way this time, with independent Africa being in a state of war with the white minority regimes.

The defiance of the Smith regime was also a negation of the principles of justice and equality independent Africa invoked to justify her existence. African countries constituted an indivisible whole. The dignity and freedom they were entitled to, was equally indivisible. And an insult to one was an insult to all. As President Nyerere stated in April 1966 - a few months after Rhodesia declared independence in November 1965 - in his article, "Rhodesia in the Context of Southern Africa," in *Foreign Affairs*:

"The deep and intense anger of Africa on the subject of Rhodesia is by now widely realized. it is not, however, so clearly understood. In consequence the mutual suspicion, which already exists between free African states and nations of the West, is in danger of getting very much worse.

Before November 11th, 1965, African states, individually and collectively, had frequently expressed their great concern about the position in Southern

Rhodesia. But it was with the unilateral declaration of independence by the Smith regime that this concern was transformed into impatient wrath.

The catalyst of this changed attitude was the rebellion against British sovereignty. This was not because Africa wished Southern Rhodesia to remain a colony; Africa's earlier demands had been for action to end colonialism. Nor was it evidence of a deep-rooted objection to illegality in the anti-colonial struggle. It is a fact that Africa prefers to use constitutional, legal and peaceful methods in the campaigns for national freedom; but if these fail then other methods are accepted. Thus, for example, an Algerian Government-in-Exile was recognized by many African states long before France conceded independence to that North African state.

And at the present time a Government-in-Exile, headed by Holden Roberto, is recognized by the Organization of African Unity as the rightful authority in Angola despite the fact that legally Portugal continues to dominate the area. Africa's objection is to this particular assumption of authority in Southern Rhodesia, not to illegality in general. It would be hypocrisy to pretend otherwise.

The hostility aroused by the Smith declaration of independence is based on a rational interpretation of its purpose and its effects in relation to the total and legitimate goals of Africa. For this rebellion is not an uprising of the people; it represents an attempt to expand the area, and strengthen the hold in Africa, of doctrines, which are inimical to the whole future of freedom in this continent. It represents an advance by the forces of racialism, fascism, and indeed, colonialism, in Southern Africa.

To the independent states of Africa this is not a development, which can be viewed with Olympian detachment. We are on the frontiers of the conflict with these forces, and our future demands their defeat.

Gradually and somewhat painfully, colonialism and racialism have been pushed out of Northern and Central Africa.

But while they remain in this continent none of us can really be free to live in peace and dignity, or be able to concentrate on the economic development, which was a large part of the purpose of our political revolution. The Smith declaration of independence represents a counter-attack by these forces, and it is in that context that Africa has reacted, and demands its defeat.

This should not be difficult to comprehend. It may have been possible for the Allied Powers to make peace with Hitler after France, Belgium, and Holland were liberated. They were not prepared to try. Still less were the Jews outside Germany willing to support any compromise which would have left their compatriots under the control of a Nazi regime - even had the ultimate horror of racial extermination been excluded. Both the states concerned, and the peoples who were being treated as racially inferior, realized that the war had to continue until Nazism was politically ended in Europe.

The parallels are almost exact. The separate freedom movements in Africa were but different arms of one liberation process. When Dr. Nkrumah said in 1957 that the independence of Ghana was incomplete until the whole of Africa was free, he spoke a truth, which is still valid for all of us. The struggle has to continue until final victory; colonialism must be wiped out in Africa before any post-colonial independent state can feel secure. And no citizen of Africa - white or black - can live in the comfort of his own self-respect while other African citizens are suffering discrimination and humiliation for being born what they are.

Yet at the present time the Portuguese colonies of Angola and Mozambique, together with South Africa, South West Africa, and Rhodesia, constitute almost one seventh of the landmass of Africa. About 12 per cent of

Africa's population lives in these areas. And each of these territories in their different way are governed on the principles of racial inequality and minority domination.

Portugal pretends that her colonies are really part of Europe, and that she abjures racial discrimination. She claims instead to be in the process of making European Gentlemen out of the African inhabitants of those areas, and talks proudly of the policy of equality for the 'assimilado.' But Africans are not European, could not become European, and do not want to become European. They demand instead the right to be Africans in Africa, and to determine their own cultural, economic, and political future. This right is what Portugal denies. The inhabitants of her colonies can certainly be 'African'; but if they are, then they are subjected to special laws, and special taxation and labour levies; their participation in the functions of their own government is ruled out.

In South Africa there is no longer even the pretence that citizens of different races are equal before the law, or in social and economic rights and duties. The 'separate but equal' concept, which was defeated in the United States in 1964, had been defeated in South Africa too; but there, inside Africa, it is the equality aspect, which has been abandoned.

In providing separate facilities for people of different races, the judges have ruled that the separate schools, housing, waiting rooms and so on, do not have to be of equal standard; it is enough that they are separate. Africans can be - and are - treated as a sub-species of mankind. No legal or political restraint now prevents the white minority government in the Union of South Africa from imposing its harsh, discriminatory will upon the African majority.

To be an African is to beg for a permit to live in your own country - or to leave it; it is to need permission to work in a particular place or in a particular job; it is to carry a pass at all times - day and night - and be subjected at any moment to arbitrary arrest. And it is to have no legal means whatsoever to participate in the determination of your own wages and conditions of employment, your own place, or conditions, of living - much less to participate in the governing of your country. To be an African in South Africa is to have permission - unlimited permission - to say 'Yes, Baas' - preferably even then in Afrikaans. It is to have permission to be humiliated by any man, woman, or child, who has a white skin just for the reason that they have a white skin.

It is conditions and attitudes of this kind, which free Africa is determined to fight. And there can be no questioning of the fact that (regardless of some reasonable criticisms of particular independent African states), the elimination of colonialism and racial domination in these countries to the South is justified by all the basic principles of mankind.

Every principle of national and individual freedom, every principle of human equality, of justice, and of humanity, make it imperative that the rule of the minorities shall be ended. For they are judge, jury, prosecuting counsel, and lawmaker in their own dispute. And the question at issue now is whether Rhodesia shall for the foreseeable future be a state governed on that same basis of human inequality, or whether the existing, at present very slightly modified, version of racial discrimination, shall be replaced by progress towards human justice and equality.

THE POLITICAL SITUATION
IN SOUTHERN AFRICA

While Africa is determined that the whole of Southern Africa shall be freed before the struggle ceases, it recognizes that the strategy and tactics of the fight will vary according to the particular circumstances of the three different areas (there are four if South West Africa in counted separately). The monster of 'unfreedom' in

Southern Africa has three heads, and although they each draw strength and sustenance from the existence of the others, it remains true that each has its own separate vulnerability to determined assault by the world forces of freedom.

The best armoured, and in many ways the most tragic of the three heads in Southern Africa is the Union of South Africa itself. There, the racialism itself has become a self-justifying religion of survival, which demands ever-increasing ruthlessness to protect its adherents against the hatred it has induced. Its doctrines of superiority are inculcated into the white community from the moment of their birth; its teaching of inferiority dominates the lives of the non-whites from a similar moment. And it is in grave danger - if it has not already done so - of convincing all South Africans that there are not human beings in the world, but whites and non-whites.

If it succeeds in this, there will also one day be learned the dreadful lesson that the whites constitute less than one fifth of the South African population, and that numbers provide strength. Yet because this religion of racialism has already been responsible for so much human humiliation and suffering, only a miracle could provide any real hope of its peaceful reversal and the growth of practical brotherhood. For it has already promoted hatred, and justified fear. It now appears inevitable that sooner or later an overwhelming internal explosion will occur in South Africa and bring the whole present edifice of apartheid to an end; we can only pray that it is not followed by a mere reversal of the racial discrimination, for that would be the logic of the doctrines which are now being propagated by the South African Government.

But if there is no hope of peaceful change from inside, it remains true that the Union of South Africa is an industrial state, inextricably involved in international commerce. It is also true that the South African Government's policies suffer the expressed disapproval of every major power political organization in the world. This disapproval, however, remains a verbal one; no action is taken to activate it. This is largely because of the international economic links of the capitalist world (and thus international business involvement in apartheid). This economic reluctance to take action is backed up by the fact that South Africa is a legally constituted, internationally recognized, sovereign nation.

Fears of the implications of intervention from outside - through the United Nations or by any other means - have thus caused the democratic, and even the anti-colonial, nations of the West, to eschew, on grounds of legality, any deliberate activity designed to reverse the apartheid policies of South Africa. It is claimed that however reprehensible these may be, there must be no outside intervention in the internal affairs of a sovereign state. Legality is given paramountcy over morality. In consequence, the only prospect for the Union of South Africa is long-drawn-out suffering, violence and bitterness. For the struggle will go on until the cause of freedom ultimately triumphs.

The position in relation to Angola, Mozambique, and Portuguese Guinea, is different. This is, or should be, a classic colonial situation. The problem is that Portugal refuses to live in the twentieth century; she persists in believing that colonialism can be maintained, even by the poorest and most backward of the states of Europe. The problem in this case is, therefore, how to wake up Portugal to the facts of politics in the modern day.

Portugal's European and American allies could, of course, have great influence upon her - particularly if they were prepared to deny her the right to use their military strength in her defence while she uses her own (and their ammunition) in suppressing incipient revolt in her colonies. They could even help her to make the transition to the twentieth century by reviving her internal economy! But if the free countries of the West fail to try, or if they fail to succeed, then Africa will have to pursue this battle on her own, or with what allies she can find. Our own weakness means that we shall have only one way of doing that; by supporting guerrilla warfare until, after suffering and destruction, Portugal wakes up to her own realities.

Until November 11th, 1965, there was a hope that Southern Rhodesia would be able to avoid this dreadful path to freedom. Certainly the *de facto* government was a racialistic, racially constituted, minority government. Certainly apartheid under other names restricted the Africans' freedom to choose their place of living and working, and certainly separate educational, health and other public services, ensured that the Africans maintained their existing lowly position. But the vital difference was that Southern Rhodesia was legally a British colony; British surrender of power to the settler minority had been tragically real, but it stopped short of legal transfer.

This meant that although she was faced with difficulties of implementation, Britain was the power responsible for the future in Southern Rhodesia. And Africa took comfort from the fact that Britain's declared policy, in relation to all her colonies, has been to bring them to democratic independence under conditions which safeguard the people from oppression from any quarter.

The legal power and responsibility of Britain therefore meant that Africa expected gradual constitutional advance towards democracy or majority rule. What appeared to be required was to make Britain realize the seriousness of a situation where Southern Rhodesia existed as an outpost of South Africa, but where she operated under the name and responsibility of the British crown. Once this was realized Africa expected that Britain would at last take steps to deal with the white settlers who were misappropriating power.

AFRICA'S DEMANDS FOR SOUTHERN RHODESIA

In other words, what Africa has been demanding from Britain in relation to Southern Rhodesia is a transition from the white minority domination in government to majority rule and, only after that, independence for the colony. This has been the position of the nationalist forces in the colony; it has been the position of all African leaders. The argument has not been about the timing of this transition - how long it would take, or how many steps are involved - but about the principle of it.

It is in that context that Africa looks at the unilateral declaration of independence by the white minority government in Rhodesia; it is because of these reasonable and justified expectations that the Smith move is of such importance. The settler regime has said, in effect, that the very existence of legal restraints upon the minority is unbearable. And as Britain refused to give them independence without asking for some assurances about the future development to majority rule, so they took the independence. And in so doing their leader had the temerity to paraphrase the greatest freedom document of all time - the American Declaration of Independence!

Mr. Ian Smith justified his seizure of power, and his quotations, by claiming that his move was 'anti-colonial,' and that his government is the defender of civilized standards - not racialistic at all. He has argued that because countries to the North with a black majority government were granted independence it is unreasonable that southern Rhodesia should remain a colony after 43 years of 'governing ourselves responsibly.'

The facts do not support Mr. Smith. The facts show that Southern Rhodesia has been governed responsibly only as far as the white community is concerned, and that every aspect of that society is based on racial distinctions to the detriment of the African community. The facts prove, once again, that any elected government is responsive to the electorate, and only to the desires of the electorate; even if its Ministers wish to consider the interests of non-voters they are virtually powerless to do anything really effective.

Writing in *Punch* recently Mr. Smith said, 'Our Parliament is open to all races, our Civil Service offers senior posts on parity terms for all races, our University opens its doors to all races, and our voters' rolls are open to all races. Merit is, and must be, the only criterion....'

The fact of the matter is that of the 65 seats in Parliament, 50 are elected by the 'A' roll, and 15 by the 'B' Roll. To get on to the 'A' Roll it is necessary to have an income of 792 pounds per annum, or an income of 330 pounds per annum plus four years' secondary school education (or certain other intermediate combinations). To get on to the 'B' Roll the figures are lower; an income of 264 pounds per annum, or a combination of being 30 years of age with an income of 132 pounds per annum plus primary education.

The registered voters in consequence showed that of the 94,080 people on the 'A' Roll, 89,278 were whites; Africans predominated in the 'B' roll with more than 10,000 voters as against 1,000 non-Africans on this Roll, but these actual figures are not very revealing as the nationalist organizations called for a boycott of the elections. The comparative population figures show that there are in Southern Rhodesia almost four million Africans, and less than 250,000 people of European descent.

The government of Southern Rhodesia is thus firmly in the hands of the white voters; and is likely to remain so. The 'B' Roll seats are not even sufficient to veto changes in the constitution. Neither are there in fact any Africans in senior positions in the Civil Service; and if there were, the existing legislation would force them to live in the designated 'African Areas' of the towns regardless of their income. And behind all this smokescreen of 'responsibility' and 'merit' is complete segregation, and absolute inequality, in the availability of education.

Schooling for non-African children is compulsory between the ages of 7 and 15 years; and in 1963 there were 19,898 European children in secondary schools out of the 53,000 total European school enrolment. Only 7,045 African pupils were attending secondary schools during that year, and only 81 of these were in Form VI where entrance to the university can be attempted. It is hard to argue that these differences of secondary school attendance are due to differences in innate ability when something like ten times more finance is allocated for each European pupil than each African pupil. The truth is that educational opportunities just do not exist for the African community in the way they do for whites. There are places in the sixth year class for only 50 per cent of the African children who attend school for the first five years; out of those who do pass that hurdle, only 25 per cent will find a place in a secondary school three years later.

It is not my purpose to deny that there are difficulties in providing the educational expansion, which is required in Africa now; Tanzania's problems are too real for that. But when this racial distinction is made in educational opportunities, it is rank dishonesty to talk of equality opportunity in other fields, which depend on an educational or income qualification. Neither is it realistic to expect the voters (i.e. the people in the upper income brackets, who have reserved educational opportunities for their own children) to break down the racial distinctions, which maintain their current privileged position.

Recent history in Southern Rhodesia supports this lack of expectation. Since 1957 there has been a steady electoral move towards political parties and groups, which have been most fierce in their declared intention to resist racial integration. The Rhodesian Front, which is the party of the present Smith regime, was elected when it opposed the United Federal Party proposal to amend the Land Apportionment Act (this, among other things, reserves 37 per cent of the land area of the country for European ownership). In its manifesto the Rhodesian Front also declared that it would bring about 'premature African dominance,' and the manifesto recognized the right of government to 'provide separate amenities for various (racial) groups.'

In fact, since the election successive Rhodesian Front governments have concentrated on political questions, and particularly on the question of independence. In the process they have gained, and used, all the powers of a police state. All African nationalist parties have been banned, and their leaders imprisoned or detained; meetings have been prohibited, demonstrations broken up by police violence. And since independence press censorship has been imposed on all media of public communication, and the harshest penalties imposed for any refusal to bow down to the behests of this minority and illegal administration. The regime has, in fact, moved consistently along the path it laid down for itself; the path which leads directly and in a short time to the imposition in Southern Rhodesia of an unabashed apartheid policy as it is operated in South Africa.

Many of these developments, and certainly the groundwork for them, had taken place before UDI. Independence merely represented a logical further stage; it had to come - legally or otherwise - or there had to be a reversal of direction. What independence under the present minority regime means, therefore, is that the Rubicon has been crossed. If this independence is sustained the hope of a peaceful (even if gradual) development to majority has been obliterated. The only hope now remaining is for the rebellion to be defeated by the legal power and a new start made on the road to peaceful progress.

THE INTERNATIONAL IMPLICATIONS OF UDI

The importance of this cannot be overestimated. A successful declaration of independence by the minority government of Southern Rhodesia represents an expansion of racialism and fascism in Africa, and a step backward in the drive for African freedom. It is as though one of the southern states in the United States of America now, in the year 1966, succeeded in enlarging and strengthening the segregation and discrimination within its area of jurisdiction. The reaction of the federal authorities, and of the civil rights organizations, can be easily imagined. They would know that their future was at stake, and that the battle was joined as surely as it was at Fort Sumter in 1861. So it is in Africa.

But the parallel does not stop there. Just as would be the case in America, so in Africa success by the Southern Rhodesian minorities would strengthen the forces of reaction in other parts of the continent. South Africa and Portugal must want the Smith rebellion to succeed. Their interest is one of ideological sympathy; but it is also of geography. The map of Africa shows their reasons for wanting white domination to be safely entrenched in Southern Rhodesia - just as it indicates the special interest of countries like Zambia and Bechuanaland that it shall not succeed.

Yet although South Africa and Portugal want white domination to be firmly established in Southern Rhodesia, the illegality of the present situation is an embarrassment to them. They cannot afford to intervene actively on the side of Rhodesia unless and until they are certain that the rebellion will succeed. For in supporting the illegal regime they are staking their own future on its success.

South Africa's strongest defence against international criticism of her policies is the legality of her government, the recognized sovereignty of her state, and the doctrine that the internal affairs of any nation are outside the competence of the United Nations or any other international official body. If she openly supports a rebellion against legal authority in another state, then it is infinitely more difficult for her to resist international intervention in her own affairs. Consequently, we have the position where the Verwoerd government claims to stand neutral in the conflict between the sovereign authority (Britain) and the *de facto* authority (the Smith regime) in Southern Rhodesia.

This official neutrality is at the moment possible because the economic sanctions are voluntary acts of each separate nation state. By refusing to participate in these sanctions South Africa is thus breaking no international commitment and infringing neither domestic nor international law. This situation would be changed if the United Nations adopted Chapter 7 of the Charter (even article 41 alone), which makes sanctions mandatory on all members. South Africa would then either have to co-operate, or she would draw upon herself the international action she is concerned to avoid. That is to say, she would either have to close her own trade with Southern Rhodesia and be prepared to answer questions about the ultimate destination of goods she is importing, or she would be liable to be included in the area covered by sanctions.

The implications of the present position are well understood by the present South African Government. They account for its failure to give the 'independent' Smith regime all the support it hoped for. Yet it is clear that white public opinion inside South Africa is willing to do at least some of the things the government fears to do - and that the government will not interfere. The 'Oil for Rhodesia' campaign depends for its success on publicity and is thus known outside Southern Africa. There is little doubt, however, that through private business deals with South African firms and citizens, the cutting edge of international sanctions against Southern Rhodesia is being - and will be - blunted. By these means South Africa is able, without risking her own position, to assist the white regime in Southern Rhodesia to survive.

Portugal, too, is hamstrung by the illegality of the present Southern Rhodesian position. She, too, is relying upon legalistic niceties to prevent Western pressure building up against her occupation of Mozambique, Angola and Portuguese Guinea. She can therefore hardly afford to defend and assist a rebellion in the territory of a major European ally. Yet again, it is (to say the least) highly probable that she is giving under-cover assistance to Rhodesia. As Sir Edgar Whitehead, a past Prime Minister of Southern Rhodesia, said in the *Spectator* of January 28th, 'Mozambique could not survive of an African nationalist government took over in Rhodesia, and would be utterly ruined if the Rhodesian economy collapsed.'

Sir Edgar went on to refer to the oil refinery at Lorenzo Marques, and the assistance, which it can give quietly to the Smith regime despite the absence of crude oil for the Umtali refinery. Once again, this position exists because there is no international 'illegality' in trading with Southern Rhodesia. The situation would be changed if Chapter 7 of the United Nations Charter were adopted. For in that case Portugal (even more than South Africa) would be forced by her own needs to cease giving active support to the Smith regime.

South Africa and Portugal are thus unable to give open support to Smith because they depend upon claims of legality to defend their own positions. There is thus a weakness in the racialist Southern African front, which could be exploited by the forces of justice.

And it is, in fact, this same question of legality which makes it imperative for Britain and the West generally to use this weakness and to defeat Smith and white domination in Southern Rhodesia.

Successive Western governments have declared their hostility to apartheid, and their adherence to the principles of racial equality. They have frequently made verbal declarations of their sympathy with the forces in opposition to South African policies. But they have excused their failure to act in support of their words, on the grounds of South Africa's sovereignty. Africa has shown a great deal of skepticism about this argument, believing that it masked a reluctance to intervene on the side of justice when white privilege was involved. Now, in the case of Southern Rhodesia, legality is on the side of intervention. What is the West going to do? Will it justify or confound African suspicions?

So far the West has demonstrated its intentions by the gradual increase of voluntary economic sanctions; there has been a refusal even to challenge South African and Portuguese support for Smith by making sanctions mandatory upon all members of the United Nations. And there have been repeated statements by the responsible authority that force will not be used except in case of a breakdown in law and order - which apparently does not cover the illegal seizure of power! What happens if the economic sanctions fail to bring down the Smith regime is left vague. The suggestion therefore remains that, despite legality, and despite the protestations of belief in human equality, the domination of a white minority over blacks is acceptable to the West.

WHAT DOES AFRICA REQUIRE IN SOUTHERN RHODESIA?

This suspicion about the sincerity of the West can only be eliminated by the defeat of the Smith regime, and a new start being made on the path to majority rule before independence. It would not be enough for Smith to resign and a different 'more liberal,' white dominated, independent government to be legally established. If Britain and her allies, with the support of Africa, defeat of Smith, then the minimum requirement must be the re-establishment of effective British authority, and an interim government, which is charged with the task of leading the colony to majority rule.

This will inevitably require the presence of British

civil servants and British troops - or, better still, United Nations administrators and forces. Experience in South Africa, and in Southern Rhodesia itself, makes it absurd for anyone to expect Africa to trust Rhodesian whites (even under nominal British sovereignty) with the task of effecting the transition to majority rule.

It is important, too, that there should be a public declaration about the intentions in Southern Rhodesia. It must be made clear that there will be a rapid move (even if in stages) to majority rule, with safeguards for human rights, and after that - but only after that - independence for the colony. This public declaration is essential. Its absence has already caused major diplomatic difficulties between Britain and Africa, because it leaves open the possibility of a simple return to the pre-UDI status quo in Rhodesia.

It is true that such a declaration would be opposed by South Africa and Portugal, and that the Rhodesian whites would be bitterly hostile. But this is what the present crisis is all about; is Southern Rhodesia to become a nation of equal citizens or is it to become an outpost of white racialism? The fears of Southern Rhodesia's minorities have been dealt with by the many assurances given by Britain about the transitional period after the rebellion comes to an end.

It is now time to consider the fears of the African majority, both inside the country and elsewhere in the continent. It is time, in other words, for Britain and the United States of America to make clear whether they really believe in the principles they claim to espouse, or whether their policies are governed by considerations of the privileges of their 'kith and kin.'

By its unilateral declaration of independence, Southern Rhodesia has come out openly in support of racialism in Africa. The rest of Africa cannot, for the sake of its own future, acquiesce in this. But circumstances have meant that Southern Rhodesia's action is also a challenge to

Britain and to the West generally. Their future relations with Africa and Africa's future attitude to them, depend upon this challenge being answered effectively. At present the world is willing to support them in meeting this challenge; for once no complications of the 'Cold War' or the 'International Communist Menace' enter into the problem.

But if the West fails to bring down Smith, or having defeated him, fails to establish conditions, which will lead to majority rule before independence, then Africa will have to take up the challenge. In that case there will be no question of a transition to majority rule. And Africa's economic and military weakness means that she would have to find allies. It is worth considering whether, if that happens, it will then still be true to say that the Cold War does not enter into the situation, and that the 'Communist Bogey' is a nonsensical red herring.

It is vital that Africa's legitimate concern in this matter should be recognized. For each sovereign African nation has had to overcome the power of racialism in order to become independent. It is, to us, the ultimate horror. We can never surrender to it, or allow it to continue unchallenged on the African continent. Our own future is too much involved.

But the United States, Britain, and all other countries of the world are also involved in the issue of racialism. Smith has thrown a challenge at the world, and particularly at the Western powers. He has thrown it on behalf of the whole of Southern Africa. Free Africa is now waiting, with some impatience, to see whether the West really intends to stand on the side of human equality and human freedom."[14]

Smith's intransigence left no room for negotiations and served as a catalyst in the liberation struggle, igniting guerrilla warfare. Although the white minority regime continued to get steadfast support from South Africa, its survival also depended on other countries including most Western nations - among them, Britain and the United States - which deliberately ignored the economic embargo imposed on Rhodesia by the United Nations. They continued to trade with Rhodesia and even more so with apartheid South Africa where they had substantial investments. But guerrilla war began to have a significant impact on Rhodesia as time went on.

The war was mostly fought by the Zimbabwe African National Union - ZANLA (Zimbabwe
African National Union Liberation Army) - guerrillas who first penetrated Rhodesia in 1966 and intensified their insurgency in 1972, launching attacks from Mozambique where they worked together with FRELIMO forces. FRELIMO was waging its own war against the Portuguese colonial rulers, but the campaign was an integral part of a wider struggle to free all the countries in southern Africa still under white minority rule.

Comprehensive economic sanctions, made mandatory by the United Nations in 1968, did not have the desired impact but continued to be advocated by a number of countries - including almost all African countries even though quite a few of them such as Malawi, Ivory Coast, Congo-Kinshasa (renamed Zaire in 1971), Liberia and others continued to trade and maintain other ties with South Africa, Rhodesia's strongest supporter on the continent. By trading with the apartheid regime, they therefore also indirectly traded - and sometimes directly - with and helped sustain the white minority regime in Rhodesia.

On March 2, 1970, Rhodesia became a republic, but no other country, besides itself, accorded it official recognition. After Robert Mugabe was released from Gwelo prison in 1974 where he spent more than 10 years for his political activities fighting against racial injustice, he assumed the leadership of ZANU, replacing Reverend

Ndabaningi Sithole, and intensified the armed struggle from bases in Mozambique.

The war had an impact on the white minority regime in Rhodesia whose South African and American allies urged rebel Prime Minister Smith to seek a negotiated a settlement to the conflict. After a meeting with American Secretary of State Henry Kissinger in Pretoria, South Africa, in September 1976, Smith announced that he had agreed to majority rule and that it would be achieved within two years. It was a shocking revelation to his white supporters in Rhodesia and elsewhere; and a major concession by a leader who had only in March the same year vowed that there shall be no black majority rule in Rhodesia, not even "in a thousand years."

Following Smith's announcement, arrangements were made for Rhodesia's main African leaders to attend a conference in Geneva, Switzerland, on the future of their country. The conference was attended by Robert Mugabe, leader of ZANU; Joshua Nkomo of ZAPU; Ndabaningi Sithole, also of ZANU, but separate from the more militant breakaway ZANU led by Mugabe which advocated intensified guerrilla warfare; and Bishop Abel Muzorewa, leader of the African National Congress (ANC). Each led his own delegation to the conference. But after some negotiations, ZANU and ZAPU agreed to form an alliance, called the Patriotic Front, in order to present a united front against Smith at the talks in Geneva and afterwards on the battlefield if the conference failed to resolve the Rhodesian crisis.

After many weeks, the delegates failed to agree on the schedule for independence on the basis of majority rule. Muzorewa and Sithole ended their exile and returned to Salisbury - obviously to pursue their own secret deals with Smith - while the more militant leaders, Mugabe and Nkomo, continued to live in exile in neighbouring countries: Nkomo in Zambia, and Mugabe in Mozambique and Tanzania.

Another attempt was made by Britain and the United States to resolve the Rhodesian crisis, and in mid-1977, British Foreign Secretary David Owen and the American ambassador to the United Nations, Andrew Young, presented the new proposals to Smith. The proposals were supposed to be a dynamic compromise intended to end the impasse and satisfy both sides.

They called for a six-month interim period in which a British-appointed commissioner would assume full control of Rhodesia; a new national army would be created out of an integrated pool of the Rhodesian forces and guerrilla armies; all whites' property rights would be guaranteed; and whites would virtually be given veto power under a power-sharing compromise which would guarantee them a disproportionate influence over any decision by the coalition government, far in excess of heir numbers in the total population. Thus, national policy would be formulated on the basis of bi-racial consensus, and not on majority basis.

It was an unacceptable formula to the African nationalists, and the war continued, as did white emigration and deterioration of the economy because of the conflict. In December 1977, Smith decided to reach an "internal settlement" to stop the downward spiral which threatened to spin out of control. He started to negotiate with Muzorewa, Sithole, and Chief Jeremiah Chirau of the Zimbabwe United People's Organization (ZUPO), a group formed by government-appointed chiefs to preserve their interests and maintain the status quo. On March 3, 1978, they signed an agreement that outlined a new constitution and created a transitional government to rule until December 31 the same year when Rhodesia would become "independent" on the basis of a compromise formula "embracing" Africans.

The African leaders - Muzorewa, Sithole, and Chirau - who signed the agreement constituted a trio, whose most influential member was Muzorewa of the United African

National Council (UANC), in pursuit of their own version of majority rule, with the black majority assuming "power" on December 31, 1978. And the signatories, including Smith, constituted the Executive Council with rotating chairmanship. But Smith retained the title of prime minister. The head of the UANC, Bishop Abel Muzorewa, joined Smith's government, and blacks were named to each cabinet ministry, serving as co-ministers with the whites already holding these posts. Zimbabwe's nationalist leaders and African countries immediately denounced the compromise as a sell-out.

And it was from the beginning. The transitional government headed by Smith was to write a new constitution which had to be approved by white voters. The Rhodesian Front, Smith's party representing white interests, had veto power in the coalition government.

The three African leaders who signed the agreement - Muzorewa, Sithole, and Chirau - agreed that whites would be automatically guaranteed 28 out of 100 seats in parliament under the new constitution, totally out of proportion with their numbers in the total population: 250,000 whites versus 6.5 million Africans by then; veto power exercised by members of the Rhodesian Front in the government, over any legislation, would last for at least 10 years; all white property and pension rights would be protected regardless of how the property was acquired, and however inequitable the allocation of pension rights - Africans had virtually none; whites would continue to control the civil service, the police, the judiciary, and the armed forces; and Smith would remain prime minister during the transitional period.

The new transitional government offered amnesty to the Patriotic Front (PF) guerrillas of Mugabe and Nkomo, but was rejected, and the war intensified. There was also schism within the coalition government, and among its few - very few - African supporters outside the government. Muzorewa and Sithole blamed Smith and other Rhodesian Front members in the government for vetoing any proposal to improve the living conditions of Africans. Faced with the prospect of increasing guerrilla warfare, continued sanctions and the collapse of the internal settlement he reached with Muzorewa, Sithole, and Chrau; Smith made an ingenious attempt in August 1978 to split the Patriotic Front and invited Nkomo to join the transitional government.

Nkomo met Smith on August 14, 1978, in Lusaka, Zambia, encouraged by President Kaunda, and by Nigerian, British and American officials to do so. The leaders of Tanzania, Mozambique, Angola and Botswana - the other frontline states together with Zambia - were not informed of the meeting. Nor was Mugabe, Nkomo's partner in the Patriotic Front. Mugabe, who was then in Nigeria, flew to Zambia the following week. He was accompanied by Nigeria's Foreign Minister Joseph Garba (he died in 2002) who told him on the way that a meeting between Smith and Nkomo had taken place in Lusaka, and another one was going on in the same city.

Feeling betrayed, Mugabe was angry and refused to negotiate with Smith secretly. The secret talks had also been held without the knowledge or approval of the Rhodesian Front members - Smith's colleagues - in the transitional government.

Just a few days before the secret meeting was revealed to the public, a civilian plane of Air Rhodesia was shot down. ZAPU guerrillas claimed responsibility. At least 48 people were killed, inflaming passions among whites, and dashing any hope that the secret talks held in Lusaka between Smith and Nkomo may bear fruit. In response to this, Smith launched sustained large-scale incursions into Mozambique and Zambia to destroy guerrilla bases and refugee camps, killing many innocent civilians as well.

The attacks on guerrilla bases and refugee camps only fuelled the conflict as Rhodesia approached "independence" scheduled for December 31, 1978. And the transitional government was compelled to postpone elections until the third week of April because of intensified guerrilla activities, yet with no sign of de-escalation in the coming months. Also, all the three African members of the Executive Council who had signed the agreement with Smith to form a transitional government - Muzorewa, Sithole, and Chirau - were rapidly losing whatever support they had among their people because of their inability to help improve the condition of the masses. And in reality, the token leadership of the three African leaders in a government dominated by whites could not claim legitimacy without electoral mandate.

In late January 1978, the new constitution written by the white-dominated parliament and government was submitted for approval in a referendum in which only white registered voters - 90,000 in total - participated. The constitution also had another concession for whites.

The country after "independence" would be renamed Zimbabwe-Rhodesia, instead of just Zimbabwe as previously agreed upon at the insistence of the three African leaders who had now lost another battle to Smith who insisted on using the hyphenated name. About 70 percent of the white voters participated in the referendum on the new constitution which received 85 percent approval. Africans - 6.5 million of them - had absolutely no say in approving the constitution in spite of the fact that they constituted the vast majority of the total population. The referendum was held on January 30, as Rhodesia continued to be hit by guerrilla attacks, and the economy continued to deteriorate.

The elections for the new parliament in 1978 lasted for four days, from April 17 - 21, and were won by Bishop Abel Muzorewa's UANC amidst tight security provided by 100,000 men under arms, mobilized by the government as a safeguard against possible disruptions by guerrilla fighters. The biggest loser was Ndabaningi Sithole, the most well known African leader living in the country at that time. He expected to win the elections and, only a few days before they were conducted, hailed them as "a great democratic experiment." But after he lost, he denounced them as "one big cheat." And the British All-Party Parliamentary Committee on Human Rights issued a searing verdict on the elections. In its report, the group said the elections were "a gigantic confidence trick," marred by intimidation and death threats against anyone who urged people not to vote.

The elections were not democratic as the government claimed, and on April 29, the UN Security Council condemned them as illegal. It also called for continued sanctions but France, Britain and the United States abstained from the vote. Yet, four days later, the American permanent representative to the United Nations, Andrew Young, denounced the elections and said they were "rigged."

On May 29, 1979, Bishop Abel Muzorewa became the country's first black prime minister, and he tried to get the sanctions lifted and his country recognized as a legal sovereign entity since he claimed to have the electoral mandate to rule, given to him by the majority of the African voters. About 1.7 million Africans voted for the first time, giving 51 parliamentary seats to Muzorewa's UANC. But Muzorewa did not have any credentials as a freedom fighter or true African nationalist, and was considered to be an accommodationist at best, compromising on the principles of genuine racial equality and helping whites retain their privileged status.

The guerrilla fighters and other Africans, inside and outside Rhodesia, considered him to be a traitor. And the war continued with the full support of African countries including Tanzania which was the headquarters of the OAU Liberation Committee and all the African liberation movements.

In early May, not long after the election, Mugabe and

Nkomo held a three-day meeting in Addis Ababa, Ethiopia, and agreed to establish a joint military command for their guerrilla armies under the umbrella of the Patriotic Front. But they also rejected a proposal by some of the frontline states that they form a provisional government which would be recognized by them and other African countries, as well as by others around the world. The two leaders refused to form such a government, not because they were opposed to the idea as a matter of principle, but because they and their organizations - ZANU and ZAPU - were not prepared to form a genuine coalition transcending personality and ideological differences.

The Zimbabwe crisis was not yet resolved and, in August 1979, the Commonwealth conference held in Lusaka, Zambia, attempted to help all the parties involved reach a final settlement. Nyerere, Kaunda, and British Prime Minister Margaret Thatcher had intense discussions in Lusaka and reached a consensus on holding another meeting in London in May the same year, attended by all the parties to the conflict. The compromise agreement reached by the three leaders was endorsed and signed by all 39 members of the Commonwealth.

The talks did not begin until September 10, 1979, under the chairmanship of British Foreign Minister Lord Carrington at Lancaster House in London. They were attended by Ian Smith, Abel Muzorewa, Robert Mugabe, Joshua Nkomo, Ndabaningi Sithole and other Zimbabwean leaders. After three-and-a-half months of tough negotiations, the leaders reached a compromise and signed the Lancaster House Agreement on December 17, 1979. It was agreed that independence would be achieved in stages. On December 21, Muzorewa and the guerrilla leaders signed a peace agreement, and a cease-fire went into effect on December 28.

In addition to the cease-fire, the implementation phase of the Lancaster House Agreement included free elections, formation of an African-majority government, and attainment of full sovereign status. In elections held from February 27 - 29, 1980, about 94 percent of Zimbabwe's black electorate of 2.9 million people voted. The results were announced on March 4, and the ZANU-Patriotic of Robert Mugabe won control of parliament with 57 of the 80 seats reserved for blacks. Mugabe's victory surprised many observers, but was well-deserved, since it was his ZANU guerrilla fighters who did most of the fighting - as the MPLA did in Angola - and therefore played the most critical role in compelling Smith to make meaningful concessions at Lancaster House.

Mugabe won 63 percent of the vote, about the same as Nelson Mandela did in South Africa's first multiracial democratic elections in April 1994 when he won 62 percent of the vote. Joshua Nkomo's ZAPU-PF won 24 percent of the vote, and 20 seats, mostly in his home region of Matebeleland in southwestern Zimbabwe, just as Mugabe did in his ethnic stronghold of Mashonaland which is also the largest with about 80 percent of the country's population. Bishop Abel Muzorewa captured 3 seats, and none of the smaller African parties won any.

On April 18, 1980, Zimbabwe became independent and Robert Mugabe its first truly elected leader, with the title prime minister, and held that title until December 31, 1987, when he became president. After the country won independence, Mugabe formed a coalition government which included his main rival, Joshua Nkomo, whose party ZAPU-PF was predominantly Ndebele, the country's second largest ethnic group constituting about 20 percent of the total population; Mugabe's ZANU-PF was equally dominated by members of his tribe, the Shona.

Nkomo became minister for home affairs in the coalition government, but security forces were kept under Mugabe's - and ZANU-PF's - control. And two other ZAPU men were also included in the government, assigned minor ministerial posts. Whites were also represented in the cabinet: David Smith was appointed minister of commerce and industry, and Dennis Norman, minister of agriculture.

Mugabe's coalition government was just one aspect of his commitment to reconciliation in order to achieve and maintain national unity across racial and ethnic lines. He left the economic structures intact, instead of restructuring them to conform to his socialist vision. He left whites in management positions, and many of them decided to stay. One of his biggest problems was the resettlement of about one million refugees who had fled to neighbouring countries during the liberation war, and the reintegration of the guerrilla fighters into the mainstream of society but who remained in their camps until the economy could absorb them.

Many people expected an exodus of whites after blacks took control of the country, but the emigration rate was far lower than had been predicted. Those who left, mainly because they just did not want to live under a black government, settled in apartheid South Africa more than anywhere else.

But despite President Mugabe's continued assurances of protection, promising whites that he would not seek retribution for the racial injustices perpetrated against blacks during white rule, many of them continued to leave in large numbers.

At independence, Zimbabwe had about 250,000 whites, mostly British. Between 1980 and 1984 alone, more than 100,000 emigrated, mostly to predominantly white countries: Britain, Australia, New Zealand, the United States, Canada, continental Europe, as well as neighbouring South Africa where the apartheid regime was still in power and assured the new arrivals of protection, guaranteeing them a privileged position over blacks and other non-whites.

By early 2002, the white population of Zimbabwe had dropped to 60,000, with further emigration prompted by the seizure of white-owned farms by Mugabe's government in his campaign to redistribute land to landless blacks in a country he had ruled for 22 years.

In March 2002, he won another six-year term in a controversial election some observers considered to be seriously flawed. In the same month, Zimbabwe was suspended from the Commonwealth for one year, although Britain and other countries did not demand the same action when the government of President Frederick Chiluba of Zambia, Zimbabwe's neighbour, rigged the election in December 2001 in favour of its candidate Levi Mwanawasa who succeeded Chiluba in spite of the fact that he won a mere 29 percent of the vote; or when other Commonwealth members had perpetrated the same injustice through the years; leading to the inevitable conclusion that the only reason why Britain and other European countries and even the United States were so determined to punish Mugabe for disregarding the rule of law - rigging elections and unleashing violences against white farmers and their black workers, and against government opponents although the opposition also used violence, sometimes in retaliation or pre-emptively - was because of the large number of whites in Zimbabwe whose farms were being seized by the government for redistribution to landless blacks.

And it is a plausible argument. But it should not in any way be misconstrued as an endorsement of violence perpetrated by the government of President Robert Mugabe and his supporters against his opponents in the Movement for Democratic Change (MDC) led by Morgan Tsvangirai and other government critics, while condemning the opposition for using the same tactics.

Both should be equally condemned when they deserve condemnation. But it is also true that the same kind of conduct has been deliberately overlooked by Britain in other African countries and elsewhere who are also members of the Commonwealth, as much as it has been by other European countries.

Military rule, rigged elections, systematic violence and other abuses of power by governments in Nigeria, Sierra Leone, Ghana, Malawi, Kenya - including ethnic cleansing instigated by President Daniel arap Moi's government - through the years, did not lead to the suspension of any of these countries from the Commonwealth. And none of these countries, except Kenya, has a significant white population; a factor that should not be overlooked in Zimbabwe's suspension from the Commonwealth.

It is also not insignificant that among all these countries - and they are only a few examples - it is Kenya, a country with a large number of whites probably no fewer than 40,000 and mostly British, which was threatened the most with severe economic sanctions through the years, especially in the 1990s, because of corruption, economic mismanagement, and suffocation of dissent. Yet Nigeria, for example, was no better off than Kenya in all those areas, but has never had a large number of whites like Kenya. And she has plenty of oil, of course.

Both factors have helped insulate her from severe condemnation by Britain, let alone expulsion from the Commonwealth; attempts to expel her during Sani Abacha's brutal dictatorship in the 1990s failed largely because of British intervention on Nigeria's behalf, thanks to oil. Other predominantly white nations, including the United States, have also soft-pedaled on Nigeria, while coming down hard on Zimbabwe.

Therefore, race is a prime factor in the equation. In fact, the countries which called for sanctions against Zimbabwe - including Britain, Australia, the United States, Germany, and France, among others - are the very same ones which opposed sanctions against apartheid South Africa. And one can't help but wonder whether they would have been just as vocal, if at all, in their condemnation had the people whose land was being taken away by Mugabe's government were black.

Would they really have been just as concerned, anymore than they were about the plight of black victims groaning under brutal dictatorship, dying from persecution and in civil wars, and suffering from other scourges, in a number of African countries? As John Kamau, a Kenyan editor, stated in his article, "Anti-Mugabe Sanctions Hypocritical," in the *Daily Nation*:

"Somebody should find a better reason for isolating Mugabe. Nobody should tell us it has anything to do with democracy. For if it had anything to do with good governance, virtually all countries in this part of Africa would be under European Union (EU) sanctions. And so the question remains: Why Zimbabwe, and not Uganda or Zambia, which also have a mockery of democratic regimes. Why not Kenya?

Most of us are wondering why the EU is shedding tears on the future of Zimbabwe. The recent elections (in January 2002) in Zambia were a total sham. Uganda's election last year was anything but democratic. We don't need a political scientist to tell us what constitutes free and fair elections and none of these states can masquerade to be democracies. And that is the reason we have to be blunt. The Zimbabwe row with Western states is about land ownership by whites and the methods Dr. Mugabe's government is using to address this land inequity.

To be frank, nobody in the West has ever cared how Africans vote or who leads what country as long as Western interests are not in jeopardy. Haven't we had Idi Amin Dada, Jean-Bedel Bokassa, Marcius Nguema, Mobutu Sese Seko, Kamuzu banda, Laurent Kabila and Siad Barre? An elementary student of history would tell you that these coconut heads were maintained by Western support.

This, however, is not to condone the kind of thuggery that ZANU-PF youths initiate in Harare in the name of protecting the government. Yet, again, Zimbabwe is not the only government, which unleashes such thugs. Just here in Nairobi, we have had the Youth for Kanu '92, Operation Moi Wins, Jeshi la Mzee (Kiswahili meaning the Old Man's Army or Militia), and so on, and none of the European Union (EU) members even dreamt of imposing sanctions on the Kanu Government.

The so-called 'smart' sanctions (against Mugabe and his colleagues) are an indicator of how the West reacts when its interests are threatened and it exposes its double standards.

Fancy this: When our own Attorney-General threatened to bring a new media Bill that would have gagged the Press in this country, these paragons of Press freedom did not speak out as they did when Dr. Mugabe tried to do the same. Journalists in this region have been jailed, beaten, harassed and even denied access to information. But the regimes that sustain this machinery go scot-free with no threat of sanctions.

If we are to believe that the sanctions were initiated out of a desire to force a free and fair election, then there must be uniformity all over.

Zimbabwe's land inequity is real and not part of Mugabe's fertile imagination. Zimbabwe has a population of about 12 million people. Of these, 98 per cent are black while 0.8 are white. The rest are Asian Indians and people of mixed races. When you look at the land distribution pattern, you find around one million black families occupy 16.3 million hectares. Compare that with 4,000 white commercial farmers who occupy 11.2 million hectares!

That means that 70 per cent of the population farm the poorest of the soil and nobody wants Dr. Mugabe's government to speak on the issue. No country, however democratic, would allow 50 per cent of its land to be occupied by a minority group that is less than one per cent of the population. The principles of natural justice demand that such inequity be addressed as fast as possible.

We all have to understand that the current crisis has its

roots in Britain's racist colonial policies, and the fact that after Zimbabwe got its new constitution, it was left with colonial laws to work with. By throwing their support to white farmers, the Western nations have shown their tail!

The EU had better look again at the terms of the Lancaster House Conference on Zimbabwe. White farmers were given up to 1990 to develop their land or hand it over to the government. All those farmers who owned land that abutted communal lands were asked to dispose of it. It was written very clearly that after 1990, the Zimbabwe Government had a right to nationalise all lands that had not been disposed of or developed. Any time President Mugabe raised the issue of land and quoted that document, the white farmers cried sabotage. Mugabe led his troops and fought Ian Smith to get back this land. Should he go to the grave without fulfilling that ambition?

According to the Western media, sanctions were imposed on Zimbabwe because Mugabe is 'clinging to power.' Now, which president in Africa is not 'clinging to power'?

The monopolisation of Zimbabwe's best land question must be addressed. And the Movement for Democratic Change leader, Morgan Tsavingirai, the man the Western media says poses the greatest danger to Mugabe's presidency (which I doubt), must come out with a clear land policy. Land, he will quickly learn, is central to African politics and any politician who masquerades otherwise and dangles IMF statistics on inflation to the electorate without promising land would lose hands down. Which is why Tsavingirai could not even win a parliamentary seat!

This brings me back to the sanctions. We have to acknowledge that Zimbabwe has little capital to buy the land and there were cumbersome legal procedures required by Britain during the independence negotiations. With the sanctions in place, Mugabe will have free rein and will conclude the resettlement in his own way, which will be bad for the country's economy. The interests of white farmers cannot be allowed to overshadow the legitimate cry of the impoverished and landless majority in post-colonial Zimbabwe. No economy is worth talking about if it is built on grave injustice."[15]

John Kamau's sentiment was echoed in other African quarters, including neighbouring Tanzania. What infuriated many Africans across the continent and elsewhere, prompting them to rally behind President Mugabe, was that his critics in the West and other parts of the world, but especially in the West, ignored the suffering of the Africans in Zimbabwe since the advent of colonial rule and the legacy of inequality they inherited and which continues to exist in the post-colonial era.

They demonized Mugabe, gave the whites under siege ample coverage, focusing on their suffering, while paying little attention to the racial injustices perpetrated by whites against the African majority. As Reginald Mhango, a prominent Tanzanian journalist and managing editor of the *Guardian,* stated in March 2002 in an editorial, "Mugabe: Teaching White Rhodesians A Final Lesson or Two":

"Robert Gabriel Mugabe, the man who in 1980, cut short white supremacist Ian Smith's 1,000 years prediction before blacks could rule themselves in Zimbabwe, the man who did what the British Government could not do; who restored the authority of the Queen of England over Rhodesia, who rid Africa of one of a scandal when a tiny settler white minority unilaterally declared independence is now high on the cross, condemned for trying to right a wrong his ancestors paid with blood.

In reality and cruel irony, some of the...opposition leaders are very young men and women, whom 78-year-old Mzee Mugabe lost his prime years in prison and the bush to liberate.... The opposition has never mentioned, raised or discussed the record of barbarism that characterised successive white regimes....

Smith with his customary arrogance declared to the world that 'never in a thousand years' would Africans rule in Rhodesia.... That was when the Nyereres and the Kaundas vowed to fight and fight they did. Like Smith in Salisbury, Nyerere and Kaunda took the liberation of Zimbabwe as a crusade. Smith saw this and made no secret of his hatred of particularly Mwalimu Nyerere, whom he labeled the communist devil. That People's China, a close ally of Tanzania was arming and training Mugabe's Zanu-PF fighters was not lost on Smith. He hated both with equal intensity....

In parliament, to which he was a member, Smith did little to hide his contempt for Mugabe and Nyerere. Mugabe too, saw his party's victory (just before independence in April 1980) as a sweet revenge on Smith and his fellow Rhodesians, as he still refers them today, 22 years after Uhuru....

Smith...openly vowed that the day Mugabe the communist was bundled out of power would be his best lived. This is the scenario Mugabe sees as happening in Zimbabwe now. He does not believe that Smith and his fellow Rhodesians are not trying to make good their vow to live for the day when his so-called communist party and government are ousted from power. Smith's own speeches in London last year and even in Zimbabwe to that effect have not helped matters.

President Mugabe himself has been quoted as saying that he will only resign from the presidency after he has taught some Rhodesians a lesson or two."[16]

His determination to win the presidential election in March 2002 showed that he still was not done teaching them a lesson or two. He felt that he needed years to do so, although with tragic consequences for the country -

starvation, death, economic destruction - because of the way he implemented the land reform programme, good intentions notwithstanding. There was need for land redistribution, but not in the way it was done. It should have been done in an orderly way without violence, farm invasions, and without disrupting the economy.

The people Mugabe tried to help are the very same ones who suffered the most. They were the most vulnerable. And many of them starved, while others - including farm workers on white-owned farms - were attacked by his supporters. Yet, he remained an icon of African liberation across the continent. Even many of his critics conceded that much and admired him because of what he did to liberate Zimbabwe and the role he played in helping liberate the rest of southern Africa, including South Africa itself, the citadel of white supremacy on the continent.

But to many suffering Zimbabweans, he became a villain, nonetheless, because of the devastation wrought as a result of his fast-track land reform programme which disrupted the economy and spawned violence across the country, forcing many people to flee their homes and seek refuge in South Africa and elsewhere, only to be turned back in large numbers by their powerful southern neighbour, where there were also strong anti-foreign sentiments especially against fellow Africans from other parts of the continent who were accused of taking jobs away from black South Africans.

And in spite of the strong opposition he faced, Mugabe claimed victory in the presidential election he saw as a struggle between the forces of change, of which he was the embodiment, and those determined to perpetuate racial inequalities at the expense of the African majority for whom he fought so hard to liberate. He also reminded friends and foes alike that he went to prison for that. He also went to war, and won.

Much as many people condemned Mugabe, hardly any

cared to construct a proportional perspective on the land crisis in Zimbabwe and on the nature of the opposition. Such bias and deliberate distortion of truth did little to facilitate a settlement of the crisis but, instead, only helped fuel the conflict. The balance sheet was clear. The government did unleash violence against its opponents and even against innocent civilians, including women and children. Mugabe's supporters must admit that.

But violence also came from the other side. Mugabe's opponents must admit that. The opposition members were not innocent bystanders as they portrayed themselves to be, when they paraded themselves before the international media most of whose reporters focused on the plight of white farmers and Mugabe's opponents more than anything else.

Mugabe's opponents, even if on a smaller scale than what the government did, also used violence as a political weapon, and not always in self-defence as some of them claimed.

They launched pre-emptive strikes. They blamed the government for all the violence across the country to make it look bad before the whole world in order to isolate it and bring it down. And they initiated violence in many cases themselves, yet denied their involvement as the culprits in these brutal attacks as if they were mere victims or some kind of saints singing hymns of martyrdom while they were being forcibly marched to their graves by Mugabe's storm troopers; all this in spite of Morgan Tsvangirai's own proclamation to the world before television cameras - broadcast by the BBC and other outlets - that "We are going to take violence to their doorsteps," and that if President Mugabe did not step down peacefully, "we will remove him violently." This is not the language of a saint or a Gandhi.

Also, a disproportionately large number of the people who bankrolled the opposition Movement for Democratic Change (MDC), led by Morgan Tsvangirai, were hardcore racists who couldn't care less if Africans were denied democratic rights, lived in anarchy, or even if the entire black population of Zimbabwe starved to death. These were the very same people who helped perpetuate white minority rule and were some of the staunchest supporters of the previous regime headed by Ian Smith.

Many of them were also members of the notorious Rhodesian security forces who were responsible for brutal attacks, torture, and indiscriminate killings of countless innocent civilians in African villages during the halcyon days of white minority rule they now remembered with nostalgia, some of them even with tears in their eyes and streaming down the cheeks. The contrast is obvious. To Africans, those were *not* the good old days. As Malcolm X used to say, "A white man's heaven is a black man's hell."

And in spite of all the achievements under Robert Mugabe, few people cared to talk about that and give credit where credit is due. Instead, Mugabe's critics were busy compiling a catalogue of his evil deeds - many of them a litany of lies - as if he had done nothing for the people in more than 20 years he had been in power. Yet here was a leader who did more for his people than all the previous colonial governments had since the conquest of Zimbabwe by white settlers - led by Cecil Rhodes and his fellow imperialists of the British South African Company he headed - from South Africa and Britain more than 100 years ago in the 1890s.

They did nothing for blacks, except steal their land, rape, kill and exploit them. And hardly any of Mugabe's critics admitted that two of his biggest enemies, Britain and the United States when they were on "good" terms with him and other Zimbabwean nationalist leaders during the struggle for independence, agreed to finance the land redistribution programme Mugabe and his colleagues demanded at the Lancaster House conference in London in 1979 which finally led to the end of white minority rule in Rhodesia.

Yet no money was provided. As the American ambassador to the United Nations, Andrew Young, who was involved in the negotiations on the transfer of power to the black majority, said when the farm invasions were taking place in Zimbabwe in the late 1990s and beyond, in an interview in July 2002 with an African-American journalist Charlie Cobb who once lived and worked in Tanzania in the late sixties and early seventies:

"I happen to like Mugabe....Mugabe is the only one who is making any effort to deal with poverty in Africa. Mugabe has politicized poverty. The land issue for Mugabe is how to enfranchise the poor. My friends in Zimbabwe who are the young intellectuals and business people did not fight in the war and they really end up being 'trickle down' economists, like the economists you have in the rest of Africa. I worry more about the gap between rich and poor in Africa than I do in America because I think the gap between rich and poor is what Gaddafi exploited in Sierra Leone and Liberia. And to some extent, Rwanda and Burundi....

Mugabe came under pressure from the war veterans (not from Tsvangirai as leader of trade unions). I was one of those who talked Mugabe out of dealing with the land question originally, saying to him that I believed that you couldn't deal with governance and land reform simultaneously....There was an agreement by the British to help Mugabe develop a land use plan and land reform programme in 1980 but that it should not start until 1990. There were specific constitutional concessions made at Lancaster House. One of them was putting off the land reform issue for 10 years.

Not one cent! Was made available. The Carter Administration pledged 70 million dollars a year for ten years. Not one penny ever got there....By the time 1990 came around there was nobody in Britain and America who was interested.

We were rightly, I think, focused on the liberation of South Africa. Mugabe was also being told by Nyerere and others: 'You can't raise these issues because we must deal with our brothers in South Africa.' So to blame Mugabe for raising the question 20 years late and not doing anything all along, I think is unfair.

It is true that he didn't push it but he was involved in the liberation of South Africa. He was involved in Namibia. He was involved even more in trying to beat back RENAMO in Mozambique. Those were the Selous Scouts from Rhodesia that fought with Ian Smith that went to South Africa who didn't want them and sent them over to Mozambique where RENAMO was continuing to try to overthrow the Mozambican government. They were also trying to undermine the Zimbabwe government.

Still, if there is any place in Africa where capitalism and democracy can work easily, it's Zimbabwe. But instead of trying to make it work, England mainly ended up demonizing Mugabe and the U.S. went along with it. And Mugabe is easy to demonize. But when I read about John Adams and Thomas Jefferson feeling threatened by the British and French and promoting an Aliens and Sedition Act and actually putting the press in jail, I say or ask, 'Was Mugabe under more pressure from the British and the South Africans than Jefferson and Adams were?' And because of the geographic proximity of South Africa, as opposed to the French and British presence in the U.S. I'd have to say a young nation in Zimbabwe was under more serious and severe pressure than Thomas Jefferson and Adams and George Washington were. In fact, King George referred to Jefferson and Adams and George Washington as hoodlums and hooligans who were only fit for hanging.

I saw so much of that British arrogance being adopted by the United States in relation to Mugabe. And even Mbeki. When Mbeki raised a legitimate question about AIDS and whether there was a political solution or whether this was a medical issue, they jumped all over him and literally forced him to try to give these drugs which proved to very toxic to Americans who are having 2 or 3 thousand calories a day....whether to give those same toxic drugs to Africans who get 2 or 3 thousand calories a week is a legitimate medical question. Mbeki said those kinds of questions ought to be left to physicians and he shouldn't make a political decision about them. But they literally forced him to come to the political position where the government is giving drugs to people without fully knowing the impact on them."[17]

Earlier in January 2001, Andrew Young was interviewed by another African-American journalist, Clarence Page, and explained that after successive British and American governments failed to deliver the funding promised to help implement land reform, Zimbabwe's war veterans who fought to free their country from white domination became impatient and "backed Mugabe into a corner."

He went on to say: "I have been a friend of Mugabe who helped convince him in 1980 to leave the land reform issue alone for the time being. We promised to take it up in 10 years, but when 1990 came, we didn't live up to the promise. Mugabe is more a solution that the problem. If you get rid of him, you still have the problem that one percent of the population (the white minority) still controls more than 70 percent of the land."[18]

Now, tell the people of Zimbabwe: that is justice, that is equality, or just be patient, change will come, 20 years after independence. It is a miracle the farm invasions did not take place sooner, much sooner, than they did two decades later after independence. The struggle for independence was over land, more than anything else. Without land, there is no independence. Yet most of the land, especially the most fertile land, remains in the hands of the white minority.

Nothing is going to be solved unless the entire matter is put in its proper historical perspective. Many may say, all that is history. It is true, it is history. But the past is also the present. There is no present without the past. It is also a warning to others. The writing is on the wall. Next will be South Africa, and even Namibia, but especially South Africa where millions of whites enjoy a privileged life style at the expense of blacks, and occupy most of the fertile land at the expense of blacks even after the end of apartheid.

If whites in neighbouring South Africa can't see this, then they will have a rude awakening. As one prominent black South African leader ominously warned in 2001, what is going to happen in South Africa is going to make Zimbabwe's conflict look like a picnic. History is not being re-written. Only historical injustices are being corrected. Therefore the past is part of the solution. As George Shire, a Zimbabwe liberation war veteran and an academic working for the Zimbabwe Open University, stated in his article, "The Struggle for Our Land: Britain is Interfering in Zimbabwe in Support of Corporate Power and A Wealthy White Minority," in the British newspaper *The Guardian* :

"The crisis currently gripping Zimbabwe has its roots in Britain's racist colonial policies, the refusal of a previous Labour government to act against the dictatorship of the white minority and the failure of Britain to stick to its promises after my people finally won independence 20 years ago. But instead of acknowledging their own responsibilities and helping overcome the legacy of the past, the British government - and her friends in the white Commonwealth - are fostering a flagrantly partisan mythology about the conflict in the country, while intervening in support of a privileged white minority and international commercial interests.

Take the continued white monopolisation of Zimbabwe's best land, which is at the heart of the upheavals and is routinely presented in Britain as a spurious pretext to keep a despot in power. In reality, the unequal distribution of land in Zimbabwe was one of the major factors that inspired the rural-based liberation war against white rule and has been a source of continual popular agitation ever since, as the Government struggled to find a consensual way to transfer land.

My grandfather, Mhepo Mavakire, used to farm on land, which is now owned by a commercial farmer. It was forcibly taken from the family after the Second World War and handed to a white man. Many of my relatives died during the Zimbabwean liberation war, trying to reclaim this land. I joined ZANU-PF, which played the central role in the war, in the late 60s and there was never any doubt in my mind that it was both a duty and an honour to fight for that land.

Land reform is now a socio-economic and political imperative in Zimbabwe. The land distribution programme of President Mugabe's ZANU-PF Government is aimed at redressing gross inequalities to meet the needs of the landless, the smallholders who want to venture into small-scale commercial farming and indigenous citizens who have the resources to go into large-scale commercial agriculture. These are modest but worthwhile objectives.

The Western-backed Movement for Democratic Change opposition, by contrast, is very reluctant to be drawn on how it would resolve the land question. Although middle England continues to be fed the tale that nothing was done about land until MDC began to challenge ZANU-PF's power base, the truth is that the white-dominated Commercial Farmers Union (CFU) has fought the Government's strategy for land distribution at every stage since the 80s.

The CFU and members of the defunct Rhodesia Front, strongly represented in the MDC, could not care less who governs Zimbabwe as long as they keep the land and continue to live in the style to which they have become accustomed. The lack of money for land acquisition, cumbersome legal procedures required by Britain in the independence negotiations and the withdrawal of international donors in recent years - as well as the explosive political restiveness and farm occupations - have all combined to force the Zimbabwean Government to speed up resettlement.

But of course a process of land acquisition and resettlement of indigenous landless people cuts across the networks that link the farmers, the producers of agricultural inputs, the banks and insurance houses, all dominated by the white minority. And this network also spreads into the international capital arena. Many Zimbabweans believe that the interests of this white network have been allowed to overshadow the morally legitimate cry of the impoverished and landless majority in post-colonial Zimbabwe.

While I unreservedly condemn all form of political violence and criminality that have come to dominate the contemporary political culture of Zimbabwe, violence is, in fact, being perpetrated by people with links to both sides of the political divide.

In the last couple of weeks alone (January 2002), three people have been killed by MDC supporters, who also went on a rampage in Harare, petrol-bombing shops belonging to ZANU-PF supporters. Senior MDC figures have been implicated in the murder of a ZANU-PF official, Gibson Masarira, who was hacked to death in front of his family. And in Kwekwe, suspected MDC supporters burnt three ZANU-PF officials' houses.

None of these events has been reported in the British media. Such MDC violence echoes the activities of the Rhodesian police and notorious Selous Scouts in the late 70s - which is perhaps hardly surprising since several are now leading lights in the MDC.

It was the Selous Scouts who killed refugees, men, women and children at Nyadzonia, Chimoio, Tembue, Mkushi, Luangwa, and Solwezi, where they still lie buried in mass graves. David Coltart, an MDC MP for Bulawayo South, was a prominent member of the Rhodesian police and he and his bodyguard Simon Spooner - recently charged with the murder of Cain Nkala, leader of the war veterans in Matebeleland - were attached to the Selous Scouts. The deputy national security adviser for the MDC, who rose to the rank of sergeant in the Rhodesian police, was likewise a handler of Selous Scouts operatives while based in Bulawayo. Mike Orret, another MDC MP, was also a senior police officer.

You would never know from the way Zimbabwean politics is usually reported in Britain that ZANU-PF supports a broadly social democratic programme, focused on the empowerment of the landless and poor, and is opposed by supporters of neo-liberal economic policies. Among ZANU-PF's often overlooked achievements is a massive expansion in education in the past 20 years - from one university to 14, and from a handful of secondary schools to hundreds of six-form colleges. Sadly, the enormous progress that had been made in public health has been reversed by the HIV/Aids pandemic, which is reducing life expectancy.

Nevertheless, the Zimbabwean Government has constructed 456 health centres, 612 rural hospitals and 25 district hospitals, as well as providing one provincial hospital in each of the country's eight provinces. Eighty-five percent of Zimbabwe's population is now within eight kilometers of a health facility. The 25 percent coverage of immunisation at independence has now been boosted to 92 percent, while antenatal coverage has risen from 20 percent at independence to the present 89 percent.

The MDC has no corresponding programme for mass public health or education, or rural electrification, or the economic empowerment of indigenous people. The MDC has remained silent when asked about what it will do with the more than 130,000 families who have been allocated land through the fast-track process if it wins the presidency. Incidentally, beneficiaries of this process include known members of MDC, not just 'friends and cronies' of president Robert Mugabe.

Contrary to the received wisdom in Britain, the best chance of completing the unfinished business of land reform, and for improvements in public services, housing, education, clean water, support for people living with illness and dying of Aids, lies with a President Mugabe victory in the presidential elections. The past few days of vigorous cross-party debate about the freedom of the press in Zimbabwe's parliament have shown what a vibrant democracy the country in fact has, with ZANU-PF reflecting a broad range of political allegiances. The longer-term challenge ZANU-PF faces is to rethink itself, in the new conditions its victory might help to bring about."[19]

Although some observers and countries said the March 2002 presidential election in Zimbabwe was deeply flawed, African countries including the Organization of African Unity (OAU) observer mission on the scene led by former Tanzanian ambassador Gertrude Mongella concluded that the election was free and fair, and Mugabe was the legitimate winner of the most bitterly contested election in Zimbabwe's history since independence.

Mugabe also rose to power after one of the bloodiest conflicts in colonial history. The guerrilla war lasted for about 15 years from 1965 - 1979 (started by ZAPU in 1965, and by ZANU in 1966), and claimed tens of thousands of lives, mostly black - including soldiers from the Tanzania People's Defence Forces (TPDF), Tanzania's national army, who joined the freedom fighters on the battlefield, as they did in Mozambique and Angola -

before the white minority regime capitulated to African might and made concessions at the Lancaster House conference which eventually led to independence on the basis of majority rule under the leadership of Robert Mugabe.

Tanzanian troops also intervened in the Seychelles in 1977 in support of revolutionary forces against an inept regime; and in 1982 saved the national government of that island nation from being overthrown by mercenaries from apartheid South Africa who, with the help of the South African security forces, captured Victoria airport in the nation's capital and largest town, Victoria, where they landed pretending to be "a rugby team."

President Nyerere also sent Tanzanian soldiers to the Comoros to reinstate an elected president who had been overthrown in a military coup. Therefore Tanzania's military involvement in the liberation struggle in Zimbabwe and elsewhere in southern Africa and other parts of the continent - including the ouster of Idi Amin by Nyerere, freeing the people of Uganda from tyranny, while other African leaders looked the other way or quietly applauded the burly Ugandan dictator; Tanzanian military officers training Congo's national army under Presidents Laurent and Joseph Kabila; and, at his insistence, the imposition of economic sanctions on Burundi in the 1990s by East and Central African countries to compel the Tutsi-dominated regime to share power with the Hutu majority on meaningful basis - was in keeping with Nyerere's Pan-African commitment he had consistently maintained throughout his tenure as president of Tanzania and as one Africa's most influential statesmen who came to be known as "The Conscience of Africa"; a point also underscored by President Robert Mugabe when he paid glowing tribute to Nyerere at his funeral for the indispensable role Tanzania played in the liberation of Zimbabwe and the rest of southern Africa.

He described Nyerere as "the revolutionary, the

visionary, the principled, indomitable and unyielding supporter of the struggle for our own and the region's independence."

Mugabe also took stewardship of one of the most developed and richest countries on the continent. As President Julius Nyerere told him: "You have inherited the jewel of Africa." He advised him to keep it that way.

Chapter notes

1. Richard Coggins, "Rhodesian UDI and the British Government 1964 - 1970," Queen's College, Oxford University, Oxford, United Kingdom. See also, "Rhodesian Crisis: Legal Issues: Constitution Test Case Appeal," in *Africa Research Bulletin, Vol. V, 1968*, p. 957 et seq.; "Constitutional Proposals: Constitutional Commission Reports," in *Africa Research Bulletin*, ibid., p. 1046 et seq.; Colin Legum and John Drysdale, *Africa Contemporary Record: Annual Survey and Documents 1968 - 1969* (London: Africa Research Ltd., 1969), pp. 689 - 711; *The Economist*, October 12, 1968. See also "Nyerere: How Much War?" in *Time*, March 17,1977; and "Nyerere's Appeal for Help," in *Time*, October 9, 1978.

2. Ken Flower, *Serving Secretly: Rhodesia's CIO Chief on Record* (Galago: 1989).

3. Akwasi A. Afrifa, *The Ghana Coup* (London: Cass, 1967); A.K. Ocran, *A Myth is Broken: An Account of the Ghana Coup D'etat of 24th February 1966* (London: Longmans, 1968).

4. Colin Legum, "Witness Seminar on Rhodesian UDI: Commentary by Colin Legum," Public Record, Kew, 6 September 2000.

5. Ibid. See also, *Africa Contemporary Record*, op. cit., pp. 370 - 383.

6. *Africa Contempoary Record*, ibid., p. 220.

7. S.A. Melville, ibid., p. 291.

8. P.W. Botha, ibid.

9. *Africa Research Bulletin, Vol. V*, p. 937 et seq.; "Rhodesian Crisis: Legal Issues," in *Africa Contemporary Record*, ibid., pp. 689 - 690. See also, Claire Palley, "No Majority Rule Before 1999," in *The Guardian*, London, November 14, 1968; "We Want Our Country!" in *Time*, November 5, 1965: "They were black...more than 6,000 of them....'Mambokadzi tinoda nyika yehu!' roared the black Rhodesians who had come to greet Harold Wilson last week. 'Your Majesty the Queen, we want our country!"

10. Julius K. Nyerere, "The Honour of Africa," in J.K. Nyerere, *Freedom and Socialism: A Selection from Writings and Speeches 1965 - 1967* (Dar es Salaam, Tanzania: Oxford University Press, 1968), pp. 115 - 133; *The Nationalist*, Dar es salaam, Tanzania, December 15, 1968; *Standard*, Dar es Salaam, Tanzania, December 15, 1968.

11. Reuben Kamanga, quoted in *Africa Contemporary Record*, op. cit., p. 372. See also *The Times of Zambia*, Lusaka, Zambia, March 1966.

12. Ian Smith, quoted in *Africa Contemporary Record*, ibid., p. 372.

13. Privy Council, ibid.

14. Julius K. Nyerere, "Rhodesia in the Context of Southern Africa," in *Foreign Affairs*, Council on Foreign Relations, New York, April 1966; J.K. Nyerere, *Freedom and Socialism*, op. cit., pp. 143 - 156.

See also Paul Redfern, "How Nyerere Tried to Stop Britain Arming South Africa in the '70s," in *The East African*, Nairobi, Kenya, February 19, 2001.

15. John Kamau, "Anti-Mugabe Sanctions Hypocritical," in the *Daily Nation*, Nairobi, Kenya, February 22, 2002.

16. Reginald Mhango, "Mugabe: Teaching White Rhodesians A Final Lesson or Two," in *The Guardian*, Dar es Salaam, Tanzania, March 15, 2002.

President Benjamin Mkapa of Tanzania was one of Mugabe's staunchest allies and one of his biggest supporters during and after the controversial March 2002 presidential election in Zimbabwe.

17. Andrew Young, interviewed by Charlie Cobb, "'Atlanta is a Model for Africa' Says Ambassador Andrew Young," in AllAfrica.com, July 22, 2002.

18. Andrew Young, quoted by Clarence Page, "Andrew Young's Newest 'Friend,'" in the *Jewish World Review*, January 22, 2001.

George Shire, "The Struggle for Our Land: Britain is Interfering in Zimbabwe in Support of Corporate Power and A Wealthy White Minority," in *The Guardian*, London, January 24, 2002.

American Involvement in Angola and Southern Africa

AMERICAN INVOLVEMENT in Southern Africa was dictated by economic interests more than anything else; rivalry with the Soviet Union and other communist-bloc countries; and strategic partnership with apartheid South Africa which was regarded as an integral part of the West and an embodiment and custodian of Western values and civilization in a non-Western region of the world. It was also influenced by racial considerations to protect the interests of the white minorities regardless of the racial injustices committed against the black majority and other non-whites.

This involvement assumed its most blatant form during the Angolan conflict in a proxy war with the Soviet Union in which American surrogates - apartheid South Africa and UNITA rebels - wreaked havoc across Angola in an attempt to oust the legitimate MPLA government from power; a government that had also been recognized by the Organization of African Unity (OAU) and other countries besides those in the communist bloc.

Although American intervention became a prime factor in determining the future of Angola especially during the war, we should not overlook the fact that the United States was not really new on the Angolan scene, although it made a dramatic "entry" during the seventies in terms of confrontation with the Soviet Union in this proxy war. American involvement in Angola goes way back to the sixties with regard to cultivating ties with potential future leaders of that country once it became independent; and long before then in terms of relations with Portugal as an ally and fellow member of NATO, while turning a blind eye to her brutal colonial policies in Angola and other Portuguese colonies in Africa.

American engagement in Angola on the nationalist side started when the United States established ties with Holden Roberto - of GRAE, later FNLA - in the sixties. The intention was not to support the liberation struggle. That's one thing the United States never did in Africa. Instead, it supported colonial and white minority regimes. But American officials felt that it was important to establish ties with potential future African leaders because Portugal would not be able to maintain colonial rule in Angola and elsewhere in Africa, including Mozambique whose nationalist leader, Dr. Eduardo Mondlane, had strong ties to the United States.

Portugal's position was contrasted with that of the apartheid regime in South Africa which American leaders believed was firmly in control of its territory, although they were proven wrong only a few years later when the racist edifice gradually began to fall apart in the seventies after the Soweto uprising by black students in 1976. The CIA and American leaders felt that Holden Roberto was their man whom they could easily buy and manipulate at will, and went on to put him on the CIA payroll around 1961 or 1962.

Yet at the same time, they continued to support the colonial regime. In the following years, the United States provided weapons and ammunition, and counter-insurgency training, the Portuguese colonial rulers needed to contain and if possible neutralize the nationalist forces of the MPLA and the FNLA, which were fighting for independence. The devastation caused by American-supplied weapons used by the Portuguese against Africans including innocent civilians - women and children being among the victims - was extensive. As John Marcum, an American scholar who walked 800 miles through Angola and visited FNLA training camps in the early sixties, wrote:

"By January 1962 outside observers could watch Portuguese planes bomb and strafe African villages, visit the charred remains of towns like Mbanza M'Pangu and M'Pangala, and copy the data from 750-point napalm bomb casings from which the Portuguese had not removed the labels marked 'Property U.S. Air Force.'"[1]

Super-power rivalry also became a prime factor because of American and Soviet involvement in Angola. But unlike the United States, the Soviet Union never supported Portugal in her war against the nationalist forces not only in Angola but in Mozambique and Portuguese Guinea (Guinea-Bissau) where Africans were also waging guerrilla warfare against the colonial armies. And that gave the Soviets credibility, which the Americans lacked, as friends of Africans helping them to become free.

The Soviets had also supported Holden Roberto but left him because, among other reasons, he had helped Moise Tshombe - a pariah on the African continent - in the Congo, and also substantially curtailed his guerrilla campaign under pressure from the United States. He was already on the CIA payroll and from 1969 was getting a $10,000-per-year retainer from the agency. His brother-in-law, President Joseph Mobutu - later Mobutu Sese Seko - of Congo, was also on the CIA payroll.

In 1964, the Soviets embraced Dr. Agostinho Neto of the MPLA as a more credible nationalist. But they also supported him for another reason: ideological. Since his student days in the 1940s in Portugal, Neto had established ties with radical elements, many of them communist, and came to embrace Marxism, the state ideology of the Soviet Union which he felt would also be appropriate for Angola and help transform the country into a better society.

Then in 1966 another nationalist party, UNITA, emerged on the scene, led by Dr. Jonas Savimbi. It was supported by the People's Republic of China, and initially also got support from Tanzania and Zambia which abandoned it later because of its ties to pro-colonial forces in the West and apartheid South Africa. At first, all three groups - FNLA, MPLA, UNITA - professed to be socialist. But only the MPLA was more committed to socialism than the other two. Yet, although it embraced Marxism, it was not really Marxist but nationalist more than anything else and ready to accept help from anywhere - including the West - to achieve its goals of liberation and economic development. In fact, in December 1962, Dr. Neto went to Washington to argue his case for Angola's independence before the American government and told American officials that it was wrong to call the MPLA communist.

American involvement in Angola dramatically increased in 1975 when the country was about to win independence. In January the same year, the CIA was authorized to give Holden Roberto and his group, the FNLA, $300,000. And shortly thereafter in March, FNLA forces attacked the MPLA headquarters in Luanda. A total of 51 unarmed, young MPLA recruits were gunned down, murdered in cold blood. The attack could not have taken place without the knowledge or approval of the United States, and it helped ignite a full-scale war in which UNITA, another American client, joined forces with the FNLA in an attempt to destroy the MPLA. Yet, it is a war in which the United States denied its involvement, let alone helping start it.

The $300,000 given to the FNLA in January 1975, and the attack by its forces that followed shortly thereafter in

March to try to destroy the MPLA, played a critical role not only in starting the Angolan civil war but in plunging the country into chaos from which it has never recovered. And the United States - not Cuba or the Soviet Union - was directly responsible for this, despite repeated denials by American officials including Secretary of State Henry Kissinger. They lied. It was only after this happened that the Soviet Union sent the first large shipment of arms to the MPLA in March. Even the investigating committee of the United States Congress conceded: "Later events have suggested that this infusion of US aid [$300,000], unprecedented and massive in the underdeveloped colony, may have panicked the Soviets into arming their MPLA clients."[2]

The Soviet Union was probably also influenced by China in its decision to send a large shipment of weapons to the MPLA. In September 1974, the Chinese sent a huge shipment of arms to the FNLA in Angola and more than 100 military advisers to neighbouring Zaire - another American client - to train FNLA soldiers only one month after the coup in Portugal which speeded up the decolonization process when the new military government of young leftist soldiers in Lisbon announced their intention to end colonial rule in Africa. The CIA escalated the conflict and further alarmed the Soviets when it sent its first major shipment of arms to the FNLA in July 1975; knowing full well that the Soviets would respond with their own shipment at least to match, if not exceed, the American infusion of military aid to Holden Roberto and his forces.

American involvement in the Angolan conflict had another dimension. Besides giving weapons to the FNLA and UNITA, the United States also trained the soldiers of the two groups, and American pilots and other personnel flew many times between Zaire and Angola on supply and reconnaissance missions. Kinshasa, the capital of Zaire, then had the largest CIA station and contingent in Africa. And their client, President Mobutu Sese Seko, did everything he could to impede the liberation of southern Africa and Angola at the behest of the United States and France and other Western powers. The CIA during that time also spent more than one million dollars to recruit and train mercenaries for its Angolan mission. Many of those mercenaries were Americans.

Others were Portuguese, French, South African, and British including the notorious George Cullen who shot 14 of his fellow mercenaries dead because they had mistakenly attacked the wrong side; the MPLA, after consolidating its position as the government of Angola, executed him.

Yet Henry Kissinger told the United States Senate that the CIA was not involved in mercenary activities in Angola, during the very same time when the agency was busy recruiting and training soldiers of fortune for the Angolan mission.

Besides the recruitment of mercenaries by the CIA, the agency also had more than 100 agents and military officers operating in Zaire, Angola, South Africa and Zambia, moving back and forth, directing military campaigns and other activities including a sustained disinformation campaign. It also recruited journalists working for major news organizations to help carry on the campaign through false reports - from the CIA - about Soviet military advisers in Angola; "atrocities" - including rape and murder - committed by Cuban soldiers against African civilians, and other lies. UNITA was one of the main sources of these reports generated by the CIA. But some major newspapers, such as *The New York Times*, *The Washington Post*, *The Guardian* (London), were on guard and pointed out that the only source of these reports was UNITA.

The implication was obvious. The papers were careful not to give credibility to such reports, implying they were fabricated. But there were other journalists who did not do this. Instead, they tried to give credence to these false reports generated by the CIA in order to discredit the Soviets and the Cubans.

Yet, in spite of all this, the CIA clients - FNLA and UNITA - had little chance of defeating the MPLA, the most organized and best led of the three groups. It also controlled the capital Luanda and was recognized by the majority of the African countries, thus casting the United States in a very bad light across the continent, while the Soviets and the Cubans gained credibility as supporters of the legitimate government of Angola.

Compounding the problem for the United States was the fact that apartheid South Africa supported the same groups - FNLA and UNITA - the Americans did. The MPLA definitely had the upper hand, but the United States still opposed a negotiated settlement of the Angolan conflict simply because the Soviet Union was on the winning side, not only of the MPLA but of the majority of the African governments who - through the Organization of African Unity (OAU) - had accorded it recognition as the government of a sovereign entity which was also a member of the OAU. And when the MPLA tried to establish relations with the United States, American officials said they would do so only if their country was allowed to replace the Soviet Union as the most influential power in Angola.

American involvement in Angola, and in southern Africa in general, assumed yet another dimension with the direct engagement of South African troops in the Angolan war with the encouragement of the United States; although the apartheid regime also had its own interests when it intervened in order to create a buffer zone between independent African countries supporting the freedom fighters and white-ruled South Africa by installing a puppet government in Angola to block guerrilla fighters from entering South West Africa (Namibia) and South

Africa itself.

The United States asked South Africa to actively intervene in Angola because it was American policy - implemented by the CIA and the National Security Agency (NSA) - since the sixties to cooperate with South Africa's intelligence service, hence the apartheid regime itself, in pursuit of Western interests in the region; including neutralizing Soviet presence and influence in Angola and elsewhere on the continent, but mainly in southern Africa which was the combat theater.

One of the main reasons why the United States wanted to actively collaborate with the apartheid regime in intelligence activities was the existence of the African National Congress (ANC) on the South African political scene as the dominant nationalist organization fighting to end apartheid, and whose most prominent leader was Nelson Mandela. Although banned, it wielded great influence not only within South Africa but in other African countries as well, and abroad, especially among anti-apartheid groups. It was also supported by the Soviet Union, thus making it a prime target for the CIA which wanted to undermine it, and, if possible, destroy it. CIA involvement in South Africa reached a dramatic point in August 1962 when Nelson Mandela, returning from Tanganyika where he met Julius Nyerere, was arrested by the South African police.

The South African authorities were able to locate Mandela based on information about his movements and disguise, and his hideout, provided by CIA agent Donald C. Rickard who worked undercover as a consular official at the American consulate in Durban from 1958 to 1963.

Rickard obtained information about Mandela that he would be disguised as a chauffeur in a car going to Durban from an informer in the African National Congress (ANC). At a farewell party for him in 1963 at the residence of the highly notorious South African and CIA mercenary Colonel "Mad Mike" Hoare who wreaked so much havoc in the Congo in the sixties, Rickard said he was supposed to meet Mandela on that night of August 5 when the nationalist leader was arrested but, instead, notified the South African intelligence service and police about Mandela's whereabouts.

Armed police flagged down Mandela's car at a roadblock outside Howick, Natal, and arrested him without resistance. In 1964, he was eventually sentenced to life imprisonment and spent almost 28 years in confinement, mostly behind bars.[3] Rickard returned to the United States to live in retirement in Pagosa Springs, Colorado, where he still lives today.

During his visit to Tanganyika in 1962, the first to an independent African country to seek financial and military assistance - Tanganyika was also the first country in eastern and southern Africa to win independence - Mandela was somewhat disappointed when Nyerere, whom he described as "very shrewd," told him that he and his organization, the African National Congress (ANC), should wait until Robert Mangaliso Sobukwe was out of prison before starting the armed struggle against the apartheid regime. Sobukwe, a professor at Witwatersrand University, South Africa's leading academic institution, was the leader of the Pan-Africanist Congress (PAC) formed in 1959 as a breakaway from the African National Congress (ANC).

Although Mandela was discouraged by Nyerere's response to his request for military help, urging postponement so that the ANC and the PAC should wage a coordinated campaign once Sobukwe was freed, he was at the same time encouraged by the fact that Nyerere told him he would get in touch with Emperor Haile Selassie and ask him to help.

So, Mandela went to Ethiopia, travelling on documents issued by the government of Tanganyika and authorized by Nyerere, where he got some military training. It was the same travel documents he used to go to other African countries and to Britain. As he states in his autobiography, *Long Walk to Freedom*, the government of Tanganyika assumed responsibility for his travel, giving him documents which said: "This is Nelson Mandela, a citizen of South Africa. He has permission to leave Tanganyika, and return here." And he did. But when he returned to South Africa, it was an entirely different story. Had it not been for the intelligence information provided by CIA agent Donald Rickard on Mandela's whereabouts and disguise, he probably would not have been found where he was hiding, and therefore would not have been arrested and sent to prison for almost three decades.

American involvement in southern Africa continued when the CIA set up a covert operation in 1975 to deliver weapons to South Africa for the South African armed forces. The weapons were also used in Angola by America's surrogate forces - FNLA and UNITA - against Soviet-Cuban-backed MPLA forces which were also supported by African countries such as Nigeria, Tanzania, Mozambique, and Congo-Brazzaville but opposed by Zaire under Mobutu, Tanzania's and Congo-Brazzaville's as well as Angola's neighbour and the most important American client state in the region and, indeed, on the entire continent.

In a reciprocal arrangement with the United States, South Africa helped transport American weapons from Zaire to Angola for the FNLA and UNITA forces in acknowledgment for the military assistance the apartheid regime was getting from the American government. Yet American officials - Dr. Kissinger, CIA Director William Colby and others - continued to deny such involvement and even lied to the United States Congress about it.

Although the United States was deeply involved in Angola, it still was unable to turn the tide against the MPLA. By February 1976, with the crucial assistance of Cuban combat forces and Soviet military hardware, the

MPLA had virtually defeated its rivals and was in full control of the capital Luanda.

There has been much controversy over the sequence of events which led to Cuban intervention, much of it generated by American denials and attempts to reverse the sequence and rewrite history. American and South African officials went in, they claim, in response to large-scale Cuban military intervention, instead of the reverse being the case; they went in surreptitiously at first. As Wayne Smith, director of the US State Department's Office of Cuban Affairs from 1977 to 1979, wrote later: "In August and October [1975] South African troops invaded Angola with full U.S. knowledge. No Cuban troops were in Angola prior to this intervention."[4]

Even when UNITA leader Dr. Jonas Savimbi tried to reach an accommodation with the MPLA, mainly because he lost the war, the United States told him to keep on fighting simply because Angola had a government American leaders didn't like and which was getting help from their nemesis, the Soviet Union; in spite of the fact that they had a reliable client next door, Mobutu, and the largest CIA station on the entire continent based in Zaire's capital Kinshasa. Zaire also had its own reasons why it was opposed to the MPLA government.

Zairean leaders wanted a government they could manipulate or influence and prevent it from allowing Katanga rebels from using Angola as a sanctuary and springboard from which to launch attacks on Zaire. In fact, Katanga *gendarmes* fled to Angola and settled there after losing the war in the sixties. Determined to keep them out of Zaire, Mobutu sent his poorly trained, but American-equipped armed forces into combat to support the FNLA against the MPLA, although Holden Roberto, Mobutu's brother-in-law, and his army were an incompetent lot, and of little use to Zaire and to the United States except as a nuisance to the Soviets and the Cubans. As Professor

Gerald Bender, a renowned American authority on Angola, said in his testimony before the United States Congress in 1978:

"Although the United States has supported the FNLA in Angola for 17 years, it is virtually impossible to find an American official, scholar or journalist, who is familiar with that party, who will testify positively about its organization or leadership.

After a debate with a senior State Department official at the end of the Angolan civil war, I asked him why the United States ever bet on the FNLA. He replied, 'I'll be damned if I know; I have never seen a single report or memo which suggests that the FNLA has any organization, solid leaders, or an ideology which we would count on.'

Even foreign leaders who have supported Holden Roberto, such as General Mobutu, agree with that assessment. When asked by a visiting U.S. Senator if he thought Roberto would make a good leader for Angola, Mobutu replied, 'Hell no!'"[5]

The United States continued to justify its intervention in Angola and southern Africa by using convoluted logic, lying, and rarely telling the truth. Secretary of State Henry Kissinger testified before Congress that one of the main reasons for the American policy in Angola was to maintain stability in Zaire under Mobutu.

Yet this was not a convincing explanation. It did not explain or justify large-scale American intervention in a third country, Angola. The United States could have directly poured massive aid into Zaire itself to strengthen Mobutu's regime. The stability and security of Zaire was, or could be maintained, within Zaire itself not in Angola. Kissinger's testimony before the US Congressional investigating committee could not be reconciled with what the United States was actually doing or how Mobutu felt after he discovered a plot to undermine his regime.

In June 1975, a month before the United States sent a large amount of weapons to the FNLA, Mobutu accused the American government and the CIA of trying to overthrow and assassinate him and expelled the American ambassador. Yet this was the very same leader Kissinger claimed the United States was helping maintain stability in his country and sustain in power.

Even when the MPLA government provided security to American and other employees of Gulf Oil and its installations, the United States was still determined to undermine it and fuel the civil war, although Gulf Oil, an American corporation, accepted MPLA's security arrangements. Instead, the CIA and the US State Department exerted enormous pressure on Gulf Oil to stop royalty payments to the MPLA government for the oil it was pumping out of the Cabinda enclave.

And contrary to what American officials said, Fidel Castro did not send Cuban troops to Angola at the behest of the Soviet Union but in pursuit of his own foreign policy objectives as a supporter of liberation movements, champion of the Third World, and as an internationalist. Hostility towards the MPLA, and refusal to accept it as the legitimate government of Angola, continued to be prominent features of American policy towards Angola even after the government had been internationally recognized by many countries as the true representative of the Angolan people, and exercising institutional authority over its territory, however tenuous in many areas because of the war. And the United States and her allies continued to work on plans to destabilize and overthrow the MPLA government. As William Blum states in his book, *Killing Hope: US Military and CIA Interventions Since World War II*:

"In 1984 a confidential memorandum smuggled out of Zaire revealed that the United States and South Africa had met in November 1983 to discuss destabilization of the Angolan government.

Plans were drawn up to supply more military aid to UNITA - the FNLA was now defunct - and discussions were held on ways to implement a wide range of tactics: unify the anti-government movements, stir up popular feeling against the government, sabotage factories and transport systems, seize strategic points, disrupt joint Anglo-Soviet projects, undermine relations between the (MPLA) government and the Soviet Union and Cuba, bring pressure to bear on Cuba to withdraw its troops, sow divisions in the ranks of the MPLA leadership, infiltrate agents into the Angolan army, and apply pressure to stem the flow of foreign investments into Angola."[6]

In pursuit of these objectives, the Reagan Administration announced in January 1987 that it was providing UNITA rebels with Stinger missiles and other anti-aircraft weapons. And, as far back as 1984, UNITA's official representative in Washington proudly stated that UNITA had "contacts with US officials at all levels on regular basis."

And when UNITA lost the election to the MPLA in September 1992, the rebel group launched a full-scale war against the government with the help of South Africa and American "private" and "relief" organizations including conservative American leaders, despite the fact that the elections had been certified to be free and fair by the United Nations, the Organization of African Unity (OAU) and other international observers. As one senior US State Department official said in January 1993 a few months before the United States finally accorded the MPLA government full recognition in May the same year: "UNITA is exactly like the Khmer Rouge: elections and negotiations are just one more method of fighting a war; power is all."[7]

And the fact that the United States and South Africa intervened in Angola months before Castro sent troops in 1975, but lied about it claiming the Cubans went in first, raises serious questions about the credibility of American - and South African - officials throughout this engagement. It also raises serious questions about American claims that Washington was concerned about the well-being of Africans when it supported groups which were trying to destroy and replace an organization - the MPLA - which did most of the fighting during the liberation war against the Portuguese colonial forces and whose government was recognized by the majority of the African countries and by the Organization of African Unity (OAU). And the devastation wrought by America's surrogate forces - FNLA, UNITA, and apartheid South Africa - with American weapons, razing entire villages and killing countless innocent civilians, shows how much Washington really cared about Africans.

If the United States cared about the well-being of Africans, she would have supported them during the independence struggle and would have exerted a lot of pressure on Portugal, her NATO ally, to relinquish power in her colonies. Instead, she did exactly the opposite, yet expected to impress Africans not only in Angola but across the continent with its military intervention against the MPLA government.

Worst of all is the fact that the lies about American involvement in Angola were used by Kissinger and the United States government to justify American intervention which plunged the country and the entire southern Africa into civil war which lasted for almost 30 years, wreaking havoc and causing untold suffering on an unprecedented scale costing at least one million lives in Angola alone; with economic devastation amounting to hundreds of millions of dollars in a country which had the potential to become one of the richest not only in Africa but in the entire Third World.

But for 30 years, all that potential went down the drain, thanks to the lies told by Dr. Henry Kissinger and other American officials to justify American intervention in an attempt to prevent the MPLA, a Soviet and Cuban ally, from assuming power.

Had the United States not intervened, the MPLA would have consolidated its position as the legitimate government of Angola from the time it routed its rivals - UNITA and the FNLA - back in 1976, and the country would have embarked on the road towards stability and economic recovery and would probably have made significant progress during the next 30 years when it was, instead, mired in conflict.

Yet American officials were so determined to prevent the MPLA from taking over Angola that they didn't care what they did to the country or what kind of lies they told; lies Kissinger continued to maintain through the years as if they were Gospel truth.

He even told the same lies in the third volume of his memoirs, *Years of Renewal*,[8] published in 2002. As Professor Piero Gleijeses in the School of International Studies at Johns Hopkins University, who used the Freedom of Information Act to uncover documents about American covert operations in Angola and who was the first American scholar to have access to the archives in Havana, Cuba, on the Angolan conflict, states:

"When the United States decided to launch the covert intervention, in June and July (1975), not only were there no Cubans in Angola, but the US government and the CIA were not even thinking about any Cuban presence in Angola.

If you look at the CIA reports, which were done at the time, the Cubans were totally out of the picture. (But in the reports presented to the US Senate in December 1975) what you find is really nothing less than the rewriting of history....

Kissinger had the CIA rewrite its report to serve the political aim of the administration, and so the poor CIA ended up lying."[9]

Not only did Kissinger deny earlier American involvement in Angola; he also maintained then, and in his memoirs almost 30 years later, that the American government did not even know that South African troops invaded Angola posing as mercenaries in 1975. And although he claimed that the United States intervened in Angola (in July 1975) in response to a massive infusion of Cuban troops earlier, about 30,000 of them, declassified CIA papers for August-October 1975 say there were only a few Cubans in Angola during that time trying to pass themselves off as tourists. As Nathaniel Davis, Assistant Secretary of State for African Affairs under Kissinger but who resigned in July 1975 over American intervention in Angola, said:

"Considering that things came to a head over covert action in the US government in mid-July, there is no reason to believe we were responding to Cuban involvement in Angola."[10]

A CIA-funded operation was launched from Zaire in July 1975 to support FNLA and Zairean forces in their invasion of Angola against the MPLA, during the same time when South African armed forces invaded the country in support of UNITA. They were not mercenaries, although the CIA leaked reports claiming that they were foreign mercenaries, probably funded by disgruntled elements in the former Portuguese colony. It was a well-coordinated attack masterminded by the CIA and the South African intelligence service.

It was not until November 4, 1975, that Cuban

President Fidel Castro decided to send troops to Angola - at the request of the MPLA in an urgent plea - in response to the South African invasion, which almost led to the capture of the capital Luanda, until the Cubans arrived in massive numbers and turned back the tide.

The arrival of 30,000 Cuban troops tilted the civil war in favour of the MPLA which was already in control of the capital. South African troops remained in Angola fighting the Cubans and the MPLA but were forced to withdraw in March 1976. They did not, however, stay out of Angola and continued to support UNITA rebels through the years, as much as the United States did, until the late 1980s.

Yet even such large-scale invasion of Angola by the South African armed forces in July 1975 was not enough to make Kissinger tell the truth when he testified before Congress in 1976 on American covert operations in Angola. As Professor Gleijeses states: "The key element of the covert operation was cooperation with South Africa. Kissinger went to the extreme of saying he only learned a couple of weeks later that South Africa had invaded."[11]

Even the former CIA station chief in Angola from August to November 1975, Robert Hultslander, conceded later that American intervention was responsible for the chaos and destruction that ensued: "It was our policies which caused the destabilisation. Kissinger was determined to challenge the Soviet Union, although no vital US interests were at stake."[12]

Hultslander also said US intelligence officers on the ground believed at the time that the MPLA was the "best qualified movement to govern Angola."[13] But Kissinger and others decided that it was not in the best interest of the United States for the MPLA to remain in power, despite its credentials as the legitimate government of Angola and the most competent group among the three contending factions (MPLA, FNLA, and UNITA).

In fact, at a National Security Council meeting on June 27, 1975, Defence Secretary Dr. James Schlesinger said the United States should "encourage the disintegration of Angola."[14] It was at that meeting that Kissinger indicated that the CIA had authorized provision of money and shipment of arms to American surrogate forces in Angola, months before the Cubans intervened in November the same year.

American intervention in Angola plunged the entire southern Africa into chaos from which it has not recovered after almost 30 years of war. The loss in human lives and destruction of property was enormous. All the countries in the region, including Tanzania, were affected one way or another. The flood of refugees alone fleeing into neighbouring countries from the civil war in Angola became a major humanitarian crisis requiring massive international relief efforts - well into the late 1990s and beyond - unprecedented in the history of the region.

Millions of Angolans became internally displaced, in addition to the one million who died, and untold numbers of others who sought refuge in Zambia, Zaire (renamed the Democratic Republic of Congo), Congo Republic (popularly known as Congo-Brazzaville), Namibia, Botswana and other countries.

America's determination to confront the Soviets wherever they were - except in their citadel, the Soviet Union itself and its satellites - turned Angola into a battleground it otherwise would not have been. As Julius Nyerere said on American television ABC programme, "Issues and Answers," when he was asked in an interview in Dar es Salaam, Tanzania, in June 1976, why he thought the CIA was behind the fighting and chaos in Angola: "Who is doing it? Who else could be doing it? Why do we keep on hearing these whispers coming from Washington saying, 'Let's create another Vietnam for Russia in Angola'?...You are causing us trouble."

And he asked in the same interview: "Why are Western countries arming South Africa?....And you expect us to sit just like that."

Nyerere also articulated his position on American involvement in the region in his article, "America and Southern Africa," published in July 1977 in *Foreign Affairs*:

"The dominant element in American foreign policy since 1946 has been opposition to communism and to the communist powers. As far as Africa was concerned, responsibility for pursuing these objectives was delegated to America's trusted allies - Britain, France, Belgium, and even Portugal - whose policies in the area were therefore broadly supported despite minor disagreements which arose as American business became interested in Africa's potential.

Inevitably this placed America in opposition to an Africa, which was trying to win its independence from those same powers; but when political freedom could be achieved peacefully, America was able to appear to Africa like a bystander. It was therefore able to adjust its policies and accept the new status quo of African sovereign states without any difficulty. Notwithstanding these adjustments, however, America has continued to look at African affairs largely through anti-communist spectacles and to disregard Africa's different concerns and priorities.

And in southern Africa events did not force any readjustments of American policies during the 1960s; so none were made. Practical support for the status quo continued unabated until after the Portuguese Revolution in April 1974. Thus, despite America's verbal criticism of Portuguese colonialism, American arms and equipment were used by Portugal in its military operations in Angola, Guinea-Bissau and Mozambique. Despite the verbal opposition to apartheid, American trade and investment in South Africa were expanded, and America opposed any effective U.N. demonstration of hostility toward the apartheid state.

The United States has also fought a hard, and largely successful, rearguard action against the demands for international intervention against South Africa's occupation of Namibia. And on Rhodesia, America has trailed behind British policies, emasculated the sanctions policies it had endorsed at the United Nations, and criticized Africa for the vehemence of its opposition to the minority Smith regime.

This general approach to African questions, and particularly to southern Africa, culminated in the American government's support for the FNLA/UNITA forces in the dispute between the Angolan nationalist movements.

Throughout the anti-colonial war in Angola that is from 1960 to 1974 America had supported Portugal, not any of the nationalist forces. Supplies to the FNLA of money and other equipment while desalinization was taking place were thus a rather blatant attempt to place 'friends' in political power in the new state. Not surprisingly, it was the least effective of the contending nationalist groups, which was open to this kind of purchase; success therefore depended upon the quick collapse of the MPLA, under assault.

But the MPLA did not collapse. Instead it asked for and received more arms from those who had been helping it for the ten years of its anticolonial war; to meet the simultaneous South African invasion of Angola, the MPLA also welcomed Cuban troops. And when the FNLA demanded more help than the American Administration alone could give it, the U.S. Congress - with the lessons of Vietnam still fresh in its mind - refused finance.

It is not cynicism, which attributes the beginnings of the 'Kissinger initiative' in April 1976 partly to this experience. Nations, like people, sometimes need to be shaken out of habitual modes of thought. Nor was the

Angolan debacle the only factor leading toward a reassessment of traditional U.S. policies in southern Africa. Some Americans had for long been urging support for the anti-racialist and anticolonial struggle, and American blacks were beginning to take greater interest in these matters.

Further, trade with independent Africa has been growing, and now includes oil from Nigeria. The possibility that this trade might be jeopardized by pro-South African actions is no longer of merely academic interest to the United States. And the guerrilla war in Rhodesia has been intensified since mid-1975, arousing fears of a repetition of the Angolan experience.

Africa welcomed the Lusaka statement by Dr. Kissinger that majority rule must precede independence in Rhodesia, and that America would give no material or diplomatic support to the Smith regime in its conflict with the African states or the African liberation movements. With some hesitation, Africa also cooperated with the Kissinger 'shuttle diplomacy' later in the year. For Africa hoped that, even at that late stage, the use of American power in support of majority rule could enable this to be attained in Rhodesia without further bloodshed.

The 'Kissinger initiative' did force Ian Smith to shift his ground, but it did not succeed in its declared objective. Neither did it remove Africa's uncertainty about the depth and geographical limitations of America's new commitment to change in southern Africa. For decades of history cannot be wiped out by one speech and a few months of highly individualistic one-man diplomacy. They cannot even be eradicated by the clear sincerity of a new President's commitment to supporting human rights, and the sympathetic understanding shown by the Ambassador he has appointed to the United Nations.

II

The United States of America is the most powerful nation on earth. Africa is weak, economically and militarily; its unity in action is still fragile. Africa does therefore naturally desire the friendship and cooperation of the United States; it does need trade, and economic assistance.

But overwhelming everything else in Africa is the sense of nationalism, and the determination of all African peoples that the whole continent shall be free and relieved from the humiliation of organized white racialism. Within Rhodesia, Namibia, and South Africa, and within the nations immediately bordering them, the commitment to the struggle against minority or colonial rule overrides all other matters.

This basic fact is important to America, as it is to the rest of the world. For power is not all-powerful. Nationalism cannot be overcome by it. Nationalist wars have no end except victory, however long that takes to achieve, whatever the cost and the inevitable setbacks. All that can be affected by the actions of its opponents is the character of the nationalist state and society after victory. The harder and longer the struggle for freedom, the more austere and radicalized the new state is likely to be. It may also be more intolerant. For wars are liable to destroy everything except hatred and mutual suspicion - which they nurture.

The United States, like other nations of the world, has a legitimate interest in the future as well as the present societies of southern Africa. It must be concerned about America's continued ability to buy the goods it needs, and its ability to sell sufficient goods to pay for its imports. America must be interested in whether or not these states will determine their own foreign policies according to their own interests after winning their freedom, or whether they will be dominated in these matters by states hostile to the United States. And America, like the rest of the world, will continue to have a legitimate interest in the status of human rights in southern Africa as well as elsewhere.

None of these things will it be able to control in a state which is really independent - that is the meaning of independence. But one would expect that current American policies toward the nationalist struggles in southern Africa would be determined with these long-term interests in mind. And it does not seem to Africa that these factors have determined American policies in the past. At least they have not done so on any intelligent assessment of the paramountcy of nationalism in shaping the future.

III

One thing is quite certain. The status of human rights could not be worse in the independent states of southern Africa than it is now. The very idea of there being 'human rights' presupposes the basic acceptance of human equality. Yet colonialism is in principle a denial of equality. It means that the interests of the colonized are subordinate to the interests of the colonizers, or at the very least are interpreted and judged by the colonizers.

Support for human rights therefore involves opposition to colonialism, regardless of how gentle, well intentioned, or selfless the colonial government may be. Greater urgency in ending this status is imparted to the situation when, as in Namibia and Rhodesia, colonialism has none of these virtues. Two hundred years after Americans fought their own kith and kin to end colonialism, it should not be necessary for Africa to try to convince America that Africans find colonialism intolerable.

Human rights are also inconsistent with the practice of racialism. They are denied by any law or practice, which distinguishes the rights and duties of men and women according to their racial origin. And in South Africa there is hardly a law, which does not make this distinction; the entire state machinery is directed at organizing and upholding the domination of one racial group over all others.

This would be inconsistent with human rights if the majority racial group were using racial discrimination as a means of controlling a dissident minority. It is not made more consistent when 83 percent of the South African population is denied elementary political, economic, and social justice by legislation and economic power used by and in the interests of the whites.

Every aspect of the South African state organization is thus inconsistent with the American philosophy of human equality and freedom. But this is not simply an internal South African matter. Without the kind of practical support, which the South African government and society have been receiving - and are still receiving - from their relations with America and its allies, the present apartheid structure could not be sustained for very long. And therefore minority rule in Rhodesia and Namibia could not continue.

Thus, for example, South Africa has a continuing and large deficit in its foreign trade, which is financed by capital imports, both long and short term. American investment in South Africa has more than tripled since 1966 and now stands at more than $1,600 million. All these investors profit from apartheid and the discriminatory wage structure - and thus have an interest in sustaining it.

Further, until now America has continued to act in the United Nations and elsewhere as if South Africa were a bastion against Soviet infiltration into southern Africa, and against the spread of communism in Africa. This image is carefully fostered by the apartheid regime, which prides itself on its anti-communism, and had defined a communist as 'anyone who supports any of the aims of communism' - including the declared aim of human equality!

Yet by identifying itself in practice with the apartheid regime and its satellites, America is liable to bring about the very things it most fears - the growth of communist influence, the radicalization of the opposition to apartheid and colonialism, and the damage to its own economic interests. For opposition to the regimes in southern Africa is inevitable.

Men will not indefinitely accept humiliation, exploitation, and tyranny. Sooner or later, by one means or another, the dominant minority will lose its ability to control the country and run the economy in its own interests. It is natural that Africa should seek American help in ending its humiliation. Americans should not find it natural when their country aids the oppressor instead of the oppressed.

The organizational and material weakness of the nationalist forces in southern Africa, which results from decades of ruthless oppression, does, however, have two consequences of international relevance. First, nationalists cannot be particular about the means through which they carry on the struggle; they have to take advantage of any opportunities, which they can find. Secondly, they have to accept help from wherever they can get it. The stronger apartheid and minority rule become, and the more supporters those forces enlist, the greater becomes the nationalists' need for outside help.

IV

When seeking external support for their struggles, it is natural that African nationalists should look first to the African countries, which have already secured their own freedom. And it is equally natural that free African states should give that support. No independent African state can rest secure while colonialism continues in Africa, for colonialism is a denial of its own right to exist. Further, the human dignity of all Africans is denied when Africans anywhere are humiliated because of their race.

On the principle of giving assistance to the freedom

movements in southern Africa, therefore, the whole of free Africa is united. But in comparison with South Africa, free Africa is weak. All African states are poor, some are almost overwhelmed by the task of trying to make independence economically meaningful and beneficial to their people.

Further, no African state has an armaments industry of its own. The nationalist movements of southern Africa therefore need more help than Africa alone can give them.

Outside Africa, however, experience has shown that communist countries are almost the only ones, which are both able and willing to assist the nationalist movements of southern Africa. The major countries of the Western bloc urge patience and nonviolence as if these had not been tried for the past 30 years; simultaneously they continue to bolster South Africa's economic and military strength by trade, investment, and political cooperation. Some of the Nordic countries give humanitarian assistance to the freedom fighters. Only the communist countries are willing to make arms and other military help available when an armed struggle becomes the only way forward.

Why the communist states are willing to assist the freedom movements is for them to say. Africa knows why it needs that assistance, and what it will be used for if it can be obtained. Anything else is, at this stage, irrelevant to us. If the West decides to give us similar aid, I for one would not question its motives. Africa is concerned with existing oppression, not with hypothetical dangers in the future. Any new threats to freedom will be dealt with after it has been won - not before! In the war against Nazism the United States and the Soviet Union were allies.

But the peoples of southern Africa are not asking others to fight their liberation battles for them. They know that a people can only free themselves; they cannot import freedom. The peoples of these countries are asking only for appropriate support for the freedom struggle they are themselves conducting. Whether that support needs to be political, economic, or military - or all three - depends upon the type of struggle, which has to be waged before, victory is achieved. It is in this respect that the differences in the political and economic situations of Rhodesia, Namibia, and South Africa become relevant to current policies for other nations of the world.

Yet although the three countries do present different problems, and opportunities, it is pointless to try to treat each one in isolation. The objective is freedom for the whole of southern Africa.

This means independence on the basis of majority rule in Rhodesia; independence on the basis of majority rule for Namibia as a single political unit; and an end to apartheid and minority rule in South Africa itself. So it is one struggle, with three geographical areas.

Therefore, South Africa cannot be regarded as an ally in the fight for majority rule in Rhodesia, any more than Rhodesia could be expected to support the anticolonial movement in Namibia. Rhodesia and South Africa are natural allies to each other. The most which could be achieved is for South Africa to recognize the differences between its own position and that of the Smith regime, and therefore to buy time for itself by refraining from direct assistance to minority rule in the British colony.

V

In Rhodesia, or Zimbabwe - to use its African name - we now have to face the fact that this is 1977, not 1965. A liberation war has started. Government 'reforms,' or reductions in the intensity of racial discrimination, which would have given hope of change fifteen or even ten years ago and thus prevented war, are now irrelevant. Options which existed at the time of Rhodesia's unilateral declaration of independence (UDI) no longer exist.

This should not be strange to Americans who know their own history. Very few inhabitants of the American colonies were calling for independence when the dispute with the British government arose in the 1760s. According to John Adams, one-third of the colonists remained opposed to the rebellion even during the War of Independence. Yet concessions made by the British government in 1770 were already too late to avert conflict. And once the war had begun it could have only one end. So it is in Rhodesia now. Ian Smith's unilateral 'package of reforms' announced in March of this year will not even buy him time.

The only question which remains open is whether independence on the basis of majority rule will be achieved by a fight to the finish, or whether that same end can be achieved by a minimum of bloodshed leading to negotiations.

Therefore negotiation cannot now be about the principle of majority rule before independence. Nor can it be about the establishment of an 'interim government' under white control. The nationalists are insisting that the 270,000 whites cannot be allowed to continue governing 5,800,000 Africans, whatever promises the former make about organizing an 'orderly transfer of power,' or anything else. For the argument now is about power, not about promises; the fighting, which has started, will not end until a transfer of power from the minority to the majority has actually taken place. A ceasefire without such a transfer of power was tried in December 1974; it led to a strengthening of the minority regime.

What was possible until the collapse of the Geneva Conference in December 1976 was a delay in independence. For in accordance with the British tradition of decolonization, the nationalists had separated independence from internal self-government under majority rule. The latter they were demanding immediately, with some minority representation in an interim nationalist government. But they had agreed on a delay of 12 months before independence, in the hope that effective British sovereignty during that period would allow members of the minority community either to adapt to majority rule, or leave the country. For in this connection it is relevant to remember that more than one-third of the 270,000 whites at present in Rhodesia have immigrated during the past 11 years - they can hardly be regarded as committed to the country.

These demands were rejected by Smith, as were the British government proposals. The British government then abandoned the Conference, showing that despite their legal responsibility for decolonization in Rhodesia, they regarded themselves merely as umpires between Smith and the nationalists, not as participants in a struggle against the Smith regime.

That opportunity for a negotiated settlement has therefore been lost. The attempt of the new British Foreign Secretary to organize talks on another basis has thus to overcome still more suspicion. And even if agreement between the British and the nationalists is reached at new talks, the removal of Smith, and the dismantling of his power structure, still have to be achieved before any political agreement can be converted into the reality of majority rule.

The world in general, and Africa in particular, does, however, still have an interest in bringing the Rhodesian war to a rapid end. Ian Smith and his supporters have no such interest. On the contrary, their objective is the continuation of war until South Africa, and possibly even the United States, come to their support.

Ian Smith recognizes that, on a long-headed assessment of South Africa's own interest, Prime Minister Vorster does not want to get directly involved in the Rhodesian conflict. But in any guerrilla war, civilian casualties are likely to occur; they are already happening in Zimbabwe. If the dead women and children begin to include large numbers of whites, then Smith knows, because Vorster has admitted it, that the Pretoria government will come under pressure from its own electorate to increase South African material support for the Smith regime. And as the casualties begin to include South African citizens who live or visit Rhodesia, Smith believes that his armed forces will be strengthened by direct South African military intervention.

Direct South African military involvement would make a great change in the balance of forces in Rhodesia. It would not defeat nationalism. But it would increase the difficulties of the freedom fighters. The nationalists would therefore be forced to seek increased external help; and it is only communist states, which are likely to give whatever assistance is required. Even if an intelligent American government is then able to withstand the consequent pressure to intervene 'against communism' and to maintain its opposition to Smith, the conflict would have been internationalized. Smith desires this. Africa does not. Whether the internationalization of a limited war of independence is in America's interests is for America to judge.

But America is not a helpless bystander to events in Rhodesia. It is a powerful nation, and influences developments there. It can frustrate Smith's attempts to escalate the war, and can even help to get the war ended.

First, it has to make it quite clear that the United States will give no support of any kind to the minority regime of Rhodesia, at any time, and regardless of the progress or possible escalation of the war.

Second, as evidence of this determination, it has to follow up the rescission of the Byrd Amendment by active steps against all sanctions-breaking (whether by American firms or others), and by greater efforts to prevent the Rhodesian recruitment of American citizens into the regime's army.

And third, the United States has to put pressure on the South African government to desist from further help to the Smith regime. It is not realistic to expect Vorster to act against Rhodesian minority rule; but he can be prevented from propping it up - at least more than he is already doing. The United States has sufficient leverage to do this without treating South Africa as if it is an ally in the struggle for justice in southern Africa.

No one is suggesting that there are quick, or painless, solutions to the problems in Rhodesia. In the 11 years, which have passed since UDI, many opportunities have been lost, and new forces have arisen which now have to be taken into account. Thus, it is true that the Zimbabwe nationalists do not control all the forces, which will influence Rhodesian events in the near and far future. But no settlement of this problem can now be reached without their participation in drawing it up, and their active support in its implementation. In 1977 it is in that context, and only in that context, that America or Britain - or Tanzania - can work for an end to war in Rhodesia.

VI

Namibia is politically different from Rhodesia in two major respects. First, if Prime Minister Vorster really accepted the principle of majority rule outside South Africa, as he has sometimes claimed, it is within his power to introduce it in Namibia. And if he really wants Namibia 'off his back,' as he once asserted, he has the power to make the necessary arrangements. Namibia is not a 'client state' like Rhodesia; it is completely under the *de facto* control of the South African government and armed forces.

Secondly, Namibia is *de jure* a Trusteeship Territory. The United Nations has, by General Assembly and Security Council decision, withdrawn the authority of South Africa over Namibia. It has established the U.N. Council for Namibia, and appointed a full-time Commissioner, whose task is to arrange for an orderly transition to Namibian independence on the basis of political unity and majority rule and periodically to report progress to the United Nations. Also the General Assembly has recognized the South West African People's Organization (SWAPO) as the sole representative nationalist movement of Namibia.

Apart from these two respects, however, the situations in Rhodesia and Namibia are becoming increasingly similar. A united nationalist party now exists, and cannot be ignored. An armed struggle has started in Namibia, although it is not as yet very intense.

South Africa is still trying to evade the necessity of negotiating the form of Namibian independence with SWAPO under the auspices of the United Nations. In response to a threat of action by the United Nations if its resolutions were not observed, South Africa organized the 'Turnhalle Constitutional Conference' in 1975. Representation was by 'ethnic group' (i.e., South African-designated racial and tribal groups), and political parties were barred. The outcome of 'Turnhalle,' not surprisingly, is a set of proposals, which basically maintain the structure of 'tribal homelands' and 'White areas,' and would leave intact the existing racialist domination by the 99,000 whites among the 850,000 population. The South African government is proposing to present the result to the United Nations as an act of 'decolonization.'

Proposals such as these will not solve the problem in South West Africa. Nationalism in Namibia cannot be overcome by establishing another independent apartheid state. The choice for the world, and for South Africa, remains unaffected by such maneuvers. The choice is: either a transfer of de facto power by South Africa to the United Nations, which can then negotiate an independence constitution with SWAPO; or negotiations between South Africa and SWAPO under U.N. auspices; or an intensified war, with all the dangers to world peace which that will bring.

Once again, America cannot control these events. But

it could use its considerable influence to avert the dangers of a serious war of liberation in Namibia. In order to do this, America would first have to accept that SWAPO is the only Namibian nationalist organization, and that no settlement is possible without its agreement. Then it would apply some pressure on South Africa to negotiate with SWAPO under U.N. auspices. Alternatively it would give active American support to the struggle at the United Nations for a South African withdrawal from Namibia, and the introduction of an effective transitional U.N. administration.

What America must not do, if it aims to prevent a major war in Namibia, is to give any encouragement to the 'Turnhalle' Conference, its participants, or South Africa's espousal of its proposals. For time is running out. If the Namibian war has to be intensified - as it will be if there is no progress - the time available for an orderly transition from minority to majority rule will again be exhausted before the work has begun.

VII

South Africa is an independent state. It is not a colony of anyone, and within the boundaries of the Republic there are no colonies to be granted independence. But its organized denial of human rights to all but 17 percent of its people, on the grounds of their race, make South Africa's 'internal affairs' a matter of world concern. For nations have learned, and mankind has learned, that the hope for world peace and justice precludes indifference in the face of organized racialism.

The official reply to all demands that the world should put South Africa into quarantine has been that apartheid is best countered by diplomatic and other contact with more open societies. Unfortunately, however, the South African whites are correct in saying that their society is unique. Nowhere else has the privileged life-style of the dominant minority ever rested so completely and exclusively on racial oppression. Other experiences of gradual desegregation, in the southern states of the United States or elsewhere, will therefore do no more to persuade the whites of South Africa to change their policies than has the polite criticism of Western statesmen since the last world war.

Policies are also based upon the argument that provided foreign investors pay a living wage to their employees; they will be increasing the pressures against apartheid because economic growth shows up the inefficiency of things like racial job reservation and migrant skilled labor. Quite apart from the fact that these are only a small aspect of apartheid, the evidence of the past 30 years - and longer - should by now have dispelled that illusion also. South Africa has been getting economically stronger and more developed at a rapid rate. Racial oppression has been increasing even faster. For the stronger the economy, the more can be spent upon suppressing the majority without any economic sacrifice being demanded of those who benefit by white supremacy. A strong South African economy strengthens the government, not the victims of its oppression.

The South African economy needs to be weakened, not strengthened, if apartheid is to be overthrown. South Africa therefore needs to be isolated economically, politically, and socially, by the rest of the world until there has been a change in political direction. The sooner that change begins, the less violence and chaos there is likely to be.

No one can doubt the desire of the people of South Africa to end apartheid. Organized opposition by the non-whites has been smashed, but the Soweto and Cape Town 'riots' are only the latest of a long series of spontaneous uprisings. And they will not be the last outburst of frustration. For despite everything which the South African state can and will do, instability is inherent in a situation where the majority of the people are excluded from the benefits of a society which depends upon their work. Change can be delayed by an intensification of oppression and human suffering. But apartheid is doomed. The only question is whether the society subsides into chaos, or whether there is an orderly but speedy movement toward justice.

At present there may still just be time for the Republic to avoid ultimate economic and social collapse if the whites can be woken up to their own danger. They would have to begin by setting free, and then entering into a dialogue with, the real leaders of the non-white peoples who are now being held in jails, detention centers, and Restriction - people like Nelson Mandela, Robert Sobukwe and their colleagues. For it is only such people who would have a chance of organizing and channeling the irresistible opposition of the black peoples to their present humiliation.

So far there has been no evidence that the South African white government intends to guide the country in this direction - on the contrary. The whites remain self-confident in their strength and their racial arrogance; and they do this partly because the world continues to talk with them and support them in action. They have not been shocked into a reassessment of their position. They have not yet realized their need to talk with non-white South Africans about their common future. Instead they are able to talk with the rest of the world, and solve their economic problems by new foreign investment, new trade, and new immigration.

VIII

Each nation has to decide for itself what will be in its own interests, and these will determine its policies. But no one is asking that America should fight for the freedom of southern Africa. Africa is simply asking that America should stop supporting racialism and unfreedom in that area.

For the penalty, as well as the opportunity, of America's great power relative to that of any other nation, is that every American action, or failure to act, has an effect upon the timing and the nature of developments outside its own borders. This is not to say that America can impose its will on an unwilling world; only that it cannot avoid involvement in events elsewhere. When Tanzania trades or fails to trade, or indicates support or opposition for another government, the world goes on unchanged and unruffled. When America does any of these things it is affecting what will happen elsewhere. One may like this or not; it remains a statement of fact.

Thus, America cannot prevent men from struggling against colonialism and racialism in southern Africa. But American actions will either ease the inevitable triumph of the freedom struggle, or strengthen the resistance to it and thus force the anticolonial and anti-racist movements into a hard, ruthless, and hostile mold. There is no way in which powerful America can avoid doing one or the other of these things, as long as it needs to have commercial and state relations with the rest of the world.

Africa is therefore asking that America should recognize the conflict in southern Africa as the nationalist struggle which it is, and that it should refuse to be taken in by the communist bogey paraded by the racialists. It is asking that America should refrain from profit making out of apartheid. South Africa needs the United States; but the United States does not need South Africa. Africa is asking that America should carry its declared support for human equality and dignity into policies which will weaken the forces of racialism and colonialism in southern Africa, so that the peoples of those areas can triumph more quickly and with less bloodshed.

With or without American support during the struggle, freedom in southern will not mean the birth of ideal democracies, where all citizens enjoy human rights, civil liberty, and a consumer society to boot. Popular governments in Rhodesia, Namibia, and later in South Africa, will face immense problems of poverty, disruption and unrealizable expectations. They will also inherit a legacy of mutual hostility and bitterness. The racial prejudice, which has been inculcated by years of deliberate indoctrination, and by bitter experience, will not disappear when majority rule begins.

But it is only after freedom has been won in the states of southern Africa that the positive struggle to build human equality and dignity can begin there. We in Africa hope that the new Administration of the United States will fulfill its early promise, and help the peoples of southern Africa to get to the position where they can make a beginning. At the very least, we hope that America will not continue to use its power and prestige to hinder the movement for freedom and humanity in the south of this continent."[15]

Nyerere's stand on southern Africa influenced the policies of the Organization of African Unity (OAU) more than that of any other African leader, especially in his capacity as chairman of the frontline states of Tanzania, Zambia, Botswana, Mozambique, and Angola in a concerted effort to end white minority rule on the continent.

White rule finally ended with the collapse of the apartheid regime in 1994, five years before Nyerere died.

Nyerere was also - although no longer president of Tanzania - one of the world leaders, including Fidel Castro whose intervention in Angola played a critical role in containing the apartheid regime, who attended the inauguration of Nelson Mandela as president of South Africa.

The end of apartheid was a crowning achievement,

culmination of an effort, in a struggle in which Dr. Julius Nyerere played a central role more than any other leader in independent Africa, and a tribute to a man who dedicated his life to the liberation of the continent during a political career that spanned almost half a century.

Chapter notes

1. John Marcum, quoted by William Blum, "Angola 1975 to 1980s: The Great Powers Poker Game," in W. Blum, *Killing Hope: U.S. Military and CIA Interventions since World War II* (Monroe, Maine: Common Courage Press, 1995).

2. "Hearings Before the House Select Committee on Intelligence (The Pike Committee)" published in *CIA: The Pike Report* (Nottingham, England, 1977), p. 199. See also Angola in *The New York Times*, September 25, 1975; *The New York Times*, December 19, 1975.

3. William Blum, *Killing Hope: U.S. Military and CIA Interventions since World War II*, op. cit.; *The Guardian*, London, August 15, 1986; *The Times*, London, August 4, 1986, p. 10.

4. Wayne S. Smith, "Dateline Havana: Myopic Diplomacy," in *Foreign Policy*, Washington, D.C., Fall 1982, p. 170.

5. Gerald Bender, in "Hearings Before the Subcommittee on Africa of the House Committee on International Relations," May 25, 1978, p. 7.

6. W. Blum, *Killing Hope: U.S. Military and CIA Interventions since World War II*, op. cit.

7. *The New York Times*, January 17, 1993, p. 5.

8. Henry A. Kissinger, *Years of Renewal* (New York: Simon & Schuster, 2000).

9. Piero Gleijeses, quoted by Andrew Buncombe, "CIA Angola Lies Exposed 25 Years Later: CIA 'Ran Covert Missions' to Stop Communist Coup," in *The Independent*, London, April 5, 2001; Anthony Boadle, "U.S. Lied About

Cuban Role in Angola - Historian," Reuters, April 1, 2002; Piero Gleijeses, *Conflicting Missions: Havana, Washington and Africa, 1959 - 1976* (Charlotte, North Carolina: University of North Carolina Press, 2002).

10. Nathaniel Davis, quoted by Andrew Buncombe, "CIA Angila Lies Exposed 25 Years Later," op. cit.

11. Piero Gleijeses, quoted by Anthony Boadle, "U.S. Lied About Cuban Role - Historian," op. cit.

12. Robert Hultslander, CIA station chief in Angola from August to November 1975, quoted by Andrew Buncombe, "CIA Angola Lies Exposed 25 Years Later," op. cit.

13. A. Hultslander, quoted by Jim Lobe, "Cuba Followed U.S. into Angola, Secret Papers Reveal," in *Imagen*, May 1, 2002.

14. James Schlesinger, ibid.

15. Julius K. Nyerere, "America and Southern Africa," in *Foreign Affairs*, Vol. 55, No. 4, July 1977, pp. 671 - 684.

The Struggle Against Apartheid: Milestones

THE struggle against apartheid was marked by successes and failures and by some of the worst tragedies in the history of the country and of the entire continent.

Some of the most important milestones involved massacres and one of the most celebrated trials in history. We are going to focus on them because of the critical role they played in highlighting the injustices under apartheid and in helping bring down one of the most brutal regimes in the history of mankind.

Sharpeville Massacre

Probably more than any other event in the history of South Africa, the Sharpeville massacre demonstrated for the first time to the rest of the world the brutal nature of the apartheid regime and how far it would go to maintain its tight grip on its nonwhite population.

It also showed how defiant the regime was, and how its indifference to the plight of the black majority and other nonwhites helped radicalise the anti-apartheid movement, forcing many of its opponents to resort to armed struggle as the only viable option to end racial injustices in South Africa which was also the bastion of white supremacy on the continent.

It was also one of the worst tragedies that befell Africa during the sixties, and only the beginning of a series of catastrophes which rocked the continent during that decade and in the following years.

The Sharpeville massacre took place on 21 March 1960 when 69 unarmed, peaceful black protesters were killed. Among those killed were 8 women and 10 children.

Most of them were shot in the back as they fled from the police. At least 180 black Africans were injured. And there are reports that as many as 300 suffered injuries at the hands of the police.

The protests were organized by the Pan Africanist Congress (PAC), a party led by Robert Mangaliso Sobukwe who was a professor of African studies at Witwatersrand University, South Africa's leading academic institution especially for English speakers.

The demonstrators lived in the black township of Sharpeville on the outskirts of the white town of Vereeniging in the Transvaal, about 30 miles south of Johannesburg.

The township was created in compliance with the country's apartheid laws to keep the races apart. And the people were protesting against the notorious pass laws which dehumanized them and forced them to carry pass books all the time.

The laws also restricted them to certain areas while whites enjoyed unlimited access to all parts of the country and enjoyed a lifestyle and privileges blacks could only dream of. As David Sibeko stated in explaining why the Pan-Africanist Congress directed its wrath against and focused its campaign on the pass laws in his article, "The Sharpeville Massacre: Its Historic Significance in the Struggle Against Apartheid":

"The pass system was deliberately chosen because: (i) it is the lynchpin of apartheid; and (ii) of all the apartheid laws none is so pervasive, and few are as perverted, as the pass laws.

They show no respect for the sanctity of marriage - men are forcibly separated from their wives or vice versa because one of them cannot obtain the permit to reside in the same area.

They tear away children from their parents: a child above the age of 16 needs a special permit to live with its parents outside the bantustan reservation, otherwise it must find accommodation in one of the location barracks they call hostels in South Africa.

They deny men and women the universal right to sell their labour to whom they choose; every African man or woman seeking employment has to obtain a special permit to look for work - within a limited period, usually 14 days; otherwise they face deportation to the 'homeland' bantustan reservation they most likely have never known.

The indignities are legion and falling foul with any of the pass law regulations leaves an African open to arrest and imprisonment. Sentences are most frequently served out on prison farms, under the most primitive conditions.

The best known African campaign before Sharpeville was the potato boycott. It came as a result of exposures in newspapers like the Post about conditions for African prisoners in the potato prison farms of Bethal, in the Eastern Transvaal.

Investigative reporters found that prisoners are dressed in nothing but sacks, they sleep on damp cement floors and are out working the potato fields with bare hands from the crack of dawn until dusk.

They are continuously whipped by jailers on horse back, and the one meal a day they eat is always half-cooked dried maize without any protein.

Many die from disease and torture before they complete the relatively short terms of imprisonment, between two and six months.

The pass laws, therefore, affect every living black

person."

Sibeko went on to explain how the campaign in Sharpeville against pass laws was organized and conducted and what the leaders, including Robert Mangaliso Sobukwe, expected and wanted to be done:

"In this non-violent campaign there is none that could have been more concerned to avoid the shedding of even an ounce of blood than the leadership of the PAC. Mr. Stanley Motjuwadi, a long-time journalist with *Drum* and its current editor, recalls in the issue of his magazine of November 22, 1972:
'A day after the Sharpeville shootings I had an interview in Johannesburg's Fort prison with Mangaliso Robert Sobukwe ... He was awaiting trial on a charge of incitement and seemed to have aged overnight. He was depressed and almost at the point of tears - the Sharpeville tragedy had really hit him hard.'
Any who have followed Sobukwe's role at the head of PAC know full well the man's courage: he went through nine years of imprisonment without flinching and all those who have seen him, during his imprisonment and now under house arrest, including Members of Parliament from the ruling National Party and the white opposition parties, testify that his convictions remain as strong and his determination as unwavering.
Mindful of the panic a threat to their power creates in despots, Mr. Sobukwe wrote to the Commissioner of Police of South Africa, on the eve of the campaign, emphasising that the PAC campaign against passes would be non-violent and imploring the Commissioner to instruct his men to refrain from the use of violence in an attempt to put down demonstrations. As a further precaution Mr. Sobukwe sternly told PAC leaders and cadres all over the country:
'My instructions, therefore, are that our people must be

taught now and continuously that in this campaign we are going to observe absolute non-violence.'"

The authorities did exactly the opposite. Their racist attitude towards blacks, and their total disregard for the lives of black people whom they did not even consider to be equal human beings, largely explains why they opened fire on the peaceful demonstrators. As Lieutenant-Colonel D.H. Pienaar bluntly put it, the mere gathering of blacks was seen as provocation by the white authorities and, by implication, justified the shooting. And typical of the stereotypes about blacks among many white racists, he bluntly stated:

"The Native mentality does not allow them to gather for a peaceful demonstration. For them to gather means violence."

That alone was enough justification for the white police to shoot the demonstrators. In justifying the shooting, Pienaar was also quoted by BBC saying:

"It started when hordes of natives surrounded the police station. If they do these things, they must learn their lessons the hard way."

The language itself, using the term "hordes" to describe blacks, and saying "they must learn their lessons the hard way" as if whites were dealing with a people who couldn't reason, was blatantly racist.

The shooting showed total disregard for the lives of black people. The life of a black person meant absolutely nothing to the white rulers and to many other whites.

The authorities didn't even care to explain what really happened or show any remorse.

They stated that the police opened fire because the police panicked and feared for their lives; a ridiculous assertion as if heavily armed security forces were indeed under siege and were threatened by unarmed, peaceful demonstrators many of whom were women and children. And as David Sibeko explains what happened on that fateful day, Monday, 21 March 1960:

"It is appropriate to focus on Sharpeville itself at this stage. Under the chairmanship of Nyakale Tsolo, the PAC branch at Sharpeville approached almost every house and the men's hostel in the township, mobilising support for the strike against passes planned for Monday, March 21, 1960.

The full story of Sharpeville is still to be told, hopefully by those who helped to make this history. I was fortunate as head of the regional executive committee of the Vaal from 1963 to work in the underground amongst many of the organisers and participants in the historic event. Like most veterans of war the people of Sharpeville hate to relive their wartime experience but I was able to learn from direct participants a great deal of what took place.

Not a single bus moved out of Sharpeville to take passengers to work on that Monday. PAC task force members started out before the break of dawn lining up marchers in street after street. By daybreak the marchers, under the leadership of the task force, were moving to a preappointed open ground, where they merged with other demonstrators.

In line with the instruction of the Party leadership, when all the groups had been assembled, the 10,000 and more men, women and children proceeded to the local police station - chanting freedom songs and calling out campaign slogans 'Izwe lethu' (Our land); 'I Africa'; 'Awaphele ampasti' (Down with passes); 'Sobukwe Sikhokhle' (Lead us Sobukwe); 'Forward to Independence, Tomorrow the United States of Africa'; and so on and so forth.

When the marchers reached Sharpeville's police station a heavy contingent of police was lined up outside, many on top of British-made Saracen armoured cars. Mr. Tsolo and other members of the Branch Executive moved forward - in conformity with the novel PAC motto of 'Leaders in Front' - and asked the white policeman in command to let them through so that they could surrender themselves for refusing to carry passes. Initially the police commander refused but much later, towards 11 a.m, they were let through.

The chanting of freedom songs was picking up and the slogans were being repeated with greater volume. Journalists who rushed there from other areas, after receiving word that the campaign was a runaway success in this mostly ignored African township, more than 30 miles south of Johannesburg, confirm that for all their singing and shouting the crowd's mood was more festive than belligerent.

But shortly after the PAC branch leaders had been let through into the police station, without warning, the police facing the crowd opened fire and in two minutes hundreds of bodies lay sprawling on the ground like debris. The joyful singing had given way to murderous gunfire, and the gunfire was followed by an authentic deadly silence, and then screams, wild screams and cries of the wounded.

Littering the ground in front of that police station in nearby dusty streets were 69 dead and nearly 200 injured men, women and children; a revolting sight which appalled decent human beings the world over as pictures of the massacre got around.

The same pattern of events had taken place in nearby Vanderbijl Park, where two Africans were gunned down by white police a few minutes later, and at Langa and Nyanga, a thousand miles away in Cape Town, where five people were shot dead by white police.

With that savagery the apartheid regime sealed the path of non-violence and PAC resolved to continue the struggle through arms in future."

Other reports including witness accounts tell basically the same story that the shooting was unprovoked, the protesters were unarmed and did not in any way threaten the police.

What is clear is that the police response and shooting was a reflex action triggered by the "natural" bias and hostility prevalent among many whites who saw black people as worthless human beings, if not just some creatures who were less than human beings; a sentiment forcefully expressed by one leader of the ruling National Party which instituted apartheid. As Sibeko wrote about the reaction among many whites, including leaders, after the shooting:

"It was a revealing comment, the one made by Carel de Wet, the Member of Parliament for Vanderbijl Park, a former cabinet minister in Mr. Vorster`s Government, who is currently serving a second term as ambassador to the Court of St. James. He complained: 'Why did the police kill only two kaffirs in my constituency?'

Clearly the mass killings were by design and they were intended to 'teach the kaffirs a lesson.'"

And the lesson assumed another dimension because of the highly symbolic value and significance of the place where it was taught, not only for blacks in Sharpeville, but for black people all over the country.

The town of Vereeniging, of which Sharpeville was an integral part as a segregated township for blacks, occupies a special place in the history of South Africa, especially in the history of white nationalism in that country.

It was in that town on 13 March 1902, that the treaty which ended the Anglo-Boer War was signed and the whites of South Africa - the British and the Afrikaners - patched up their differences in pursuit of a common objective to consolidate their position as the dominant racial group in the country at the expense of blacks and other non-whites.

Almost 60 years later, the same place became the scene of bloodshed and one of the worst racial incidents in South African history when powerless blacks protested against the inhuman treatment they endured everyday at the hands of their white oppressors. And the words "Sharpeville massacre" were indelibly etched on the consciences of many people around the world as a constant reminder of the brutal treatment black Africans suffered under the apartheid regime.

The government viewed the protest against the pass laws as a challenge to its authority and the legitimacy of the abominable institution of apartheid whose walls finally came tumbling down more than 40 years later in 1994 when the country held its first multi-racial democratic elections and Nelson Mandela, the leader of the African National Congress (ANC), was elected president of a country that had been dominated by whites for more than 300 years.

The consistency of the reports from different sources and by different people of different backgrounds and political persuasions including news reporters lends credibility to the conclusion that the shooting of the protesters was unprovoked and the Sharpeville massacre could have been easily avoided had the police reacted with restraint and concern for the well-being of the demonstrators.

But because the protesters were black, it was an entirely different story, and their fate was sealed simply because of who and what they were. As the assistant editor of *Drum* magazine, Humphrey Tyler, who was at the scene described what happened:

"Protestors were chanting 'Izwe Lethu' which means 'Our land' or gave the thumbs up 'freedom' salute, and shouted 'Afrika.,' nobody were afraid, in actual fact they were in a cheerful mood. There were plenty of police and more ammunition than uniforms.

A Pan Africanist leader approached us and said his organization and the marches were against violence and were demonstrating peacefully. Suddenly I heard chilling cries of 'Izwe Lethu' it sounded mainly like the voices of women. Hands went up in the famous black power salute. That is when the shooting started.

We heard the clatter of machine guns one after the other. The protestors thought they were firing blanks or warning shots. One woman was hit about 10 yards away from our car, as she fell to the ground her companion went back to assist, he thought she had stumbled.

Then he tried to pick her up, as he turned her around he saw her chest had been blown away from the hail of bullets. He looked at the blood on his hand and screamed 'God she had been shot.'

Hundreds of kids were running like wild rabbits, some of them were gunned down. Shooting only stooped when no living protestor was in sight."

The protesters were told by the leaders of the Pan-Africanist Congress to leave their passes at home and to offer no bail, seek no defence, and pay no fine, if arrested. About 5,000 people - some reports say 7,000 or more - are said to have participated in the protest that morning, marching through Sharpeville to the municipal offices at the entrance of the township.

Before the protests, Sobukwe wrote the police commissioner on 16 March 1960, stating that the Pan-Africanist Congress would hold a five-day, disciplined, peaceful protest against the pass laws starting on March 21st. And he further stated at a press conference on March 18th that he was sure the protesters would conduct themselves in a peaceful manner. As he put it:

"I have appealed to the African people to make sure that this campaign is conducted in a spirit of absolute non-violence, and I am quite certain they will heed my call.

If the other side so desires, we will provide them with an opportunity to demonstrate to the world how brutal they can be."

And they did.

Sobukwe was sentenced to three years in prison for leading the demonstrations against the pass laws. He was released on 3 May 1963, but was immediately rearrested and sent to Robben Island where he spent six years in detention and solitary confinement without trial.

The provision of the law which empowered the government to continue detaining anyone found guilty of "incitement" came to be known as the "Sobukwe clause."

He was released from Robben Island on 8 May 1969 but was not really free. He was placed under house arrest in Kimberley until his death on 27 February 1978. He was 54.

Born to poor Xhosa parents on 5 December 1924, he was an excellent student and a gifted orator. He also earned more degrees, in econmics and law, from the University of London after he was released from Robben Island and will always be remembered for the Sharpeville massacre and as the most prominent black leader in South Africa besides Mandela. He was also a man of peace.

Had the apartheid regime agreed to talk to him, and with Mandela and other anti-apartheid leaders, there would have been no Sharpeville and other bloody incidents including the Soweto uprising.

The Sharpeville massacre was one of the most significant events in the struggle against apartheid and was not even eclipsed years later by the events in Soweto when hundreds of school children were massacred by the South African police and security forces in June 1976, an event that is widely acknowledged as having signalled the beginning of the end of apartheid. As Ambrose Reeves, a minister in South Africa, stated in "The Sharpeville Massacre: A Watershed in South Africa":

"History records that on May 13, 1902, the treaty which ended the Anglo-Boer war was signed at Vereeniging, then a small town some thirty miles from Johannesburg. Nobody could then have realised that some fifty-eight years later the whole world would learn of another event occurring in that part of the Transvaal; this time in the African township of Sharpeville.

As with most towns on the Reef, as the white population of Vereeniging grew so did the township for Africans on the outskirts of the town....

The events at Sharpeville on March 21, 1960,... shocked the world and...are still remembered with shame by civilised men everywhere.

Early that morning a crowd of Africans estimated at between 5,000 and 7,000 marched through Sharpeville to the municipal offices at the entrance to the township.

It appears that much earlier that day members of the Pan Africanist Congress had gone around Sharpeville waking up people and urging them to take part in this demonstration. Other members of the PAC prevented the bus drivers going on duty with the result that there were no buses to take the people to work in Vereeniging.

Many of them set out on bicycles or on foot to their places of work, but some were met by Pan Africanists who threatened to burn their passes or "lay hands on them" if they did not turn back. However, many Africans joined the procession to the municipal offices quite willingly.

Eventually this demonstration was dispersed by the police, using tear gas bombs and then a baton charge, some sixty police following them into the side streets. Stones were flung and one policeman was slightly injured.

It was alleged that several shots were fired by Africans and that only then some policemen opened fire without an order from their officer to do so. Fortunately nobody was hurt.

I was not at Sharpeville when the shooting occurred but it was familiar territory to me. Time and again I officiated at the large African Anglican church there and knew intimately many of the congregation, some of whom were to be involved in the events of that tragic day. I could so well visualise the scene.

Near my home in the northern suburbs of Johannesburg was a large zoo situated in acres of parkland. By a curious anomaly the lake near the zoo was the meeting place for Africans working in the northern suburbs on a Sunday afternoon.

Work finished for the day they would leisurely make their way there in small groups - a gay, colourful, jostling crowd - families and individuals - some political, some not, chatting, laughing, singing, gesticulating and occasionally fighting.

The thud of home-made drums could be heard shattering the Sunday calm, and over all the plaintive notes of the penny whistle - shrill and penetrating.

It could so easily have been like that on that crisp autumn morning in Sharpeville. Like that, but so very different.

During the morning news spread through the township that a statement concerning passes would be made by an important person at the police station later that day.

The result was that many who had been concerned in the earlier demonstration drifted to the police station where they waited patiently for the expected announcement. And all the time the crowd grew.

Reading from the police report on what subsequently happened the Prime Minister told the House of Assembly that evening that the police estimated that 20,000 people were in that crowd.

This seems to have been a serious exaggeration. From photographs taken at the time it is doubtful if there were ever more than 5,000 present at any particular moment, though it may well be that more than this number were involved at one time or another as people were coming and going throughout the morning.

They were drawn to the crowd by a variety of reasons. Some wanted to protest against the pass laws; some were present because they had been coerced; some were there out of idle curiosity; some had heard that a statement would be made about passes.

But whatever may have brought them to the police station, I was unable to discover that any policeman ever tried either to find out why they were there or make any request for them to disperse.

And this in spite of the fact that the presence of this crowd seems to have caused a good deal of alarm to the police.

So much so that at ten o'clock that morning a squadron of aircraft dived low over the crowd, presumably to intimidate them and encourage them to disperse. This was surely a most expensive way of trying to disperse a crowd.

The police claimed that the people in the crowd were shouting and brandishing weapons and the Prime Minister told the Assembly that the crowd was in a riotous and aggressive mood and stoned the police. There is no evidence to support this.

On the contrary, while the crowd was noisy and excitable, singing and occasionally shouting slogans it was not a hostile crowd. Their purpose was not to fight the police but to show by their presence their hostility to the pass system, expecting that someone would make a statement about passes.

Photographs taken that morning show clearly that this was no crowd spoiling for a fight with the police. Not only was the crowd unarmed, but a large proportion of those present were women and children. All through the morning no attack on the police was attempted.

Even as late as one p.m. the Superintendent in charge

of the township was able to walk through the crowd, being greeted by them in a friendly manner and chatting with some of them. Similarly, the drivers of two of the Saracen tanks stated subsequently that they had no difficulty in driving their vehicles into the grounds surrounding the police station. And their testimony was borne out by photographs taken of their progress.

As the hours passed the increasing number of people in the crowd was matched by police reinforcements. Earlier there had only been twelve policemen in the police station: six white and six non-white. But during the morning a series of reinforcements arrived until by lunch time there was a force of nearly 300 armed and uniformed men in addition to five Saracens.

Yet in spite of the increased force that was then available, no one asked the crowd to disperse and no action was taken to arrange for the defence of the police station. The police just strolled around the compound with rifles slung over their shoulders, smoking and chatting with one another.

Scene was set for explosive situation

So the scene was set. Anyone who has lived in the Republic of South Africa knows how explosive that situation had already become. On the one side the ever-growing crowd of noisy Africans - the despised Natives - the Kaffirs who, at all costs, must be kept down lest they step outside the place allotted to them. On the other side the South African police.

Every African fears them, whether they be traffic police, ordinary constables or members of the dreaded Special Branch. Most policemen expect unquestioning deference from Africans. If this is not forthcoming they immediately interpret it as riot and rebellion.

In part this is due to the widespread prejudice of white people the world over to those who happen to have a different coloured skin than their own.

But in South Africa it is underpinned by the hatred, fear and contempt that so many white police have for all non-white people.

The only action taken during that morning appears to have come not from the police but from two Pan Africanist leaders who urged the crowd to stay away from the fence around the perimeter of the compound so that they did not damage it.

Then Lieutenant Colonel Pienaar arrived in the compound. He appears to have accepted that he had come into a dangerous situation and therefore made no attempt either to use methods of persuasion on the crowd or to attempt to discover what the crowd was waiting for.

Instead, about a quarter of an hour after his arrival he gave the order for his men to fall in. A little later he said, "Load five rounds". But he said no more to any of his officers, or to the men.

Later, Colonel Pienaar stated that he thought his order would frighten the crowd and that his men would understand that if they had to fire they would not fire more than five rounds. Unfortunately, this was not understood by the policemen under his command.

During this time Colonel Spengler, then head of the Special Branch, was arresting two of the leaders of the Pan Africanist Congress. Afterwards he arrested a third man. Colonel Spengler said subsequently that he was able to carry out his arrests because while the crowd was noisy it was not in a violent mood.

It is extremely difficult to know what happened next. Some of the crowd near the gate of the police station compound said later that they heard a shot. Some said that they heard a policeman say, "Fire". Others suddenly became aware that the police were firing in their midst. But all agreed that practically all of them turned and ran away once they realised what was happening.

A few, it is true, stood their ground for some seconds,

unable to understand that the police were not firing blanks. Lieutenant Colonel Pienaar was quite clear that he did not give the order to fire. Moreover, he declared that he would not have fired in that situation. It was stated later that two white policemen opened fire and that about fifty others followed suit, using service revolvers, rifles and sten guns.

Police action caused devastating consequences

But whatever doubts there may be of the sequence of events in those fateful minutes, there can be no argument over the devastating consequences of the action of the police on March 21, 1960, in Sharpeville. Sixty-nine people were killed, including eight women and ten children, and of the 180 people who were wounded, thirty-one were women and nineteen were children.

According to the evidence of medical practitioners it is clear that the police continued firing after the people began to flee: for, while thirty shots had entered the wounded or killed from the front of their bodies no less than 155 bullets had entered the bodies of the injured and killed from their backs.

All this happened in forty seconds, during which time 705 rounds were fired from revolvers and sten guns.

But whatever weapons were used the massacre was horrible. Visiting the wounded the next day in Baragwanath Hospital near Johannesburg, I discovered youngsters, women and elderly men among the injured. These could not be described as agitators by any stretch of the imagination.

For the most part they were ordinary citizens who had merely gone to the Sharpeville police station to see what was going on. Talking with the wounded I found that everyone was stunned and mystified by what had taken place. They had certainly not expected that anything like this would happen.

All agreed that there was no provocation for such

savage action by the police. Indeed, they insisted that the political organisers who had called for the demonstration had constantly insisted that there should be no violence or fighting.

Arrests follow massacre

To make matters worse, some of the wounded with whom I spoke in hospital stated that they were taunted by the police as they lay on the ground, being told to get up and be off. Others who tried to help were told to mind their own business.

At first there was only one African minister of the Presbyterian Church of South Africa who tried to help the wounded and the dying. It is true that later the police assisted in tending the wounded and summoned ambulances which conveyed the injured to Vereeniging and Baragwanath Hospitals. Later still, 77 Africans were arrested in connection with the Sharpeville demonstration, in some cases while they were still in hospital.

In fact, it was clear on my visits to the wards of Baragwanath Hospital that many of the injured feared what would happen to them when they left hospital. This wasn't surprising, for Baragwanath Hospital was an extraordinary sight.

Outside each of the wards to which the wounded were taken were a number of African police, some white policemen, and members of the Special Branch in civilian clothes.

The attitude of the South African Government to the event at Sharpeville can be seen from its reaction to the civil claims lodged the following September by 224 persons for damages amounting to around 400,000 arising from the Sharpeville killings.

The following month the Minister of Justice announced that during the next parliamentary session the Government would introduce legislation to indemnify itself and its officials retrospectively against claims resulting from action taken during the disturbances earlier that year.

This was done in the Indemnity Act, No. 61 of 1961. Not that money could ever compensate adequately for the loss of a breadwinner to a family or make up for lost limbs or permanent incapacity. But it would have been some assistance.

It is true that in February 1961 the Government set up a committee to examine the claims for compensation and to recommend ex gratia payments in deserving cases. But this is not the same thing, and in fact by October 1962 no payments had been made.

Failure of police to communicate with the people

Few commentators since Sharpeville have attempted to justify the action of the police that day. In fact, many of them have drawn special attention to the complete failure of the police to attempt to communicate with the crowd at the police station. If it had been a white crowd the police would have tried to find out why they were there and what they wanted.

Surely their failure to do so was due to the fact that it never occurred to them, as the custodians of public order, either to negotiate with the African leaders or to try to persuade the crowd to disperse. Their attitude was summed up by the statement of Lieutenant Colonel Pienaar that "the Native mentality does not allow them to gather for a peaceful demonstration. For them to gather means violence."

The same point was demonstrated even more graphically by one of his answers at the Court of Enquiry under Mr. Justice Vessels. When he was asked if he had learnt any useful lesson from the events in Sharpeville, he replied, 'Well, we may get better equipment.'

Not that all members of the South African Police Force are cruel or callous. No doubt many of them were shocked by what happened. At the same time what happened at Sharpeville emphasises how far the police in South Africa are cut off from sympathy with or even understanding of Africans. And this is underlined by the fact that at no time did the police express regret for this tragic happening.

Yet it would be folly to attempt to fasten the whole blame for the events at Sharpeville on the police. By the mass of repressive legislation which has been enacted every year since 1948, the South African Government has given the police a task which ever becomes more difficult to fulfill.

The pass laws

It was this legislation which was indirectly responsible for the tragedy of Sharpeville, and in particular the "pass laws". Indeed, the immediate cause of many in the crowd assembling at the police station was the growing resentment of Africans to the system of passes.

This system originated in 1760 in the Cape Colony to regulate the movement of slaves between the urban and the rural areas. The slaves had to carry passes from their masters.

Subsequently, the system was extended in various forms to the whole country and was eventually collated in the Native (Urban Areas) Consolidation Act of 1945.

This Act made provision for a variety of passes including registered service contracts and for passes permitting men to seek work in particular areas. But through the years an increasing number of Africans had been given exemption from these laws.

This was the situation which obtained until 1952 when a new act ironically called 'The Abolition of Passes Act' made it compulsory for every African male, whether he had previously had to carry passes or no, to carry a reference book.

If the holder had previously been exempted from the

pass laws he was now privileged to carry a reference book with a green instead of a brown cover! But the contents were identical.

The advent of the reference books meant that technically there were no longer any such things as passes. But, as will be understood, to the Africans reference books are passes for they contain all the details which were previously entered on the various pass documents. They contain the holder's name, his tax receipt, his permit to be in an urban area and to seek work there, permits from the Labour Bureau, the signature each month of his employer to show that he is still in the employment he was given permission to take, as well as other particulars.

Even more objectionable than having to possess a reference book is the fact that this book must be produced on demand to any policeman or any of the fifteen different classes of officials who may require to see it. Failure to produce it on demand constitutes an offence for which an African may be detained up to thirty days while inquiries are being made about him.

What this means in practice can be seen from the fact that in the twelve months ending June 30, 1966 no less than 479,114 Africans were prosecuted for offences against the "pass laws". At the time of Sharpeville there were 1,000 prosecutions a day for these offences. By 1966, this had risen to over 1,300 a day. These figures speak for themselves.

In 1960 a new development occurred when the Government of South Africa decided for the first time in South African history to extend the pass laws to African women. In their case another fear was added that they might be subjected to manhandling by the police with a further loss of human dignity. In fact, by the time of Sharpeville it was estimated that three-quarters of African women were in possession of reference books.

But many of the women who had not obtained reference books were strenuously opposed both to the pass system and to its extension to themselves. To them reference books stood for racial identification, and therefore for racial discrimination.

Intolerable economic situation

But this was by no means the only reason for unrest in Sharpeville. Anyone who knew the township at that time was aware that there had been increasing tension among the inhabitants because in that area wages were too low and rents were too high. Prior to March of that year rent had been increased in Sharpeville and this had added to the burdens of Africans living there.

The previous year (1959) a study of the economic position of Africans in Johannesburg had shown that 80 per cent of Africans were living at or below the poverty datum line. The probability is that the lot of Africans in Sharpeville was worse than in Johannesburg.

A survey carried out by the Johannesburg Non-European Affairs Department in 1962 in Soweto showed that 68 per cent of families there had an income below the estimated living costs.

A subsequent study in 1966 showed that this figure remained the same. So in spite of the increased prosperity of South Africa the economic position of a high percentage of Africans does not seem to have improved much since Sharpeville.

African wages in Sharpeville in 1960 were low, partly because African trade unions were not (and still are not) recognised for the purpose of bargaining with employers. But also, the continuing colour bar in commerce and industry meant, and still means, high minimum wages for white workers and low maximum wages for the black workers who make up the great majority of the labour force.

All this means two wage structures in South Africa which have no relation to one another: in the fixing of the black wage structure the workers frequently have no say at all.

Several months before the tragic events at Sharpeville it was becoming obvious that those living in the township were facing an intolerable economic situation. It is too easy to dismiss the Sharpeville demonstration at the police station as the work of agitators and the result of intimidation. All that those who led the demonstration did was to use a situation which, for political and economic reasons, was already highly explosive.

Growing resistance

Not that Sharpeville was an isolated incident. The ten years before Sharpeville had seen feverish activity by the opponents of apartheid. By means of boycotts, mass demonstrations, strikes and protests, the non-white majority had attempted by non-violent means to compel those in power to modify their racist policies. For example, on June 26, 1952, the Campaign of Defiance against Unjust Laws had been launched.

The same day three years later (June 26, 1955) 3,000 delegates had adopted the Freedom Charter which had been drafted by the Congress Alliance. This took place at a massive gathering at Kliptown, Johannesburg.

The following year the Federation of South African Women held a series of spectacular demonstrations against the extension of the pass system to African women. These culminated in a mass demonstration at the Union Buildings, Pretoria, on August 9, 1956. Some 10,000 women gathered there in an orderly fashion to present 7,000 individually signed protest forms.

Again, from January 7, 1957, many thousand African men and women for months walked eighteen to twenty miles a day to and from work in Johannesburg in a boycott of the buses. Although in this particular case they gained their objective, all the various endeavours by Africans to secure change by peaceful means brought little tangible result.

The surprising thing was that in all this activity there was very little violence on the part of boycotters, demonstrators and strikers. In spite of great and frequent provocation by the police, Africans remained orderly and disciplined.

They were in truth non-violent. As could be expected there were, however, occasions when the resentment and frustration of Africans spilled over into violence.

One such occasion was at Cato Manor near Durban on June 17, 1959. On that day a demonstration of African women at the beer hall destroyed beer and drinking utensils and was dispersed by the police. Several days later the Director of the Bantu Administration Department met 2,000 women at the beer hall. Once they had stated their grievances they were ordered to disperse.

When they failed to do so the police made a baton charge. General disorder and rioting followed, with the result that damage estimated at 100,000 (Rands) was done to vehicles and buildings.

Later that day Africans attacked a police picket and were driven off with sten guns.

After this, things remained comparatively quiet in Cato Manor until a Sunday afternoon in February, 1960, when the smouldering resentment of Africans there again burst into flame. An ugly situation developed in which nine policemen lost their lives. This was a deplorable business.

Whatever may be said of the actions of the South African police these men died while carrying out their duties. The blame for their deaths must in the first instance lie on those who murdered them.

The fact that these deaths occurred in Cato Manor only a few weeks before the demonstration at Sharpeville must have been well known to the police gathered at the police station in Sharpeville that morning. Certainly more than one spokesman of the South African Government linked these two affairs together.

There is not the slightest evidence, however, that there was in this sense any connection between the tragedies of Cato Manor and Sharpeville.

But in another sense they were both intimately connected because more indirectly they both arose out of the action of those in power during the previous decade, who had taken every possible step to ensure that the whole life of the millions of Africans was encased within the strait-jacket of compulsory segregation.

Civilisation without mercy

Yet there the similarity ended. The crowd at Sharpeville was not attacking anything or anyone. Further, there is abundant evidence to show that they were unarmed. While nothing can justify the killing of police at Cato Manor, that incident cannot in any way exonerate the vicious action of the police at Sharpeville. As the late Sir Winston Churchill pointed out in a debate in the British House of Commons on July 8, 1920:

"There is surely one general prohibition which we can make. I mean the prohibition against what is called 'frightfulness'. What I mean by frightfulness is the inflicting of great slaughter or massacre upon a particular crowd of people with the intention of terrorising not merely the rest of the crowd, but the whole district or the whole country." (This is precisely what the police did at Sharpeville).

On that occasion Sir Winston concluded his speech with some words of Macaulay - "... and then was seen what we believe to be the most frightful of spectacles, the strength of civilisation without mercy." These are words which aptly summarise all that happened at Sharpeville that March morning.

Many people inside South Africa, though shocked for a time by the events at Sharpeville, ended by dismissing them as just one incident in the long and growing succession of disturbances that down the years have marked the implementation of apartheid. Certainly the Government of South Africa, though badly shaken in the days immediately following Sharpeville, soon regained control of the situation.

On March 24, the Government banned all public meetings in twenty-four magisterial districts. On April 8, the Governor-General signed a proclamation banning the African National Congress and the Pan Africanist Congress as unlawful organisations, the result being that they were both driven underground. But neither of them became dormant.

At the same time the Government mobilised the entire Citizen Force, the Permanent Force Reserve, the Citizen Force Reserve and the Reserve of Officers, and the whole of the Commando Force was placed on stand-by. Already on March 30, in Proclamation No. 90, the Governor-General had declared a state of emergency which lasted until August 31, 1960.

During that time a large number of prominent opponents of government policy of all races were arrested and detained without being brought to trial. In addition some 20,000 Africans were rounded up, many of whom were released after screening.

So after some months eventually, at least superficially, life in South Africa became at least relatively normal. But underneath the external calm dangerous fires continue to smoulder: fires that can never be extinguished by repressive measures coupled with a constant and growing show of force.

Outside South Africa there were widespread reactions to Sharpeville in many countries which in many cases led to positive action against South Africa: action which still continues. But here, too, most people, even if they have heard of Sharpeville, have relegated what happened there to the archives of history, just one of the too many dark pages in the human story.

Sharpeville marked a watershed in South Africa

Yet it is my personal belief that history will recognise that Sharpeville marked a watershed in South African affairs. Until Sharpeville, violence for the most part had been used in South Africa by those who were committed to the maintenance of the economic and political domination of the white minority in the Republic. Down the years they had always been ready to use force to maintain the status quo whenever they judged it necessary to do so.

When the occasion arose they did not hesitate to use it. Over and over again, non-white civilians were injured by police action or by assaults on them when in prison.

Until Sharpeville the movements opposed to apartheid were pledged to a policy of non-violence. But on March 21, 1960, when an unarmed African crowd was confronted by 300 heavily armed police supported by five Saracen armoured vehicles, an agonising reappraisal of the situation was inevitable. Small wonder is it that, having tried every peaceful method open to them to secure change without avail, the African leadership decided that violence was the only alternative left to them.

Never again would they expose their people to another Sharpeville. As Nelson Mandela said in court at his trial in October 1962:

"Government violence can do only one thing and that is to breed counter-violence. We have warned repeatedly that the Government, by resorting continually to violence, will breed in this country counter-violence among the people till ultimately if there is no dawning of sanity on the part of the Government, the dispute between the Government and my people will finish up by being settled in violence and by force."

Outwardly things may go on in South Africa much as before. Visitors may find a booming economy, the white minority may seem secure in their privileged position for any foreseeable future, some urban Africans may have higher living standard than formerly. But all this ought not to deceive anybody.

The fact is that for the first time both sides in the racial struggle in South Africa are now committed to violence; the white minority to preserve the status quo; the non-white majority to change: change from society dominated by apartheid to one that is non-racial in character. Already there are clear indications that the opponents of apartheid are turning deliberately to violence.

The fact that at the moment this is being expressed through small bands of guerillas who may be neither very well trained nor well-equipped does not mean that they ought therefore to be dismissed as having little significance. After all, we have the examples of Algeria, Cuba and Viet Nam before us as powerful reminders of what may result from very small and weak beginnings.

In spite of the present calm in South Africa and a prosperity unparallelled in its history, within the Republic the seeds of violence have already been sown. Unless there is a radical change in the present political and economic structures of South Africa, that which has already been sown will be harvested in a terrible and brutal civil war which might easily involve the whole African continent in conflict before it ends.

Indeed it may be that in the present situation in the Republic of South Africa are hidden forces which will involve humanity in a global racial conflict unless the present racist policies there are changed radically.

The choice before the international community has been a clear one ever since Sharpeville. Either it takes every possible step to secure the abandonment of the present policies in South Africa or the coming years will bring increasing sorrow and strife both for South Africa and for the world.

Sharpeville was a tragedy showing most plainly that the ideology of apartheid is a way of death and not of life. Can the nations recognise this before it is too late?"

The apartheid regime obviously did not recognise that and was reinforced in its belief that it would survive because some of the most powerful countries in the world, especially the industrialized nations of the West, continued to support it.

It did not take the massacre seriously. It believed that the white power structure was invincible, virtually an impregnable fortress that could withstand the most sustained assault even by its fiercest opponents.

And it invoked the inspired canon of scripture to justify its diabolical policies - and iniquities - as if they had been sanctioned by God and white people had divine mandate to rule members of "the lesser breed": black people and other non-whites.

Shortly after the massacre, the apartheid regime declared a state emergency which lasted from March 30 to August 31, 1960.

The emergency declaration was prompted by widespread demonstrations, protests ans strikes across the country in condemnation of the massacre and what the apartheid regime perceived to be a threat to the nation's security and white domination of the country.

More than 18,000 people including most of the country's leading anti-apartheid politicians of all races were arrested when the emergency was declared. And on April 8, both the African National Congress (ANC) and the Pan Africanist Congress (PAC) were declared illegal, forcing them to go underground and resort to other means to try and bring about change.

The establishment of Umkhonto we Sizwe (The Spear of the Nation), the military wing of the African National

Congress; and of Poqo, PAC's armed wing, was largely inspired by the massacre and by the government's refusal to negotiate with the opponents of apartheid and find ways to achieve racial equality in the country without resorting to violence.

Although both the ANC and the PAC were banned in South Africa, they remained active in the country and from their operational bases in other countries such as Tanzania and Zambia. It was not until 40 years later, in 1990, that they were unbanned.

Thus, instead of bringing about fundamental change, the government became even more repressive following the Sharpeville massacre.

And in October 1960, the white electorate voted for a republican form of government under the leadership of the National Party dominated by Afrikaners and which instituted apartheid in 1948. South Africa withdrew from the Commonwealth in March 1961. And on May 31st the same year, it became a republic.

The withdrawal of South Africa from the Commonwealth was a result of a concerted effort by African leaders to keep the apartheid regime out of this community of nations, once former British colonies. The campaign was led by Julius Nyerere who made it clear that if South Africa remained a member, his country Tanganyika would not join the Commonwealth once it became independent. As he stated: "To vote South Africa in, is to vote us out."

There is no question that the Shaperville massacre galvanized the anti-apartheid movement worldwide.

It drew worldwide condemnation and played a critical role in changing the attitude of many African leaders who had earlier embraced non-violence as a means to achieving racial justice in the land of apartheid.

After the massacre, armed struggle was seen a viable alternative that could be used to compel the apartheid regime to accept fundamental change and was effectively used through the years as a complementary strategy, along with diplomacy, to achieve this goal.

Rivonia Trial

The Rivonia Trial was one of the most important milestones on the long road to freedom and was preceded by a series of events in the struggle against apartheid.

One of those events was Nelson Mandela's tour of independent African countries when he slipped out of South Africa in early 1962 and attended a conference of African heads of state and government in Addis Ababa, Ethiopia, where he sought help for the liberation struggle in South Africa.

He addressed the conference and won support from the African leaders who went on to play a critical role in the following years in the campaign against racial injustices under the apartheid regime.

African leaders who attended the conference, and even those who were not in Addis Ababa, agreed to provide moral, diplomatic, material and financial support to the African National Congress (ANC) and other liberation movements in countries which were still under colonial domination or white minority rule.

And when Mandela was in Ethiopia, he received some military training and went to Algeria where he underwent further training. He also visited other African countries where he was promised support for the liberation struggle in South Africa.

He returned to South Africa in July 1962 and was arrested in Natal on August 5th when he was in a car on his way to Durban from where he would proceed to Johannesburg.

The South African police and intelligence service got information and details about his travels and whereabouts from the CIA. According to *The Washington Post*, 6

November 1990, (p. A18), a CIA officer claimed "we have turned Mandela over to the South African security branch."

The CIA officer was Donald C. Rickard who was working undercover as a consular official at the US Consulate in Durban, Natal. He tipped off the Special Branch of the South African police on Mandela's itinerary, telling them that Mandela would be disguised as a chauffeur in a car going to Durban. The CIA agent got the information from an informer in the ANC.

After getting the information, plainclothes and intelligence officers got on Mandela's trail and arrested him at a roadblock outside Howick, Natal, when the police flagged down his car.

It was a big victory for the police and for the South African government. Mandela had eluded capture for 17 months and had been able to sneak out of the country during those months.

When he was still in South Africa before leaving to attend the conference in Addis Ababa, he was able to disguise himself and move about freely without being detected.

CIA's involvement in Mandela's capture had been known right from the beginning. In 1963, at a farewell party for Donald Rickard who had been in South Africa since 1958, the CIA agent said he was, in fact, going to meet with Mandela the night Mandela was arrested but, instead, tipped off the South African Special branch on Mandela's itinerary.

The meeting, which never took place, had been arranged by the CIA informer in the African National Congress. And the farewell party was held at the residence of a South African mercenary, the highly notorious Colonel "Mad Mike" Hoare who wreaked so much havoc in the Congo in the sixties.

Rickard returned to the United States in 1963 and went to live in Pagosa Springs, Colorado, where he was still living n the late 1990s, and may be even at this writing.

Mandela's arrest led to a five-year prison sentence. Then the South African police went on to arrest other ANC leaders and the leaders of other anti-apartheid groups in a crackdown that virtually decapitated the entire anti-apartheid movement in the country. Almost the entire leadership was arrested or fled into exile.

In October 1963, Mandela again, with the other anti-apartheid leaders who had been arrested, went on trial for treason. It came to be known as the Rivonia Trial, named after the highly affluent suburb of Johannesburg where the anti-apartheid leaders had their headquarters at a secret location. That is also where they were arrested when the South African police raided the house in which they were having a meeting.

In June 1964, Mandela was sentenced to life imprisonment together with a number of other anti-apartheid leaders including Walter Sisulu, Govan Mbeki, Andrew Mlangeni, Elias Motsoaledi, Raymond Mhlaba, Dennis Goldberg, and Ahmed Kathrada.

But although the ANC leadership fell in a single swoop, as did some of the leaders of the other anti-apartheid organisations, the struggle against apartheid did not lose its potent force although it may have been temporarily interrupted.

The repressive nature of the apartheid state itself proved to be a catalyst for the liberation movement. It galvanised the movement and helped to propel it, enabling it to go forward and gain momentum as the people became more and more determined to end apartheid.

What happened after the leaders were arrested, in terms of mobilisation of forces against the apartheid regime, was that the movement was forced to go even deeper underground. It also vigorously sought support from the independent African countries and elsewhere among its supporters around the world.

The Rivonia Trial was a landmark and one of the most

important chapters in the history of the liberation struggle against apartheid.

It will also be remembered as one of the major events in the history of Africa which included the Zanzibar Revolution and the unification of Tanganyika and Zanzibar, a union that led to the creation of the United Republic of Tanzania in 1964. And the year will also be remembered as the year of the Rivonia Trial.

The Rivonia Trial was a significant event, not only for South Africa but for the entire continent. It was a defining moment in the struggle against apartheid and it influenced the course of African history during the post-colonial era because of the involvement of other African countries in the liberation struggle throughout southern Africa, and not just in South Africa.

But South Africa posed special problems because it was the strongest nation and the bastion of white supremacy on the continent. And the Rivonia Trial provided an opportunity for the opponents of apartheid to expose the evils of this diabolical system of racial oppression.

The trial also showed that the apartheid regime was determined to maintain its grip on the country, especially on the restive black majority, and was not ready to make any concessions to its opponents.

The most prominent of those opponents was Nelson Mandela, leader of the African National Congress (ANC) and commander of Umkhonto we Sizwe, the Spear of the Nation, which was the military wing of the ANC.

The Rivonia Trial took place between 1963 and 1964 involving 10 leaders of the African National Congress, including Mandela.

It was a treason trial. The accused were tried for 221 acts of sabotage intended to start a violent revolution and overthrow the government.

It all started with the arrest - at one location - of almost all the major leaders of the anti-apartheid movement.

On 11 July 1963, 16 leaders of the African National Congress were arrested at Liliesleaf Farm in Rivonia, a Johannesburg suburb.

The farm was owned by Arthur Goldreich and was used as a private meeting place and hideout for the leaders of the African National Congress.

Among those arrested were Walter Sisulu, Govan Mbeki, Raymond Mhlaba, Andrew Mlangeni; Elias Motsoaledi, trade union and ANC member; Ahmed Kathrada; Dennis Goldberg, a Cape Town engineer and leader of the Congress of Democrats; Lionel "Rusty" Bernstein, architect and member of the South African Communist Party (SACP); Bob Hepple, Arthur Goldreich; Harold Wolpe, a prominent attorney and activist; and James "Jimmy" Kantor, brother-in-law of Harold Wolpe.

Charged together with those who were arrested at Liliesleaf Farm were Nelson Mandela and Walter Mkwayi.

Mandela was brought to the trial in Pretoria from Robben Island where he was already serving a five-year sentence since 1962 for sabotage and leaving the country illegally.

Most of those who were charged in the Rivonia Trial were black. Four of them - Goldberg, Bernstein, Hepple and Goldreich - were Jews. And one, Ahmed Kathrada, was Indian.

The prosecutors and the police considered Goldreich, the owner of Liliesleaf Farm, to be "the arch-conspirator" and were infuriated when he and Wolpe managed to escape from prison on 11 August 1963 after they bribed a guard.

The people who were arrested at the farm owned by Goldreich had been forced to go underground by the apartheid regime's repressive laws.

The ANC had been operating underground from the time it was outlawed in April 1960, one month after the Sharpeville Massacre. The police had collected hundreds of documents from the ANC hideout at Rivonia about

Operation Mayibuye - Operation Comeback - which they used against the defendants.

Under the new General Law Amendment (Sabotage) Act of 1962 and the Suppression of Communism Act, the defendants faced the threat of the death penalty.

But defence lawyers did not have enough time to prepare their case. They were unable to see their clients until two days before the indictment on October 9th.

The defence team was led by Bram Fischer, a prominent Afrikaner lawyer. He was assisted by George Bizos, Joel Joffe, Harold Hanson, and Arthur Chaskalson who became a distinguished judge after the end of apartheid.

In June 1994 President Mandela appointed Chaskalson the first president of South Africa's new Constitutional Court. And on 22 November 2001, he became the Chief Justice of South Africa.

At the end of October 1964, Bob Hepple was struck off the list of the accused and left the dock after he agreed to testify for the prosecution. He later fled the country.

The prosecution team was led by Dr. Percy Yutar, a Jew, who was the assistant attorney-general of the Transvaal, the northern province.

His conduct of the case was reminiscent of the Rosenbergs' trial in New York in the United States in the early 1950s in which Julius Rosenberg and his wife Ethel were accused of spying for the Soviet Union and giving the Soviets secret information on the atomic bomb.

Both the prosecutor and the judge in this case were Jews who are said to have been too harsh on the Rosenbergs to prove to the American government that although they were Jews themselves like the accused, their patriotism could not be questioned; they were good American citizens and fiercely loyal to the United States of America and the star-spangled banner.

The prosecutor was Assistant US Attorney Roy Cohn. And the judge was Irving Kaufman.

The Rosenbergs were convicted and sentenced to death in April 1951 and were executed in June 1953, although many observers believed that Ethel was innocent of espionage and played only a minor role, if any, in helping her husband provide Soviet agents with nuclear secrets.

Dr. Yutar also, as Jew, may partly have been motivated by his desire to prove to the Afrikaner-dominated government that he was a true patriot by seeking a harsh sentence for the defendants in the Rivonia Trial, among whom were some Jews opposed to apartheid.

The charges against the accused were:

- Recruiting persons for training in the preparation and use of explosives and in guerrilla warfare for the purpose of violent revolution and committing acts of sabotage.

- Conspiring to commit the aforementioned acts and to aid foreign military units when they invaded the Republic.

- Acting in these ways to further the objects of communism.

- Soliciting and receiving money for these purposes from sympathizers in Algeria, Ethiopia, Liberia, Nigeria, Tunisia, and elsewhere.

- Production requirements for munitions for a six-month period were sufficient, Prosecutor Percy Yutar said in his opening address, to blow up a city the size of Johannesburg.

It was the most celebrated, and most sensational, trial in the history of South Africa.

The trial began on November 26, 1963, and ended on June 12, 1964, when the defendants were sentenced to prison. Each of the 10 accused pleaded not guilty.

James "Jimmy" Kantor was discharged at the end of the prosecution, and Lionel "Rusty" Bernstein was acquitted. But Bernstein was rearrested, released on bail, and placed under house arrest. He later fled the country.

The case had some dramatic aspects including daring escapes.

Arthur Goldreich escaped from prison disguised as a

priest; Walter Mkwayi escaped during the trial; and Harold Wolpe and James Kantor also escaped.

The trial was condemned by the UN Security Council but nothing was done to punish the apartheid regime, although the Security Council members talked about imposing sactions on the South African government. It was more rhetoric than action. And race played a critical role in this.

The three Security Council members with veto power - the United States, France and Britain - besides the Soviet Union, were allies of apartheid South Africa. And their actions were motivated by racial considerations, not just geopolitical interests vis-a-vis the Soviet Union. As President Julius Nyerere, whose remarks were also appropriate with regard to the apartheid regime, stated in his article, "Rhodesia in the Context of Southern Africa" published in *Foreign Affairs* in April 1966:

"It is time for Britain and the United States of America to make clear whether they really believe in the principles they claim to espouse or whether their policies are governed by considerations of the privileges of their 'kith and kin'....

Despite the protestations of belief in human equality, the domination of a white minority over blacks is acceptable to the West."

As the treason trial continued, there was a distinct possibility that many of the accused, if not most or all of them, would get capital punishment.

In fact, Mandela was warned by his lawyers before the trial started not to bluntly tell the judge in his opening statement that he's ready for capital punishment; chances were he could get it since the judge would see that as a challenge to him.

That is why, as he stated in his autobiography *Long Walk to Freedom*, he qualified his remarks, "I am prepared to die," with "if needs be."

Although the prosecution would have preferred capital punishment, and had in fact originally requested the death penalty, worldwide protests against the trial and the ingenuity of the defence team helped to influence the outcome of the case.

The death penalty was dropped and eight defendants, including Mandela, were sentenced to life imprisonment. One was acquitted.

Dennis Goldberg was sent to Pretoria Central Prison, at that time the only place where white political prisoners in South Africa were confined. He served 22 years.

The rest were sent to Robben Island, the most harsh imprisonment facility in the South African penal system.

Probably the most dramatic moment during the trial was on 20 April 1964 when Nelson Mandela read his statement from the dock at the opening of the defence case in the Pretoria Supreme Court, "I Am Prepared to Die."

On 11 June 1964, at the conclusion of the trial, Mandela and seven others - Walter Sisulu, Govan Mbeki, Raymond Mhlaba, Elias Motsoaledi, Andrew Mlangeni, Ahmed Kathrada and Denis Goldberg - were convicted of treason.

But although Mandela was found guilty on four charges of sabotage and like the others was sentenced to life imprisonment, he and his colleagues did not give up the fight.

In fact, Mandela was even offered freedom in the 1960s if he was going to abandon the struggle and return to his home region, the Transkei, and live a quiet life.

But he turned down the offer and said he would be back in prison as soon as they let him out if the government was not going to allow blacks and other non-whites to enjoy the same rights and freedom enjoyed by whites.

It was not until almost 30 years later that Mandela and his compatriots were released from prison, undefeated, after the government finally agreed to start dismantling apartheid. It was a major concession by the government and a victory for the anti-apartheid movement. Mandela was freed on 11 February 1990.

In fact, the 1964 Rivonia Trial was a warning to the architects and adherents of apartheid that this abominable institution would one day come tumbling down under the sustained assault of its opponents as long as the anti-apartheid forces refused to compromise on fundamental issues of freedom and justice for all.

And it did.

Soweto Uprising

The Soweto uprising marked the beginning of the end of apartheid. probably more than any other event in the struggle against this abominable institution.

Soweto was already a place seething with anger. It had poor living conditions. It had rampant disease. Many houses were made of mud and cardboard and the streets were flooded with gangs. And it was overcrowded. By 1978, about two years before the uprising, the population of Soweto had reached one million.

It was already a tinderbox waiting to explode into flames. All that was needed was a spark to start the inferno. And it was the apartheid regime which provided that spark, igniting a conflagration that proved impossible to extinguish. and which finally consumed the apartheid regime itself.

So, the Soweto uprising was not an isolated incident or simply a random act of "terror." It had its roots in the injustices black people suffered under apartheid.

It was sparked by the government's decision to force African students to use Afrikaans as a medium of instruction together with English. But the problem was deeper than that. It didn't just start in 1976.

The seeds for the uprising had been planted years earlier. It had its roots in apartheid's racist policy of Bantu education.

The irrational decision by the apartheid regime to force black students to learn Afrikaans, the language of their racist oppressors, and use it in school only lit the fuse of a dangerous powder keg which had been around for quite some time. And when it blew up, it sounded a death knell for apartheid.

The indifference of the apartheid regime to the concerns and well-being of black people, including young black students, was also demonstrated by the arrogance and imperious attitude of the deputy minister of Bantu Education, Punt Janson, when he bluntly stated during that period just before the uprising: "I have not consulted the African people on the language issue and I'm not going to."

The decree was deeply resented by blacks even before it was implemented. It was also highly symbolic of the asymmetrical relationship between blacks and whites and the inequity of power in a society dominated by whites. As Desmond Tutu stated, Afrikaans was widely viewed by blacks as "the language of the oppressor."

And organisations of black teachers in the country, such as the African Teachers Association of South Africa, strongly objected to the decision by the government to use Afrikaans in black schools.

Black people already had to contend with the problem of inferior education, and the decree by the government that they also – without their consent and approval – had to use the language of the people who oppressed them only made things worse.

Bantu Education, mandated as official policy, had its roots in the Bantu Education Act of 1953 which established a Bantu Education Department under the Department of Native Affairs.

The department was charged with the responsibility of

designing a curriculum that suited "the nature and requirements of the black people."

It was therefore clearly a racist policy right from the beginning. And it could not have been anything but that under apartheid, a racist regime. And its intentions were clear: to provide inferior education to blacks.

That is why the government talked about "the nature and requirements" of black people as if they were subhuman or were a different species from the rest of mankind – definitely "different" from whites, according to the apartheid regime.

The author of the Bantu Education Act was Dr. Hendrik Verwoerd who was then minister of Native Affairs. An uncompromising champion of apartheid, he later became prime minister of South Africa.

He had profound influence on the provision of inferior education to blacks as the author of the Bantu Education legislation and because of his position as a cabinet member who was in charge of the "well-being" or "welfare" of black people under the department of Native Affairs.

And he made it clear that blacks were inferior to whites. As he bluntly stated when explaining the goals of Bantu education: "Natives [blacks] must be taught from an early age that equality with Europeans [whites] is not for them."

Besides the "inferior nature" of black people, as the apartheid regime saw it, which made provision of good education to them meaningless, there was another reason why they were not entitled to it.

There were jobs in society which blacks were not allowed to have. Therefore, educating them for such positions was meaningless and a waste of money. Those jobs were reserved for whites.

They were, instead, to receive education designed to provide them with skills to serve their own people in their own tribal homelands or to work under whites, doing menial work or whatever subordinate positions their white masters felt they were suited for as an "inferior" people who did not have the same rights as whites.

The inferior Bantu education black students got was made even worse by a severe lack of facilities. The students did not have the right books to use and, when they had them in a few cases, they were not enough.

They also did not have enough and well-qualified teachers. In fact, black schools ranked the lowest in terms of teacher-to-student ratios.

Also, their classrooms were overcrowded and used on rotational basis because they were not enough for all the students.

And there were other problems which, individually or collectively just like the ones just mentioned, could have sparked the uprising: the racist content of the school syllabus or curriculum, inadequate and poorly maintained facilities – libraries, latrines, playgrounds and others - besides classrooms; and high dropout rates.

In fact black schools had the highest dropout rates among all the schools in the country. And for a large number of the students, the reason was simple. They felt that even with education, they had no future in such a racist society.

All that led to pent-up fury. It was a disaster waiting to happen. All it needed was a trigger. Yet the government kept on fuelling anger and frustration among blacks, building up tensions which would one day reach breaking point.

The students were simply sick and tired of being oppressed, and of seeing their parents and other blacks oppressed and exploited by whites and their white racist government.

They were tired of being denied freedom. And they felt they had nothing to lose.

And they took action, fuelled by the ideology of the black consciousness movement which had permeated the schools not just in Soweto but in other parts of the country as well.

The government's homeland policy of requiring Africans to live in their tribal homelands, and forcing those living in the cities to "go back" where they came from although a very large number of them had never even been there since they were born and brought up in the cities and other urban centres, compounded the problem. It was clearly a racist policy.

Between 1962 and 1971, no new schools were built in Soweto. The students were required to move to their tribal homelands and attend school there.

But in 1972, the government reversed its policy, somewhat. Businesses wanted better trained black workers and the private sector brought pressure to bear upon the government to improve Bantu education. As a result, 40 new schools were built in Soweto.

And between 1972 and 1976, there was a dramatic increase in the number of secondary school students, from about 12,600 to more than 34, 600. One in five Soweto children were attending secondary school.

The dramatic increase in the number of students in Soweto had a profound impact on the lives, attitudes and perceptions of the youth in this black township.

A wave of high expectations swept through the community. But probably more than anything else, the increase in secondary school attendance transformed youth culture in Soweto. It politicised the youth to a degree they had not been before.

Before then, many young people spent their time in gangs after leaving primary school if they didn't get jobs and when they were looking for jobs. And they had to be very lucky to get employed. Jobs for them were scarce and unemployment very high.

The only guaranteed form of employment for many of them was being gang members. Most gang members thought mostly about themselves, for their own survival, and did not have the kind of political awareness and consciousness many of their counterparts who were in school did.

The dramatic increase in the number of secondary school students not only helped politicise – and in some cases even radicalise – the students; it also helped them form and strengthen solidarity among themselves, especially with the increasing number of clashes between the students and gang members which already was or became an integral part of life for many of them.

But while the number of students increased, the government continued to deny them funds for their education.

The economic depression that hit the country in 1975 was used by the government as an excuse to say it did not have enough money to pay for the education of black students although it always found the money to educate white children.

The government spent R644 a year on education for a white child but only R42 for a black.

It was a yawning gap. And the apartheid regime had no intention of closing it.

The Department of Bantu Education then announced that it was removing the Standard Six year from primary schools, a decision that was to have a dramatic impact on black children in more than one way.

It meant that the majority of the students could now go straight from primary school to secondary school.

Before then, Standard Six was a major stumbling block. Students had to pass a tough examination in Standard Six, obtaining first or second class, before being admitted into secondary school. That hurdle was now cleared.

The result was a sharp increase in the number of students going to secondary school.

In 1976, the year of the Soweto uprising, 257,505 students entered Form I, which is the first year in secondary school.

But there was enough space for only 38,000. Therefore, the vast majority of the students could not go to secondary school.

It was a recipe for disaster and chaos ensued.

The students felt that they were being denied education they were entitled to. And the only reason they felt they had been denied this opportunity was because they were black.

There could have been no other rational explanation for people who lived under apartheid, a racist regime, and when they saw that the government had no problems finding money for white students.

All those injustices played a critical role in raising the political consciousness of the black students who already had legitimate grievances. All they needed was a vehicle or some kind of mechanism to help them articulate their grievances and focus their energy on fundamental change. And they had to channel their energy in a constructive way to achieve their goals.

They found this channel in the African Students Movement (ASM).

Founded in 1968 to express the grievances of African students, the African Students Movement changed its name in January 1972 and came to be known as the South African Students Movement (SASM). And it pledged itself to building a national movement of high school students who would work with the black consciousness organisation at black universities and colleges. This organisation was the South African Students' Organisation (SASO).

It was a highly significant link. The philosophies and teachings of the black consciousness movement permeated black schools. They instilled black pride in the students as a people who had their own identity to be proud of, and rights to which they were entitled as equal human beings. And it helped to politicise them and articulate their grievances forcefully.

So when the issue of Afrikaans came up, with the government decreeing that black students had to learn the language and use it in school, they were ready to respond. And they responded accordingly.

They already knew the symbolic significance of Afrikaans as the language of their oppressors. They needed no one to tell them that.

Embracing it would have turned them into flag bearers of Afrikanerdom, which would have been tantamount to submission to the ideology and institution of white supremacy: apartheid.

Instead, they chose to fight back. And with the political consciousness that had been raised amongst them, facilitated by the black consciousness movement whose most prominent leader was Steve Biko, they were much more prepared to articulate their grievances in a much more organised way than before.

The language issue - use of Afrikaans in black schools - which ignited the conflict was a highly volatile issue, and the situation in Soweto and other black townships was already volatile.

Not only were the students vehemently opposed to being taught in Afrikaans; many of the teachers, who were now required to teach their subjects in Afrikaans, did not even know the language. They could not speak Afrikaans and did not understand Afrikaans.

There may also have been a perception, which would probably have been well-grounded fear, among many black students and black teachers that the Afrikaner-dominated government wanted some "higher" or "harder" and "better" or "more important" subjects to be taught in Afrikaans; while most of the "lower" or "softer" and "less important" subjects would have to be taught in English, the language of their rivals, the British, who also once ruled the country and dominated Afrikaners.

Afrikaners were also fully aware that English was the

dominant language in the world and the language of business – in commerce and industry – and the medium of instruction in most institutions of higher learning even within South Africa itself. They resented that and wanted to relegate it to a lower status while elevating Afrikaans to an eminent status, if they could, or on the same level with English and even higher if possible.

They were also fully aware that English was the language of choice among most black students and teachers across the country.

The government decree, which was issued in 1974, demanded that all black schools were to use Afrikaans and English in a 50-50 bilingual programme of instruction effective January 1st 1975.

Afrikaans was to be used for mathematics, arithmetic, and social studies from Standard Five. And English would be used for general science, and for practical subjects: woodwork, metalwork, needlework, homecraft, art, and agriculture science. Indigenous or tribal languages were to be used for religion, music, and culture.

The concession to English as the medium of instruction for general science, and even for agriculture science, was simply a pragmatic decision on the part of the government. Most text books, in fact for all subjects, were written in English. The apartheid regime wanted to strike a medium between the two - English and Afrikaans - and, if possible, even reverse that.

Opposition to using Afrikaans was overwhelming among blacks. A poll conducted in 1972 found that 98 per cent of young Sowetans did *not* want to be taught in Afrikaans. In fact, blacks in general associated Afrikaans with apartheid. Accepting to be taught in Afrikaans was tantamount to condoning apartheid.

Even the governments of "Bantustans" - black tribal homelands set up by the apartheid regime to separate the races as much as possible – did not use Afrikaans as an official language. They chose English, instead, and an indigenous African language that was appropriate for each of the homelands.

There had, in fact, been a decline in the use of Afrikaans among Africans – many of them knew and spoke the language as a practical necessity to deal with and communicate with their Afrikaner employers, as they still do today – and the 1974 decree was partly intended to forcibly reverse that.

The discriminatory nature of the decree, used against Africans, came into sharper focus when blacks learnt that while all schools had to use both English and Afrikaans to teach black students, white students were allowed to learn other subjects in their own language. Thus, Afrikaners used Afrikaans for those subjects, while South Africans of British origin used English.

Black students resented all that. And when the school year started n 1976, many teachers refused to teach in Afrikaans.

The defiance of the students also assumed a militant tone. And they firmly believed that they had the right not to obey unjust laws. Defying such laws was not only taking a firm stand against apartheid; it was also morally right. As one student in Soweto wrote to *The World* newspaper:

"Our parents are prepared to suffer under the white man's rule. They have been living for years under these laws and they have become immune to them. But we strongly refuse to swallow an education that is designed to make us slaves in the country of our birth."

The resentment against the language decree and the policies of the apartheid regime in general reached its peak on 30 April 1976 when children at Orlando West Junior Secondary School (also known as Phefeni Junior Secondary School) in Soweto went on strike. They refused to go to school.

It was the beginning of the uprising. Their boycott spread to seven other schools in Soweto. The Department of Bantu Education responded by sending in police.

At one of the high schools, Naledi High School, students wanted to speak to the regional director of education to express their grievances. The government responded by sending members of the Special Branch.

A student from Morris Issacson High School, Tsietsi Mashinini, proposed a meeting on Sunday, 13 June 1976, to discuss what should be done about the government's decision to force black students to learn Afrikaans and use it in school, and how the students should respond to that. The meeting was held on that day and was attended by 400 students or so.

Students formed an Action Committee, later known as the Soweto Students' Representative Council, which organised a mass rally for 16 June 1976 to articulate their grievances and make themselves heard.

Mashinini, a leader of a South African Students Movement (SASM) branch, called for a mass demonstration against the use of Afrikaans. The demonstration was scheduled to take place on June 16th and the students made a pact not to get their parents involved because they feared the parents would try to stop it.

On June 16th thousands of students assembled at different points throughout Soweto. Carrying placards emblazoned with different slogans to express their frustrations and exhort people to action, they then walked to Orlando Stadium at Orlando West Secondary School to protest against the use of Afrikaans in school. They also pledged their solidarity to the liberation cause and sang Nkosi Sikeleli 'iAfrika.

Tsietsi Mashininini led students from Morris Isaacson High School to join up with others who walked from Naledi High School. The students began the march only to find out that police had barricaded the road along their intended route.

Political protests had already become an established part of life in the township and therefore not many citizens of Soweto were alarmed or surprised by the student protest, although some of the older people might have tried to stop the students from holding the demonstration, fearing that the government would react violently, as it surely did. But that was the price that the people, including the students, were willing to pay to win their freedom.

The leader of the action committee asked the crowd not to taunt or provoke the police or do anything that would instigate the authorities to respond with violence. And the march continued on another route, eventually ending up near Orlando High School.

The crowd of between 3,000 and 10,000 students made their way towards the area of the school; at the same time police called for reinforcements of officers.

Witnesses later said that between 15,000 and 20,000 students marched.

Many students who later participated in the protest arrived at school that morning without prior knowledge of the protest, yet agreed to become involved.

The protest was intended to be peaceful and had been carefully planned by the Soweto Students' Representative Council's (SSRC) Action Committee, with support from the wider Black Consciousness Movement. Teachers in Soweto also supported the march after the Action Committee emphasized good discipline and peaceful action.

There are various accounts of what started the massacre which followed. The police had weapons and tear gas while the students were unarmed. Some reports later claimed that the school children were throwing stones, while others claim the protests were peaceful with no violent actions from the children at all.

Members of the Bureau of State Security (BOSS), which was in charge of South Africa's internal security, were caught unaware.

A police squad was sent in to form a line in front of the marchers. The police ordered the crowd to disperse. When the students refused to do so, police dogs were released, then teargas was fired.

The police threw canisters of tear gas to disperse the students who then began throwing stones and bottles in retaliation. The gas forced the crowd to draw back a little, but they continued singing and waving placards with slogans including "Down with Afrikaans," "Blacks are not dustbins – Afrikaans stinks," "Viva Azania," "If we must do Afrikaans, Vorster must do Zulu," "Afrikaans is oppressors' language," and much more.

The peaceful protest broke into violence when the Soweto police started firing what most protesters thought were plastic bullets at the protesters. Yet, when children began dropping to the cement soaked in blood, the protesters fled. While attempting to flee, some smaller children were trampled to death by other protesters and witnesses attempting to flee.

Trying to protect themselves, the students responded by throwing sticks, stones, rocks, bricks, bottles - and whatever they could pick up from the ground - at the police. Journalists later reported seeing a policeman draw his revolver and shoot without warning into the crowd, causing panic and chaos. Other policemen also started shooting.

One of the people who witnessed the shooting was a young boy, Mark Mathabane, who also lived in Soweto with his parents, a younger brother and a younger sister. He later attended school in the United States and became a successful author. As he stated in his book, *Kaffir Boy*:

"They opened fire. They did not give any warning. They simply opened fire. Just like that. Just like that. And small children, small defenseless children, dropped down to the ground like swatted flies. This is murder, cold-blooded murder." – (Mark Mathabane, *Kaffir Boy*, p. 260).

The students started screaming and running and more gunshots were fired. At least four children were shot, the first being Hastings Ndlovu followed by 13-year-old Hector Pieterson.

One of the reporters who covered the uprising was Nat Serache of the South African *Rand Daily Mail*. Quoted in a report by BBC, he recalled what happened:

"All of a sudden about six policemen armed with sten guns and rifles turned onto the crowd and most of them fired shots into the air.

But unfortunately one of them fired into the crowd and two kids were hit: One a five-year-old girl who was hit in the head and died on the spot, and a nine-year-old boy who was shot through the chest and also died on the spot."

The students then started setting fire to symbols of apartheid, such as government buildings, municipal beer halls and liquor stores, Putco buses, and vehicles belonging to white businesses.

The violence escalated as the students panicked further. Bottle stores and beer halls were targeted because many students believed that alcohol was used by the government to control black people.

Even adults joined the protest.

Anti-riot vehicles and members of the Anti-Urban Terrorism Unit arrived. Army helicopters dropped teargas on gatherings of students. Roadblocks were set up at all entrances to Soweto. The battle between the students and the police continued into the night.

And in what amounted to government endorsement of brutal police tactics, including murder, Prime Minister John Vorster warned on television during the uprising:

"The police have been instructed, regardless of who is

involved, to protect lives and property with every means at their disposal.

This government will not be intimidated and instructions have been given to maintain law and order at all costs."

At least 23 people, including three whites, died on the first day of the uprising in Soweto.

Among them was Dr Melville Edelstein who had devoted his life to social welfare among blacks. He was stoned to death by a mob of blacks and left with a sign around his neck proclaiming 'Beware Afrikaaners'.

Emergency clinics were swamped with injured and bloody children as ambulances rushed them in. Almost all of the children who were brought in had sustained bullet wounds.

The violence had, however, abated with nightfall. Police vans and armored vehicles patrolled the streets throughout the night.

Emotions ran high after the massacre on June 16th. Hostility between the students and the police was intense, with officers shooting at random and more people joining the protesters. The township youth had been frustrated and angry for a long time and the riots became the opportunity to bring to light their grievances.

The 1,500 heavily armed police officers deployed to Soweto on June 17th carried high-powered weapons, including automatic rifles, stun guns, and carbines. They drove around in armoured vehicles with helicopters monitoring the area from the sky.

The South African Army was also on standby as a tactical measure to show military force. Basic crowd control methods were not a part of South African police training at the time, and many of the officers shot indiscriminately, killing many black students. This only intensified the students' anger.

But even without training in riot control, the police

would have done better than that. Had the demonstrators been white students, they probably would not have been shot and mowed down the way black students were.

For three days the protests spread from one township to another before the authorities regained control.

The students were also fully aware that the success of the liberation movements in neighbouring countries – Angola, Mozambique and Zimbabwe – had a profound impact on the apartheid regime. They showed that white-minority regimes in the region could be defeated, and South Africa was no exception. And if their black brethren in those countries could win freedom, there was no reasons why they couldn't theirs.

Both Angola and Mozambique won independence in 1975, and the freedom fighters in Zimbabwe were applying intense pressure on the white minority rulers in that country which later forced them to make concessions to Africans, and finally relinquish control in 1980.

The apartheid state itself was virtually under siege and the students used the issue of Afrikaans to confront the regime in the struggle for racial equality. If their brethren in Angola and Mozambique could be free *now*, why not them? Why wait?

When the students took to the streets, they were dramatising the plight of all blacks and other nonwhites groaning under apartheid and were ready to make sacrifices, including giving up their lives for the cause of freedom.

This was also demonstrated by the fact that as the police continued to shoot randomly, more people joined the protesters. It was a struggle for all.

They also sought freedom by any means available, including guerrilla warfare.

By November 1976, Murphy Morobe, one of the original leaders of the student revolt was back in Soweto, having received military training, attempting to build a cell of Umkhonto we Sizwe, the military wing of the African

National Congress (ANC).

Others also returned. Some of those who were arrested were sent to Robben Island where Nelson Mandela was serving a life sentence. He said some of them told him they had received military training in Tanzania, as he stated in his autobiography, *Long walk to Freedom*.

It was the African National Congress which made arrangements for them to leave South Africa and get military training in other countries.

The uprising made international headlines, showing the brutal nature of apartheid.

One photograph which became a powerful symbol of the struggle against apartheid and of the injustices perpetrated by the white-minority racist regime against black people and other nonwhites was that of Hector Petersen. It was taken by Samuel Nzima, showing Mbuyisa Makhubu carrying the body of 13-year-old Hector Petersen, who had been shot, with Hector's sister running next to him.

This is how Nzima described what he saw:

"The first shot was fired before children started throwing stones. Then absolute chaos broke out. The children ran all over the place and stoned the police."

A postmortem revealed that Hector had been killed by a shot fired directly into him, not a bullet ricocheting off the ground as the police later stated.

The dawn of June 17th revealed burnt-out cars and trucks blocking the roads, virtually every liquor store, beer hall, and community centre burnt to the ground; and dead bodies lying in the streets.

The official death toll was 23; others put it as high as 200. Hundreds, probably thousands, were injured on the first day.

Students again poured into the streets. Parents stayed away from work to watch over their families. Police patrolled the streets. By the end of the third day of the uprising, the minister of Bantu Education had closed all schools in Soweto.

And the death toll was much higher than 200. It was later reported to be at least in the hundreds, with thousands seriously injured.

The rioting soon spread from Soweto to other towns on the Witwatersrand, Pretoria, to Durban and Cape Town, and developed into the largest outbreak of violence South Africa had experienced.

Coloured and Indian students joined their black compatriots. And unlike the anti-apartheid Defiance Campaign of 1952 and the Sharpeville demonstration of 1960, the police were unable to quell the protesters, even with force.

Students showed reckless disregard for their own safety to vent their frustrations. As soon as the upheavals were suppressed in one area, more flared up elsewhere. And so it continued for the rest of 1976.

The uprising galvanised the anti-apartheid movement within South Africa as never before. And the government had to contend with an increasingly restive population many of whose members, especially the youth, became more and more militant.

Together with the African National Congress and other anti-apartheid forces, they were determined to make the country ungovernable.

Before the uprising, the anti-apartheid struggle was largely being waged from external bases. The war was now being fought from within.

The uprising caused political and economic instability, a situation that was aggravated by an international boycott of South Africa. And the government never succeeded in restoring the relative peace and stability the country enjoyed before the uprising.

Encouraged by the uprising, black resistance to apartheid continued to grow and get more support from the people and governments in other countries.

In many cases, the isolation of the apartheid regime became a reality, although the regime continued to get support from its traditional allies.

But to a substantial segment of the international community, it became a pariah. And the Soweto uprising played a critical role in putting the apartheid regime in that unenviable position.

The regime even lost support from many whites in the country. Many white South African citizens were outraged at the government's actions in Soweto, and about 300 white students from the University of the Witwatersrand marched through Johannesburg's city centre to protest the killing of children. Black workers went on strike as well and joined them as the campaign progressed.

Right from the beginning, there was a high probability that the uprising would spread far beyond Soweto. And it did.

Student organisations in Soweto and other parts of the country directed the energy and anger of the youth towards political resistance.

Students in Thembisa organised a successful and non-violent solidarity march, but a similar protest held in Kagiso led to police stopping a group of participants and forcing them to retreat, before killing at least five people while waiting for reinforcements. The violence only died down on June 18th.

There were also protests abroad. Images of the violent attacks by the police, and of the students being beaten and shot, spread all over the world, shocking millions. The photograph of Hector Petersen's dead body caused international outrage and condemnation of the apartheid regime; a mere child killed for crying for freedom.

There were protests against the regime in many Western countries and elsewhere around the world. The United Nations imposed even more sanctions on South Africa and many countries responded with boycotts of the regime.

A new generation had made their voice of opposition to apartheid heard. And they were determined to bring the regime down.

Many left South Africa to join the armies of the exiled political movements in Tanzania, Zambia and other countries. Those who stayed behind ensured the exiled organisations could count on support from within the townships. June the 16th would never be forgotten.

After the uprising ended, it was reported that the death toll reached 600, with thousands seriously injured.

South Africa was never to be the same again.

During the uprising, Winnie Mandela, the wife of then-imprisoned ANC leader Nelson Mandela, had this to say:

"The people are unarmed. They are faced with a heavily-armed government who will succeed in suppressing it now as is always the case. But it is just the beginning."

And it was.

The uprising signified the beginning of the end of apartheid, although it was not until almost 20 years later that it finally ended.

The uprising also had an impact on the lives of whites. The majority supported their government. But there were those who did not. They were against apartheid.

One white student, Hamilton Wende, recalled the uprising years later in a report, "How Soweto Changed Everything," published by BBC, London, on 10 June 2006. He was a pupil at a white boarding school during that time and had this to say on the 30th anniversary of the Soweto uprising:

"This month Soweto will celebrate the 30th anniversary of the uprisings.

"Riots in Soweto". The words tumbled anxiously

across the country on that cold southern winter morning.

No-one knew what to believe at first.

I was 14 years old and at boarding school in Grahamstown, in the eastern Cape province, nearly a 1,000 miles (1,600 km) away from Soweto.

As the day wore on, the fear of what might happen grew.

The teachers tried, I suspect, to rein in the worst of the rumours, but they too had little or any idea of what was happening.

Refracted through the narrow prism of guilt and fear that defined our isolated, teenage world of white privilege, the gossip became more and more frenzied.

"Tonight is 'kill a white night'," somebody began saying.

Wave of rage

In the dormitories that night, arguments broke out among the boys.

The rumours were exaggerated, but the riots and bloodshed were real

Those who had liberal views said that the story was nonsense. Many others went to bed clutching cricket bats or hockey sticks, ready and eager to spring awake and fight the blacks.

There was breathless talk of the shooting team being put on "special alert" in case the blacks came sweeping down on us in their hordes from the nearby township.

Morning came and the cricket bats were returned sheepishly to their lockers.

The front page of the newspaper carried a picture of a plume of dark smoke across the Soweto skyline.

The rumours were exaggerated, but the riots and bloodshed were real.

The government death toll was 23 but many people on the streets of Soweto said it was much higher.

That day saw a wave of black rage that swept across the country.

Late the next night we were woken by army trucks driving through the streets of white Grahamstown to set up a cordon around the black township.

The violence lasted for almost a year and nearly 500 people were killed.

It was the beginning of the end for apartheid... and our lives had changed forever in South Africa.

Rocks and bricks

A day or so later, my housemaster summoned me to his study.

There was a phone call from my parents in Johannesburg.

I knew something was wrong.

I had not understood on the phone just how close she had come to death, but now I could see it for myself.

My mother's voice was calm but I could tell she was holding back her feelings.

Suddenly I felt dizzy, as I remembered that she and some of her friends worked as volunteers at a creche in Soweto.

She told me that she had been in Soweto on the morning the riots broke out, and that she had been confronted by a crowd of angry young students.

However, one of the student leaders had taken control of the situation and had prevented the others from attacking her.

Her friend Jen, the mother of my friend Chris, was not so lucky.

She and two other white women were trapped by a crowd.

The students started pelting the car with rocks and bricks. They smashed the windscreen, but in an act of extraordinary courage, Jen hunched herself over the woman who was driving to protect her from flying debris.

Jen was hit by many missiles but the driver remained unhurt and managed to steer the car out of the crowd.

They were finally rescued by the police.

Faced with reality

A few weeks later our parents came down for half-term.

Jen and my mother sat us boys down in the seaside cottage where we spent the weekend.

I was shocked at the deep bruising that still disfigured Jen's face. Both her arms were in plaster casts.

I had not understood on the phone just how close she had come to death, but now I could see it for myself.

It might easily have been my own mother who was so bruised and shattered.

I did not know what to think.

I no longer recall the precise details of what Jen and my mother told us that day. But I remember that their voices were measured.

They talked of the injustice of apartheid and why it had led to such violence. And of how, too, there were black people there that very morning who had tried to protect them.

Personal inspiration

Jen and my mother were not heroes of the struggle against apartheid, but ordinary middle-class women who, 30 years ago, unexpectedly found themselves faced with the terror of an ugly death at the hands of a crowd.

It was the courage and wisdom of what they told us that set the tone in my life to hope for reconciliation between black and white in the future and not a cycle of violence and counter-violence.

It would have been so easy for them to retreat into the

angry cliches of defending white privilege, but instead, they chose to show their children the possibility of looking beyond their fears."

The effects of the uprising echoed across the country. And in spite of the repression which intensified after the Soweto uprising, the government was still unable to contain the situation.

Popular unrest and opposition to apartheid continued to grow until the end of the 1980s.

Finally, local and international pressure led to a negotiated settlement between the government and its opponents in the early 1990s until apartheid finally collapsed in 1994.

It was the dawn of a new era. And the Soweto uprising played a major role in bringing about this fundamental change.

The Soweto uprising is commemorated every year in South Africa. June 16th is celebrated as Youth Day and in remembrance of those who sacrificed their lives upon the altar of freedom.

Appendix

The Land Question

THE struggle to end white minority rule in the countries of southern Africa may have been successful in the political arena. Multiracial governments, predominantly black, came into power after winning democratic elections. But in the economic arena, whites are still in control, virtually dictating terms to the black majority and influencing in varying degrees – decisions by governments whose leaders derive their mandate from the majority of the people who put them in power.

The most contentious subject in this continuing struggle for justice and equality is land ownership. Whites, although a minority, still own most of the land; it is also the most fertile.

Unless the land question is resolved, and the majority of Africans get back the land that was forcibly taken from them and from their ancestors by the white rulers who conquered them, there will be no justice – and genuine peace – in any of those countries. And the future of race relations will remain uncertain as black people who constitute the overwhelming majority of the population in the countries of southern Africa continue to demand restoration of their right to land ownership without which independence is meaningless.

Decades after the end of white minority rule, they

continue to invoke the slogan, "The struggle continues."

Africa's Racial Land Divide

Zimbabwe Confronts White Grip on Fertile Farms

By Jon Jeter
Washington Post Foreign Service
Monday, February 21, 2000; Page A01

GLENDALE, Zimbabwe— Allistair Booth's farm seems to stretch practically into another day, beginning at the paved road and ending 2,000 acres later on the banks of the Mwenje River. He and his wife moved here from England 51 years ago when this country was the British colony of Rhodesia, and the rich soil has provided them with a good living. The couple has, in fact, more land than they can use.

Just beyond Booth's prosperous cornfield, past his neighbors' cornfields and orange groves and the sprawling tobacco plantations owned almost entirely by white commercial farmers, the road ends and Kandal Masvi and her six children try to scratch a living from shallow, stingy soil on a spit of land that covers maybe four acres. Their farm does not produce enough to feed them, and if the family had only a few more acres, Masvi said, they would have enough corn and beans to last the year and, perhaps, a surplus to sell so that she could pay her son's school fees.

"It's painful to know that we have so little," Masvi, 53, said recently while sitting on a stool in front of her mud hut, "when a few have so much."

This country of 12.5 million people won its independence from Britain 20 years ago, but the balance of economic power remains unchanged. Only 70,000 whites remain here, down from 280,000 at the time of independence, yet they own 70 percent of the land in a nation roughly the size of Texas. Four thousand white farmers own nearly a third of Zimbabwe's most fertile farmland, while blacks like Masvi squeeze onto tiny plots that yield little more than misery.

The problem is not unique to Zimbabwe. Across Africa, the most bountiful soil remains disproportionately in the hands of an elite minority. In South Africa, for instance, blacks represent nearly three-quarters of the population, but occupy less than 15 percent of the land. Similarly, whites in neighboring Namibia account for about 7 percent of the population but own 44 percent of all private land.

Without question, warlords and tyrants, corruption and disease have eaten away at the promise of a sub-Saharan Africa free of its colonial rulers and Cold War patriarchs. But just as vexing for the continent is the unresolved legacy of the European settlers who stole land at gunpoint and never returned it.

As Africa tries to strengthen its economies with free-market reforms, appeals for reparations have crescendoed. The calls for repayment are similar to those of some African Americans whose ancestors were never paid for slave labor. But Africa's abiding poverty and history of oppression, which is still fresh in the minds of many people, lend the issue a sense of urgency that is unmatched in the United States.

In Africa, reparations are as much a practical matter as a moral one. The concentration of vital lands among Africa's white minority is having a direct impact on the continent's future, economists say, arresting the development of former colonies such as Zimbabwe, South Africa, Zambia, Kenya, Malawi and Namibia. Unless more people can gain access to land, analysts say, there can be little expansion of an indigenous African middle class--something the continent badly needs to reduce poverty and political instability.

"Land is the key to accumulating wealth in an agrarian

society," said Shadrack Gutto, a law professor at the University of the Witwatersrand. "You cannot possibly improve Africa for future generations without somehow addressing the need to return to its rightful owners the land that has been unlawfully taken from them over the course of 300 years. What you have is a very small segment of the population ready to jump to the industrial phase, and everybody else gets left behind."

Neither blacks nor whites here publicly dispute the need to redistribute land, but the way it should be done is a divisive and emotional issue, complicated by politics, race and history.

In Zimbabwe last week, voters rejected President Robert Mugabe's proposed revisions to the constitution that would have given his government authority to seize lands from the descendants of British settlers without compensation. Mugabe's ruling party exhorted black voters to approve the changes, issuing black nationalistic appeals that were openly scornful of whites. "Don't follow [whites] back to the dark past, when they were queens and kings while you suffered," read one newspaper advertisement.

While Zimbabwe's black population is mostly rural and widely in support of land reform, they focused their anger on Mugabe's failed fiscal policies and mismanagement, which many blame for steering the country into its worst economic crisis. Moreover, both blacks and whites typically agree that three years ago, Mugabe's cabinet bungled an effort to acquire nearly 1,500 white-owned farms through eminent domain. Only about 50 of the properties were bought, because the government failed to meet legal deadlines.

"The truth of the matter is that the government doesn't want to resolve the land issue because it would deprive them of a key political issue," said Jerry Grant, a vice president for the Commercial Farmers' Union, which represents more than 4,000 farmers, most of them white.

"Mugabe makes a meal out of us at every opportunity, and a lot of whites are just scratching their heads wondering: 'What the hell did we do so wrong to deserve this?'"

British settlers began shoving blacks off their farmland from virtually the moment they arrived in this southern African country in the 1890s, resettling about half the population onto barren communal properties similar to Indian reservations in the United States.

"As you drive through Zimbabwe," said Rogier Van den Brink, director of the World Bank's land project here, "the more rocky and infertile the land gets, the more black people you see."

Land ownership was at the heart of Zimbabwe's liberation war in the 1970s, but when the colonial government and Mugabe's guerrillas negotiated the transfer of power in 1979, the rebels--eager to assume power--agreed that land could only be acquired from white settlers through fair-market purchases. Namibia's rebels struck much the same deal with the white minority regime in 1990, and South Africa followed suit in 1996 when it negotiated a new constitution two years after the country's first all-races election.

The arrangements have hampered each black majority government in its efforts to remedy the disparities in land ownership. Inheriting from their predecessors a neglected population badly in need of improved housing, hospitals, schools and jobs, the new governments discovered their resources were stretched too thin to buy much land at market rates. Zimbabwe has bought, on average, just 50 properties annually since 1992. South Africa devotes less than 2 percent of its federal budget to the purchase of land.

The idea of seizing lands is widely unpopular with whites, who argue that it would reinforce the image of maturing African governments as unstable with volatile economies. And, many argue, it would be impractical to dislodge experienced farmers who sometimes employ up to 200 workers and hand over thousands of acres of farmland to blacks who are unfamiliar with large-scale farming.

"I haven't seen many black farmers who can compete with European farmers," said Booth, who purchased his farm from a British family that had owned the estate since the turn of the century. "Most of it is they just lack the resources, but experience is a factor, too."

The redistribution of land likely would fail without investment in training, said Nokwamzi Moyo, an organizer for Zimbabwe's Indigenous Commercial Farmers' Union. But that would be no more than the colonial government provided whites, he said. British soldiers returning from World War II were offered free plots of land in Rhodesia. Thousands accepted, even though many had no experience as farmers.

The government gave them training, low-interest loans and subsidized crops, Moyo said. When a beginner had a hard time catching on, the Rhodesian government often forgave each government loan until he turned a profit, Moyo said.

"It was affirmative action before affirmative action got a bad name," Moyo said.

Historically, the efficient use of agricultural lands has been a crucial factor in developing economies, agricultural economists say. Much like America's Homestead Act in the 1860s, which gave settlers up to 160 acres of land for a nominal fee, the redistribution of land in Africa would create wealth, help families educate their children and prepare them for the industrial and technological developments that typically follow, economists predict.

"If you look at most successful markets today," said Van den Brink of the World Bank, "there has been some sort of efficient land use policy and liberalization of markets that are key features in every one: the United States, Singapore, China, South Korea, Japan, Taiwan. That's really how to broaden your economic base."

Stephen Ndiyamamba, 34, is a farmer in search of a

farm. For two years, he has leased 20 acres about 160 miles northeast of Harare. If he could afford 400 acres of fertile land, he said, he could quit his job in the mines and farm full time, growing enough corn and beans to provide for his wife and young son.

One of nine children, he grew up in a village on about three acres, farmed first by his grandfather and then his father. His grandfather got him interested in becoming a commercial farmer by telling him stories about his great-grandfather.

"My great-grandfather had a really big farm near Mutare, which is good for growing tobacco," Ndiyamamba said. "Acre on acre, apparently, and he grew a little bit of everything."

"But then the settlers came."

Namibia: Landless In The Land Of The Brave

By Mabasa Sasa
New African
15 February 2015

Namibia's national anthem includes these lyrics: "Namibia, land of the brave/ Freedom fight we have won/ Glory to their bravery/ Whose blood waters our freedom." But today – 23 years after independence from apartheid South Africa – very few indigenous Namibians own land in the "Land of the Brave". From Windhoek, Mabasa Sasa looks at what has been hindering land reform in Namibia, and the options available to the people and the government.

At the close of Namibia's ruling party, SWAPO's fifth congress on 2 December 2012, party leader and state president Hifikepunye Pohamba disclosed that a raft of major issues had been highlighted during deliberations and these would be dealt with expeditiously. Among them were "accelerated land reform and land redistribution" and "addressing the access and affordability of residential land in urban and peri-urban areas."

A few statistics will put the criticality of the land issue into perspective: White Namibians make up about 6% of Namibia's population of 2.4 million people, other non-black groups (mostly mixed race) make up less than 8%, and the rest (about 76%) are black Africans.

But whites control nearly 90% of the land in what is the world's 34th largest country by area. And around 50% of the arable land is in the hands of just about 4,000 white commercial farmers.

In this country of skewed land ownership, experts say the GDP per capita in 2005 was $2,334 (Africa's average was $681), but the richest 5% of the population – mostly whites – take about 71%. At the same time, the poorest 55% account for 3% of GDP.

This has seen Namibia characterised as one of the most unequal societies on Earth, something that is rarely mentioned in the media. The whites who enjoy all this wealth are mostly descendants of German and South African colonisers, and many of them are absentee landowners who live permanently in South Africa, Italy, Germany and other places.

According to Dr Wolfgang Werner, who soon after Namibia's independence in 1990 served as director of lands in the Ministry of Lands, Resettlement and Rehabilitation: "The racially-weighted distribution of land was an essential feature in the colonial exploitation of Namibia's resources, directly affecting the profitability not only of settler agriculture, but also of mining and the industrial sector.

"As in pre-independence Zimbabwe, the whole wage structure and labour supply system depended critically on the land divisions in the country. Access to land determined the supply and cost of African labour to the colonial economy. So, large-scale dispossession of black Namibians was as much intended to provide white settlers with land, as it was to deny black Namibians access to the same land, thereby denying them access to commercial agricultural production and forcing them into wage labour."

It is against this background that at its December party congress, President Pohamba (pictured left) and SWAPO included the land issue amongst the most pressing in Namibia. But how is it that this situation prevails 23 years after independence?

When apartheid South Africa finally succumbed to local military and international diplomatic pressure in 1990 and left Namibia, the new government tried to institute a process of land reform.

However, as in all independence pacts, crucial clauses were inserted in the constitution to ensure that "private property" remained protected and the status quo was preserved.

In Namibia's case, this was Article 16(2) of Chapter 3 of the constitution, which says: "The state or a competent body or organ authorised by law may expropriate property in the public interest subject to the payment of just compensation, in accordance with requirements and procedures to be determined by [an] Act of Parliament."

More broadly, this is interpreted as the "willing-buyer, willing-seller" system, in which the state cannot acquire land for redistribution unless the landholder actually wants to let go of it. Crucially, the seller has to agree to the price offered by the government.

This condition, it is widely accepted, came about as a result of the efforts of the "Contact Group", which comprised the UK, USA, Canada, Germany and France, as a means of ensuring SWAPO could not deliver on its key liberation grievance of large-scale land redistribution.

As such, between 1990 and 2002, only 1% of commercial land changed hands from whites to blacks, and by the mid-1990s less than 20 freehold farms had been purchased for redistribution.

Available figures indicate that as at November 2011, the government had bought 293 farms covering some 1.8 million hectares at about $66m. This translated to 4,790 families resettled against a waiting-list of nearly 200,000. Namibia's First National Development Plan (1995-2000) committed $2.4m per year for purchasing commercial farms, and a similar figure was set aside for the same purposes under the Second National Development Plan (2001-2005).

The annual budget for land acquisition was increased to $5.9m in 2003, and there are indications that this could soon be doubled. Even then, going by what was paid for 293 farms in the first 12 years of independence, the figure could turn out to be woefully inadequate as land prices rise.

The government says it aims to acquire 15.3 million hectares of land by 2020; 5 million for direct resettlement and the rest through an Affirmative Action Loan Scheme. With the current pace of redistribution, such a target remains unlikely – unless radical reforms are instituted.

The government has responded to the land pressure by coming up with new regulations that it hopes will speed up the process of acquisition. However, it remains a willing-buyer, willing-seller system. In essence, the new model allows commercial farmers to tell the government they are not interested in selling land in a shorter space of time.

According to a Lands and Resettlement Ministry newsletter, farmers can now withdraw their offer of selling land to the state if they do not like the initial offer price or how negotiations are proceeding. The government then moves on to the next farmer.

"This model opens the way for flexibility and negotiations between government and the landowner before the ministry makes a final counter-offer," the Lands Ministry says. Previously, once a farmer made an offer of sale to the state, s/he could not withdraw it and the two parties would be locked in never-ending negotiations with the Lands Tribunal standing available for price determination.

"The [new] mechanism has been rigorously tested since then and has proved to be doable and beneficial to all parties," the Lands Ministry insists.

This means farmers can easily price the land out of the government's reach much quicker than previously, something that Namibia's founding president, Dr Sam Nujoma, fumed about in an interview with the regional weekly paper, The Southern Times. "We thought that when we have adopted the policy of national reconciliation, those whites who remained with us in Namibia, [would] also accept our policy of land reform, but we see now they are sabotaging land reform," said a furious Dr Nujoma.

Land reform remains premised on the National Resettlement Policy and Resettlement Criteria, which are thankfully now under review.

The criteria stems from the 1991 National Land Reform conference, which adopted 24 "consensus resolutions" that inform the laws and policies governing tenure changes. Apart from the willing-buyer, willing-seller system, there can be no claims on the grounds of "ancestral land" and priority is on expropriating farms from absentee landlords. Amendments through a proposed Land Bill, to peg maximum farm sizes in communal areas to 20 hectares and to identify under-utilised land among other measures, could also mean more people getting access to land. But the question is: why are the farm sizes of the already disadvantaged being limited in a country where it is not unusual for a white farmer to own 20,000 or more hectares of land?

Zero cases in 20 years!

There are several legal and political routes that the state can pursue to meet its obligations to the land hungry, one of which is using the Lands Tribunal more effectively. The Tribunal was established to act as an arbiter in disputes between the willing-buyer and the willing-seller.

According to the Ministry of Lands and Resettlement:

"The Lands Tribunal is mainly tasked with the determination of the purchase price of farms in the event where the farm owner concerned [does] not agree [with] the counter-offer made by the minister in respect of the farm offered and the owner makes an application to the Lands Tribunal."

The Ministry's website gives the Lands Tribunal's jurisdiction as:

*Deciding any appeal lodged with it in terms of any provision of the Act.
*Considering and giving a decision on any application made to it in terms of any provision of the Act.
*Generally inquiring and adjudicating upon any matter which is required or permitted to be referred to it under any provision of this Act or any other law.

The Tribunal has as much authority as the High Court of Namibia, and thus carries sufficient weight to ease things along. But according to the chair of the Tribunal, Advocate Dirk Conradie, the institution is yet to hear a single case. That's right, zero cases in 20 years!

In an interview with *New African (see pages 42-43)*, Conradie could barely hide his frustration, both as a Namibian and as a professional, at the under-use of the

Lands Tribunal. In his view, the state is yet to exhaust the options available to it.

"The government can simply state maximum farm sizes and start reallocating the 'excess' land," he says. "There is no justice in one person having 70,000 hectares of land – which was illegally seized from indigenous populations during colonialism – when hundreds of thousands of people have nothing.

"After that, the state must go after absentee landlords. This has been done to some extent but the mechanisms must be tightened. Why should a person own 20,000 hectares that they use as a holiday resort for two months of the year and then spend the other 10 months in Germany or wherever else?"

Conradie adds that a major area that needs revisiting to unlock land access is that of "illegally obtained land". According to him: "Any transfer of land requires a waiver from the Ministry of Lands and Resettlement, even if that land is owned by a closed corporation. But what we have are white lawyers in this country facilitating the transfer of land from one closed corporation to another without seeking clearance from the state.

"The Ministry of Trade should avail a register of the properties of closed corporations, so that if they own land no asset transfers can be done without the Ministry of Lands being aware."

What he means is this: a private company that owns farmland can sell out to another private company, and ownership of that land is thus transferred without the government being aware of it.

Since no waiver has been granted for the transfer of that land, the land is "illegally obtained" and should thus be automatically forfeited to the state.

Conradie thinks "the government should conduct an audit on which companies own what land and how they acquired it."

Another major handicap in the present system is that of the jurisdiction of the Lands Tribunal. While it enjoys the same status as the High Court, it also appears to share jurisdiction with that institution.

This means an aggrieved party can opt to take a land dispute to the High Court rather than the Lands Tribunal, and that is more likely to happen as Conradie's views on land reform are well known. As long as white farmers can get recourse to the High Court, they will not go to the Lands Tribunal. President Pohamba knows that Namibia is sitting on a timebomb.

In an interview with *Al Jazeera* last year, the president said: "Inequality exists... people are not happy, and when you talk about people not being happy, what do you expect? They can react. And when they react, then those who have the land will not have the land, people will take over the land."

Political and legal options are there for Namibia, but will they be taken? The late Prof Archie Mafeje of the University of Cape Town (South Africa) once cast aspersions on the political will of Namibia's rulers and the wealthy.

"The whole debate about land in Namibia is not about the livelihood of the dispossessed in the countryside but about how best to maintain the status quo," he said. "This could be true of white farmers, the government, as well as the black notables in the so-called communal areas."

But how long can this situation continue?

In South Africa, Land Apartheid Lives On

By Bernadette Atuahene and Alfred L. Brophy

The New York Times
January 15, 2015

CHICAGO — Friday marks the 150th anniversary of Gen. William Tecumseh Sherman's famous field order to confiscate 400,000 acres of land from former slave-owners and distribute it to former slaves — the promise of 40 acres and mule that we so often hear about.

In the wake of the Civil War, the United States could have provided a solid foundation for black economic development. But the government failed to follow through with General Sherman's ambitious land reform initiative; instead his order was repealed by President Andrew Johnson in the fall of 1865 and former slaves were drawn into various forms of peonage, which kept them in economic bondage.

Today, 21 years after the end of apartheid, South Africa finds itself at a moment of comparable significance. The country has a land reform program, but its implementation is in many ways undermining instead of promoting black economic development.

Due to colonial and apartheid-era land theft, when South Africa held its first democratic election in 1994 whites owned about 87 percent of the country's total land, although they constituted just over 10 percent of the population. The post-apartheid state has tried to address past land theft through a multifaceted land reform strategy that includes land restitution — a program providing compensation to individuals and communities dispossessed of land after 1913 as a result of racially discriminatory laws and practices. Although the South African government has made significant investments in land reform, the ruling African National Congress has made decisions and promoted policies that are calcifying the existing economic order rather than transforming it.

In the course of 150 interviews with people who received compensation through the land restitution program, it became clear that the government's policy is deeply flawed.

Of the nearly 80,000 claims filed primarily by blacks, the post-apartheid state has settled about 70 percent by distributing a Standard Settlement Offer, which is symbolic monetary compensation that is unrelated to the current or past market value of the property confiscated. Such compensation was particularly unjust for former owners like the Majolas, a black family that had owned property in Sophiatown — a once-vibrant, mixed-race community near downtown Johannesburg, which apartheid authorities uprooted to create a white suburb called Triumph. (We have used a pseudonym to protect the family's privacy.)

South Africa's land restitution authorities did not give the dispossessed residents of Sophiatown the option of receiving land in their former neighborhood or elsewhere. Instead, the state paid them a mere 40,000 rand per claim (approximately $3,500). In the case of the Majola family, the law mandated that each of the six surviving siblings receive about 6,600 rand ($570), since their deceased parents owned the home. As one family member said, "It was a case of take the money and go type of thing." Sadly, these small sums were all the Majolas and their former neighbors were offered, despite the fact that several houses in Sophiatown are currently on the market for upwards of 700,000 rand ($60,000), about 20 times the value of the compensation the siblings received.

Although the situation is deeply unfair for families like the Majolas, defenders of the current policy argue that the South African government has no viable alternatives because it has a limited budget and it must spend on other costly priorities like education and health. Others believe that this is the price South Africans had to pay to end apartheid without a full-scale civil war and keep the economy intact.

The problem is that white South Africans are receiving far more compensation than blacks.

When the post-apartheid state wants to put the Majolas and other dispossessed blacks back into their homes, it pays the current owners market-related compensation through voluntary exchange or by exercising eminent domain. This most often involves amounts that are several orders of magnitude higher than a typical settlement offer proposed to dispossessed blacks. For instance, this month a white farmer was paid nearly 1.5 million rand ($130,000) for 165 hectares in the northern Mpumalanga region. It is patently unfair for current owners (who are mostly white) to systematically receive higher compensation than owners dispossessed by prior governments (who are mostly black).

Furthermore, when the government allows current owners to keep their property, they receive a significant additional benefit. The modest payment given to families like the Majolas negates any outstanding claims to their former properties — effectively sanitizing the property rights of current owners by removing the stench of past land theft, but without properly compensating blacks.

Given the state of public opinion, this inequity could have devastating consequences for South Africa's future. Professor James Gibson of Washington University, St. Louis, surveyed 3,700 South Africans and found that two of every three blacks agreed with the statement: "Land must be returned to blacks in South Africa, no matter what the consequences are for the current owners and for political stability in the country."

South Africa may have avoided civil war during the transition to democracy two decades ago, but that does not mean the country's impoverished majority is content with their lot or that the risk of instability has disappeared.

The United States failed to institute meaningful land reform when it had the opportunity 150 years ago, and today we are living with the consequences in the form of persistent racial inequalities.

South Africa must not make the same mistake. The country began its second round of land restitution in June 2014; this time the government must get it right.

Land inequality in SA a 'ticking time bomb'

Fran Blandy
Mail & Guardian
Johannesburg, South Africa
19 November 2007

For more than a decade, Molefi Selibo has been sent from pillar to post by the South African authorities in a futile quest to own a plot of land for his family.

"Land to us, it is a very key issue. There is a hunger for land in South Africa," says Selibo as he looks out across the rolling green hills of Muldersdrift which he still one day hopes to transform into a thriving village.

"It is very, very, very frustrating. It is more than 10 years. People become disillusioned, they start questioning whether this thing is progressing," says Selibo, eyeing the land which lies fallow.

His frustration is indicative of a wider sense of disillusionment about the pace of land reforms in post-apartheid South Africa.

Thirteen years on from the end of white rule, the World Bank is warning the issue of land ownership, which has already proved toxic across the border in Zimbabwe, is "a time bomb" that could blow up if not defused.

The land at Muldersdrift, about 30km west of Johannesburg, is the third property the Ethembalethu (Our Hope) community has tried to buy and develop in a ten-year battle with stubborn white land-owners, conflicting government policies and miles of bureaucratic red tape.

South Africa's land ministry admitted earlier this month that drastic measures were necessary to save the country's land reform programme, whose slow delivery has sparked anger and fears of Zimbabwe-style land grabs.

Despite the government maintaining it is "committed to stability" and using a system of payment for land and negotiation with white farmers, patience is wearing thin for those awaiting land.

At the onset of democracy in 1994, about 87% of agricultural land in the country was owned by white South Africans, who form less than 10% of the population.

Thirteen years later only 4% of land, or four-million hectares has been transferred to black South Africans, and the ministry's annual report says it will be a "serious challenge" to reach its target of 30%—25-million hectares —by 2014.

In 1996, Selibo and others living in Muldersdrift had a dream to become self-sufficient.

A group of about 250 families started putting away R100 a month, until they saved enough to make their first purchase offer.

The community has since faced numerous obstacles, two cancelled sale agreements, court battles, as well as an out-of-court settlement where white landowners paid them not to move into their neighbourhood.

Now, since 2001, they have an agreement to occupy the 30,8ha property owned by the municipality, but have still not won the right to develop or farm on the land.

"It has cost us almost all the money we have saved," said Selibo.

"It has gone to paying the consultants to do the studies that are required. We have been going from pillar to post."

The land ministry has come under fire for its chaotic record-keeping, its failure to fill staff vacancies and the dismal state of its financial affairs, with the department's director general ousted last month.

Chief land claims commissioner Tozi Gwanya said that land reform had been hampered by opposition from landowners who dispute the validity of land claims and demand exorbitant prices.

He said when the government tried to fast-track the process, "prophets of doom" suggested the country was going the same route as neighbouring Zimbabwe.

"We do not want to see what has happened in Zimbabwe and we will always ensure that our land reform programme remains socially, economically and politically sound."

However Rogier van den Brink, World Bank country economist to South Africa, said time was running out to resolve the land issue peacefully.

"The World Bank has always said that a land inequality of this magnitude is a ticking time bomb, at some point some politician will run with this.

"What happened in Zimbabwe, little did we know it was the president of the country who would run with this issue. You cannot predict when and how a land crisis will emerge."

Back at Muldersdrift, Selibo says the community has been battling an absence of any clear policy to help black South Africans buy land in areas near towns.

However over the hill, a high-income development which will eventually include 120 houses, has surged ahead, easily gaining planning permission.

"Each and every landowner is opposing this development. People go far to prevent others from having a better life," said Selibo, who is employed as a civil servant dealing with land issues.

He said the community did not want to build another township where people lived in appalling conditions.

"We have now allocated a site for a primary school. We also planned to have community facilities, a hall and a taxi rank.

"The difference is here we also look at the agricultural side. Here there are no shacks."

Van den Brink says the country is missing out on massive growth opportunities by not using agriculture or land reform to its full potential.

"Countries with more equal land distribution grow faster, permanently," he said.

Can South Africa avoid doing a Zimbabwe on land?

By Pumza Fihlani
BBC News, Eston, KwaZulu-Natal
24 June 2013

Land reform is a thorny issue in South Africa; for some it conjures up images of Zimbabwe-like land grabs and raises tensions in small farming communities.

The 1913 Natives Land Act divided the country into white and black areas and a century later, most of the country's best land remains in the hands of a few thousand white commercial farmers, while tens of thousands of black peasants are crammed together in less fertile areas.

While some fear this powderkeg could explode, the sugarcane industry seems to be proving that reform can happen amicably.

Fifth-generation sugarcane farmer Alan Bruscow has been training his new neighbours, a group of 36 black farmers who were awarded a farm through the land reform policy four years ago.

The two farms, the Bruscow farm and the Zibophezele farm, outside Pietermaritzburg in KwaZulu-Natal are about 50m (164ft) apart.

There is nothing separating them – if you didn't know you would think it is all one big farm.

Mr Bruscow describes his relationship with the black farmers as one of "trust and working together." It is a rare but admirable sight.

"I'd say that trust is a key element here and you build trust by working with people," says Mr Bruscow.

"They need to see that you're for them and they are for you, and you are there to try and make them as successful as possible and vice versa."

Set to fail?

One of the main problems with South Africa's land reform so far, experts say, is a lack of capital to sustain the farms under new ownership.

The other is that many of the black farmers who win land claims have no skills to run a farm, let alone turn it into a successful business – these farms end up unproductive.

A study presented at the Land Divided conference in March showed that many land transfer projects were failures.

Peter Jacobs of the Human Sciences Research Council reported that only 167 land-reform beneficiaries from a sample of 301 farms were actively farming. And many of them used only a small piece of their land for agricultural activities.

But this is not the case on the Zibophezele farm, where Sipho Xulu is working his land with a tractor in preparation for this season's harvest.

Being a landowner has given him a sense of security.

"Land is extremely important n – there is virtually nothing one can do without it. We live off the land – our children will also benefit from it. It has given me a real chance to leave a legacy for my family," he explains.

Mr Xulu says the mentorship he has received has been invaluable.

"There is a lot of suspicion about white farmers in this part of the world but our mentor has proven to be a good man – we wouldn't be where we are without his teachings," explains Mr Xulu.

Land or cash?

In South Africa, agriculture, land and labour are closely entwined.

The South African Sugarcane Association (Sasa) says the only way of securing the future of this industry is through partnerships between new and old farmers.

This is why Sasa took the pioneering decision to set up its own land reform unit.

"Unless both black and white farmers commercial farmers cross that barrier and understand that we need one another for our mutual successful and for the benefit of the country, we won't get very far," says Sasa land reform unit head Anhwar Madhanpal.

Of South Africa's 1,500 commercial sugar farms, about 300 are now black-owned and most are said to be doing well.

South Africa's land reform programme is divided into four pillars: Redistribution, restitution, development and tenure, according to Land Reform and Rural Development Minister Gugile Nkwinti.

The emphasis so far has been on redistribution – buying land from white owners and redistributing it to black people whose families were forced off it during white minority rule.

But Mr Nkwinti says more people have opted for restitution – cash payments – than having their land back.

The government says that in today's increasingly

urbanised South Africa, choosing a financial settlement this "is a reflection of poverty, unemployment, and income want."

Nineteen years after the end of apartheid, there are no official figures on what proportion of land is white-owned.

Mr Nkwinti said his department is now working on getting a breakdown of private land ownership according to race and even nationality.

Racial tensions

Despite the progress made in the sugarcane industry, the government has had to concede that it will not meet its target of transferring 30% of South Africa's land to black hands by 2014.

To date less than 10% of white-owned land has been handed over, with the delays blamed on the government's "willing buyer, willing seller" policy, under which white farmers are not compelled to sell their land.

"This policy has so far allowed property owners to block redistribution efforts, as it allows property owners to refuse to have their property expropriated and also allows them to hold the government to ransom by demanding that the state pay exorbitant prices for property intended for expropriation," says constitutional expert Pierre de Vos.

In the face of the lack of progress, some activists are calling for a more drastic approach, including taking land from white farmers without compensation – something which the South African constitution makes provision for.

But many look at Zimbabwe's economic meltdown after it seized most of the country's white-owned commercial farms and caution against this approach.

Some 8.5 million South Africans depend directly or indirectly on agriculture for their livelihood.

"We have to co-operate because finding a solution is for the benefit of all South Africans, black and white," former ANC Chief Whip Mathole Motsekga told parliament recently.

"We can't guarantee peace in this country unless we find an equitable solution."

Mr Xulu and Mr Bruscow hope their model can be copied across the country to prevent the situation coming to that.

"It's about thinking of the future," says Mr Bruscow.

"A government settlement is temporary but the relationships you can build with people are forever. Our children will grow up to run these farms one day and we owe it to them to make sure that they are around for them."

www.ingramcontent.com/pod-product-compliance
Lightning Source LLC
Chambersburg PA
CBHW071308150426
43191CB00007B/541